Agents of Orthodoxy

Agents of Orthodoxy

Honor, Status, and the Inquisition in Colonial Pernambuco, Brazil

James E. Wadsworth

ROWMAN & LITTLEFIELD .
Lanham • Boulder • New York • London

Published by Rowman & Littlefield
A wholly owned subsidiary of The Rowman & Littlefield Publishing Group, Inc.
4501 Forbes Boulevard, Suite 200, Lanham, Maryland 20706
www.rowman.com

Unit A, Whitacre Mews, 26-34 Stannary Street, London SE11 4AB, United Kingdom

Copyright © 2007, 2017 by Rowman & Littlefield

All rights reserved. No part of this book may be reproduced in any form or by any electronic or mechanical means, including information storage and retrieval systems, without written permission from the publisher, except by a reviewer who may quote passages in a review.

British Library Cataloguing in Publication Information Available

The Library of Congress has cataloged the hardcover edition of this book as follows:

Wadsworth, James E., 1968–
  Agents of Orthodoxy : honor, status, and the Inquisition in colonial Pernambuco, Brazil / James E. Wadsworth.
      p. cm.
  Includes bibliographical references and index.
  1. Inquisition—Brazil—Pernambuco. 2. Pernambuco (Brazil)—Church history. I. Title.
  BX1733.B6W33 2007
  272'.2098134—dc22

2006025483

ISBN: 978-0-7425-5445-0 (cloth : alk. paper)
ISBN: 978-0-7425-5446-7 (pbk : alk. paper)
ISBN: 978-0-7425-6965-2 (electronic)

Printed in the United States of America

∞™ The paper used in this publication meets the minimum requirements of American National Standard for Information Sciences—Permanence of Paper for Printed Library Materials, ANSI/NISO Z39.48-1992.

Printed in the United States of America

To my wife, Jessica, and our four wonderful children,
Mark, EmmaLynn, Sidney, and Abigail
and
to my father and mother
for their love and support

Contents

	List of Figures	ix
	Acknowledgments	xi
	A Note on Portuguese Orthography, Currency, and the Inquisition	xv
	List of Abbreviations	xvii
Chapter 1	Introduction	1
Chapter 2	In the Name of the Holy Office	19
Chapter 3	The Inquisition at Work in Pernambuco	37
Chapter 4	Qualifying for Office: Procedures and Costs	53
Chapter 5	Qualifying for Office: The Problems of Honor	73
Chapter 6	Genealogical Fraud and Political Reform	95
Chapter 7	Nobility of Blood	119
Chapter 8	Corporate Privileges: The Familiares do Número	143
Chapter 9	Corporate Institutions: Brotherhoods and Militias	161
Chapter 10	Impostors, Abusers, and Obstructers	187
Chapter 11	Decay and Decline	209

Chapter 12	Conclusion	229
	Bibliography	237
	Index	255
	About the Author	269

Please see the book's website for additional materials:
http://www.rowmanlittlefield.com/isbn/0742554465

Figures

1.1.	Map of Brazil c. 1780	7
3.1.	Familiares in the Portuguese Empire and Pernambuco, 1580–1820	39
3.2.	Familiar Applications and Appointments in Pernambuco, 1740–1800	40
3.3.	Sentences and Appointments of Familiares in the Portuguese Empire, 1580–1820	41
3.4.	Distribution of Those Denounced to and Punished by the Inquisition from the Captaincy-General of Pernambuco by Morphological Zone, 1590–1810	48
4.1.	Family Tree Submitted with Application for Office	55
4.2.	Carta de Familiar: Letter of Appointment to the Inquisition	61
4.3.	Average Cost of Applications from Pernambuco in mil-réis, 1611–1820	64
7.1.	Place of Residence of Familiares in the Captaincy-General of Pernambuco by Morphological Zones, 1613–1820	123
7.2.	Place of Residence of Clerical Officials from the Captaincy-General of Pernambuco by Morphological Zones, 1613–1820	124
7.3.	Ages of Familiares at Appointment in Pernambuco, 1613–1820	134
7.4.	Minors Appointed as Familiares in Pernambuco, 1613–1820	135

9.1.	The Igreja do Corpo Santo	165
9.2.	The Corpo Santo Just Prior to Its Demolition	166
9.3.	Coat of Arms of the Inquisition, Évora, Portugal	167
9.4.	Companhia dos Familiares Uniforms, c. 1800	174

Acknowledgments

I wish to express my deep and enduring gratitude to those who have not only made this study possible, but have also made it enjoyable. I have often wondered why in acknowledgments the people who most deserve the thanks are left to the last. I should like to change that tradition by first thanking my wife, Jessica. She has gracefully suffered the long, and often trying, years of graduate school and research and their accompanying economic and emotional struggle. She and our children have endured the absence of a husband and a father as I have wandered through the myriad twists and turns of inquisitional history and the history of colonial Pernambuco. They have also endured many hours of discussions on topics they probably did not find particularly interesting. Likewise, Jessica has read every word of this book, not once, but several times, through its many drafts, and has contributed her editorial skill and comments. To her I owe the deepest debt of gratitude.

My parents have also provided much-needed emotional support throughout all the long years of research, never doubting that I could finish the work. Their visit to Portugal while I was researching allowed me to share with them not only this project, but also my love for the Portuguese people, language, and culture.

I would also like to thank all who have contributed their expertise and skill to the preparation of the manuscript. I would especially like to thank Bert Barickman, who endured my many failings and offered acute and penetrating commentary on my work that challenged me to dig deeper, to think and write more clearly, and to avoid ranging too far afield. His careful readings and commentary have only made this a better book. I have learned a great deal from him, and I remain in his debt.

Helen Nader and Kevin Gosner also read this work and contributed their insights and support. Luiz Mott pointed me in the right direction when I first began the project and offered valuable information and advice along the way. David Higgs offered his long experience and vast knowledge about Portugal, Brazil, and the Inquisition and was always available to field my many questions. David Higgs and Guilherme Pereira das Neves shared my interest in Bernardo Luís Ferreira Portugal, Joaquim Marques de Araújo, and Bishop Azeredo Coutinho, offered much-needed knowledge and insight, and kindly shared their work on these men with me. Maria Beatriz Nizza da Silva kindly gave her support to the project, gave me relevant articles, and invited me to share some of my work at a colloquium in Lisbon while I was still researching. Bruno Feitler has been a constant source of information, debate, and friendship. The anonymous reviewer for Rowman & Littlefield provided much-needed suggestions for revising and improving the final version of the manuscript. Likewise, many other friends and colleagues, too many to name, have offered guidance and companionship along the way. To all of you, I say thank you.

I also express my gratitude to the little band of Brazilian researchers who shared my corner of the Torre do Tombo, with whom I laughed and worked, and who shared their knowledge and friendship with me and helped me wade through some of the difficult Portuguese paleography. Likewise, the staff of the Torre do Tombo, the Arquivo Ultramarino, and the Biblioteca Nacional, where I spent many hours, were kind and helpful and provided me with documents that would otherwise have been inaccessible. Their friendship and kindness were essential, not only to the completion of this work, but also to the enjoyment that I derived from it.

I am likewise indebted to the institutions that so graciously offered their financial support for this research. The Tinker Grant and the fellowship with the Luso-American Development Foundation and the Portuguese National Library provided the financial assistance that allowed me to get the research off the ground in the summer of 1998. A Fulbright Full Grant and another Luso-American Development Foundation fellowship with the Torre do Tombo from September 1999 to August 2000 permitted me to complete the research in Portugal. A Dean's Dissertation Fellowship from the University of Arizona allowed me write full-time during the 2001–2002 school year. A summer research grant from Stonehill College allowed me to complete my research in Brazil and to finalize the major revisions of the manuscript. To all of those mentioned here and to a multitude of others—scholars, friends, and colleagues—whom I cannot mention individually, I offer a heartfelt thanks and the hope of a long and continued association. I remain, of course, responsible for any residual errors.

Portions of chapters 2 and 3 were published in "In the Name of the Inquisition: The Portuguese Inquisition and Delegated Authority in Colonial Pernambuco, Brazil," *Americas* 61, no. 1 (July 2004): 19–54. Portions of chapter 7 were published in "Children of the Inquisition: Minors as Familiares of the Inquisition in Pernambuco, Brazil, 1613-1821," *Luso-Brazilian Review* 42, no. 1 (2005): 21–43. Portions of chapter 8 were published in "Os familiares do número e o problema dos privilégios," *A Inquisição em Xeque: temas, controvérsias, estudo de caso*, ed. R. Vainfas, L. Lage, and B. Feitler (Rio de Janeiro: edUERJ, 2006), 97–112. (2006). Portions of chapter 9 were published in "Celebrating St. Peter Martyr: The Inquisitional Brotherhood in Colonial Brazil," *Colonial Latin American Historical Review* 12, no. 2 (Spring 2003): 173–227.

A Note on Portuguese Orthography, Currency, and the Inquisition

Orthography

I have preserved the original spellings and punctuation in the titles of documents, books, and articles. In the text, I have attempted to modernize and standardize the spellings of proper names. Where a widely used and accepted English equivalent exists for an individual or place-name, I have employed it (e.g., Philip for Felipe). But since Portuguese names are most frequently left in their original Portuguese, I have continued that practice here. I have also left the titles for the inquisitional officials in Portuguese, although I have modernized the spellings. In the case of the *familiares*, no good English equivalent exists. In the case of the *notários* and *comissários*, the English equivalents carry too many connotations that simply do not apply to these officials and would serve only to confuse their meaning. For example, *notário* is usually rendered *notary*. The notários who worked in the tribunals did carry out what we would understand to be notarial activities, but in Brazil they served most frequently as auxiliaries to the comissários. Likewise, the English equivalent of *comissário* is *commissioner* or *commissary*. Neither of these terms is useful in conveying the administrative and inquisitorial activities that most frequently occupied the comissários. For these reasons, I have retained the Portuguese titles of these nonsalaried officials. That said, the titles of the inquisitor general (*inquisidor geral*), the deputies (*deputados*), and the names of the various councils have been translated because English equivalents do not confuse the meaning and are often already widely used in English.

Portuguese Currency

The basic unit of currency in colonial Brazil was the *real* (plural *réis*), written $100 rs or Rs.$100. Larger sums were often calculated in *mil-réis* (one thousand réis), written 1$000 rs or Rs.1$000, which equaled one *conto de réis*, written 1:000$000 rs or Rs.1:000$000. Other denominations included the *pataco* ($320 réis), the *tostão* ($100 réis), the *vintém* ($020 réis), the *meia pataca* ($160 réis), and the *cruzado*. The value of the cruzado vacillated over time. It was valued at around $400 réis until 1642, at which time it became $750 réis. In the 1660s, it was valued at 1$000 réis. By 1718, it had become 4$800 réis.

The Inquisition

The proper name of the Inquisition was the Holy Office of the Inquisition (Santo Ofício da Inquisição). Contemporary references to the institution often used the term Holy Office as a shorthand for the Inquisition generally. Where possible, I have distinguished between the various tribunals of the Inquisition in Portugal (i.e., Lisbon Tribunal or Coimbra Tribunal) and the General Council of the Portuguese Inquisition. Where it is impossible to make these distinctions, the terms *Inquisition* or *Holy Office* have been employed interchangeably. These terms are also used as a general shorthand for the Inquisition as an institution without reference to specific tribunals or functions. I have also used the adjective *inquisitional* in place of the more commonly used *inquisitorial* as the adjectival form of the word *Inquisition* for three reasons. First, the word *inquisitional* is the correct adjectival form of the word *Inquisition*. Second, the term *inquisitorial*, although also an adjective, is more closely associated with the office of an inquisitor and with the actual trial itself. Since none of the resident officials in Brazil were inquisitors and none of them performed trials, the term does not seem appropriate. Third, in using the term *inquisitorial* to speak of the activities of inquisitional officials in Brazil, we run the risk of perpetuating myths about who these men were and what they did in colonial Brazil. This arrangement will not satisfy everyone, but it is an honest attempt to clarify the sometimes-confusing language used to discuss the Inquisition and to avoid the perpetuation of historical stereotypes and myths. Unless otherwise specified, all discussions concerning the Inquisition in the following pages refer specifically to the Portuguese Inquisition.

Abbreviations

AMP	*Anais do Museu Paulista*
AHM	Arquivo Histórico Militar
AHR	*American Historical Review*
AHU	Arquivo Histórico Ultramarino
ANTT	Arquivo Nacional/Torre do Tombo
APEJE	Arquivo Público Estadual Jordão Emerenciano, Pernambuco
BNL	Biblioteca Nacional, Lisbon, Portugal
BPE	Bispado de Pernambuco
CGSO	Conselho Geral do Santo Ofício
Cod.	Codice
cx(s).	caixa(s)
D.	Dom or Dona
doc(s).	document(s)
fol(s).	folio(s)
Freg.	Freguesia
HAHR	*Hispanic American Historical Review*
HI	Habilitações Incompletas
HSO	Habilitações do Santo Ofício
IAHGPE	Instituto Arqueológico Histórico e Geográfico Pernambucano
IC	Inquisição de Coimbra
IE	Inquisição de Évora
IL	Inquisição de Lisboa
JLAS	*Journal of Latin American Studies*

LARR	*Latin American Research Review*
LBR	*Luso-Brazilian Review*
m.	maço
MCO	Mesa da Consciência e Ordens
ML	Manuscritos da Livraria
MNEJ	Ministério dos Negócios Eclesiásticos e da Justiça
MR	Ministério do Reino
NH	Novas Habilitações
no(s).	number(s)
NT	Número de Transferência
OC	Ordem de Cristo
PA	Papeis Avulsos
PB	Padroado do Brasil
PE	Pernambuco
RH	*Revista de História*
RHI	*Revista de História das Ideias*
RHES	*Revista de História Econômica e Social*
RIHGB	*Revista do Instituto Histórico e Geográfico Brasileiro, Rio de Janeiro*

CHAPTER ONE

Introduction

In 1695, the hopeful Antônio Gonçalves Carneiro applied to work for the Holy Office of the Inquisition as a familiar (lay official).[1] Antônio immigrated to Brazil from Portugal in the second half of the seventeenth century, married into an established local family, and set himself up as a *senhor de engenho* (owner of a sugar plantation). He lived on his sugar plantation, the Engenho de Maciape, in the parish of São Lourenço da Mata in the bishopric of Pernambuco and served as a lieutenant in the local militia unit. By all outward signs, Antônio Gonçalves had successfully integrated into the local landowning elite. But he still lacked something. He needed the formal recognition of the status he had achieved. His attempt to acquire a position as a lay official of the Inquisition represented an effort to acquire the "proof" of his purity and status.

On the orders of the Portuguese Inquisition, the local parish priest interviewed eleven of Antônio's fellow sugar planters, who gave a positive review of his background and character. His application, however, encountered serious problems when the inquisitional officials on the Ilha Terceira in the Azores could not find any information on his grandmother or her family. This failure stalled out his application for twenty years.

In desperation, Antônio sent a letter to the General Council of the Inquisition in Lisbon complaining that his personal credit and good reputation had suffered great damage. The stalled application had apparently raised embarrassing questions about the "purity of his blood" (*limpeza de sangue*; i.e., no non-Christian ancestry). His sons also suffered because those who had testified in Antônio's inquiry knew that he had not received the appointment, and they spread the rumor that the Inquisition had discovered a "defect" in the family. Because of the rumors, Antônio's sons were rejected for the priesthood. Antônio pleaded with the General Council "for the love of God" to defer to him for these "just reasons" and grant him the position of familiar.[2] But silence prevailed from across the Atlantic. The General Council never responded to his request.

One thousand forty-six men such as Antônio Gonçalves Carneiro applied to work for the Inquisition in the Captaincy-General of Pernambuco, one of Portugal's oldest, wealthiest, and most densely populated colonies in Brazil, between 1613 and 1821. They did not all share the same fate, but they shared similar interests, goals, and beliefs. Their collective history reveals the institutional structure of the Inquisition in colonial Pernambuco and how it articulated with deep-seated social ideals to facilitate the production and legitimation of honor, prestige, and status—thus contributing to social promotion. The inquisitional procedures and practices of selection, the institutional organizations, the privileges, and the rich symbolic repertoire all contributed to the construction of a relatively closed status group.

The term *status group* is used here in the Weberian sense of a group of people within a larger community who retain "effective claim to social esteem in terms of positive or negative privileges," which create both distance and exclusiveness. Status is here understood as a "quality of social honor or a lack of it" and is often based on style of life, occupation, formal education, and prestige.[3]

Through these techniques and others, the Inquisition also constructed its own power and authority. The Inquisition needed to produce power ("the perception that one can enforce one's desired goals") because its ability to use force ("direct physical [or legal] action to compel one's goals") was always constrained.[4] It was constrained by regulation, by custom, by distance, by popular resistance, and by competing powers. The Inquisition spent considerable time and energy actively constructing perceptions of its power because power is always a more efficient way of accomplishing one's goals. It is more efficient because it requires the people to police themselves and each other, thus freeing the Inquisition from the costly use of force. Power may be more efficient, but it is not perfect, and force must often be used.

Inquisitional power grew out of the activities of the Inquisition's members, in regard to its "strategies, techniques, resources and organization," and to the structures of the society in which the Inquisition functioned. The manner in which these resources articulated with one another facilitated and constrained the actions of the Inquisition, its officials, and the people it sought to control.[5]

Power can also be seen as a form of production. The Inquisition had to draw from the raw material available to it in colonial Pernambuco, which was already organized into "various competing and cooperating social groups, and transform them . . . into organized groups that [could] produce the desired commodity."[6] In this case, the commodities were status, prestige, honor, power, and authority.

The Inquisition assumed this role more forcefully toward the end of the eighteenth century in what became a radical shift in focus from social control to social promotion. Thus it became one of several institutions that supplied the necessary "proofs" of purity and status that many families and individuals, such as Antônio Gonçalves Carneiro, needed to legitimate and maintain their social standing and increase their chances of social mobility. However, by the end of the eighteenth century, a complex combination of forces coalesced to force open the status group. This opening contributed to a decline in inquisitional power and prestige and an accompanying decline in the prestige value of inquisitional appointments and the Inquisition's ability to produce and maintain its status group.

The inquisitional ideals of purity and comportment also articulated with existing cultural values and social ideals to produce honor and prestige in colonial Pernambuco. The fulfillment of this important social function helps explain similar dynamics elsewhere in Latin America where the Inquisition persisted even when limited geographic reach and increasingly limited repressive capacity no longer seemed to justify its continued existence.

In effect, the Inquisition became a tool for the men who achieved inquisitional appointments at least as much as they were tools of the Inquisition. The men who worked for the Inquisition in Pernambuco successfully adapted a metropolitan and imperial institution and reshaped and appropriated it to utilize it in local conflicts. Their experience challenges long-held notions within the historiography, of the innate hostility between merchants and planters and immigrants and native-born Brazilians in colonial Brazil and of the existence of rigid social hierarchies.[7]

Likewise, many of these men did not belong to the Pernambucan or Brazilian elite. As a group, they shared a common desire to work for the Inquisition, but not necessarily a common class background. Many of them belonged to the upper echelons of society and many did not. This complicates the study of this group because they do not fit neatly into any of the categories scholars have created to study social groups in Brazil or elsewhere. It is precisely this heterogeneity that makes them truly interesting for historical analysis. As a group, they represent a broad cross-section of Pernambucan society and defy our attempts to categorize them under unambiguous stereotypical labels. Consequently, any study of this group must also be an exploration in social mobility. As will become clear later in this work, by the end of the seventeenth century, the Inquisition became useful both to the established elite and to those upwardly mobile groups who sought social, economic, and political advantage.

Although I have had to reconstruct the institutional structures that supported the creation and maintenance of inquisitional personnel, many other aspects of the Inquisition have received only cursory notice or none at all. The focus here is on the men who sought inquisitional appointment, why they did so, and why, during the last quarter of the eighteenth century and the first quarter of the nineteenth, this 285-year-old system collapsed. I have only dealt peripherally with the techniques used to control or repress heretical behaviors or beliefs, but those techniques have been well documented elsewhere.[8] This is the story of an ongoing dialogue between the Inquisition, potential candidates for inquisitional office, and the society in which they lived.

Sources and Methodology

I have employed a modified prosopographical methodology (or collective biography) because it allows us to study populations that left very little in the way of personal records and to perceive larger historical patterns.[9] It also permits us to make more valid generalizations regarding the officials of the Inquisition than has been possible through the small nonrepresentative samples employed in the past.

I have modified this methodology out of necessity. The documents required for a full prosopography that would permit a detailed account of their economic, political, and social roles within colonial society simply do not exist. Documents such as wills, municipal records, militia lists, political appointments, and *engenho* records are extremely difficult to find for colonial Pernambuco. Despite the challenging documentation, I hope that this study will encourage others to take the officials of the Inquisition seriously and attempt regional studies that will fill in what remains a history of shadowy outlines and fragmented sketches.

The 1,046 men included in this study lived between 1613 and 1821 in the Captaincy-General of Pernambuco, including its five subordinate captaincies: Ceará (1654–1799), Rio Grande do Norte (1701–1799), Paraíba (1755–1799), Itamaracá (incorporated into Pernambuco in the mid-1700s), and Alagoas (1654–1817). They were either clerics or laymen who sought to work as *comissários* (clerics in charge of inquisitional activities in Brazil), *qualificadores* (officials in charge of censure), *notários* (notaries or assistants to the comissários), and *familiares* (lay officials). In addition, I have utilized information on the 359 women who applied to be qualified by the Inquisition either as wives of proposed candidates for a position as familiar or as the fiancée or wife of someone who had already received an appointment. Despite their diverse economic and social backgrounds, all of these men shared the common feature of either serving as inquisitional officials, with the accompanying privileges, responsibilities, and challenges, or of wishing to do so.

Studying the officials of the Inquisition in any given geographic region is complicated by the large number of applications, inadequate indexes, and scattered documentation. No existing registry lists them by place of residence, and the only index for their applications is incomplete and often inaccurate. Likewise, the applications are not all found in one location but are spread throughout three different collections and scattered in uncataloged and unnumbered boxes. Consequently, I had to use a variety of sources to winnow out the officials from Pernambuco from the more than twenty thousand applications for inquisitional office and to double-check my findings.

The core documentary base consists of the inquisitional investigations into the conduct and ancestry of every person who petitioned to work for the Inquisition or petitioned to marry a familiar. These investigations, called *habilitações*, *diligências*, or *processos*, were intended to assure that inquisitional officials were of good character and "pure blood." They contain all of the biographical and genealogical information gathered by the Inquisition on each official. This information is surprisingly complete, which makes these documents perfectly suited for collective biographical research. The documents provide the quantitative data and much of the qualitative data employed in this study. They also provide rare insights into the daily administration of the Inquisition and the social, political, and religious structures that permitted and conditioned the regular functioning of the Inquisition for nearly three centuries. In addition, they provide important information regarding the historical development of the Inquisition and its officials.

Using data gathered from the diligências and a wide variety of documents collected from the Biblioteca Nacional (National Library), the Arquivo Nacional/Torre do Tombo (National Archive), the Arquivo Militar (Military Archive), the Arquivo Histórico Ultramarino (Overseas Historical Archive), and the Biblioteca da Ajuda (Library of Ajuda) in Lisbon, the Arquivo Público Estadual de Pernambuco (Public State Archive of Pernambuco), and the Instituto Arqueológico Histórico e Geográfico Pernambucano

(Pernambucan Archaeological, Historic, and Geographic Institute) in Recife, I have constructed a chronological, geographic, and social profile of inquisitional officials in Pernambuco between 1613 and 1821. The detailed biographical and genealogical data I have gathered also help map out the social contours of Pernambucan society, one of the most productive and populated sugar captaincies in colonial Brazil.[10]

Despite what some have asserted, a comprehensive history of the *habilitação* (qualifying inquiry for appointment) and of the officials of the Inquisition is possible.[11] In order to accomplish it, however, one must move beyond a rigid adherence to the indexes of the Portuguese National Archive and branch out into other inquisitional and non-inquisitional sources as I have done.

Captaincy-General of Pernambuco

D. João III established Pernambuco in 1534 as one of several captaincies intended to counter French dyewood poachers and to establish a firm Portuguese presence in Brazil.[12] It was the second largest captaincy and became one of only two of the original captaincies to succeed economically. Eventually, Pernambuco became a captaincy-general with several subordinate captaincies. The captaincy-general was bounded on the south by the São Francisco River and on the north by the Parnaíba River. It stretched inland to the line of Tordesillas, encompassing at least three main morphological zones (see figure 1.1).

The eastern littoral lowlands, called the Zona da Mata, are hot, humid, and subject to two regular seasons: one rainy, the other dry. The southern part of the Zona da Mata is especially humid. On the western edge are the rolling hills of red, fertile soil called *massapé* that is excellent for sugarcane production. The part of the Zona da Mata in the captaincy of Alagoas, to the south of Pernambuco, was heavily forested. These forests were protected as a royal preserve whose timber was used for ship construction, but the forests have now disappeared. Sugar production in the northern captaincies of Rio Grande do Norte and Paraíba was concentrated in the river valleys, which formed corridors of tropical climate suitable for sugar production. The Zona da Mata continues to this day to be the zone of sugar, cotton, and tobacco production and of population concentration.

Between the Zona da Mata and the Borborema plateau, which rises up about seventy kilometers from the coast, is the region known as the Agreste. The Agreste is a transitional region between the Zona da Mata and the Sertão (backlands) and, as such, contains wet, dry, and semiarid regions. It occupies

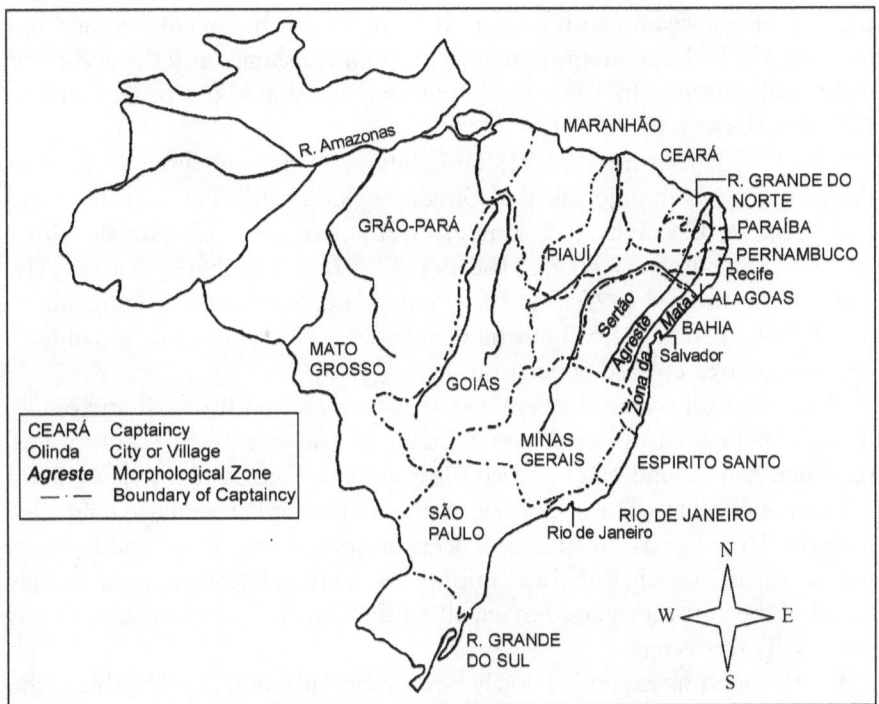

Figure 1.1. Map of Brazil c. 1780.

the eastern part of the Borborema plateau and is roughly equal in size to the Zona da Mata. During the colonial period, the Agreste was used mostly for raising livestock, but agriculture also occurred in the wetter regions.

The Agreste eventually gives way to the Sertão, which encompasses most of the captaincy-general—particularly the captaincies of Rio Grande do Norte and Ceará, where it reaches almost to the beach. The Sertão is arid or semiarid, with scant vegetation, including a wide variety of cacti, and is subject to occasional and prolonged droughts. The primary activity in the region is cattle ranching, but cotton and other crops have been grown there.

The captaincies of Pernambuco and Alagoas were the first to be settled by the Portuguese and the first to produce sugar. Paraíba (1585), Rio Grande do Norte (1599), and Ceará (1603) were all settled later. Population statistics are scarce until the last quarter of the eighteenth century, but by 1600 there were about fifteen thousand inhabitants, excluding the subjugated Indian population. The Dutch occupation of much of northeastern Brazil between 1630 and 1654 disrupted the population and economy considerably, but by the end of the seventeenth century the population had recovered and was growing, while the economy remained in a relative slump until the end of the eighteenth century. In 1693, the population stood at about 62,415, and in 1700 it was about 67,280.[13]

The 1777 census listed 363,238 inhabitants in the Captaincy-General of Pernambuco (the municipality of Olinda, including Alagoas, and Itamaracá had 226,254; Ceará 61,468; Paraíba 51,169; and Rio Grande do Norte 24,347), excluding, of course, the nonconverted Indian population. The 1782 census showed 239,713 just for Pernambuco, and by 1819 Pernambuco had 368,465 people, 97,633 of which were slaves.[14] In addition, Pernambuco had a large, free colored population.

Pernambuco became the center of sugar production in Brazil and one of the most populated and wealthiest colonies. By the seventeenth century, Pernambuco had around one hundred sugar mills worked by many slaves, both African and Indian. The apex of sugar production for Pernambuco coincided with the 1630 Dutch invasion and occupation of Pernambuco and much of the northeast, which they held until 1654. Pernambucans remain fiercely proud of the part they played in expelling the Dutch, but the sugar economy never fully recovered.

Cattle ranching expanded slowly into the arid interior, aided by those who fled the Dutch occupation, until the discovery of gold in Minas Gerais in 1695 increased the demand for meat and leather, which became important commodities in the internal economy. Rio Grande do Norte served as an important producer of salt and dried meat for this internal economy. In the last quarter of the eighteenth century, cotton became increasingly important in the northeast, and toward the end of the colonial period it became the primary export commodity.

Indigenous slave labor formed the bulk of the labor force in the sixteenth century, but African slave labor soon replaced it. Pernambuco also had a large and growing free and racially mixed population who worked in all sectors of the economy. Most of that population, both slave and free, was concentrated along the Zona da Mata, while the arid interior remained only sparsely settled.

The settlement of the captaincies generally occurred from east to west or, in the case of Ceará, from north to south, following the river valleys. The principal settlements of Pernambuco were the city of Olinda and the port town of Recife. Olinda had been established in 1537 and served as the seat of secular and ecclesiastical government in the colony. After the Dutch occupation, Recife eclipsed Olinda in size and importance, and it successfully petitioned to be elevated to a town in 1710. The landed aristocracy who controlled the *câmara* (municipal council) at Olinda feared the loss of their civil, ecclesiastical, and economic power to the port of Recife, which had become the hub of trade and commerce. The rural landowners refused to accept the elevation of Recife, and they rose up in rebellion against the governor in a conflict known as the *guerra dos mascates* (the peddlers' war). Eventually, a new governor arrived from Portugal and settled the conflict in favor of Recife and the merchants.

The secular jurisdiction of the Captaincy-General of Pernambuco more or less paralleled the ecclesiastical jurisdictions for much of the colonial period. Until 1676, Pernambuco remained subordinate to the bishopric of Bahia when that diocese became an archdiocese. After 1676, the bishopric of Pernambuco essentially included all of the Captaincy-General of Pernambuco and much of the interior as far as Minas Gerais. Of course, as other bishoprics were established, large portions of the bishopric of Pernambuco were shifted to other jurisdictions and the subordinate captaincies were eventually either absorbed, as in the case of Itamaracá, or severed from Pernambucan secular jurisdiction.

To control what would otherwise be a confusing and shifting set of boundaries for the study, I have chosen to confine the study geographically to the region encompassed within the bishopric of Pernambuco or the Captaincy-General of Pernambuco for most of the colonial period. Consequently, much of the upper Rio São Francisco watershed that had been part of the bishopric of Pernambuco, but later fell under that of Mariana, and the secular jurisdiction of Bahia and Minas Gerais have been excluded. At the same time, I have retained Alagoas (1654–1817), Ceará (1654–1799), and Paraíba (1755–1799), even though they were separated from the Captaincy-General of Pernambuco at the end of the colonial period.[15] Even then, the boundaries of the captaincies were often ill defined, and at times considerable confusion exists as to the location of certain small towns and villages, which either disappeared, were renamed, or were absorbed into larger municipalities.

The Myth of the Inquisition

Before proceeding with the endeavor to understand the men who ran the Inquisition, we must first recover them from the "myth" of the Inquisition. The "existing studies [of the Inquisition] furnish a frequently 'fleshless' image of the tribunals of faith."[16] As a result, the Inquisition has become a great faceless and emaciated beast. We tend to see an endless stream of accusations, interrogations, trials, torture, and burning, with shadowy characters whose identities we do not know lurking behind the scenes. We see an

Inquisition churning out heretics almost of its own accord, with little or no consideration for the men and the society who kept the inquisitional machinery running for 285 years. It is now time to fatten up the inquisitional beast. But this requires a systematic study of the officials of the Inquisition and setting aside the inquisitional myth.

Júlio Dantas's 1909 play, *Santa Inquisição* (Holy Inquisition), contains all of the elements of the myth of the Inquisition. It has the cold, calculating comissário, the mechanically emotionless notário, the rich, innocent victim, the confiscation of his property, his beautiful wife and helpless children turned out into the streets, the money-hungry Jew, the nameless familiares, the sensual and corrupt inquisitor general, unrestrained power and greed, and of course torture and terror.

In the play, the aged inquisitor general has lost his passion for physical torture and sensuality and wants to regain his youthful relish for them both. Through the advice of his old friend, the physician, he undertakes an experiment in moral torture. "Experience, Your Eminence," cajoles the physician,

> The interrogation of a victim. . . . To feel a soul shatter and crack in your hands. . . . To see it palpitate with pain, fiber by fiber! The torture of the body is brutal. It is coarse. For the soul of an Italian artist, such as Your Eminence, the elegance resides in the moral torment.[17]

The inquisitor general finds his new art both satisfying and rejuvenating. The rich victim and his beautiful wife become his hapless pawns as he forces each of them to publicly admit the shame brought upon them by the Inquisition's rapacious greed. All the while, the inquisitor general revels in their agony and finds the rejuvenation he seeks.

Those who embark on a study of the Inquisition immediately confront this myth.[18] The myth developed in the sixteenth century as Protestant war propaganda against the imperial and religious power of Spain in Europe. The myth soon enveloped Portugal, which remained a bastion of Catholic power.[19] It drew on exaggerated reports and focused only on a narrow set of inquisitional practices, particularly the techniques of secrecy, torture, and the confiscation of property. In doing so, it created an image of a tyrannical institution that was the enemy of all true religion, artistic expression, scientific and intellectual inquiry, and political liberties, and the cause of the supposed political, economic, and cultural deterioration of the states that sustained it.[20] The Inquisition was portrayed in opposition to society as an outside, unwanted, and unjust imposition.

The myth became even more widespread as the Inquisition became one of the whipping boys of the Enlightenment. Voltaire used the Inquisition as evidence to support his claim for the need to "crush the infamy," by which he meant the Catholic Church.[21]

This image remained popular well into the nineteenth century. Only in the last half of the nineteenth century, when inquisitional records became more readily available and historians were able to distance themselves from the heated polemic of the preceding centuries, did more or less unimpassioned studies of the institution begin to appear. Even then, they retained the structure of the myth.

After several decades of renewed disinterest in inquisitional studies in the first half of the twentieth century, the myth of the Inquisition resurfaced. This disinterest arose, in part, from the turmoil of two world wars, the relocation of the inquisitional archives in Spain, and a shift in the direction of historical research. After 1945, when researchers began to turn to social and economic history, they rediscovered inquisitional records and found that, in them, they could discover "the people without history."

The old myth was no longer needed, but it reappeared in a new form—reworked, rehabilitated, and reincarnated to serve the political interests of modern novelists, playwrights, journalists, politicians, and philosophers. The rich and powerful imagery the myth had inspired provided a symbolic framework for critiquing and explaining the powerful and threatening ideologies and practices that so complicated politics and international relations in the twentieth century. Thus at least one play produced in Brazil in the 1960s used the Inquisition as a metaphor for intolerance and state-supported repression by the military dictatorship then in power. A Portuguese play also staged in the 1960s relied on the same metaphor to criticize the dictatorial regime of Dr. Salazar.[22] New reinvigorated versions of the myth also came to be applied to the United States during the McCarthy era, to Fascist Italy, to Soviet Russia, and to Communist Poland.[23]

Likewise, it should come as no surprise that the new reinvigorated myth appears in loose and unsystematic comparisons sometimes made between the Inquisition and Nazi Germany.[24] Certainly, one can find similarities in every repressive system, but these loose comparisons generally obscure more than they reveal, and they do not go very far in helping us understand the Inquisition or Luso-Brazilian society. At least in terms of scale, any comparisons of the Iberian Inquisitions with either Nazi Germany or Soviet Russia are inaccurate and inappropriate. Even combined, the Iberian and Latin American Inquisitions came nowhere near to an attempted genocide—"culturecide" perhaps, but certainly not genocide.

The best estimates show that 1,175 people were executed as a result of Portuguese inquisitional activity, or less than 4 percent of those punished by the Inquisition.[25] Certainly, nearly 1,200 executions is no small number, but it is not the rampant and psychotic pyromania of the thirteenth century, nor the genocidal barbarism of Nazi Germany. This repression, which stretched out over nearly three centuries, has more in contrast than in comparison to the horrific spectacle of the concentrated genocide and repression of Nazi industrial slaughter and Russian political purges.

Much of the historical production on the Inquisition of the past three decades has inadvertently perpetuated the myth by focusing on the victims and techniques of inquisitional repression.[26] Like much of the recent work on other areas of the Iberian world, studies using the inquisitional records for colonial Brazil have generally focused on understanding the mechanisms of inquisitional repression and control or the study of otherwise difficult topics, such as popular religiosity, sexuality, or New Christians and crypto-Jews. Consequently, despite the fact that we now know much about the groups the Inquisition selected for prosecution, we still do not know who served the Inquisition or why they did it.

The attempt to understand or interpret the Inquisition and "its history in terms of merely one of its functions is to interpret it anachronistically."[27] The continuing fascination for witches, New Christians, homosexuals, errant priests, and bigamists, or any other category of the accused as defined by the Inquisition or modern-day researchers, tends to blur the Inquisition's larger program and its application and manipulation of power and the motivations behind inquisitional service.[28]

The rising tide of inquisitional studies has already begun to wash away much of the myth, but one area in particular remains shrouded in myth, exaggeration, misrepresentation, and literary hyperbole—the officials of the Inquisition. To date, no book-length study has investigated the officials who served the Portuguese Inquisition, whether in Portugal or in Brazil, and only a handful of articles have appeared.[29] Inquisition officials continue to be portrayed as a "reckless and evil-minded" "social scourge" and as ruthless spies and unprincipled bandits who acted at will, protected by the cloak of inquisitional immunity.[30] As a result, in the smattering of articles and chapters in longer works, the officials of the Portuguese Inquisition continue to appear as shadowy footnotes and as faceless, largely nameless agents of repression and intolerance. They are seen as the agents of Catholic orthodoxy who inspired fear and respect and who wielded the terrible power of the Inquisition with impunity. They haunt the pages of inquisitional studies as fanatics and spies who infiltrated society, denounced their neighbors, and dragged them away to inquisitional prisons.[31]

An attempt to set aside the myth and understand the Inquisition and its officials on their own terms and in the context of their own times need not be equated with an effort to rehabilitate the Inquisition, as some have suggested.[32] Such an attempt does not presuppose a denial of the naked brutality and coercion inherent in the system or the prejudice and intolerance that fed it. Indeed, those who continue to insist that the only legitimate focus of inquisitional studies is the sensational, repressive, and perverse side of the institution while ignoring a more holistic approach are perhaps guilty of rehabilitating an outdated myth that began as Dutch Protestant war propaganda against Spanish imperial domination.

Nothing in this work can or ought to be construed as a defense of, or justification for, the Inquisition—far from it. My intention is to deepen our understanding of how and why the Inquisition managed to persist for so long and to understand the men who ran it. To do so requires research into the lives of the men who staffed the Inquisition, to shake off the myths that surround them and to fatten up our inquisitional beast. Only then can we truly see the shallow human interests that not only produced, in some cases, immense pain, suffering, and fear, but also facilitated the acquisition of a type of honor, prestige, and status that was constructed on the disenfranchisement of many thousands and upon the ashes of the dead. This is a humanized vision of the Inquisition. The officials of the Inquisition are here portrayed as real people with real beliefs, motives, goals, and weaknesses. Their activities must be seen in the broader context of the societies in which they lived and the interpersonal relationships that occupied their time and attention.

The Inquisition was not an outside imposition on a weak and unsuspecting society. Rather, it was an integral part of that society and reflected and reinforced deeply held social and religious values. In this sense, the story of the officials of the Inquisition can reveal much about modern forms of state-supported intolerance and how they reproduce themselves. This is the first systematic and empirical study of the officials of the Portuguese Inquisition. Although I do not generally deal with the myth explicitly in the text, it is always implicit.

Notes

1. In Spain, many familiares came from the Third Dominican Order, and it has been assumed that they received the title *familiar* because they associated so closely

with the inquisitors whom they protected. See Henry Charles Lea, A *History of the Inquisition of the Middle Ages*, 3 vols. (New York: MacMillan, 1922), 1:381–85; Lea, *A History of the Inquisition of Spain*, 4 vols. (New York: MacMillan, 1922), 2:273–82; Jaime Contreras, *El Santo Oficio de la Inquisición en Galicia, 1560–1700* (Madrid: Akal Editor, 1982), 67; and Stephen Haliczer, *Inquisition and Society in the Kingdom of Valencia, 1478–1834* (Berkeley: University of California Press, 1990), 151–52. This is not entirely true, however. The term had been used in the Iberian peninsula since at least the tenth century to refer to those laypersons who joined religious orders, donating their possessions and becoming a part of the religious family, subject to the authority of the prelate. In return, they often continued to live on the estates they donated or lived at the monastery, receiving food, clothing, and burial in the monastery's cemetery. See Joaquim de Santa Rosa de Viterbo, *Elucidario das palavras, termos e frases que em Portugal antigamente se usaram e que hoje regularmente se ignoram*, ed. A. J. Fernandes Lopes, 2nd. ed. (Lisbon: Em casa do Editor A. J. Fernandes Lopes, 1865), s.v. "Familiares," 304–5.

2. ANTT, HSO, Antônio, m. 209, n. 3127.

3. See Max Weber, *Economy and Society: An Outline of Interpretive Sociology*, ed. Guenther Roth and Claus Wittich, 2 vols. (New York: Bedminster, 1968), 1:305–7; Max Weber, "Class, Status, and Party," in *Class, Status, and Power: Social Stratification in Comparative Perspective*, ed. Reinhard Bendix and Seymour Martin Lipset (New York: Free Press, 1966), 21–27.

4. Ross Hassig, *Mexico and the Spanish Conquest* (London: Longman, 1994), 22–23.

5. James Given, *Inquisitional and Medieval Society: Power, Discipline, and Resistance in Languedoc* (Ithaca: Cornell University Press, 1997), 3–4, 23–24, and Given, "The Inquisitors of Languedoc and the Medieval Technology of Power," in *AHR* 94, no. 2 (April 1989): 337.

6. James Given borrows Foucault's "technology of power." Given, *Inquisitional and Medieval Society*, 23–24. See also Weber, *Economy and Society*, 1:53, and Michel Foucault, *Power/Knowledge: Selected Interviews and Other Writings 1972–1977*, ed. Colin Goerdon (New York: Pantheon, 1980), 119, 141, 412.

7. See, for example, Alan K. Manchester, "The Rise of the Brazilian Aristocracy," *HAHR* 11, no. 2 (May 1931): 145–68; A. J. R. Russell-Wood, *Fidalgos and Philanthropists: The Santa Casa da Misericórdia of Bahia, 1550–1755* (Berkeley: University of California Press, 1968); John Norman Kennedy, "Bahian Elites, 1750–1822," *HAHR* 53, no. 3 (August 1973): 415–39.

8. See Anita Novinsky, *A Inquisição* (São Paulo: Brasiliense, 1982); António José Saraiva, *Inquisição e Cristãos-Novos*, 6th ed. (Lisbon: Editora Estampa, 1994); Francisco Bethencourt, *História das Inquisições: Portugal, Espanha, e Itália* (Lisbon: Temas e Debates, 1996); and collections of studies on the Inquisition, such as Anita Novinsky and M. Luiza Tucci Carneiro, eds., *Inquisição: Ensaios sobre mentalidade, heresias e arte* (Rio de Janeiro: Expressão e Cultura, 1992), and Maria Helena Carvalho dos Santos, ed., *Inquisição*, 3 vols. (Lisbon: Universitária Editora, 1989).

9. For prosopography as a methodology, see Stuart B. Schwartz, "State and Society in Colonial Spanish America: An Opportunity for Prosopography," in *New Approaches to Latin American History*, ed. Richard Graham and Peter H. Smith (Austin: University of Texas Press, 1974), 3–35; and Roderick Barman and Jean Barman, "The Prosopography of the Brazilian Empire," *LARR* 13, no. 2 (1978): 78–97. For examples of prosopographical studies in Brazil, see the well-known trilogy, John D. Wirth, *Minas Gerais in the Brazilian Federation, 1889–1937* (Stanford: Stanford University Press, 1977); Robert M. Levine, *Pernambuco in the Brazilian Federation, 1889–1937* (Stanford: Stanford University Press, 1978); and Joseph L. Love, *São Paulo in the Brazilian Federation, 1889–1937* (Stanford: Stanford University Press, 1980). See also José Murilo de Carvalho, *A construção da ordem: A elite política imperial* (Rio de Janeiro: Editora Campus, 1980).

10. Important works on Pernambucan society include Evaldo Cabral de Mello, *Imagens do Brasil holandês 1630–1654* (Rio de Janeiro: Ministério da Cultura, Fundação Nacional ProMemoria, 1987); Mello, *Olinda restaurada: Guerra e açucar no Nordeste, 1630–1654* (São Paulo: Editora Forense-Universitária, 1975); Mello, *Rubro veio: O imaginário da restaurção Pernambucana* (Rio de Janeiro: Editora Nova Fronteira, 1986); Mello, *O Nome e o Sangue: Uma fraude genealógica no Pernambuco colonial* (São Paulo: Editora Schwarz, 1989); José Antônio Gonsalves de Mello, *Restauradores de Pernambuco: Biografias de figuras do século XVII que defenderam e consolidaram a unidade brasileira* (Recife: Imprensa Universitaria, 1967); José Antônio Gonsalves de Mello, *Tempo dos flamengos: Influência da ocupação holandesa na vida e na cultura do Norte do Brasil* (Rio de Janeiro: Livraria José Olympio Editora, 1947).

11. Elvira Cunha de Azevedo Mea claims that such a study is impossible, in *A Inquisição de Coimbra no século XVI: A insitutição, os homens, e a sociedade* (Porto: Fundação Eng. António de Almeida, 1997), 179.

12. The discussion about the geography of this region has been taken largely from Manuel Correia de Andrade, *The Land and People of Northeast Brazil*, trans. Dennis V. Johnson (Albuquerque: University of New Mexico Press, 1980).

13. Bruno Feitler, *Inquisition, Juifs et Nouveaux-Chrétiens au Brésil: le Nordeste XVIIe et XVIIIe Siecles* (Louvain, Belgium: Leuven University Press, 2003), 87–89.

14. For the 1777 census, see AHU, Pernambuco, cx. 127, doc. 9665. "Mapa, Que Mostra o Numero dos Habitantes das Quatro Capitanias Deste Governo, a Sabe, Pernambuco, Paraíba, Rio Grande, e Ceará, 30 Sept. 1777." See also Dauril Alden, "The Population of Brazil in the Late Eighteenth Century: A Preliminary Survey," *HAHR* 43, no. 2 (May 1963): 173–205.

15. Ceará and Paraíba became independent of Pernambuco on January 17, 1799. The new governors remained subordinate to Pernambuco in matters of defense, but could carry on direct trade with Portugal. Alagoas became an independent captaincy in 1817. See AHU, Cod. 585, fol. 40–43.

16. Bethencourt, *História das Inquisições*, 11.

17. Júlio Dantas, *Santa Inquisição* (Lisbon: Arthur Brandão, 1909), 95. Voltaire employed the ruthless, self-serving, and sensual side of this myth in *Candide* (1759).

See François Marie Arouet de Voltaire, *Candide and Related Texts/Voltaire*, trans. David Wooton (Indianapolis: Hackett, 2000).

18. For the history of this myth, see Edward Peters, *Inquisition* (Berkeley: University of California Press, 1988).

19. See Charles Dellon, *Narração da Inquisição de Goa*, trans. Miguel Vicente de Abreu (Lisbon: Edições Antígona, 1996); Hippolyto Joseph da Costa Pereira Furtado de Mendonça, *Narrativa da perseguição de Hippolyto Joseph da Costa Pereira Furtado de Mendonça*. . . . 2 vols. (London: W. Lewis, 1811); and David Nieto, *Noticias Reconditas del procedimento de las Inquisiciones de España y Portugal con sus Presos* . . . (London: 1720). For a discussion of Dellon, Nieto, and anti-Portuguese propaganda, see Augusto da Silva Carvalho, "Dois processos da Inquisição interesantes para a história da propaganda contra êste tribunal," *Anais da Academia Portuguesa da História* 9 (1945): 47–91.

20. See L. M. E. Shaw, *Trade, Inquisition and the English Nation in Portugal, 1650–1690* (Manchester: Carcanet, 1989), and Célia Freire A. Fonseca, "Comércio e Inquisição no Brasil do século XVIII," in *Inquisição: Ensaios sobre mentalidade, heresias e arte*, eds. Anita Novinsky and M. Luiza Tucci Carneiro (Rio de Janeiro: Expressão e Cultura, 1992), 195–207.

21. See Voltaire, *Candide*.

22. See George W. Woodyard, "A Metaphor for Repression: Two Portuguese Inquisition Plays," *LBR* 10, no. 1 (June 1973): 68–75, for a discussion of Alfredo Dais Gomes's 1966 *O Santo Inquérito*, first staged during the Brazilian military dictatorship, and *O judeu*, by Portuguese playwright Bernardo Santareno, which was first staged in Lisbon during the Salazar dictatorship and was released as a film in 1996 as *The Jew*, directed by Jom Tob Azulay. For works dealing with Bernardo Santareno's play, see José Carlos Sebe Bom Meihy, "Antônio José da Silva: O teatro judaizante. História ou Literatura?" in *Inquisição: Ensaios sobre mentalidade, heresias e arte*, ed. Anita Novinsky and M. Luiza Tucci Carneiro (Rio de Janeiro: Expressão e Cultura, 1992), 583–607; Paulo Pereira, "O riso libertador em Antonio José da Silva, 'o judeu'," in *Inquisição: Ensaios sobre mentalidade, heresias e arte*, ed. Anita Novinsky and M. Luiza Tucci Carneiro (Rio de Janeiro: Expressão e Cultura, 1992), 608–20; Isolina Bresolin Viana, "Antonio José da Silva, 'o judeu', e as *Obras do Diabinho da Mão Furada*," in *Inquisição: Ensaios sobre mentalidade, heresias e arte*, ed. Anita Novinsky and M. Luiza Tucci Carneiro (Rio de Janeiro: Expressão e Cultura, 1992), 621–37; Francisco Maciel Silveira, "*O Judeu*, de Bernardo Santareno: O poder das trevas e o santo ofício da ficção," in *Inquisição: Ensaios sobre mentalidade, heresias e arte*, ed. Anita Novinsky and M. Luiza Tucci Carneiro (Rio de Janeiro: Expressão e Cultura, 1992), 638–45.

23. Peters, *Inquisition*, 297.

24. See, for example, Anita Novinsky, "A Inquisição: Uma revisão histórica," in *Inquisição: Ensaios sobre mentalidade, heresias e arte*, ed. Anita Novinsky and M. Luiza Tucci Carneiro (Rio de Janeiro: Expressão e Cultura, 1992), 8–9; Novinsky, "A Igreja no Brasil colonial: Agentes da Inquisição," *AMP* 33 (1984): 19; and Michael Baigent and Richard Leigh, *The Inquisition* (London: Viking, 1999), 75.

25. Fortunato de Almeida, *História da Igreja em Portugal*, 4 vols. (Porto: Livraria Civilização, 1971), 4:287–318. See also Bethencourt, *História das Inquisições*, 272–75.

26. See Ronaldo Vainfas, *A Heresia dos índios: Catolicismo e rebeldia no Brasil colonial* (São Paulo: Companhia das Letras, 1995); Vainfas, *Trópico dos pecados: Moral, sexualidade e Inquisição no Brasil* (Rio de Janeiro: Campus, 1989); Laura de Mello e Souza, *O diabo e a terra de Santa Cruz: Feitiçaria e religiosidade popular no Brasil colonial*, 2nd ed. (São Paulo: Companhia das Letras, 1994); Souza, *Inferno atlântico: Demonologia e colonização séculos XVI–XVIII* (São Paulo: Companhia das Letras, 1993); Anita Novinsky, *Cristãos novos na Bahia: A Inquisição*, 2nd ed. (São Paulo: Editora Perspectiva, 1992); José Antônio Gonsalves de Mello, *Gente da nação. Cristãos novos e judeus em Pernambuco, 1542–1654* (Recife: Editora Massangana, 1989); Luiz Mott, *Homosexuais da Bahia: Dicionário Biográfico (Séculos XVI–XIX)* (Salvador: Editora Grupo Gay da Bahia, 1999).

27. Peters, *Inquisition*, 99.

28. Stuart B. Schwartz, "Somebodies and Nobodies in the Body Politic: Mentalities and Social Structures in Colonial Brazil," *LARR* 31, no. 1 (1996): 128.

29. See Novinsky, "A Igreja no Brasil colonial," 17–34; Luiz Mott, *Inquisição em Sergipe* (Aracajú: Editora Fundesc, 1989); Mott, "Um nome . . . em nome do Santo Ofício: O Cônego João Calmon, comissário da Inquisição na Bahia setecentista," *Universitas, Cultura* 37 (July–September 1986): 15–31; David Higgs, "Á recepção da revolução francesa em Portugal e no Brasil," in *Actas do Colóquio A recepção da revolução francesa em Portugal e no Brasil II em 2 a 9 Novembro de 1989* (Porto: Universidade do Porto, 1992), 227–46; Higgs, "Comissários e familiares da Inquisição no Brasil ao fim do período colonial," in *Inquisição: Ensaios sobre mentalidade, heresias e arte*, ed. Anita Novinsky and M. Luiza Tucci Carneiro (Rio de Janeiro: Expressão e Cultura, 1992), 374–88. José Veiga Torres, "Da repressão religiosa para a promoção social: A Inquisição como instância legitimadora da promoção social da burguesia mercantil," *Revista Crítica de Ciências Sociais* 4 (October 1994): 109–35; and Daniela Calainho, "Em nome do Santo Ofício: Familiares da Inquisição portuguesa no Brasil colonial" (M.A. thesis, Universidade Federal do Rio de Janeiro, 1992). By contrast, the officials of the Spanish Inquisition have received far more attention. See, for example, Lea, *History of the Inquisition of Spain*, 2:263–84; Contreras, *Santo Oficio*, 67–178 (probably the best study on the topic available); Haliczer, *Inquisition and Society*, 151–208; E. Mier, *El conflicto del poder y el poder del conflicto. El familiar de la Inquisición, Toribio Sánchez de Quijano de Cortés* (Spain: Santander, 1992); and José Enrique Pasamar Lázaro, *Los familiares del Santo Oficio en el distrito inquisitorial de Aragón* (Zaragoza: Ebro Compsición, 1999).

30. Lea, *History of the Inquisition of the Middle Ages*, 1:381–85; Lea, *History of the Inquisition of Spain*, 2:273–82; Contreras, *Santo Oficio*, 67; and Haliczer, *Inquisition and Society*, 151–52.

31. Novinsky, *A Inquisição*, 4; Novinsky, "A Inquisição," 4; Calainho, "En nome do Santo Ofício," 118. Henry Kamen also argues that the officials of the Inquisition in Spain did not act as spies, nor did they function as a form of social control. See

Henry Kamen, *The Spanish Inquisition: An Historical Revision* (London: Weidenfeld, 1997), 145–48.

32. Novinsky, "A Inquisição," 8. For a good discussion of inquisitional critics and apologists, see Frédéric Max, *Prisioneiros da Inquisição: Relato de vítimas das inquisições espanhola, portuguesa e romana transcritos e traduzidos com anotações e precedidos por um levantamento histórico*, trans. Jusmar Gomes and Susie Fercik Staudt (Porto Alegre: L&PM, 1991), 51–75.

CHAPTER TWO

In the Name of the Holy Office

The Portuguese Inquisition came to Brazil late in the sixteenth century, but did not establish a permanent or significant presence in the colony until the end of the seventeenth century. In the interim, it created a symbiotic relationship with local secular and ecclesiastical authorities that endured until the abolition of the Inquisition in 1821. After 1690, local resident officials began to appear in larger numbers and inquisitional activity shifted largely to their control. A study of the early Inquisition in colonial Pernambuco demonstrates that the Inquisition created a significant presence for itself in colonial Pernambucan society by relying on non-inquisitional personnel to carry out its business.

The Portuguese Inquisition officially began in 1536[1] with the papal bull *Cum ad nil magis*.[2] This was a time of dramatic change for Europe and the world, a time of accelerating exploration and exploitation of non-European peoples and lands. New knowledge and new wealth flowed into Europe. Ferdinand Magellan's men had sailed around the world, and the colonial settlement of Brazil was only beginning. The Portuguese had trading stations all down the African coast and throughout the Indian Ocean where they attempted the impossible task of monopolizing the spice trade. The Protestant Reformation had already ripped Europe apart, and the Council of Trent would soon publish its long-needed reforms of the Church and the clergy. The Spaniards had finally removed the last Moorish kingdom from the peninsula in 1492 and expelled the Jews, who flooded into Portugal, swelling its already substantial Jewish population. This population provided much of the fodder for the inquisitional machinery in the Portuguese Empire for two centuries.

When the Inquisition came to Portugal in 1536, Portuguese Brazil did not really exist, but the continuing growth of the Portuguese Empire eventually required the extension of inquisitional authority and the adaptation of inquisitional practices to the colonies. In the 1530s, Brazil remained almost completely unexplored and unsettled by Portuguese colonists and contained little more than the isolated trading posts, called *feitorias* (factories), that trafficked in exotic goods such as parrots and red dyewood, called *pau-brasil* (brazilwood), from which the country eventually took its name. The rich stands of brazilwood attracted challengers to Portuguese control of the region. French dyewood poachers traded directly from their ships and sent agents to live among the Indians to establish positive trade relations. By 1530, D. João II concluded that the only way to secure Brazil from French poachers was to create permanent settlements that could act as a coast guard against foreign incursions.

To that end, D. João III created fourteen captaincies and gave them, in the form of grants, to twelve upwardly mobile soldiers of fortune, merchants, bureaucrats, and intellectuals. The king divided all of Brazil into huge strips of land called *capitanias donatárias* or *hereditárias* ("donatary" or hereditary captaincies) that stretched westward from the coast all the way to the line of Tordesillas. All but two of the captaincies—São Vicente under Martim Afonso de Sousa and Pernambuco under Duarte Coelho—had failed by 1550. The settlements struggled with serious problems, including Indian attacks, poor location, disease, inadequate finances, and difficulty in attracting and keeping sufficient settlers.

By the late 1540s, Portugal's resources came to be seriously stretched and the crown groped for new sources of revenue. Losses in Africa and Asia, rumors of gold and silver in Brazil, the continuing French threat, and the death of the donatary captain of Bahia combined to push the crown toward a more aggressive policy in Brazil. To gain greater control and to assert royal authority in the colony, the crown sent Tomé de Sousa as governor-general of Brazil. Tomé de Sousa effectively established royal government in the colony.

The establishment of ecclesiastical jurisdiction over Brazil also occurred in the mid-sixteenth century through the *padroado real*, or royal patronage. The Order of Christ (whose grand master was the king himself) and the Mesa da Consciência e Ordens (Board of Conscience and Orders) administered the royal patronage in the colony. Among other things, the Mesa reviewed candidates for ecclesiastical benefices, vicarships, and canonships of the cathedral chapters.

The Church in Brazil remained directly subordinate to the archbishopric of Funchal, Madeira, until the first diocese was established in Bahia in 1551. Pernambuco did not become a diocese until 1676, when Bahia became an archbishopric. Throughout the entire colonial period, Bahia remained the only archbishopric in Brazil, although six bishoprics were eventually established. For Pernambuco, this meant that until 1676 the highest local ecclesiastical officials were the vicars generals, the rectors of the Jesuit college, and the priors of the Benedictine, Franciscan, and Carmelite convents.

The effective settlement and growing economic importance of the colonies required the expansion of the Inquisition overseas. To that end, in 1551, the Tribunal of Lisbon gained jurisdiction over all the empire except that portion of Portugal under the jurisdiction of Évora. Later developments created other tribunals, Coimbra and Porto, which shrunk the size of the Lisbon Tribunal in Portugal; but Lisbon retained jurisdiction over Brazil, the Atlantic islands, and Africa.[3] These tribunals came to be administered by inquisitors who relied upon an army of lesser officials. The inquisitor general assumed the centralizing role of president of the General Council, which oversaw the activities of all the other tribunals. The members of the General Council were called deputies. In questions of policy and procedure, the inquisitor general and the General Council reigned supreme, unless the pope or the king ruled differently.

The Inquisition, however, could not simply be transplanted to Brazil. It lacked two important things—a tribunal and resident officials on the ground. Portugal never established a tribunal in Brazil, and it took almost one hundred years for the Inquisition to overcome its initial unwillingness to permit resident officials in the colonies. Once it overcame that obstacle, it had to create a network of officials large enough to carry out its work. The Inquisition did not succeed in doing this until the eighteenth century. In the meantime, it developed a different strategy for functioning effectively in Brazil, which included the use of a variety of ecclesiastical and secular officials.

The Inquisition in Pernambuco Pre-1700

By the end of the seventeenth century, the number of inquisitional officials remained small, considering the vast territory they were expected to cover. For this reason, the Inquisition initially, to fulfill its responsibilities to police the religious and moral orthodoxy of the colonial population, chose to rely on infrequent temporary tribunals, called *visitas* (investigations or inspections), that visited Brazil only occasionally, and on the existing political and religious establishment. All civil and religious authorities were legally bound to obey the orders of inquisitional officials and to honor the privileges the crown had granted them. This permitted the Inquisition to rely on civil and ecclesiastical authorities to support its various activities. For example, the Inquisition used secular authorities during the famous *autos-da-fé* (acts of faith). These autos-da-fé served as public demonstrations of inquisitional power where the convicted were formally punished and reconciled with the Church. Those whom the Inquisition sentenced to death were "relaxed" (i.e., delivered) to the secular authorities, who carried out the punishment. The secular authorities either garroted those who preferred to meet the flames as Christians and "confessed" their sins or set the torch to those who refused all reconciliation and defiantly met the scorching flames alive. This reliance on secular and ecclesiastical authority went beyond support at the autos-da-fé and extended into almost every aspect of the Inquisition's activity.

Except for the very rare visitas sent from Lisbon that visited Brazil only three times and Pernambuco only once, it would appear that the inquisitional presence in Brazil was slight indeed until the beginning of the eighteenth century. To be sure, these visitas were the most visible and dramatic demonstrations of inquisitional power in Brazil, but they were infrequent and limited in their geographic reach. The specially appointed inquisitors established temporary tribunals to receive denunciations, interrogate suspects to extract confessions, carry out trials, confiscate goods, and hold autos-da-fé.

The first temporary tribunal arrived in Bahia under D. Heitor Furtado de Mendonça in 1591 and remained there until 1593, at which time it shifted to Pernambuco, where Mendonça remained until 1595.[4] Inquisitor D. Marcos Teixeira visited Bahia between 1618 and 1620.[5] An inquisitor did not visit Brazil again until 1763–1769 under D. Giraldo de Abranches in Grão Pará.[6] These visitas were infrequent, and it is doubtful that they had much of a long-term impact on the morality and religious orthodoxy of the colony.[7]

Compilations known as *regimentos* (bylaws or regulations) governed inquisitional activity and were updated and revised periodically to incorporate new regulations and to adapt to the demands of political and social change. The first general instructions for the Portuguese Inquisition appeared in 1541. The 1552 bylaws followed and began to lay out inquisitional procedures in more detail and to centralize the Inquisition's hierarchy.[8] The next three regimentos (1613, 1640, and 1774) continued this trend toward centralization and bureaucratization.

These regimentos also controlled the creation of the network of officials. The 1613 Regimento permitted appointment of familiares and limited the numbers of comissários and scribes in the principal settlements in the Portuguese Empire to one each. It did not limit the number of familiares. The

1640 Regimento retained the limitation of one comissário and his scribe to each of the most "notable cities, villages, and places," but the 1774 Regimento simply dismissed all limitations and left the numbers to the inquisitor general to determine.[9] In practice, these limitations were generally ignored.

The Inquisition, however, did not permit permanent local officials in Brazil until after the regimento of 1613. For example, in 1611, two men applied to become familiares and were both rejected (a clear sign that the Inquisition still did not want permanent officials in the colony). The 1613 concession came in recognition of the growing economic and demographic importance of Brazil, but very few individuals there took advantage of the opportunity. No other applications were made from Pernambuco until 1638, and between that date and 1690 only twenty-two men applied.

The earliest verifiable appointment of a familiar in Brazil is that of Francisco Vieira in 1621 in Bahia.[10] In Pernambuco, João Rodrigues Chaves became the first approved familiar in 1641.[11] The first comissário appeared in Brazil in 1654.[12] The first application for a position as a comissário in Pernambuco came in 1686, the first comissário was appointed in 1692, the first qualificador in 1697, and the first notário in 1709.[13]

The tardy growth of a network of familiares and other officials in Brazil helps account for the strong presence of New Christians in the colony. It is also a manifestation of the disruption caused by the Dutch wars (1630–1654) and the relatively thin Christianized population that clung to the coastline. By the early seventeenth century, the sugar economy boomed and the colonial population rose, which made the colony more interesting economically, politically, and religiously to Portugal. This became particularly true after the Dutch had ransacked the Portuguese trading post empire in Asia and Portuguese interest began to shift more decisively toward Brazil in order to recoup lost revenues and stabilize its tottering seaborne empire.

Reports from Brazil in the early seventeenth century indicated that the situation was serious. A priest who spent nine years in Brazil working in the upper echelons of the bishopric decried the awful state of things in the colonies in a report to the General Council in 1632. There were far too many New Christians who practice Judaism openly and without fear, he claimed. Those investigations that did occur were undermined by the lack of secrecy. Witnesses' names were revealed, and their lives were threatened. Many stated that they preferred to swear falsely rather than lose their lives. And the officials who had been sent during the visitation between 1618 and 1620 were corrupt and self-serving. All of this could be remedied, the priest claimed, by simply establishing a tribunal in the colony. In this way, the people could be relieved of the stress of having to risk their lives to serve the

Inquisition. Bishops would receive more respect. Ecclesiastical officials would be esteemed and not reviled. And, most importantly, the near continuous procession of sin could be corrected.[14]

The inquisitional inspections of Bahia and Pernambuco in the late sixteenth and early seventeenth centuries seemed to corroborate this dismal view of the moral fiber of the Brazilians. By 1621, the crown seriously considered establishing a tribunal in Brazil because the population had grown considerably and because of the "quality of the people that live there." The king also declared that he wanted to have resident officials of the Inquisition in Brazil to promptly punish those who were delinquent in caring for the "purity and conservation of our Catholic faith."[15] It should be remembered that between 1580 and 1640 Portugal existed as a semiautonomous kingdom under the Spanish crown. The Spanish/Portuguese crown had already established tribunals in Mexico City (1570), Lima (1570), and Cartagena (1610). In a letter dated July 22, 1621, the king instructed the inquisitor general to establish a tribunal in Brazil. The king ordered him to appoint the bishop of Brazil, D. Marcos Teixeira, as the inquisitor (he had served as the inquisitor of the 1618–1620 inquisitional inspection to Bahia). The king also ordered the inquisitor general to appoint members of the high court of Bahia as his adjuncts and to create the other necessary offices for the functioning of an inquisitional tribunal.

Apparently, the inquisitor general did not approve of the plan and suggested some revisions. The king again ordered the establishment of a tribunal on November 8, 1622, but again the inquisitor general proved recalcitrant.[16] Three years later, the matter still had not been resolved. In June 1623, the king ordered the inquisitor general to explain why he had not yet sent the necessary orders for the creation of the tribunal in Brazil.[17] We have yet to discover why the inquisitor general dragged his feet and erected obstacles, but whatever the reason he managed to forestall indefinitely the creation of a tribunal in Brazil. The lack of a tribunal meant that the Inquisition had to function differently in Brazil than it did in Portugal and that the Inquisition could not simply be transplanted in the colonies.

At any rate, by the early seventeenth century, the Inquisition had developed a system for policing the orthodoxy of the colony that relied on close coordination with non-inquisitional institutions and personnel. This system continued into the nineteenth century in locations where inquisitional officials were not present or were unavailable. For that reason, we need to understand this earlier system.

This system relied on local ecclesiastical and secular authorities who received denunciations, performed investigations, arrested accused heretics, and sequestered their goods. Together with the yearly reading of the edicts of faith, this practice permitted the Inquisition to extend its influence and its authority into regions where it did not have a formal presence. This practice also allowed them to compensate for their numerical deficiency in the colony.

The registries of correspondence sent to Brazil from the Lisbon Tribunal give us a glimpse of how that system functioned during the seventeenth century.[18] This correspondence shows that, between 1590 and 1690, the Lisbon Tribunal selected ecclesiastical personnel to perform most of the work, and only occasionally called upon secular authorities to carry out orders of imprisonment and confiscation of goods. Of the 126 letters recorded as having been sent to Brazil between 1590 and 1690, 103 (81.7%) went to ecclesiastical authorities. Twelve (9.5%) went to officials of the Inquisition, and six (4.8%) went to secular authorities.

The Inquisition clearly preferred to work with the secular clergy where possible. Seventy-one letters (56.3%) were sent to upper-level secular clergy such as the bishops (19.8%) and the vicars general (12.0%). In 1682, the vicar general of Pernambuco, Antônio Alves Teixeira, forwarded ten investigations of prisoners held in the Olinda prison, all of which had been performed by local vicars.[19] The remaining 25.4 percent of the letters went to regular clergy, with the Carmelites predominating.

Ecclesiastical magistrates and vicars general were used most frequently in Pernambuco probably because they were the highest ecclesiastical authorities in the region before it was elevated to a bishopric in 1676. These clerical authorities also represented the most educated class in Pernambuco at the time. For that reason, and because of their high ecclesiastical offices, they held a certain amount of prestige in colonial society.

Except for the priests and vicars, the secular clergy delegated to work for the Inquisition were all associated with the Episcopal seat, and most sat on the cathedral chapter, which assisted the bishop in governing the diocese. The deacons, schoolmasters, ecclesiastical magistrates, and vicars general all sat on the cathedral chapter and held positions of considerable authority. They were responsible for the daily oversight and administration of the diocese under the direction of the bishop. In the case of the vicars general and the ecclesiastical magistrates, they also held responsibility for policing the behavior and orthodoxy of the diocesan fold, including the power to detain suspected deviants, adjudicate their cases, and pronounce sentence.

Another source of information about non-inquisitional officials that provides a more global view and allows us to see patterns of change over time are the investigations for qualification to work for the Inquisition. In them we find the men who were, by the eighteenth century, frequently referred to as *juiz comissário, comissário delegado*, or the *comissário desta diligência* (judge comissário, delegated comissário, or comissário of this investigation).[20] The term *comissário* in these cases refers simply to someone who had received a commission to do something; it should not be misconstrued as official comissários of the Inquisition. The orders sent from the Inquisition to perform investigations and inquiries were called "commissions" (*comissões*). The one who received the commission was the commissioner (or comissário). The Inquisition made frequent use of these delegated comissários in Pernambuco, particularly up to the 1760s in the populated areas and until the nineteenth century in more remote areas. In Pernambuco, Jesuits were some of the most important delegated comissários from 1690 until they were expelled in 1759.[21] The Inquisition preferred rectors of the Jesuit colleges and vicars. They preferred these men because, in many cases, they were educated and capable of performing inquisitional investigations. Likewise, the Inquisition saw its authority as predominantly ecclesiastical and preferred to use other individuals who possessed ecclesiastical authority.[22]

The men they selected tended to be in positions of influence and authority over the Catholic fold. Vicars pertained to the parish community as assigned by the bishop. Together with the parish priest, they held responsibility for the spiritual welfare of the parish. In this role, they were well placed to have access to local sources of information. The Jesuit rectors oversaw the Jesuit colleges that had become centers of culture and education responsible for the formation of the local clergy. By the end of the seventeenth century, the Jesuit order also enjoyed vast privileges in the missionary field and in education. It had also become one of the wealthiest and most powerful institutions in Portuguese America. Utilizing Jesuit rectors, then, allowed the Inquisition to tap into that authority and to enjoy the services of the most educated men in the area. Some of the Jesuit rectors could be very active *comissários delegados* because the Inquisition recognized and appreciated their abilities. For example, Antônio de Matos, Manuel de Siqueira, and Felipe Coelho performed more than half of the extrajudicial (informal) inquiries done by rectors and all but two of the judicial (formal) inquiries.

After the Jesuits were expelled from the Portuguese Empire in 1759, the Inquisition shifted its delegated authority to the secular clergy. Vicars and parish priests acted most frequently as *comissários delegados* after 1760. These ecclesiastical authorities were involved in every aspect of inquisitional activity. They performed investigations, administered oaths of office, published Edicts of Faith, and arrested suspects.

The Lisbon Tribunal used secular authorities much less frequently between 1590 and 1690. The Lisbon Tribunal instructed secular officials to apprehend suspects and to sequester goods, but they could also be asked to perform investigations and monitor the penance imposed by the Inquisition on convicted heretics. Before the creation of a viable network of comissários and familiares in Pernambuco, this practice permitted the Inquisition to extend its reach beyond the areas where it had officials on the ground. In other words, anywhere the Church or the crown had a presence, the Inquisition could also reach.

The Inquisition, then, relied heavily on secular clergy before 1690, made increasing use of the Jesuits after 1690, and shifted back largely to secular clergy after 1760 with the expulsion of the Jesuits. It should also be noted that, by the end of the seventeenth century a more effective resident force of inquisitional officials was being established and began to take over the work of the Inquisition in the areas where they lived. In those towns and villages where inquisitional officials were not available, however, the old system of using non-inquisitional personnel persisted into the nineteenth century.

Bishops and archbishops also played a fundamental role in this system of close cooperation in colonial Brazil. Because the jurisdiction of the Inquisition overlapped with that of the bishops, it could not avoid them, even though it often would have preferred to do so. The bishops in Brazil retained their jurisdiction over the prosecution of most forms of heresies and remained important in carrying out inquisitional activity.[23] Indeed, the Constitution of the Bahian Archbishopric of 1707 declared that all heretics and their accomplices of every social status should be denounced either to the purveyor, the vicar general, or an inquisitor, if one were present in the archbishopric. It also commanded that all crimes of heresy, Judaism, and apostasy be denounced directly to the Inquisition "because the punishment of all of these crimes pertains to the said Tribunal of the Inquisition." The fifth book of the constitution goes on to describe the crimes against the faith for which the archbishopric had jurisdiction and lists the punishments to be applied in these cases. The list includes infractions that also clearly fell under the jurisdiction of the Inquisition, such as blasphemy and witchcraft. It also includes infractions over which the Inquisition retained no jurisdiction, such as incest and simony.[24]

In 1579, the king granted the bishop of Brazil, together with the Jesuits, the authority to deal with cases pertaining to the Inquisition and to send their findings to Lisbon.[25] This helps account for the important role that the Jesuits played before their expulsion in 1759. Likewise, none of the papal decrees establishing the Inquisition ever revoked responsibility for heresy from the bishops, to whom it had solely belonged. But in 1561, the pope granted the inquisitor general of Portugal, Cardinal Infante D. Henrique, the authority to assume responsibility for heresies from the bishops when it became necessary. This was not a blanket grant, but it came to be used as such.[26]

In addition, between 1627 and 1819, the bishops and archbishops of Brazil regularly named the senior inquisitor as their procurator to the General Council of the Inquisition. This gave the Inquisition authority over everyone under the bishop's jurisdiction in cases of heresy. It also gave the senior inquisitor the authority to vote in the bishop's place when their votes were necessary.[27] Although these transferals of authority certainly did not eliminate the bishops' responsibility or authority over heresy within their jurisdictions, they strengthened the Inquisition's hand in determining how inquisitional power would be used in the colony. Likewise, the 1774 Regimento declared that the inquisitors took precedence over the bishops in matters concerning the Inquisition.[28]

Despite these apparent retractions of Episcopal authority, the Inquisition could not simply ignore the bishops, and these prelates continued to exercise their jurisdiction in Brazil. The Inquisition, however, often interfered in the inquisitional activities of the bishops. For example, on March 24, 1605, in response to the king's pardon, the Lisbon Tribunal ordered the bishop of Bahia to release all prisoners held for offenses against the Inquisition. It also ordered him to refrain from arresting suspects unless he had cause to fear that they might flee.[29] The tribunal sent a similar order to the deacon of the bishopric of Pernambuco, Nicolau Pais Sarmento, in 1687, because the bishop had detained prisoners in the name of the Inquisition when he should not have.[30] Likewise, on November 8, 1766, the Lisbon Tribunal ordered Antônio Alves Guerra to forward its order to the bishop of Pernambuco to release Father Ventura de Albuquerque, because it did not have any credible accusation against him.[31] In 1690, the bishop of Pernambuco received instructions not to forward bigamy cases to Lisbon unless the existence of plural marriage had been verified.[32]

Sometimes the bishops' enthusiasm could be excessive—at least from the Inquisition's perspective. Their eagerness to send suspects to Lisbon evoked an order from the Lisbon Tribunal in 1743 that forbade all the bishops in the colony from sending prisoners to Lisbon without first sending a summary of their crimes and permitting the tribunal to determine their guilt. At the same time, it sent letters to all the comissários ordering them to refuse to send any prisoners to Lisbon that the bishops delivered to them. The Inquisition instructed the comissários to use the orders they had received from the Inquisition to excuse their disobedience to the bishops.[33]

Nonetheless, the Inquisition often worked harmoniously with the bishops. For instance, in 1639, the bishop of Brazil requested permission to sentence several prisoners of the Inquisition in Brazil rather than send them to Lisbon because the journey was inconvenient and because the prisoners were too poor to pay for it. His request was granted.[34] Later, in 1760, the Lisbon Tribunal sent a letter to the bishop of Pernambuco instructing him to make an inquiry into eight Indians imprisoned by the *capitão-mor* (captain major) and governor of Rio Grande do Norte, Pedro de Albuquerque e Melo. The prisoners had been taken at the instigation of his own son and still had not been formally charged. The tribunal instructed the bishop to determine whether there was any cause to hold them, to release those who were innocent, and to send those who had substantial evidence against them to Lisbon.[35]

In remote areas, however, regular clergy still monopolized the exercise of inquisitional activity and resisted attempts by local secular clergy to have themselves appointed as officials of the Inquisition. For example, when Antônio Rodrigues Portela, the parish priest from Paraíba, applied to become a comissário in 1755, the Jesuit, Antônio dos Reis, conducted an investigation in Paraíba to determine Portela's qualifications for office. Antônio dos Reis concluded that Portela was unsuitable, but did not explain his conclusion. The deputies of the General Council in Lisbon questioned the Jesuit's motives for finding Portela unsatisfactory. "It has been shown through experience," they said, "that in the lands where there are no comissários, and for this reason the Holy Office entrusts investigations to the Jesuits, these Jesuits try to maintain this authority [for themselves] by keeping anyone else from acquiring it."[36]

As this statement indicates, the system of delegated authority did not always function well. The individuals to whom inquisitional authority had been delegated often did not fully comprehend their responsibilities and consequently made perplexing mistakes. Many of them became involved in local conflicts. Consequently, inquisitional prisoners often became the victims of personal rivalries and the pawns in larger political and social maneuvering. Sometimes these conflicts and tensions permitted inquisitional prisoners to escape.

Problems of Delegation

Delegated authorities could cause difficulty for the Inquisition by failing to follow instructions or by overstepping the bounds of the authority given them.[37] The vicar of São Lourenço da Mata, Luís Inácio de Morais, is a case in point. He received an order in 1769 from the comissário Antônio Ribeiro Maio to perform an informal inquiry.

Luís Inácio did not understand the limits of his authority and made a formal inquiry without authorization to do so. In addition, the little information he gathered was incorrect. The comissário, Antônio Ribeiro, reported the failure to the General Council with considerable discomfiture because it meant that the informal inquiry had to be done again and that the Inquisition's shield of secrecy had been breached.[38]

Often conflicts between local ecclesiastical and secular authorities impeded the smooth functioning of the Inquisition and permitted inquisitional prisoners to escape, as in the case of Antônio Teixeira da Motta. In 1748, D. João V appointed Antônio Teixeira da Motta as the *juiz de fora* (crown judge or magistrate) of Olinda, Brazil. Almost upon arriving, Antônio entered into conflict with the ecclesiastical authorities. In 1749, he sent a letter to the vicar general ordering him to present the legal proceedings and charges against the prisoners held in the public prisons on the orders of the ecclesiastical authorities. Antônio wanted to see if their sentences were legal. He informed the vicar general that he would release the prisoners in twenty-four hours if he did not receive an accounting of why they were being held. When the vicar general failed to respond to the order, the juiz de fora released the prisoners in Olinda and Recife on January 1, 1750.

According to the vicar general, at least three of the twenty prisoners Antônio released were being held for crimes that fell under the Inquisition's jurisdiction. Antônio claimed that he had not been informed of that fact. And in any case, he argued, if they had been inquisitional prisoners, they should have been sent to Lisbon on the fleet instead of being left to rot in the ecclesiastical prisons in Brazil. This had been a problem since at least the late seventeenth century. The comissário Nicolau Paes Sarmento complained in 1686 that when he assumed the position of vicar general in Olinda he found many prisoners locked up in the public prison of Olinda for five years without any resolution.[39]

Despite the magistrate's defense of his conduct, the bishop of Pernambuco excommunicated him. Both the bishop and the vicar general denounced the juiz de fora to the Lisbon Tribunal and to the Overseas Council (Conselho Ultramarino). Antônio made an accounting to the Lisbon Tribunal that seems to have satisfied it, as no action appears to have been taken against him. In any event, prisoners who were awaiting an inquisitional trial in noninquisitional prisons managed to escape because of conflicts between secular and ecclesiastical authorities.[40]

Prisoners of the Inquisition could also become pawns in power struggles and personal rivalries, especially at the local level.[41] These tendencies appear in the arrests of at least 141 Paraíban New Christians between 1729 and 1741 for Judaizing.[42] Most of the arrests took place in two large operations. During 1728–1729, the familiar and field marshal of Olinda, Antônio Borges da Fonseca, captured twenty individuals in Paraíba. He coordinated the arrests with the bishop and the *ouvidor geral* (superior magistrate) of Paraíba and carried them out with such success that the Lisbon Tribunal commended him for his intelligence and zeal. In April 1730, the Lisbon Tribunal ordered him to imprison another thirty-one individuals and send them to Lisbon.[43]

During the first mass imprisonment of 1729, Antônio Borges da Fonseca called upon the familiar Teodoro de Lemos Duarte, from Paraíba, to assist in the detention of the prisoners. The ouvidor geral, acting as the *juiz do fisco* (fiscal judge), assigned Teodoro to take an inventory of the property confiscated from the prisoners.[44]

Antônio Borges also enlisted the assistance of a local colonel and his soldiers. They proved useful, but they muddled the inventory and allowed a few suspects to escape. Teodoro claimed that he found the property of several prisoners simply piled up in a room in absolute confusion and disorder—in so much disorder that he had to ask each prisoner what belonged to them.

The soldiers also transported prisoners and their goods across a flooding river, leaving their property in the "worst possible disorder." They had simply slaughtered the prisoner's livestock, and one soldier had stolen an earthen jug, a silver platter, and a gold ring from the prisoners. One woman offered some gold coins to another soldier to bribe him into letting her escape.

Afterward, Antônio Borges gave certificates of service to everyone who had participated in the imprisonment. Teodoro claimed that he even gave certificates to people who had not participated, including the son of the captain major of Paraíba. Antônio Borges did this because he had contracted to marry the captain major's daughter after she obtained proof of her pure blood, and now he sought to ingratiate himself to the family. Teodoro earned the enmity of the entire clan by publicly stating that they had always been rumored to be New Christians. Antônio Borges struck back at Teodoro by leaving behind two prisoners that Teodoro had to take all the way to Recife at his own expense. Teodoro also claimed that Antônio Borges intended to falsify the inventories to make them more ridiculous than they already were because of the confusion caused by the soldiers, who were only interested in stealing the prisoners' property. Teodoro eventually traveled to Lisbon to defend himself against accusations of mishandling the inventories.

This episode demonstrates that inquisitional activity, filtered as it often was through high-ranking secular and ecclesiastical authorities, some of whom were also inquisitional officials, could result in complications and conflicts that left the wretched prisoners as pawns in personal rivalries and power struggles. This insertion of personal interest into inquisitional activity decreased the efficiency and effectiveness of the institution.

The Inquisition also struggled with inadequate facilities to house prisoners in Brazil. Beyond the simple terror and paralyzing delay of inquisitional justice, the difficulties and uncertainties faced by inquisitional prisoners in Brazil inspired many to attempt to escape from the clutches of the Inquisition. Of course, many individuals succeeded in escaping before the Inquisition could arrest them, but many also escaped after their incarceration.

Even with, and sometimes because of, the assistance of local ecclesiastical and secular authorities, the plight of prisoners remained a constant problem for the Inquisition in Brazil. This problem became particularly acute toward the end of the eighteenth century, when the prisoners tended to be of more humble origins and the confiscation of goods as a punishment decreased. The Inquisition did not maintain any prisons in Brazil and had to rely on the secular and ecclesiastical prisons to hold their prisoners until they could be sent to the inquisitional prison in Lisbon.

These prisoners were held in the public prisons, in one of the convents, or in the homes of the familiares. For example, the priest José Aires, accused of taking prisoners and sequestering goods without orders from the Holy Office in 1744, was detained under lock and key in the Jesuit college in Olinda. He was confined in a room with a bed and table for thirty-seven days before he was shipped to Lisbon.[45] Ironically, prisoners such as José Aires were fortunate. Those who were not priests or were of humble origins could not hope for such lodgings. Instead, they were usually held in public prisons—poorly ventilated, unhealthy places where the prisoners suffered much from the heat of the tropical sun and from their shackles.

The Brazilian prisons themselves were a serious problem. In 1791, the comissário Manuel Garcia Velho do Amaral reported that the prisons in Brazil were generally very weak, which permitted frequent jailbreaks. This was particularly a problem for the ecclesiastical prison in Olinda, Manuel Garcia claimed, because the prisoners suffered such misery that their lives were in danger. For this reason, they spent considerable energy in contriving ways to escape.[46]

Indeed, inquisitional prisoners could and did escape from the prisons in Brazil, sometimes becoming quite creative in the process. For example, an unnamed mulatto being held in Olinda reportedly attempted to escape by acquiring milk from a woman named Maria so that he could work the necessary witchcraft to break out of prison.[47] Perhaps not as fantastic but no less original was the successful escape of Antônio da Silva Maciel. On August 18, 1778, the imaginative, and possibly desperate, Antônio escaped from the ecclesiastical prison in Olinda through the pipes of the latrine![48]

The comissário Manuel Garcia Velho do Amaral reported to the Inquisition that Antônio's case was not unique. In fact, on at least one occasion, all of the prisoners had escaped together from the supposedly secure underground cells of this same prison. The warden of the prison found himself banished to Angola for letting it happen. In 1791, Manuel Garcia claimed that ten of the thirteen prisoners in the ecclesiastical prison were inquisitional prisoners. He urged the Lisbon Tribunal to speed up their investigations so that the prisoners could be sent to Lisbon without further embarrassment.[49]

Throughout the colonial period, the Inquisition in Brazil relied on a system of close cooperation with non-inquisitional personnel and institutions. This system permitted the Inquisition to extend its reach beyond the localities where it had resident officials. But the system had its drawbacks. The Inquisition often found that local rivalries, conflicts, and human frailties complicated the Inquisition's already complex work. That is not to say that inquisitional officials and institutions were foolproof. Not only did prisoners successfully avoid imprisonment and escape from inquisitional officials and prisons, but those officials could also prove to be unreliable and given to abuse of their authority.

By the beginning of the eighteenth century, the Inquisition succeeded in setting up an extensive network of officials on the ground in Pernambuco and elsewhere to carry out its activities. Placing officials in all of the numerous towns and villages of the empire, however, proved impossible, especially in the vast interior of northeastern Brazil. Consequently, the Inquisition had no choice but to rely on non-inquisitional personnel to carry out its orders. Inadequacy of and lack of cooperation among non-inquisitional officials and institutions proved to be at least as much of a liability as their cooperation was a strength to the efforts of the Inquisition.

This structural ambiguity in the functioning of the Inquisition, and in the administration of the empire more generally, will come as no surprise to students of colonial Brazilian history. Overlapping and often competing authority structures were common, resulting in long-standing and repeated disputes over jurisdiction and maneuvering for position within colonial society. The interests and the structures of the Church and the state did not necessarily coincide with those of individuals or even the dominant social groups in the colony. Because these social groups were able to wield power through colonial institutions, the ambiguity of inquisitional power in colonial Brazil reflected the same ambiguity that existed in the shifting alliances and enmities between members of colonial society, the Church, and the state.[50]

Nonetheless, the Inquisition successfully created a complex system of close coordination and cooperation with non-inquisitional personnel that extended the reach of inquisitional authority deep into colonial Brazilian society. After 1690, more officials became available to carry out the Inquisition's business, and in the more settled areas they almost completely dominated inquisitional activity.

Notes

1. Alexandre Herculano, *History of the Origin and Establishment of the Inquisition in Portugal*, trans. John C. Branner (Stanford University Press, 1926). Other accounts can be found in J. Lúcio de Azevedo, *História dos Cristãos-Novos Portugueses*, 3rd ed. (Lisbon: Clássica Editora, 1989). Saraiva, *Inquisição e Cristãos-Novos*; Sonia Siqueira, "O momento de inquisição (I)," *RH* 42, no. 85 (January–March 1971): 49–73, and Siqueira, "O momento de inquisição (II)," *RH* 43, no. 87 (July–September 1971): 43–85.

2. See *Documentos para a história da Inquisição em Portugal* (Porto: Arquivo Histórico Dominicano Português, 1984), 1–27.

3. Assertions that the Lisbon Tribunal did not retain jurisdiction over Brazil are unfounded. When the officials were in Brazil, they were under its jurisdiction and could not legitimately engage in inquisitional activity without the tribunal's consent. See Sonia A. Siqueira, *A Inquisição portuguesa e a sociedade colonial* (São Paulo: Editora Ática, 1978), 141.

4. José Antônio Gonsalves e Mello, "Um Tribunal da Inquisição em Olinda, Pernambuco (1594–1595)," *Revista da Universidade de Coimbra* 36 (September 1991), 369–74.

5. The Inquisition may have sent a visita to Paraíba in 1619 under Antônio Teixeira Cabral, but it is not known whether Cabral actually held a tribunal in Paraíba. See ANTT, CGSO, NT, 4149.

6. See João Capistrano de Abreu, ed., *Primeira Visitação do Santo Offício às partes do Brasil pelo licenciado Heitor Furtado de Mendonça. Confissões da Bahia, 1591–1592* (São Paulo: Paulo Prado, 1922); Abreu, *Primeira Visitação do Santo Offício às partes do Brasil pelo licenciado Heitor Furtado de Mendonça. Denunciações da Bahia, 1591–1593* (São Paulo: Paulo Prado, 1925); Rodolfo Garcia, ed., *Primeira Visitação do Santo Offício às partes do Brasil pelo licenciado Heitor Furtado de Mendonça. Denunciações de Pernambuco 1593–1595* (São Paulo: Paulo Prado, 1929); José Antônio Gonçalves de Mello, ed., *Primeira Visitação do Santo Ofício às partes do Brasil. Confissões de Pernambuco, 1594–1595* (Recife: Universidade Federal de Pernambuco, 1970); Rodolfo Garcia, ed., "Livros das Denunciações que se fizeram na Visitação do Santo Ofício à Cidade de Salvador da Bahia de Todos os Santos do Estado do Brasil, no ano de 1618," *Anais da Biblioteca Nacional do Rio de Janeiro* 49 (1927): 100–392; Eduardo de Oliveira França and Sonia Siqueira, eds., "Segunda visitação do Santo Ofício às partes do Brasil pelo inquisidor e visitador Marcos Teixeira. Livro das Confissões e

Ratificações da Bahia, 1618–1620," *AMP* 17 (1963): 123–547; and José R. do Amaral Lapa, ed., *Livro da Visitação do Santo Ofício da Inquisição ao Estado do Grão-Pará, 1763–1769* (Petrópolis: Vozes, 1978).

7. For failure to impose orthodoxy, see Luciano Raposo de Almeida Figuereido, *Barrocas Famílias: Vida familiar em Minas Gerais no século XVII* (São Paulo: Editora Hucitec, 1997).

8. I have cited Sonia A. Siqueira's transcriptions in "Os Regimentos da Inquisição," *RIHGB* 157, no. 392 (July–September 1996): 495–1020.

9. See Siqueira, "Os Regimentos da Inquisição," 615–16, 694, 885–86 (1613 Regimento, Book I, Title I, Paragraph II; 1640 Regimento, Book I, Title I, Paragraph 1; 1774 Regimento, Book I, Title I, Paragraph 1).

10. ANTT, HSO, Francisco, m. 2, no. 48.

11. ANTT, HSO, João, m. 4, no. 153.

12. ANTT, HSO, Miguel, m. 2, no. 36.

13. ANTT, HSO, Nicolau, m. 5, no. 80; Antônio, m. 31, no. 812; ANTT, HI, m. 30, doc. 1; ANTT, HSO, Leandro, m. 1, no. 5.

14. ANTT, IL, Livro 216, fol. 45–48.

15. ANTT, CGSO, Livro 88, doc. 125. Also published in Isaías Rosa Pereira, *A Inquisição em Portugal: Séculos XVI–XVII-Período Filipino* (Lisbon: Vega, 1993), 116–17.

16. António Baião, "Tentativa de estabelecimento duma Inquisição privativa no Brasil," *Brotéria* 22 (1936): 480–81.

17. ANTT, CGSO, Livro 88, doc. 145. Also published in Pereira, *A Inquisição em Portugal*, 129.

18. Extracted from ANTT, IL, Livros 18–19. See also James E. Wadsworth, "In the Name of the Inquisition: The Portuguese Inquisition and Delegated Authority in Colonial Pernambuco, Brazil," *Americas* 61, no. 1 (July 2004): 19–54.

19. ANTT, IL, Livro 255, fols. 310–408.

20. See, for example, Fernanda Mayer Lustosa, "Raízes judaicas na Paraíba colonial: Séculos XVI–XVIII" (master's thesis, University of São Paulo, 2000), 85.

21. During the inquisitional visits to Brazil, Jesuits often served as deputies and assessors. See Serafim Leite, *História da Companhia de Jesus no Brasil* (Rio de Janeiro: Civilização Brasileira, 1938), 2:388–89.

22. This relationship developed in the sixteenth century. See Giuseppe Marcocci, "Inquisição, Jesuítas e Cristãos-Novos em Portugal no Século XVI," *RHI* 25 (2004): 247–326.

23. See Baião, "Tentativa," 477.

24. *Constituiçoens primeiras do arcebispado da Bahia* . . . (Lisbon: Miguel Rodrigues, impressor do Eminentissimo Senhor Cardeial Patriarca, 1765), 8–9, 334–35 (Book I, Title 6, Paragraph 15; Book 5, Title 1, Paragraphs 886–887).

25. António Baião, *A Inquisição em Portugal e no Brasil: Subsidios para a sua história: A Inquisição no século XVI* (Lisbon: Arquivo Histórico Portuguese, 1920), documento 70.

26. Fortunato de Almeida, *História da Igreja em Portugal* (Porto: Livraria Civilização, 1971), 2:421–22.
27. ANTT, IL, Livro 191, fol. 853.
28. See Siqueira, "Os Regimentos da Inquisição," 890 (1774 Regimento, Book I, Title I, Paragraph 13).
29. ANTT, IL, Livro 18, fol. 254.
30. ANTT, IL, Livro 19, fol. 171v.
31. ANTT, IL, Livro 23, fol. 325.
32. ANTT, IL, Livro 19, fols. 244v–245.
33. ANTT, IL, Livro 817, fol. 121; IL, NT 2125.
34. ANTT, IL, Livro 151, fols. 369–370.
35. ANTT, IL, Livro 23, fol. 134v.
36. ANTT, HSO, Antônio, m. 213, no. 3164.
37. See, for example, ANTT, IL, Livro 18, fol. 206v.
38. ANTT, HSO, Jerónimo, m. 12, no. 186.
39. ANTT, IL, Livro 255, fol. 310–311.
40. ANTT, IL, m. 10, doc. 105; ANTT, IL, Livro 301, fols. 255–264; ANTT, Papeis do Brasil Avulsos, m. 1, no. 2, fol. 100; AHU, Pernambuco, cx. 99, doc. 7769; AHU, Pernambuco, cx. 73, doc. 6118. See ANTT, Manuscritos do Brasil, 1, no. 35.
41. Lustosa, "Raízes judaicas na Paraíba colonial," 82–109; Bruno Feitler, "Cristãos-Novos da Paraíba: Do tempo dos judeus ao tempo da Inquisição" (typed manuscript, Paris, 2002); Feitler, *Inquisition, Juifs et Nouveaux-Chrétiens au Brésil.*
42. See ANTT, IL, Livro 156, fol. 171.
43. ANTT, IL, Livro 21, fols. 347–347v.
44. Taken from his account to the Inquisition. See ANTT, IL, m. 31.
45. ANTT, IL, Processo 8059. See ANTT, IL, m. 30, doc. 11.
46. ANTT, IL, m. 10, doc. 69.
47. ANTT, IL, Livro 255, fol. 370, no date.
48. ANTT, IL, m. 10, doc. 69.
49. ANTT, IL, m. 10, doc. 69.
50. Stuart B. Schwartz, *Sugar Plantations in the Formation of Brazilian Society: Bahia 1550–1835* (Cambridge: Cambridge University Press, 1985), 258–63.

CHAPTER THREE

The Inquisition at Work in Pernambuco

The system of close coordination with non-inquisitional institutions and personnel created in the sixteenth and seventeenth centuries persisted throughout the entire colonial period. Although the Inquisition permitted resident officials in Brazil as early as 1613, applications and appointments lagged for almost eighty years. After 1690, however, the Inquisition began to establish a network of permanent resident officials in Brazil. The growing interest in working for the Inquisition and the Inquisition's growing desire to construct an effective network of officials signaled the growing importance of the Inquisition as a social institution. It also permitted a transition in inquisitional focus from social control to social promotion. These officials took over much of the work of the Inquisition and strengthened its presence there. During the colonial period, the Inquisition maintained a significant presence in colonial Pernambucan society and became an important colonial institution.

Quantifying the Officials

Until recently, no one had any real idea how many officials had been appointed by the Portuguese Inquisition or who those officials were. José Veiga Torres found that 20,057 familiares were appointed between 1580 and 1820—3,114 familiares were appointed for all of Brazil. He also found 2,561 comissários for the Portuguese Empire.[1]

Pernambuco and Bahia were the two captaincies with the highest numbers of officials in Brazil.[2] Pernambuco had 885 applicants for a position as a familiar, 663 of whom received appointments. Bahia had at least 828 applicants to become familiares, while Rio had at least 658 and Minas Gerais at least 345.[3] In all, Brazil had at least 178 comissários, sixty-six of whom lived in the Captaincy-General of Pernambuco.[4] The highest concentrations of comissários were in the captaincies of Pernambuco and Bahia—113 of the 178 (63.5%) between them. Of the 1,046 individuals who applied to work for the Inquisition in Pernambuco between 1613 and 1820, 663 familiares, sixty-six comissários, fifty-eight notários, and thirteen qualificadores received appointments.

A comparison of appointments in Pernambuco with those for the Portuguese Empire reveals the larger patterns. As seen in figure 3.1, the data from Pernambuco show that the number of appointments to familiares began to rise after 1690 and continued to do so more or less steadily until the 1760s. In that decade, the number of appointments almost doubled. Where the empire experienced a decrease of nearly one-half in the decade of the 1770s, Pernambuco witnessed an increase that almost doubled the number of appointments of the previous decade. The same is true for the 1780s. Real decline set in only during the 1790s in Pernambuco. Appointments in the empire had dropped to 347, the lowest since the 1630s, and appointments in Pernambuco dropped from 182 to 56.

The decline in Pernambuco really set in after 1794. As shown in figure 3.2, applications for inquisitional office rose steadily until a dramatic jump in 1775, and they remained high until 1790. Appointments follow a similar pattern with about a two-year delay. Applications plummeted after 1794 and appointments followed in 1796. From then on, applications and appointments continued, but only in very small numbers.

So the decline of interest in inquisitional appointment that was already beginning in Portugal by the 1770s was delayed in Pernambuco, where inquisitional appointment remained attractive for another twenty-five years. The persistence of interest in inquisitional appointments in Pernambuco was due, in part, to the fact that the Inquisition had shifted its emphasis from social control to social promotion, so these appointments had not yet lost their currency in Pernambucan society.

A comparison of inquisitional sentences with the appointments of familiares (figure 3.3) demonstrates that the Inquisition had, in fact, shifted its focus after 1690. Beginning in the 1680s, following the restoration of the Inquisition after a papal suspension, the numbers of familiares receiving appointments surpassed the number of individuals being sentenced. The appointment of officials then dominated inquisitional activity until the Inquisition's abolition in 1821.

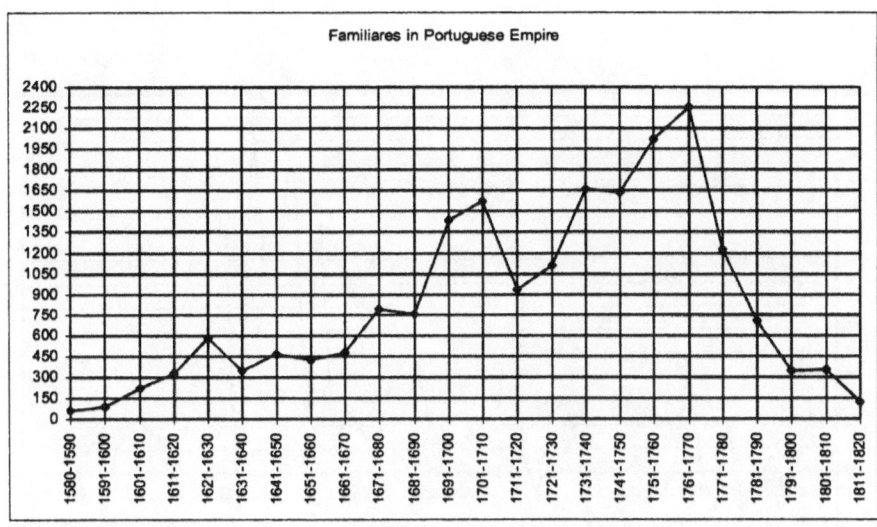

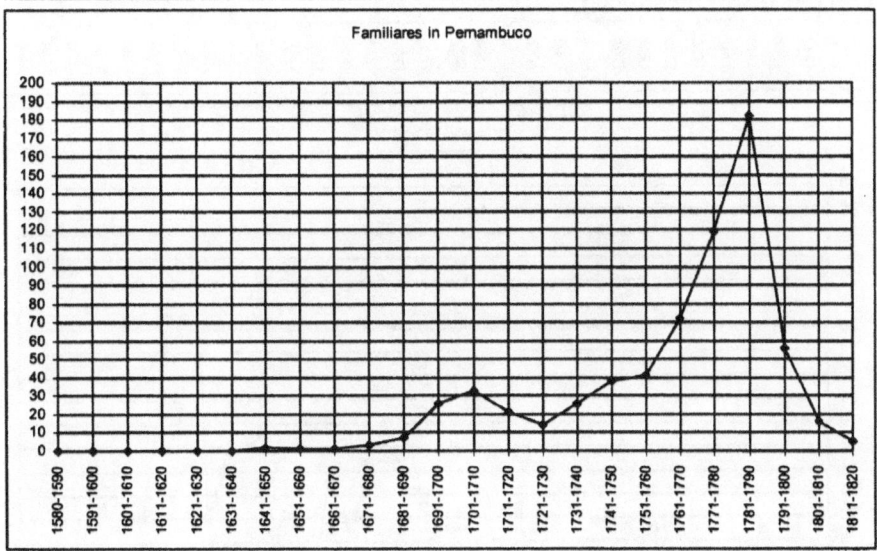

Figure 3.1. Familiares in the Portuguese Empire and Pernambuco, 1580–1820. *Sources:* Torres, "Da repressão religiosa," 133 for the Portuguese Empire; Processos de habilitação for Pernambuco, 1611-1820 [ANTT].

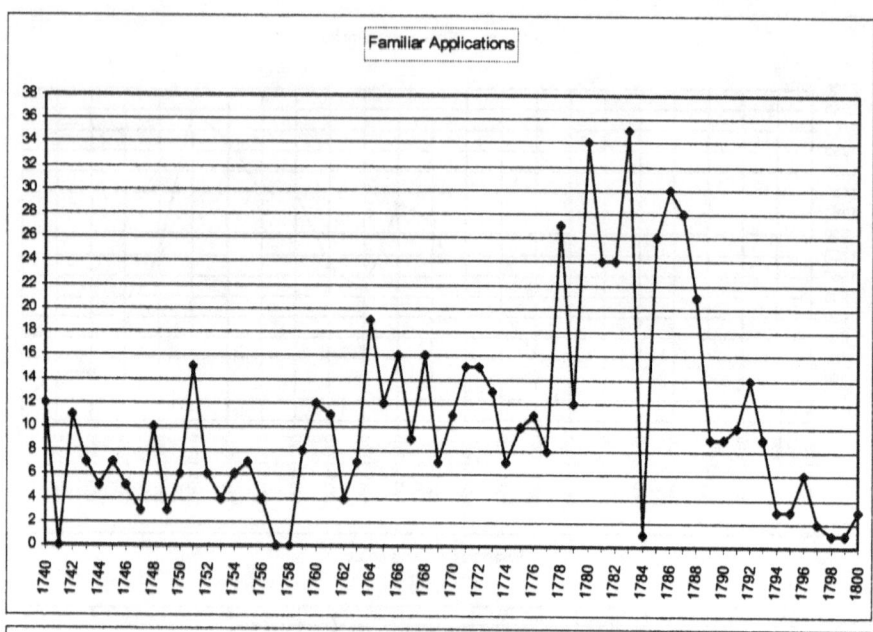

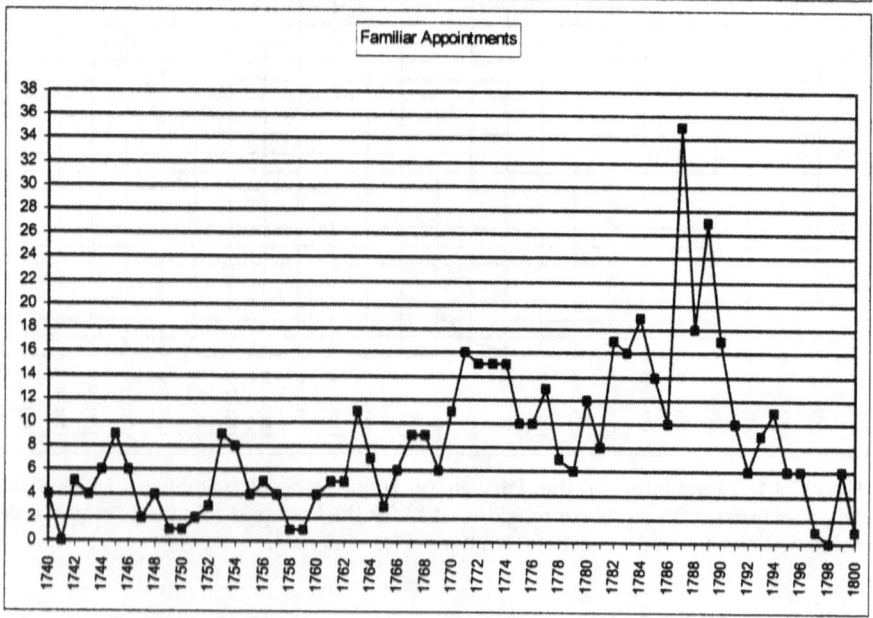

Figure 3.2. Familiar Applications and Appointments in Pernambuco, 1740–1800.
Source: Processos de habilitação for Pernambuco, 1611–1820 [ANTT].

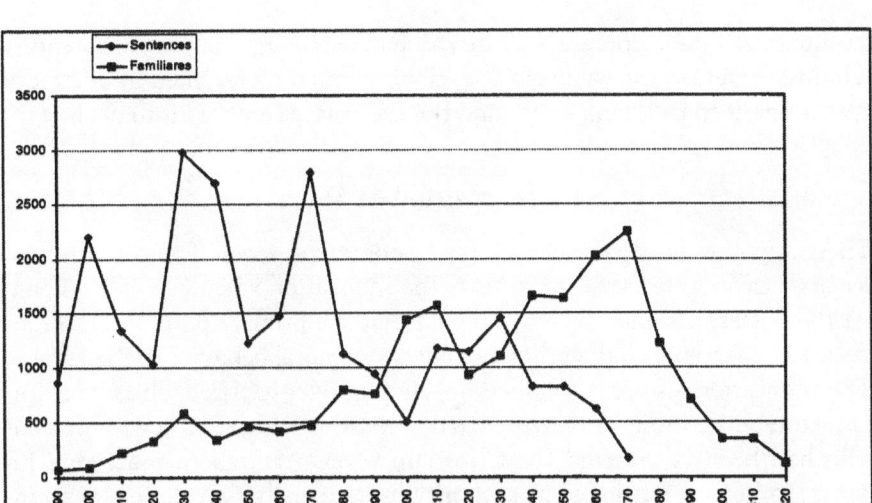

Figure 3.3. Sentences and Appointments of Familiares in the Portuguese Empire, 1580–1820. *Source:* Torres, "Da repressão religiosa," 135.

It seems clear that, after a period of weakness, the Inquisition attempted to strengthen its popular support among the aristocracy and social elite by increasing the number of familiares. At the same time, the traditional elite and the newly ascendant elite began utilizing the institution as an avenue for access to privilege, social promotion, and social legitimation.[5] Thus, at the same time that the Inquisition was seeking new sources of support and income, socially mobile groups were seeking new methods of social promotion, and they were willing to pay for it. The Inquisition found in this popular interest an opportunity to expand its own base of popular support.[6]

This shift is also evident in the growing numbers of comissários, notários, and qualificadores, which paralleled those of the familiares. The Inquisition needed more of these officials so that it could churn out certificates of pure blood in ever-larger numbers and distribute the "symbolic capital that facilitated" the acquisition of status and honor and "legitimated social promotion."[7] That capital resided primarily in the discriminatory practice of pure blood (*limpeza de sangue*). But the ideology of pure blood served more than one function. Not only did it serve as a vehicle for social, political, and economic marginalization, but it also acted as a positive and legitimate authentication for social distinctions by controlling access to religious and military orders, education, and public office. The decline of inquisitional power in the last quarter of the eighteenth century, due in part to mid-eighteenth-century reforms, decreased the value of the symbolic capital represented by a letter of appointment to the Inquisition, and the Inquisition entered into decline.

The Inquisition at Work

These appointments were not simply honorary, however. The officials who received them were expected to serve the Inquisition whenever called upon. At the outset, it should be remembered that the primary purpose of the Inquisition was to police the religious beliefs and moral behavior of the empire. The Inquisition also only retained jurisdiction over baptized Christians. Initially established to root out suspected crypto-Jews (those of Jewish descent who had been "converted" to Christianity yet persisted in practicing Judaism), it quickly expanded its authority over virtually every aspect of an individual's religious and moral life. In colonial Brazil, the denunciation served as the primary mechanism for discovering religious and moral unorthodoxy.

Inquisitional officials in Brazil faced the continual challenge of educating the public as to what they should denounce and encouraging them to do so. No clear distinction existed in colonial Brazil between crime and sin. Indeed, most kinds of wrongdoing were both sinful and criminal. The practice of denunciation remained very common at all levels of colonial government and formed a fundamental part of the Portuguese system of social and political policing. All members of colonial society were expected to inform the proper authorities of the misconduct of their friends, neighbors, and family members. The Inquisition joined the ecclesiastical hierarchy in using denunciations to police the piety and orthodoxy of the Catholic congregation. The bishops held ecclesiastical tribunals and organized periodic visitas within their dioceses, receiving denunciations and trying cases. In addition, not all crimes against Christian morality fell under the jurisdiction of the Inquisition. For example, denunciations of incest made to the Inquisition usually received the brief marginal note, "does not pertain to the Inquisition."[8]

To educate the masses, the Inquisition published the *éditos-da-fé* (edicts of faith). The comissários had the primary responsibility for disseminating these printed edicts sent from Lisbon, and they regularly sent the familiares to distribute them to all the churches and convents. The colonial clergy were supposed to read the edicts aloud in the parish churches and monasteries every year on the first Sunday of Lent, and occasionally during the Conventual Masses, and then post them in the sacristy as a perpetual reminder.[9] The Inquisition used Lent because it was traditionally the period of fasting, prayer, and penitence in preparation for Easter and was the appropriate time to clear one's conscience. Sometimes the parish priests failed to read the edict every year. For example, in 1719, the cathedral chapter of Olinda complained that this failure caused much scandal, principally in the Sertão (arid backlands of northeastern Brazil), where crimes were not denounced because the people remained ignorant of this obligation.[10]

The edict listed the crimes for which the Inquisition had jurisdiction in hierarchical order. These were the crimes that the faithful were obligated to denounce. Of course, these lists changed over time as the political and religious context in Portugal evolved. By 1792, the crimes listed included all doubts or ill will toward the Catholic Church; the use of reason and philosophy to "blaspheme" God, his mysteries, and the Virgin Mary; practicing Islam, Judaism, Lutheranism, or Calvinism; denial of the mortal sins and the necessity of works; thinking ill of, or mocking, the sacraments, vows, and ceremonies of the Church; doubting the obligation to confess; denying the existence of purgatory and the Church's power to grant indulgences; denying the veneration of saints; solicitation; sodomy; astrology; witchcraft; superstitions; pacts with the devil; freemasonry; buying, selling, or reading prohibited books without license; and false testimony to the Inquisition. Bigamy also fell under inquisitional jurisdiction because it was seen as a denial or abuse of the sacrament of marriage. Despite the great mixture of African, Indian, and Portuguese varieties of religious expression in the Brazilian colonies, the Inquisition never felt that it was necessary to revise the edict for Brazil, as they did for both Goa and Angola.[11]

The edict required all Catholics to come forward within thirty days of the public reading and denounce all that they knew regarding any of these issues or confess their own infractions. If they did so, the Inquisition offered them greater mercy and lenience. If they failed to do so, or impeded another from so doing, they would be excommunicated and prosecuted by the Inquisition. Excommunication severed the offender from the Christian community and was not to be courted lightly.[12]

To make a denunciation, an individual communicated either personally or through an intermediary to the nearest comissário. If there were no comissários, then he could make the denunciation to his confessor, who would then relay it immediately to the Inquisition. When comissários received denunciations, they made the denouncer swear an oath and sign the recorded denunciation. The comissário then sent the denunciation to the Lisbon Tribunal. When the Tribunal determined that sufficient evidence existed to justify a formal inquiry, it sent an order to one of its officials in the colony, usually a comissário, or a non-inquisitional authority. The comissário then ordered a familiar or group of familiares to arrest the suspects, sequester their property, and detain them until they could be sent to Lisbon for trial. In most cases, they called upon secular authorities to provide military support and the magistrate general (ouvidor geral) to act as the fiscal judge for the Inquisition and keep a record of and administer all sequestered property.

The comissários formed the backbone of inquisitional power in Brazil, and all other inquisitional officials were subordinate to them.[13] They held responsibility for carrying out all inquiries sent to them, either to investigate accused heretics or to qualify potential officials. At the direction of the comissários, the familiares summoned witnesses, took prisoners, escorted them to the ships that were to carry them to Lisbon, and sometimes accompanied them across the Atlantic. The familiares also escorted the comissários when they had to travel to perform inquiries and assisted the comissários with all of their work.[14] The notários often served as scribes for the investigations, carefully taking down the witnesses' testimony. When a comissário was either not present or unable to perform the inquiry, the notários could also do so. The qualificadores technically reviewed written works to see whether they broke the rules of inquisitional censorship; but in Brazil, where printing presses were not allowed until 1808 and few libraries existed, they found very little employment in this area. More often, they simply worked as comissários.

The officials of the Inquisition operated under strict limitations, although comissários in Brazil had slightly expanded authority. The great distance separating Lisbon from Brazil and the significant time lag between the sending of denunciations to Lisbon and the response of the tribunal necessitated expanded authority for comissários in the colony. Potential witnesses in these cases could die or move to another area, and suspects could flee, thus avoiding punishment. For these reasons, comissários in Brazil received permission to do judicial inquiries and ratify all denunciations given to them. This meant that they had the authority to have informants give recorded testimony in front of witnesses. This did not mean they could try cases, only that they could investigate and collect judicially recorded testimonies in those that seemed urgent enough to warrant such action.[15]

Comissários could legitimately detain suspects without orders only if three conditions had been met: a clear cause that pertained to the Inquisition, sufficient evidence, and reason to believe that the individual might flee. Instructions sent to comissários in Brazil included the conditions that the crime was sufficiently grave to warrant such action, that it was done according to the law, and that recorded and ratified testimonies had been taken.[16] Otherwise, they had to send the information to Lisbon and await instructions.

Sometimes the comissários sought an extension of their authority in this area. For example, in 1796 Comissário Henrique Martins Gaio asked for permission to act immediately on denunciations of those who possessed, sold, read, or purchased "pernicious" books or papers. He wanted to be able to go right away to the home of the accused, apprehend the offending literature, and send it to Lisbon before the accused could hide it. The General Council denied his request.[17]

Comissários also could not sequester property without specific instructions to do so from the Inquisition. When they did sequester property, a notário or familiar made two copies of the inventory, one that remained with the comissário and another that was given to the juiz do fisco, who received and administered the sequestered goods. They also had no jurisdiction over civil cases, nor could they obstruct other ecclesiastical or secular jurisdictions without instructions from Lisbon. In practice, of course, this authority was often abused. In addition, comissários did not retain jurisdiction over each other. If a comissário were guilty of a crime, then other comissários could take no action on their own, but had to inform Lisbon.[18]

All the officials, including the familiares, were required to denounce any crimes that they were aware of, just like everybody else; but there is no evidence that they ever acted as spies for the Inquisition in Brazil, as has sometimes been asserted.[19] The Inquisition had little reason to create a private network of spies, in any case, because all Catholics were obligated to denounce crimes against the faith. Likewise, familiares could not legitimately engage in any inquisitional activity without instructions from the comissário or the tribunal in Lisbon.[20]

Quantifying Inquisitional Activity

We do not know exactly how many individuals passed through the Inquisition's clutches, but we have a good idea of how many were tried (*processado*) and "relaxed" (*relaxado*, meaning delivered to the secular authorities for execution) by the four inquisitional tribunals of Lisbon, Coimbra, Évora, and Goa.[21] The period of most intense inquisitional activity occurred between 1584 and 1674, after Portugal fell under the Spanish crown and before the papal suspension of inquisitional activity between 1679 and 1681. Between 1606 and 1674, the Inquisition investigated 22,481 cases and sent 863 individuals, either in person or in effigy, to the civil authorities for execution. The next one hundred years saw a marked decrease in this type of inquisitional activity. Between 1675 and 1767, 12,142 cases came before inquisitional tribunals, and 446 faced the flames either in person or effigy.[22]

The lists of the autos-da-fé show how many individuals were sentenced in those proceedings and reveals that the number of individuals actually executed by the Inquisition was fewer than is usually thought. Of the 28,266 who appeared in the autos-da-fé, 1,817 were relaxed: 1,175 in person (4.2%) and 642 in effigy (2.2%).[23] Most of the actual executions occurred in the sixteenth and seventeenth centuries, and several years often passed between executions. Of the 44,817 individuals who were investigated, 28,266 (63% of those who came before the Inquisition) were punished and 1,175 (2.6%) actually perished in the flames.

Within this larger field of inquisitional activity, Brazil became an important arena for the prosecution and punishment of crimes against the Inquisition. The rhythms of inquisitional activity in Brazil have not yet been mapped out in their entirety, but we can sketch the general outlines. As in Portugal, New Christians formed the primary raw material for inquisitional activity. A report submitted to the General Council in the early seventeenth century reflected the general perception of the Brazilian sugar-producing regions as a haven for crypto-Jews. The report claimed that New Christians sought out Pernambuco and Bahia because they could live without fear, practice their ceremonies without discovery, and be served by "Negro brutes" who knew nothing of Christianity. Many New Christians owned sugar mills and had become wealthy and influential members of colonial society.[24] Likewise, the Inquisition regularly banished its prisoners to Brazil. Between 1540 and 1720, 590 prisoners were sent to Brazil. These represented 49.7 percent of all those banished by the Inquisition to overseas colonies.[25]

The lists of the autos-da-fé held by the Lisbon Tribunal demonstrate that Brazil served as a significant zone of inquisitional activity, which suggests that the close cooperation with non-inquisitional personnel was at the very least marginally successful. They also allow us to locate the areas of most intense inquisitional activity and the groups selected for inquisitional prosecution.

Of the 556 individuals from Brazil punished in autos-da-fé, the most frequently punished "crimes" were Judaism and bigamy, but they also included many of the other crimes against the faith.[26] Most of those punished for Judaism came from two relatively intense periods of activity in two regions of Brazil. Between 1709 and 1728, most of those punished in the autos-da-fé were New Christians from Rio de Janeiro, many of whom were related.[27] Between 1731 and 1741, a large group of related individuals from Paraíba was also punished.[28] Men represented the majority of those punished in Lisbon (372 or 66.9%), while women represented 33.1 percent (184).[29]

Consequently, more than one-half of those punished in the *autos* were from Rio, followed by Bahia, Paraíba, and Pernambuco. Most of the punishments handed down were limited to prison terms and wearing the coarse sleeveless habit known as the sanbenito. Bigamists and sodomites received special treatment: most of them were sentenced to be whipped and sent to the galleys. Most of the New Christians punished for Judaizing received prison sentences and the sanbenito. Nineteen individuals were relaxed, five in effigy and fourteen in the flesh. All but one of those were convicted of Judaizing. The other was convicted of Calvinism.

Until recently, estimates of how many people from Brazil were tried by the Inquisition were very low.[30] One thousand eight hundred nineteen men and women were accused or suspected by the Inquisition of Judaizing in Brazil in the eighteenth century alone.[31] At least 1,076 prisoners, both men and women, were sent from Brazil to Lisbon.[32] At least 148 men and women were accused of homoerotic behavior during the colonial period.[33] Indeed, the evidence from the *autos* suggests that during the eighteenth century, inquisitional activity in Brazil provided a significant portion of the total inquisitional activity in the empire.

From 1709–1737, Brazil provided a substantial number of those punished in the autos-da-fé, sometimes exceeding 50 percent. Brazilians continued to appear in significant numbers for the rest of the eighteenth century. Between 1600 and 1787, fully 13.85 percent of those punished in the autos-da-fé came from Brazil. Of those punished in the autos of the eighteenth century, 21.25 percent were from Brazil. The very high percentage of individuals from Brazil being punished at the autos-da-fé suggests the increasing importance of Brazil as a locus for inquisitional activity.

Denunciations to the Inquisition came from all over the Captaincy-General of Pernambuco as did the individuals who were punished in the autos-da-fé, but they tended to concentrate in the Zona da Mata (93.4% of the denunciations and 72.0% of those punished) and the more urban areas (see figure 3.4).[34]

Judaism (37.9%), bigamy (12.1%), witchcraft (8.2%), and heretical propositions (6.4%) were the most frequent "crimes" denounced to the Inquisition in Pernambuco. Judaism remained the most frequently denounced crime during the seventeenth century and up until about 1740. After 1740, most of the denunciations were for bigamy, heretical propositions, and disrespect for the sacraments and images of the saints. After the mid-eighteenth century, the so-called philosophical heresies and freemasonry drew considerable attention from the Inquisition.[35] Accusations of Judaism never disappeared entirely, however, even after the 1773 pure-blood law did away with the distinction between New and Old Christians. The latest case I found was from 1799. The pure-blood law did not make Jewish practices legal; it only eliminated the distinction between New and Old Christians and legal

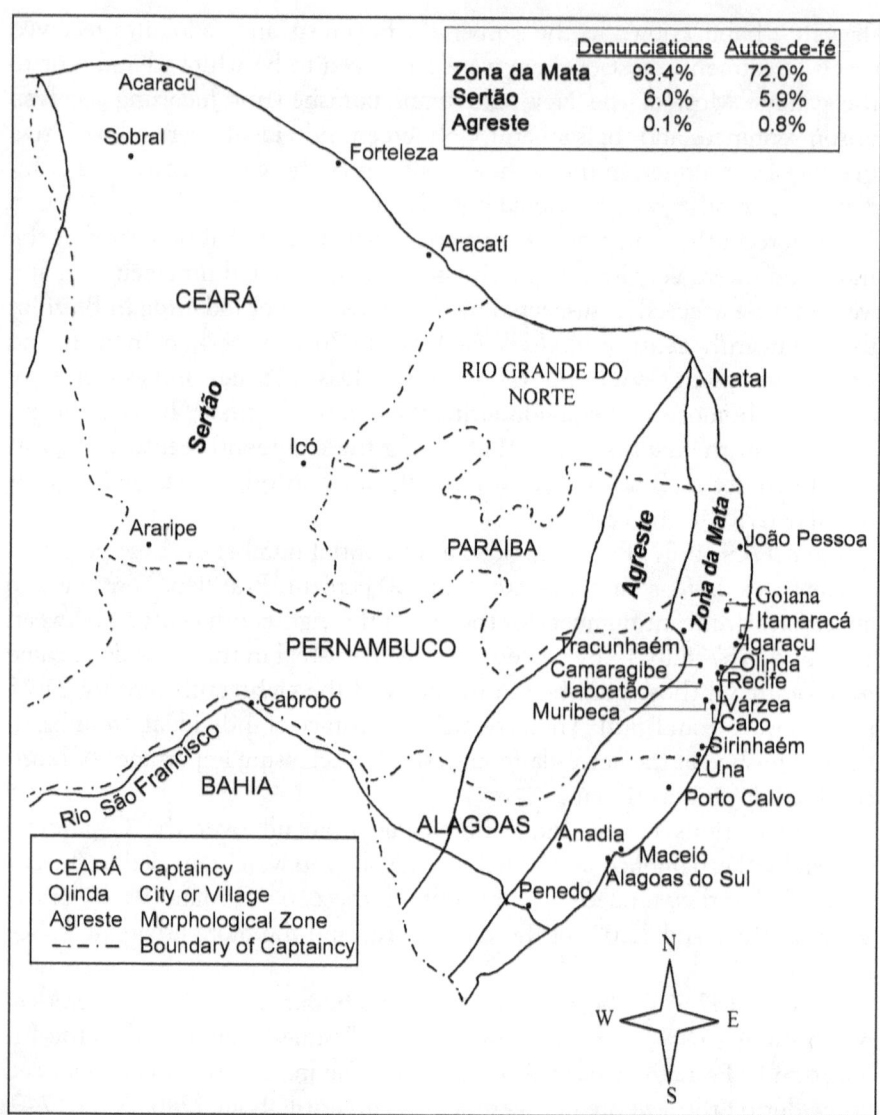

Figure 3.4. Distribution of Those Denounced to and Punished by the Inquisition from the Captaincy-General of Pernambuco by Morphological Zone, 1590–1810.

discrimination against New Christians. Judaism, if practiced by baptized Christians, remained a heresy. All of this suggests that the Inquisition remained active for much of the colonial period in Brazil and was generally effective in using its cooperative system to carry out its activities. To be sure, problems, weaknesses, abuses, and failures existed. Overall, however, the system proved to be remarkably effective and resilient.

The creation of a network of officials on the ground in Pernambuco in the eighteenth century responded to increasing popular interest and the Inquisition's own desire to garner more popular support. It also signaled a shift in inquisitional focus from repression to promotion as individuals began to use the Inquisition in increasing numbers to legitimate their social status.

But inquisitional appointments were not merely honorary. They required service to the Inquisition. Officials were responsible for instructing the populace regarding what constituted crimes against the faith, in investigating those crimes, and in bringing deviants to inquisitional justice. The activities of the Inquisition in Brazil show that Brazil constituted an important focus of inquisitional activity and that within Pernambuco that activity concentrated within the Zona da Mata, where the bulk of the population and officials of the Inquisition lived. That activity was not limited to the populated region and could and did penetrate into the interior.

No matter how much a man might desire to work for the Inquisition, however, he could not legitimately do so until he had passed through the refining and socially purifying fires of an intense inquisitional investigation into his conduct and ancestry. The challenge of this fire lay in its ability not only to burn off the dross of impure and irresponsible men, but also to scorch and purify those "honorable" men who wanted to publicly proclaim their purity by daring to pass through its flames.

Notes

1. See Torres, "Da repressão religiosa para a promoção social." Previous attempts to quantify the familiares have been inadequate. See Siqueira, A Inquisição portuguesa, 163, 168, 181, and Calainho, "Em nome do Santo Ofício," 67–68, 70, 73.

2. It is likely that between four and five thousand men applied from Brazil and around 3,500 were accepted. For previous attempts to quantify the officials, see Siqueira, A Inquisição Portuguesa, 140, footnote 3. Bethencourt, História das Inquisições, 51.

3. These numbers are based on my study of the applications for appointment (habilitações) in the Torre do Tombo, novas habilitações (new habilitações), the

habilitações incompletas (incomplete habilitações), and the *livros de juramentos* (the books where the oaths were recorded).

4. Sonia Siqueira's tabulations are extremely low for Pernambuco and probably elsewhere. A quick run of the habilitações revealed the following: comissários, at least 184 in Brazil (Rio de Janeiro had at least 39, Bahia 38, Minas Gerais 10, Grão Pará 9, Maranhão 8, São Paulo 7, Mariana 3, Espírito Santo 2, Matto Grosso 1, Goiás 1, and Pernambuco 66); notários, at least 89 in Brazil (Pernambuco 58, Bahia 13, Rio de Janeiro 10, Minas Gerais 3, Maranhão 2, Mariana 2, and Grão Pará 1); qualificadores, at least 39 in Brazil (Pernambuco 13, Bahia 15, Rio de Janeiro 8, Maranhão 2, and Sergipe 1). These numbers are probably still low because a thorough search has yet to be made. For Siqueira's numbers, see A *Inquisição portuguesa*, 163, 168, 181.

5. Bethencourt, *História das Inquisições*, 51.

6. Siqueira, "Os Regimentos da Inquisição," 560.

7. Torres, "Da repressão religiosa," 114.

8. David Higgs, "Sacred and Secular Law in Late Colonial Brazil" (paper presented at the Latin American Studies Association, Chicago, 1998), 1–6.

9. See ANTT, CGSO, m. 19, no. 76; CGSO, m. 6, no. 27; CGSO, m. 7, no. 34; CGSO, m. 4, no. 28; CGSO, m. 40, no. 40; IL, NT 2125, 2146, 3135; IL, m. 33 and 54. The officials sometimes requested more edicts to replace old ones that were falling to pieces. See ANTT, IL, m. 4, no. 3.

10. ANTT, IL, Livro 20, fol. 246v–249.

11. The edict for Goa dealt with the problems of syncretism with Hinduism, Buddhism, Islam, and other religions. For Angola, the edict included direct references to the various practices and ceremonies of African culture and religion. See Higgs, "Sacred and Secular Law," 2. The edict for Angola can be found in ANTT, IL, m. 52.

12. ANTT, CGSO, m. 30, no. 2.

13. For comissários in Spain, see José Enrique Pasamar Lázaro, "El comisario del Santo Oficio en el distrito inquisitorial de Aragón," *Revista de la Inquisición* 6 (1997): 191–238.

14. See Siqueira, "Os Regimentos da Inquisição," 758–59 (1640 Regimento, Book I, Title XXI, Paragraphs 2 and 4).

15. ANTT, IL, Livro 20, fol. 242–254.

16. ANTT, IL, Livro 20, fol. 243.

17. ANTT, CGSO, NT 4195.

18. "Instrução que hão guardar os Comissários do Santo Officio da Inquisição nas cousas, e negocios da fee, e no demais que se offerecerem." See ANTT, CGSO, m. 12, no. 28.

19. See Novinsky, "A Inquisição," 4; Novinsky, "A Igreja no Brasil colonial," 19. Henry Kamen also rejects the "familiares as spies" argument for Spain. See Kamen, *Spanish Inquisition*, 145.

20. ANTT, CGSO, m. 12, no. 28.

21. See José Veiga Torres, "Uma longa guerra social: Os rítmos da repressão inquisitorial em Portugal," *RHES* 1 (January–June, 1978): 55–68; Torres, "Uma longa

guerra social: Novas perspectivas para o estudo da Inquisição portuguesa a Inquisição de Coimbra," RHI 8 (1986): 59–74; and Torres, "Da repressão religiosa."

22. Bethencourt, História das Inquisições, 275.

23. Almeida, História da Igreja, 4:287–317.

24. ANTT, IL, Livro 216, fols. 45–48. See Anita Novinsky, Cristãos-Novos na Bahia: A Inquisição, 2nd ed. (São Paulo: Editora Perspectiva, 1992). See also Gonsalves de Mello, Gente da nação, 7.

25. See Geraldo Pieroni, Os excluídos do reino: A inquisição portuguesa e o degredo para o Brasil colonial (Brasília: Editora Universidade de Brasília, 2000), 14–15. See also his other two books on banishment to Brazil, Banidos: A Inquisição e a lista dos Cristãos-Novos condenados a viver no Brasil (Rio de Janeiro: Bertrand Brasil, 2003) and Vadios e ciganos, heréticos e bruxas (Rio de Janeiro: Bertrand Brasil, 2000).

26. BNL, Cod. 166–169; ANTT, CGSO, Livro 435; IL, Livros 30, 31, 32, 159, 327; Processos 56, 111, 112, 306, 436, 514, 720, 1324, 1335, 1480, 2304, 5306, 5534, 5546, 5579, 5674, 6344, 8657, 8675, 11035.

27. Lina Gorenstein Ferreira da Silva, Herético e impuros: A Inquisição e os cristãos-novos no Rio de Janeiro século XVIII (Rio de Janeiro: Secretaria Municipal de Cultura, Departamento Geral de Documentação e Informação Cultural, Divisão de Editoração, 1995).

28. This wave of inquisitional activity in Paraíba began with the denunciation of two New Christians against members of their own families, probably motivated by revenge. See Lustosa, "Raízes judaicas na Paraíba colonial," 84–109, and Feitler Inquisition, Juifs et Nouveaux-Chretiens au Bresil.

29. In the sixteenth and seventeenth centuries, it was typically "a white, Portuguese-born man of middle age and middle income who appeared before the Tribunal. Few women appeared." See Patricia Aufderheide, "True Confessions: The Inquisition and Social Attitudes in Brazil at the Turn of the XVII Century," in LBR 20, no. 2 (December 1973): 212.

30. See Bethencourt, História das Inquisições, 129.

31. Anita Novinsky, Rol dos Culpados: Fontes para a história do Brasil, século XVIII (Rio de Janeiro: Expressão e Cultura, 1992).

32. Anita Novinsky, Inquisição: Prisioneiros do Brasil, Séculos XVI - XIX (Rio de Janeiro: Expressao e Cultura, 2002).

33. Mott, Homosexuais da Bahia.

34. These numbers are incomplete because the records are incomplete. See ANTT, CGSO, Livros 435 and 529; ANTT, CGSO, m. 8, no. 4; IL, Livro 23, 31–32, 65, 159–162, 255, 263, 265, 268, 280–281, 299, 300–301, 306, 315–317, 322–323, 327–329, 818, 922; IL, m. 3, no. 21, m. 19, no. 53, m. 26, no. 58, m. 27, nos. 16, 20, 30, m. 30, no. 11, m. 40; IL, NT 2123, 2132, 2160, 3135; IL, Processos 12, 56, 78, 111, 112, 132, 226, 306, 402, 436, 514, 720, 820, 885, 936, 1061, 1324, 1332, 1335, 1377, 1406, 1439, 1462, 1480, 1770, 1829, 1847, 1958, 2304, 2439, 2686, 2776, 2778, 3693, 4044, 5212, 5306, 5534, 5546, 5586, 5579, 5674, 5840, 5844, 5863, 6344, 6625, 7276, 7533, 8059, 8657, 8675, 9747, 10401, 10890, 11035, 11575,

12991, 13817, 14321, 16460, 17213, 11362; 12945, 17213; Novinsky, *Rol dos Culpados*.

35. Luís A. de Oliveira Ramos coined the phrase *heréticos de filosofia* and made the same argument. See Luís A. Oliveira Ramos, "A Inquisição pombalina," *Brotéria* 115, no. 2–4 (August–October, 1982): 173–74.

CHAPTER FOUR

Qualifying for Office: Procedures and Costs

Officials of the Inquisition necessarily came from the men who chose to apply for appointments. The Inquisition, of course, had to rely on this raw material to construct the network of officials who could then carry out inquisitional business and see to the reproduction and maintenance of inquisitional power and prestige within the colony. To that end, the Inquisition constructed over time a set of standards and procedures that tried to guarantee the selection of the best available candidates. These exclusionary practices permitted the Inquisition to construct the image of honor and prestige that it wanted to portray and that attracted potential officials. It also contributed to the strength of the institution.

The procedures and the costs of an application for inquisitional appointment help us understand the accessibility of inquisitional office and the techniques of selection that contributed to the construction of social honor and status. These investigations for qualification had to be paid for, and over time the Inquisition developed an increasingly efficient system for collecting its fees. But the cost of the investigation limited the accessibility of an appointment to those groups who had sufficient surplus income to spend on an appointment that was not guaranteed to bring large financial returns.

The Processo

The process by which potential officials of the Holy Office were qualified and approved first appeared in the 1613 Regimento, but was not fully systematized until the 1640 Regimento. The 1640 Regimento provided greater bureaucratic efficiency, taking advantage of the growing centralization of the Inquisition, and reflected the growing intolerance within Portugal.

The investigations were supposed to proceed under the *estilo* of the Holy Office.[1] The term *estilo*, translated as "style" or "custom," referred to the practices and traditions, both written and unwritten, that governed the manner in which the Inquisition proceeded against the accused. In other words, the same method by which the Inquisition determined the veracity of denunciations against accused heretics would be applied to those who wished to work for the Holy Office. In form, at least, this proved to be true; but the history of the application process shows that, in practice, the Inquisition functioned differently when it came to the qualifying inquiries into potential officials of the Inquisition.

The Inquisition could upgrade the application process in the seventeenth century because it had adopted the "technology of documentation." The 1613 Regimento mandated the careful collecting and organizing of inquisitional records for rapid and easy access of information about both accused heretics and potential officials. These records included registers of denunciations, confiscation of goods, and the creation of inquisitional officials and were used regularly in the investigations. Elaborate indexes permitted the rapid retrieval of information. This technology of documentation served not only as an aid to memory, but also as a tool to create information, coerce suspects, and legitimate inquisitional procedure.[2]

The actual requirements of office developed over nearly one hundred years and reached their final form, or nearly final form, in 1640. According to the 1640 Regimento, officials of the Inquisition had to be

> natives of the kingdom, Old Christians of pure blood, without Moorish or Jewish race, or newly converted people to our holy faith, and without fame to the contrary; who have not been involved in any public infamy of deed or law, nor imprisoned nor punished by the Inquisition. Nor are they descendants of persons who have one of the aforementioned defects. They will be of good quality and customs, capable of being entrusted with any business of importance or secrecy. The same qualities should also be found in the people that the *ordinário* [referring to the bishops] names to assist in the completion of the investigations of the people within its jurisdiction . . . .[They all should be able] to read and write. If they are married, their wives and children should have the same purity.[3]

These requirements did not change until the 1774 Regimento eliminated the requirement for purity of blood.

Qualifying for Office: Procedures and Costs ~ 55

To apply for inquisitional office, a formal application was submitted through the local comissário to Lisbon, where a scribe prepared a formal petition. The petition contained all relevant genealogical information, including the place of birth, marriage, and residence, for the applicant and his wife, their parents, their grandparents, and sometimes their great-grandparents (see figure 4.1).[4] Likewise, any official who wanted to marry needed to have his future wife qualified by the Inquisition before doing so.

The process included two major steps. The first step in the investigation included a search of the records of the tribunals of Coimbra, Évora, and Lisbon to ensure that neither the applicant nor his wife nor any of their ancestors or relatives had been condemned for any crimes against the Holy Office. If any crimes were discovered, the notários briefly summarized the crime and the outcome of the proceedings in the margin of the request and appended the text to the diligência. If the applicant had indicated that a relative was an official of the Inquisition, a search was also made among the records of the General Council and his letter of appointment was copied and placed in the diligência.

The second step involved the investigations undertaken in both the applicant's place of birth and place of residence, as well as those of his wife and their ancestors. This step had two parts. The first part, known as the extrajudicial, involved an informal inquiry by an official at the applicant's place of birth and residence into the purity of the applicant's blood, his customs

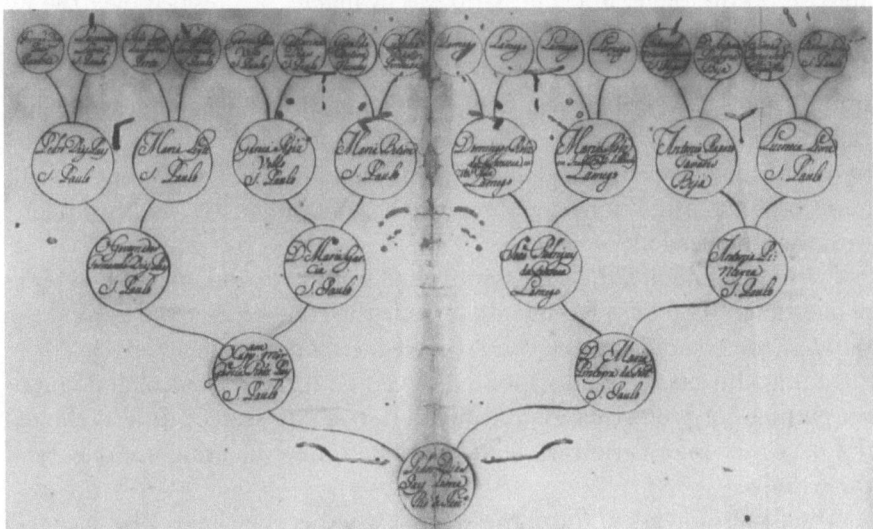

Figure 4.1. Family Tree Submitted with Application for Office. *Source:* ANTT, HSO Pedro, m. 25, no. 476, fol. 30.

and behavior, and his financial situation. After the 1690s, comissários most frequently performed the extrajudicial, but notários did them as well. Less frequently, familiares could also do so.[5]

The official performing the extrajudicial usually interviewed between four and twelve informants and then submitted his report with a list of the witnesses questioned. If the extrajudicial turned up any questionable ancestry or behavior, the General Council often sent another extrajudicial for further clarification. If further inquiry confirmed the questionable information, the application could be discontinued. Likewise, if the official could not find information regarding the individual or his family, the application could sit for decades without any further inquiry or be permanently discontinued.

Several reforms of the mid-eighteenth century focused on this part of the procedures. For example, an April 25, 1759, order stated that the official should ask all the necessary questions regarding the applicant's customs, capacity, yearly income, age, literacy, marriage status, children, public opinion, and ancestry without omission. On February 13, 1758, the General Council decreed that, in order to avoid dishonesty on the part of the comissários, the formal, or judicial, inquiry should not be sent to the same individual who had done the extrajudicial. And all of these should be given to comissários of known capacity, judgment, and secrecy.[6]

The Inquisition called the second part of the inquiry the judicial. In this formal inquiry, a familiar summoned the witnesses, who were made to swear an oath on the Bible. If a comissário was available, he presided over the judicial inquiry, but notários and qualificadores could and did carry them out, as did other ecclesiastical authorities specifically commissioned by the Inquisition to do so. A scribe, most frequently a notário but sometimes a qualificador, familiar, or comissário delegado, always attended the judicial inquiry to record the questions asked and the testimony given.[7] In all cases, the Inquisition sent instructions detailing which questions to ask, and how many witnesses to question.[8]

During the inquiry, the comissário asked eight to twelve witnesses a series of questions.[9] The 1774 Regimento forbade the comissários to go beyond the terms of the commission they had received, either in asking questions or in recording answers.[10] The questioning served both the rhetorical and practical purposes of protecting inquisitorial prestige and secrecy. It also elicited the necessary information while at the same time evaluating the quality of the witness.

The comissário asked the witnesses first whether they knew why they had been summoned. Then they asked several specific questions regarding the applicant's ancestry and behavior. The Inquisition wanted to know whether the applicant was an illegitimate child, whether he had any illegitimate children, and whether he or his ancestors were heretics or had committed crimes against the king or the Inquisition. Finally, the witnesses were asked whether they had any reason to hate or dislike the applicant. The Inquisition had reservations about testimony given by a witness who had any animosity toward an applicant. If animosity could be shown to exist, the witness was effectively impeached and the testimony could be thrown out.[11]

The Inquisition relied on Old Christians and familiares as witnesses where possible.[12] The 1640 Regimento instructed the comissários to go to the homes of the very old to take their testimony.[13] The Inquisition did this because these witnesses had the longest memories in a largely illiterate society that still placed great weight on the truth-value of oral testimony.[14]

The witnesses were white, and they were usually men. Women testified in only thirty-nine inquiries for potential candidates and twenty-three inquiries for their spouses (144 women in all). The comissários had to take care to question women in a manner that would not tarnish the women's honor or their own. Women were, of course, not allowed to go to the home of the comissário (who was always a cleric), but had to be questioned in a church. This certainly complicated the taking of female testimonies and may help explain their less-frequent participation in the inquiries.

Familiares also played a significant role as witnesses. They testified in 195 judicial cases for potential officials and sixty-five for women. More importantly, they almost always testified in extrajudicial inquires. Comissários and notários only appeared occasionally.

The significance of this practice of calling local witnesses should not be underestimated, especially when we attempt to understand the presence and influence of the Holy Office in Brazil. This practice gave men and women a very real relationship with the Inquisition—one that extended beyond pageantry and overt oppression. The people not only participated in inquisitional inquiries, but they also had the power to influence the outcome of petitions for office. Expanding the sheer numbers of familiares necessarily expanded the inquisitional base of support and also drew ever-larger numbers of people into overt collaboration with the Inquisition.

Likewise, using inquisitional officials not only to perform the inquiries but also to act as witnesses allowed these officials to have significant input into who could join their status group, thus contributing to the Inquisition's closed and exclusive nature. This was particularly true because familiares almost always appear in the extrajudicial stage, where the primary weeding out of candidates took place. More importantly, however, the selection of witnesses indicates that the Inquisition actively engaged the local population and cannot be seen strictly as an outside imposition. This engagement of the local population also shows that the problems that applicants encountered arose from rumors of impurity reported by their own peers.

At the conclusion of the questioning, the witnesses' testimonies were read to them before they signed them. The comissários then wrote a brief summary of the testimonies, commenting on the trustworthiness of the witnesses and giving their assessment of the candidates.[15] Their conclusions carried considerable weight, and very seldom did the deputies override them.

The comissários paid close attention not only to the words spoken but also to the body language of witnesses. For example, Father Rodrigo Gaioso noted that two of his witnesses in his inquiry on Marcos Soares de Oliveira were not reliable. One witness, Manuel da Paz Barreira, showed a certain repugnance to answering the questions, and by his manner of speech he appeared to be hiding something about Marcos's ancestry. The comissário later found that Manuel had revealed information about the inquiry after having been sworn to secrecy. Likewise, the witness Sergeant Major Zacarias de Oliveira Ribeiro showed a certain amount of fear in responding to the questions. It turned out that he was afraid because he had heard that a priest in Paraíba had made a denunciation to the Jesuits and had been thrown into prison by the governor for five years without ever knowing why.[16]

Generally, the comissários did not perform inquiries on their own family members. For example, the judicial inquiry on Bernardo Raimundo de Souza was originally sent to his brother Francisco Fernandes de Souza. Francisco informed the Inquisition of the relationship, excused himself from the inquiry, and delivered it to the comissário, Henrique Martins Gaio. But some comissários, such as Joaquim Marques de Araújo, had no such scruples in these matters. He performed the inquiries on two of his nephews and a niece.[17]

The officials who performed the inquiry were also required to search for all relevant baptismal and marriage certificates and send copies of them with the diligência. The inability to find these records was one of the main causes for delay in the process.

The inquiries performed on wives or potential wives of the familiares followed the same general format, but there were slight differences. If they were already married and they applied together, then she went through exactly the same process of extrajudicial and judicial testimony as her husband and their accounts were tallied together. But women who applied to marry familiares after the familiar had already received the appointment were not sent to the extrajudicial. That stage was simply skipped, and they went straight to the judicial, which not only accelerated the process, but made it cheaper as well.[18]

Accusations of impurity or misconduct frequently arose during the inquiries, and the need to maintain some semblance of order and legitimacy in these investigations caused the Inquisition to develop a complex system for determining the veracity of such accusations. In doing so, the Inquisition sought two types of evidence—oral testimony and written records. Oral testimony was gathered during the extrajudicial and judicial proceedings. Written evidence included searching the records of the Inquisition, collecting baptismal and marriage records, and consulting genealogies. The Inquisition also used previously collected oral testimonies that had been written down in inquiries for the priesthood or for military or religious orders, which was one of the reasons applicants noted in their applications all relatives who had been ordained or served in any honorary position.

The Inquisition began to develop these practices in the mid-sixteenth century, barely a century after the printing presses of Europe had revolutionized the nature of knowledge and the written word began to supersede the oral word in terms of validity and truth-value. The Inquisition valued both forms of evidence, and depending on the circumstances, one form might take precedence over the other. When baptismal and marriage records were not available, oral testimony could supersede the lack. In cases where oral testimony was insufficient to establish paternity or fraternity, a baptismal record could fill the void.

Accusations of impurity or misconduct were verified or refuted through the use of these two types of evidence. The Inquisition, however, had to rely heavily on oral testimony because most of the officials who applied from Pernambuco and elsewhere came from nonnoble origins and their ancestors did not normally find their way into the written record beyond baptismal and marriage records—and even those could be woefully incomplete. Even when records existed, real weight rested on public opinion or *fama pública*. To verify the authenticity of public opinion, the Inquisition tried to determine whether a rumor was truly public and generally accepted as true, and it tried to establish the origins of the rumor. In doing so, the Inquisition had to rely on local memories and records, neither of which were infallible.

When other sources of information were lacking, the Inquisition sought out previous investigations into purity of blood by other institutions that had similar statutes to resolve questions of impurity. But such testimony was not automatically accepted. The general rule was that witnesses taken in one tribunal were not valid in another. But the deputies of the General Council remained free to accept such testimony if they felt it was necessary.[19] The Inquisition used these non-inquisitional investigations to clear up rumors of impurity. Another method of clarifying rumors of impurity was to send to the candidate's place of origin to see if there was any truth to the rumor. In the case of Lourenço Gines Pacheco Ferrás in 1763, rumors of impurity raised in his place of residence were not verified in further inquiry at his place of birth, and so they were rejected.[20]

This systematic and skillful use of oral testimony and documentation contributed to the perception that an inquisitional investigation possessed more rigor than that of other institutions. This perception contributed to the popularity of seeking inquisitional office and enhanced the prestige of those who achieved it.

After all the information had been gathered, the deputies of the General Council reviewed the inquiries and offered their opinions. The deputies retained the ability to resubmit the inquiry for further clarification on any point they thought necessary. If they approved the application, then a letter of appointment was drawn up, and it was signed by the inquisitor general. These letters of appointment, known as the *carta de familiar* (the letter of familiar) or *provisão* (an official document conferring an office), were intended to convey not only the authority but also the dignity and honor of the office. Consequently, they were beautifully extravagant and dignified. They were written in black ink on bleached rawhide in beautiful script and tied with a bright green ribbon and contained in a small, hollow, dark wood box with a lid. The box held, in red or green wax, a stamped impression of the coat of arms of the Holy Office (see figure 4.2). Familiares also received a golden medallion carved with the arms of the Inquisition that they wore around their necks during official activities as outward signs of their position.[21] Together with the habit bearing the crusading cross with the fleur-de-lis on each end, these insignia legitimated the new official's claim to authority, pure blood, status, and entrance into the ranks of the defenders of the faith.

After the applicant successfully ran the inquisitional gauntlet and paid the necessary fees, he then took the oath of office—first introduced in the 1613 Regimento. Technically, all officials were supposed to go to Lisbon and take the oath in front of an inquisitor. For those who lived in Brazil, however, such a journey proved impractical. So the Inquisition permitted candidates from Brazil to take the oath in Brazil or to have their procurators in Lisbon take it for them. But each applicant had to petition to have this privilege because the 1640 Regimento declared that this dispensation could only be received by special license from the General Council.[22] Of the 247 individuals for whom I have information on where they took their oaths, thirteen took them personally in Lisbon, usually while they there on other business. Forty took them in Pernambuco in front of a comissário or a high-ranking ecclesi-

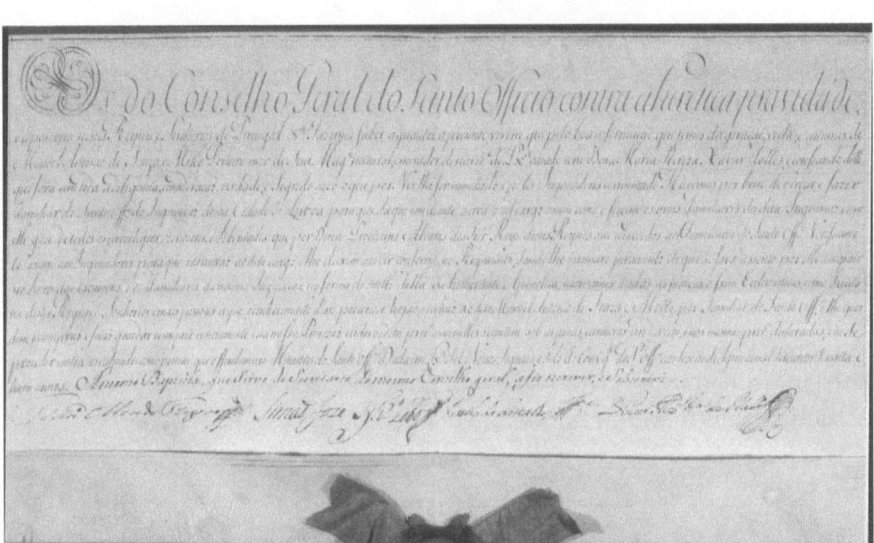

Figure 4.2. Carta de Familiar: Letter of Appointment to the Inquisition. *Source:* ANTT, HSO, Manuel, m. 182, no. 1935.

astical authority. The vast majority, however, 194, sent to have their procurators take the oath for them in Lisbon.

In the late seventeenth century, when there were still very few comissários, the Inquisition utilized Jesuit rectors, vicars general, and bishops to administer the oaths.[23] Sometimes fathers or brothers took the oaths in the place of their relatives when they could not be present.[24] When taking the oath, the official knelt before the comissário and placed his hands on the Bible. Besides swearing obedience and fidelity, he also promised not to receive gifts from anyone or befriend any New Christian. The oath remained essentially the same for all the officials.[25] After a familiar had been appointed, taken the oath of office, and received the tokens of his position, the Inquisition notified the resident comissário of the area in which the new familiar lived so that he could serve the Inquisition when necessary.[26]

To ensure that all officials knew their obligations and duties, the Inquisition gave them a copy of the section of the regimento that dealt with their respective office at the time they took the oath. The regimento instructed inquisitional officials that they were expected to maintain a high standard of modesty and decency in accordance with their station and to be good examples. They were not to cause offense or vexation to anyone through the power of their office, or with the pretext of privileges, nor to permit their family members or servants to do so. They were to take care not to extend the hatred that all should have for crimes against the faith to the people who committed them. Nor were they to have personal communication with anyone under suspicion or under investigation by the Inquisition. They were also forbidden to accept gifts or presents, even if they were small. And they were not to accept offers to pay lower than market prices for the goods and medicines they received. Nor could they take loans from Jews or contract debts that could cause complaints or diminish the authority they possessed. They were likewise admonished that everything regarding the Inquisition required the utmost secrecy and was of the utmost importance.[27] The fact that these restrictions had to be listed so clearly indicates that officials had been guilty of such infringements of honor and dignity.

Costs

How much did an appointment cost and what did the cost mean in terms of the accessibility of an appointment? To date, no one has attempted an analysis of the cost of a petition for office, which has permitted exaggerated claims that only the very wealthy could afford to work for the Inquisition. An analysis of the cost not only allows us to evaluate the accessibility of an inquisitional appointment, but it also reveals the increasingly bureaucratic nature of the inquisitional system.

For 781 of the processos utilized in this study, an account tabulation existed or one could be constructed from marginal notations. The costs fell into two broad categories: the expenses of the General Council and the tribunals and the expenses of the officials in the field who performed the inquiries. The first category included charges for the carta itself, for the recording of the oath, and for every type of letter, request, or order the General Council or the tribunals sent out, for the paper they were written on, and for the officials who wrote them. The second general category included the daily stipends given to officials who made the inquiries in the field. They were also paid for each witness questioned and each marriage or baptismal certificate extracted.[28]

In addition, several hidden costs associated with the applications do not appear in the accounts. The payments made to the familiares are one of the costs so curiously missing. Familiares carried the summons to call witnesses, and yet their $500 réis per diem compensation never appears in the accounts. Likewise, the deputies of the General Council each received 1$000 réis for each habilitação they reviewed. If all the deputies were not present or did not review the habilitação, then a note would be made to credit it to the account of the candidate. Each applicant also paid a one-time fee of 2$000 réis, which was divided between the *promotor* and the *notários*. Officials also paid the *porteiro* (doorkeeper) of the Lisbon Tribunal about $500 réis and the obligatory 2$400 réis fee to join the brotherhood of St. Peter Martyr. This fee doubled toward the end of the eighteenth century.[29] All of this means that, in most cases, the applications probably cost at least 10$000 to 15$000 réis more than the accounts show.

For example, the concluding accounts for José Duarte Sedrim indicated that he owed 5$200 réis as the cost of the investigation. He had already deposited 25$000 réis in 1781, and he had sent in another 12$800 réis in 1782. Even if the 5$200 réis were discounted from his deposits, he should have had 32$600 réis left over.[30] Where had the rest of the deposit gone? There were clearly other costs associated with his processo that do not appear in the account balances. Nonetheless, the account information gives us some idea of the costs incurred by those who sought inquisitorial office.

After each applicant passed on to the judicial stage, he made a deposit against the costs of the proceedings.[31] The average deposit was about 40$000 réis, although they ranged from 20$000 to as high as 100$000 réis. The deposit paid for the expenses of the diligências. When the process was complete, if anything remained of the deposit, it was refunded to the applicant. If the deposit had been insufficient, then extra funds were requested and the carta would be withheld until the money was received.[32]

The relative cost of obtaining an inquisitional appointment allows us to evaluate the affordability and hence the accessibility of an inquisitional appointment. Of the 781 applications for which we have account information, many fall below 5$000 réis. These are most likely the result of incomplete reporting, although some of the applicants were the children of familiares. Fully 46 percent of the applicants paid between 5$000 and 20$000 réis, but occasionally the costs could be very high indeed. In 1771, Manuel Pereira Azevedo de Farjado paid the large sum of 120$100 réis for his appointment.[33]

Despite the occasional very expensive carta, the average cost of an application was 18$865 réis.[34] But if we adjust for the hidden costs, the average would be around 30$000 réis. As shown in figure 4.3, the average cost of an application continued to increase until 1770, when it dropped back down to the levels of the 1730s and '40s. After 1800, the average cost began to rise again.

The slow but steady increase during the seventeenth century came from the Inquisition's increasing efficiency in collecting the fees.[35] The much stronger increase after 1720 was partly the result of increased stipends given to the officials and inflation. By 1700, the compensation increased for the

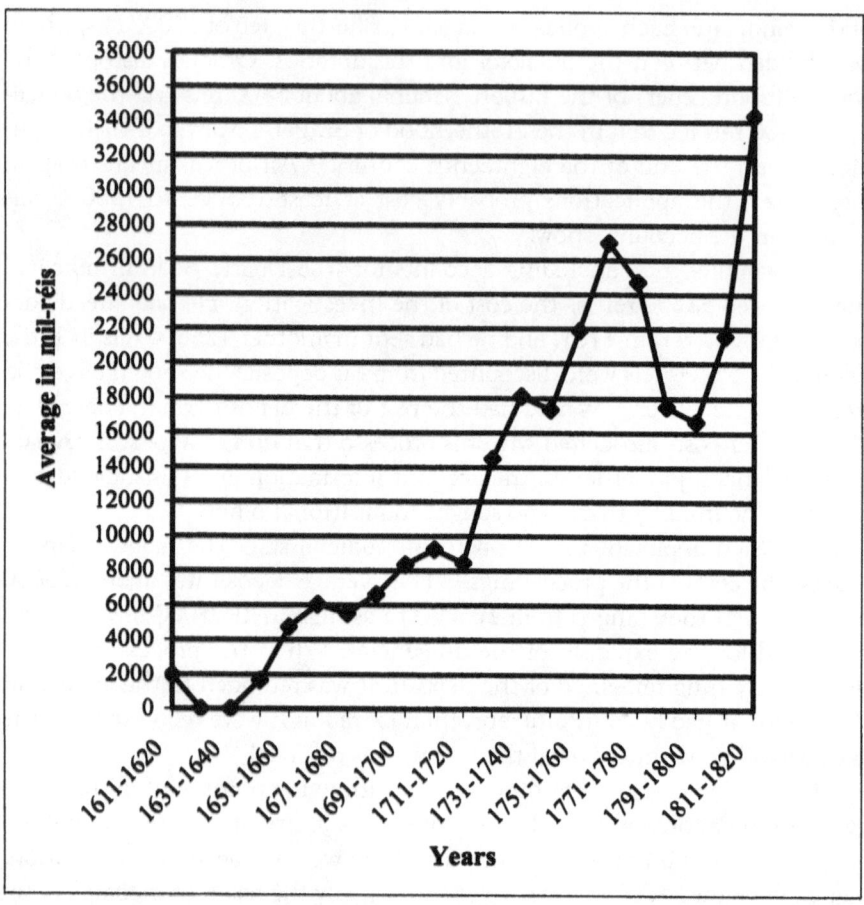

Figure 4.3. Average Cost of Applications from Pernambuco in mil-réis, 1611–1820.
Sources: Processos de habilitação for Pernambuco, 1611-1820 [ANTT, HSO; NH; HI].

comissários for work performed outside of their city of residence. Comissários received $600 réis, scribes $400.[36] In 1714, the comissários and notários complained that this compensation was insufficient to meet their costs, and so they were granted an increase of $200 réis, but only for work on the habilitações.[37] These fees appear to have continued unchanged until the abolition of the Inquisition in 1821.[38]

Another way to look at the cost is the percentage of those over 10$000 réis. Between 1715 and 1750, 79 percent of the applications cost more than 10$000 réis, and between 1751 and 1770, 73 percent were above 10$000 réis. But from 1771 to 1790, only 58 percent were over 10$000 réis, and from 1791 to 1810, only 55 percent were over 10$000 réis.

The apparent decline in average cost after 1770 can be misleading. The decline in cost was due, in part, to the increase in applications from the children of familiares and from long-term residents of Pernambuco. Consequently, fewer inquiries needed to be made, thus reducing the cost. Also, the Inquisition became more lenient and permitted more inquiries to be done in Lisbon without sending to Brazil. This became the practice for most applicants who had fathers who were already familiares. The decrease is thus misleading because the lower costs were mostly for the increasing numbers of applicants whose families had already been qualified. Thus the costs decreased for the sons of familiares, but not necessarily anyone else.

The cost of the application stimulated some candidates to find ways to decrease the cost of the investigation. Sometimes officials tried to decrease the cost by applying in groups or requesting to have the inquiry done in Lisbon. For example, in 1786, the brothers Domingos Lopes Guimarães and Padre José Lopes Guimarães applied together, which meant that fewer inquiries had to be performed. They were accepted.[39] Applying together could, however, have its drawbacks. If one of the applicants encountered problems, it could affect the others. In fact, most people who applied together experienced some difficulty. In 1786, five brothers applied together but none of them received an appointment because they failed to pay the 100$000 réis deposit.[40] Likewise, Antônio Martins da Cunha Souto Maior and his son with the same name applied together, but after a wait of ten years they were finally rejected because the Inquisition could not find information on Antônio's grandfather. Had his son applied separately it is likely that he would have been approved because the Inquisition did not generally go beyond an individual's grandparents.[41]

Another common strategy to decrease the cost of an appointment was to request that the inquiry be made in Lisbon instead of Pernambuco. To facilitate this process, the applicants often forwarded notarized copies of baptismal and marriage certificates so that there would be no need to send to Pernambuco for information.[42] Others made the same request because they had not lived in the colony very long and people in Lisbon knew them better. Usually the Inquisition attended to these requests, but occasionally it sent to the colony anyway. Often the Inquisition even sent the judicial to Lisbon without any request on the part of the applicant. This practice usually occurred when the applicant was a minor or from a well-known family. Eighty-two applications had the judicial taken in Lisbon—most of them after 1770. When these attempts were successful, they did decrease both the cost and the time it took to complete the diligências.

To get some feel for the real cost of a carta, it is worthwhile to compare it with the cost of important colonial commodities such as a healthy male slave or manioc flour, and with the yearly salaries of day laborers, professionals, and upper clergy. Between 1700 and 1740, a male slave could be purchased for 40$000 to 200$000 réis depending on the slave, the location, and inflation.[43] These high prices can be deceiving, however, because during the eighteenth century, slave ownership was not limited to the wealthy or to the white minority. Slave ownership sank deep roots in Brazilian society and was widespread even among Brazilians of very modest means. Widows, poor manioc farmers, and free blacks and mulattos all owned slaves, though in very small numbers.[44] If these groups could afford to purchase slaves, it seems likely that they could have saved enough to afford an appointment to the Inquisition had they wanted it. As I have already noted, however, cost was not the only factor in acquiring a position as a familiar. The poverty, social status, and often the ethnic-racial background of these groups certainly would have served as impediments. In addition, when living on the edge of subsistence, the prestige associated with the carta would have done little to lighten the workload, to satisfy an empty belly, or to pay the bills.

Manioc flour was a basic food commodity that virtually everyone consumed in colonial Pernambuco. If they could afford it, Brazilians would eat about nine to ten *alqueires*[45] of manioc flour a year, which could range in price from 3$200 to 40$000 réis during the eighteenth century.[46] Likewise, the average yearly wage of an unskilled rural laborer in 1817 in Pernambuco was 48$000 réis. A deacon of the Olinda cathedral received 200$000 réis in the 1790s, and the canons received 160$000 réis. A lawyer in Bahia in 1750 received 130$000 réis. Even if an appointment could be acquired for 20$000 or 30$000 réis, it clearly remained beyond the reach of the day laborer, even if his social standing had not been an impediment. It also continued to be relatively expensive, although not prohibitively so, for the professional classes and the higher clergy if they had to rely solely on their salaries.[47] Moreover, inquisitional appointments fell well within the reach of well-off merchants and the planter elite.

Applying to work for the Inquisition, then, could be an expensive and risky endeavor. Any number of difficulties could arise that could delay the process for years, decades, or even indefinitely, thus increasing the cost. Distance from Lisbon, the vast expanse of Pernambuco, bad weather, illness, lack of information, and rumors of impurity or poor conduct often delayed processos and increased their cost. During the colonial period, the round-trip from Pernambuco to Lisbon and back again could take from seven months to a year. Mishaps could also occur on the voyage. For example, the first judicial inquiries on Antônio de Souza Barroso never made it to Lisbon, but were sent to England by accident and never returned.[48]

Qualifying for Office: Procedures and Costs ~ 67

The inquisitional authorities in Lisbon also did not have a clear conception of how large Brazil was, and they often sent commissions to officials who lived a great distance from where the inquiry needed to take place. Sometimes they simply tried to get as close as they could. When that happened, the officials either traveled to the area or sent the commission on to the local clergy or someone else they trusted to maintain secrecy and use proper judgment in calling and questioning witnesses. For example, in 1782, the Comissário Delegado Father José Rimígio Ferreira performed an inquiry in the interior that was more or less typical of such diligências.

> I certify that, in the execution of this diligência, the Reverend Juiz Comissário spent five days outside of his residence. On the first, he traveled two and half leagues from his residence until the Engenho Santa Ana in whose chapel he questioned the first witness. On the second day, [he traveled] four and one half leagues until the Chapel of Santa Luzia of the Engenho dos Tabacos where other witnesses were questioned. And on the third day, [he traveled] one league to the Engenho Santa Ana where the Reverend Comissário had retired until the Engenho Santo Antônio where he questioned one witness in his house because he was ill. On the fourth day, he traveled four and one half leagues from the residence of the Reverend Juiz Comissário until the Chapel of Santiago of the Engenho do Pouxi where other witnesses were questioned and on the fifth day two and one half leagues from his residence to the chapel of the same Engenho Novo de Santa Ana where the last witness was questioned.[49]

These kinds of inquiries increased the cost of diligências because the officials were paid more for the time they had to spend outside of their town of residence.

The most extreme example of inquisitional delay was that of Antônio Gonçalves Reis, who applied in 1728 and waited forty-one years. He heard nothing until 1769, when he received a request from the General Council for a deposit of 32$000 réis. By then, he was too old and no longer wanted the appointment.[50]

Lack of information on ancestors could also delay the processo and increase the cost. Indeed, the cost of the most expensive processo from Pernambuco, that of Manuel Pereira Azevedo de Farjado, was due partly to a lack of information. His petition lasted for ten years between 1761 and 1771 and cost 120$100 réis.[51]

Other considerations besides cost could weigh more heavily in the minds of the men who sought appointment. Men such as Antônio Gonçalves Carneiro often claimed that delays in their investigations damaged their honor and reputations. For example, João Rodrigues Teixeira applied in 1740 with the stated purpose of removing the damage caused to his family's reputation because of his father's rejection for lack of information on his great-grandparents. The mesa approved him for notário in 1745 and actually noted that one of the reasons for approving him was to remove the damage the family had received as a result of the lack of information.[52] Not all applicants enjoyed such a sympathetic ear. Marcos Soares de Oliveira, for example, applied for a comissário position in 1760 and was rejected eleven years later, in 1771, for New Christian ancestry. In 1764, he wrote a letter claiming that he was experiencing considerable injury to his credit and honor and begged "for the love of God and for Catholic piety" that his petition be approved.[53]

The procedures and criteria of the qualification emphasized the conduct and ancestry considered honorable by the Inquisition. In submitting to an investigation into his conduct and ancestry, a candidate also submitted himself to the public scrutiny of popular opinion. Witnesses testified what they knew or had heard about the applicant. Those witnesses often came from the applicant's own peers, which meant that the very people who testified in an inquiry would be the ones with whom the new official worked and over whom he exercised inquisitional authority. Whether true or not, their opinion mattered, and the Inquisition took it seriously.

Not just anyone could apply, however. Even if they met all of the other requirements, applicants still had to muster the 20$000 to 30$000 réis to pay for the investigation. It is clear that, when compared with the price of important commodities and various salaries at the time, inquisitional office was generally beyond the reach of the working poor. Although not inexpensive, it was still within the reach of the better-off portions of the merchant population, the clergy, planters, and some artisans.

Because the qualifications focused on honorable characteristics, the investigation became a test of the applicant's honor. For that reason, delays in the investigation led to complaints of loss of honor, which points to the importance of the Inquisition as a mediator of honor and status.

Notes

1. Siqueira, "Os Regimentos da Inquisição," 616 (1613 Regimento, Book I, Title I, Paragraph II).
2. Given, *Inquisitional and Medieval Society*, 25–51.
3. Siqueira, "Os Regimentos da Inquisição," 694 (1640 Regimento, Book I, Title I, Paragraph 2).
4. ANTT, HSO, José, m. 176, no. 4192.

5. The familiar Antônio José Victoriano Borges da Fonseca received an extrajudicial to do while he was serving as governor of Ceará in 1773 on Francisco Vas Leite. See ANTT, HI, m. 6, no. 50.

6. ANTT, IL, Livro 817, fol. 8. This order was reiterated on June 12, 1759. See ANTT, IL, Livro 157, fols. 22, 227.

7. In some cases, the scribe could also be a witness in the same inquiry. See, for example, ANTT, HSO, José, m. 162, no. 400 and Felix, m. 5, no. 69.

8. After 1762, these forms were printed forms with blanks left to fill in names and places. See, for example, ANTT, HSO, Manuel, m. 190, no. 2021.

9. These questions remained the same until the 1774 Regimento removed all references to New and Old Christians. Azevedo Mea has published the questions in *A Inquisição de Coimbra*, 180–81, footnote 264.

10. Siqueira, "Os Regimentos da Inquisição," 898 (1774 Regimento, Book I, Title VIII, Paragraph 3).

11. See, for example, ANTT, HSO, Manuel, m. 122, no. 218.

12. "Instrução que hão guardar os Comissários do Santo Officio da Inquisição nas cousas, e negocios da fee, e nos demais que se offerecerem," ANTT, CGSO, m. 12, no. 28.

13. Siqueira, "Os Regimentos da Inquisição," 740 (1640 Regimento, Book I, Title XI, Paragraph 3).

14. See, for example, ANTT, HSO, José, m. 146, no. 2856; HSO, Antônio, m. 159, no. 2500.

15. Siqueira, "Os Regimentos da Inquisição," 740 (1640 Regimento, Book I, Title XI, Paragraph 4).

16. ANTT, HSO, Marcos, m. 3, no. 44.

17. ANTT, HSO, Bernardo, m. 12, no. 469; José, m. 168, no. 4084; Manuel, m. 251, no. 1621; Pedro, m. 38, no. 655.

18. Of the 342 women who applied to be qualified, 286 were accepted. Twelve were rejected and forty-four were left incomplete.

19. See ANTT, HSO, Roberto, m. 1, no. 4, and ANTT, HI, m. 6, no. 147.

20. ANTT, HSO, Lourenço, m. 9, no. 139.

21. Comissários oversaw the manufacture of these medallions in Brazil. See ANTT, IL, Livro 299, fol. 397.

22. Siqueira, "Os Regimentos da Inquisição," 695 (1640 Regimento, Book I, Title I, Paragraph 5).

23. ANTT, IL, m. 52.

24. ANTT, HSO, Manuel, m. 249, no. 1566.

25. ANTT, CGSO, m. 4, no. 6, fols. 20–21.

26. ANTT, IL, Livro 20, fols. 246v-249.

27. ANTT, IL, Livro 20, fols. 246v-249.

28. ANTT, CGSO, NT 4192.

29. Familiares who took the oath personally in Lisbon paid a fee of half a gold coin (about $500 réis) to the porteiro. By 1730, so many cartas were being granted outside of Portugal that the porteiro of the Inquisition complained that he was losing

income. In response, the Lisbon Tribunal required all familiares to pay the fee to the porteiro of the Inquisition in Lisbon. See ANTT, IL, Livro 156, fols. 151–152. For the fee assessed for joining the brotherhood, see ANTT, IL, Livro 79, fol. 207; IL, NT 2142; CGSO, m. 17, no. 21.

30. ANTT, HSO, José, m. 150, no. 2922.

31. It appears that they may have sent in a sum with the application, but I was unable to uncover any details on that account.

32. At least once, the Inquisition even requested more money from an applicant who had died during the processo to pay for the work that had been done even after his death. See ANTT, HSO, Antônio, m. 20, no. 613.

33. ANTT, HSO, Manuel, m. 229, no. 1331.

34. I calculated the average cost from the total expenditures of 14:733$902 divided by 781.

35. None of the *regimentos* detailed the costs of an inquiry. The 1552 Regimento only stated that notários should be compensated according to the ecclesiastical regulations of each diocese and receive $100 réis for each night spent away from their place of residence. See Siqueira, "Os Regimentos da Inquisição," 601–2 (1552 Regimento, Capítulo 92–93). The 1613 Regimento raised the notário's stipend only to $400 réis for each night. See Siqueira, "Os Regimentos da Inquisição," 674 (1613 Regimento, Book I, Title VIII, Paragraph 10–11). The 1640 Regimento granted the notários one *vintém* (20 réis) for each seal they placed on a letter or piece of paper. They were paid by the page at the completion of the processo. The comissários and their scribes, whether they were notários or not, received $400 réis for diligências outside their residence. The familiares received $500 réis per day, and anyone they took with them was paid according to the customs of the place. See Siqueira, "Os Regimentos da Inquisição," 733, 738–39, 741, 759 (1640 Regimento, Book I, Title VII, Paragraph 19; Title X; Title XXI, Paragraph 13; and Title XXI, Paragraph 5).

36. ANTT, CGSO, m. 4, no. 5, fol. 26.

37. ANTT, IL, Livro 154, fol. 258; CGSO, m. 43. See also ANTT, CGSO, m. 43.

38. See Siqueira, "Os Regimentos da Inquisição," 895–900 (1774 Regimento, Book I, Title V, Paragraph 9; Title VIII, Paragraphs 9 and 11; Title IX, Paragraph 6). The comissários, of course, were not supposed to number the pages or add up the accounts. See ANTT, CGSO, Livro 157, fols. 131–132v.

39. ANTT, HSO, Domingos, m. 56, no. 881 and José, m. 157, no. 303.

40. ANTT, HI, m. 36, no.9.

41. ANTT, HSO, Antônio, m. 211, no. 3146 and HI, m. 15, no. 8. See also ANTT, HSO, Simão, m. 6, no. 115; HSO, João, m. 165, no. 1409; José, m. 158, no. 3051; NH, m. 10, no. 48; and IL, Livro 206.

42. For example, ANTT, HSO, João, m. 168, no. 1454; Joaquim, m. 21, no. 282; Joaquim, m. 13, no. 163; Antônio, m. 98, no. 1770; Manuel, m. 46, no. 1034; Inácio, m. 6, no. 96.

43. See Guillermo Palacios, *Cultividores libres, estado y crisis de la esclavitud en Brasil en la época da la Revolución Industrial* (Mexico City: Fondo de Cultura Economica,

1998), 49, and Stuart B. Schwartz, "Plantations and Peripheries, c. 1580–c. 1750," in *Colonial Brazil*, ed. Leslie Bethell (Cambridge, reprint 1991), 83.

44. See Bert Barickman, *Bahian Counterpoint: Sugar, Tobacco, Cassava, and Slavery in the Recôncavo, 1780–1860* (Stanford: Stanford University Press, 1998), 52–53, 142–45, 150–53. See also Sheila de Castro Faria, *A colônia em movimento: Fortuna e família no cotidiano colonial* (Rio de Janeiro: Editora Nova Fronteira, 1998), 248.

45. An alqueire is roughly equivalent to a bushel or about 36.27 liters.

46. Manioc flour was rationed to soldiers and slaves at about one-fortieth an alqueire per day. Prices of manioc flour fluctuated in Recife, but in very good years they could be as low as $320 réis. In times of scarcity, they could soar to 4$000 réis per alqueire. Thus, the yearly ration of manioc flour alone could range from 3$200 to 40$000 réis. See Dauril Alden, "Price Movements in Brazil Before, During, and After the Gold Boom, with Special Reference to the Salvador Market, 1670–1769," in *Essays on the Price History of Eighteenth-Century Latin America*, ed. Lyman L. Johnson and Enrique Tandeter (Albuquerque: University of New Mexico Press, 1990), 335–59; Palacios, *Cultivadores libres*, 207–23; and Barickman, *Bahian Counterpoint*, 46.

47. For the yearly income of the day laborer, see Peter L. Eisenberg, *The Sugar Industry in Pernambuco: Modernization without Change, 1840–1910* (Berkeley: University of California Press, 1974), 188. For the salaries of ecclesiastical officials, see ANTT, OC, PB, m. 12; AHU, Pernambuco, cx. 263, doc. 17594; and Pernambuco, cx. 264, doc. 17688. For the salary of a Bahian lawyer, see A. J. R. Russell-Wood, *Fidalgos and Philanthropists: The Santa Casa de Misericórdia of Bahia, 1550–1755* (Berkeley: University of California Press, 1968), 380.

48. ANTT, HSO, Manuel, m. 27, no. 132.

49. ANTT, HSO, Felipe, m. 7, no. 97. See also Antônio, m. 196, no. 2924. The Portuguese *légua*, or league, varied from 5,555 meters to 6,600 meters. Foul weather and poor health could also delay inquiries. See ANTT, HSO, José, m. 103, no. 1465, HI, m. 6, no. 129, and HSO, Jerónimo, m. 12, no. 86. The Lisbon earthquake of 1755 also delayed inquiries. See ANTT, HSO, Joaquim, m. 21, no. 282.

50. ANTT, NH, cx. 25, m. 22–23.

51. ANTT, HSO, Manuel, m. 229, no. 1331.

52. ANTT, HSO, João, m. 86, no. 1503.

53. ANTT, HSO, Marcos, m. 3, no. 44.

CHAPTER FIVE

Qualifying for Office: The Problems of Honor

Claims of the loss of honor as a result of delayed inquiries demonstrate the importance of the Inquisition as a producer of social honor and prestige in Pernambuco. The Inquisition used the procedures and criteria outlined in the previous chapter as exclusionary tools. Through the inquiries into the ancestry and behavior of the applicants, the Inquisition sought to control the quality of its officials and to exclude those groups or individuals whose ancestry or behavior could bring disrepute upon the Inquisition. Because of the nature of the criteria, problems encountered during the inquiries were widely perceived as challenges to the individual's honor and status. The system through which these problems were raised, investigated, and refuted or corroborated demonstrates how inquisitional inquiries articulated with existing codes of honor and how social honor and status were constructed. The production of inquisitional officials was also tied to social promotion as families and individuals used the inquiries to further their own claims to honor, status, and prestige.

Ethnic-Racial Discrimination and Honor

The concept of honor in the Luso-Brazilian world came to be tied to ethnic-racial discrimination. Anti-Jewish and ethnic-racial discriminatory sentiment in Portugal and Brazil had a long gestation and was continually fed by members of the royal court and the clergy who resented the privileged treatment some Jews received at the hands of the crown and the aristocracy.[1] Legalized discrimination began at least as early as 1446 and received a heavy impetus from the royal expulsion of the Jews and Moors from Portugal in 1497.[2]

After the expulsion, most Jews stayed or were forced to stay, and D. Manuel refused all attempts to introduce the Inquisition into Portugal. It was not established there until 1536. D. Manuel sought instead to integrate Jewish converts into the Christian community, and he contrived to keep them in Portugal through a series of draconian measures, sugar-coated with concessions. First, he ordered the baptism of all Jewish children less than fourteen years of age and took them from their families to be raised by Christian families.[3] Then he made it difficult for Jews to leave the country by allowing them to leave only through the port of Lisbon. Once they had gathered there, he forcefully baptized them in mass. He sugar-coated this bitter pill with an exemption of the Jews from any religious investigations for the space of twenty years, which effectively postponed any creation of the Inquisition until at least 1517. On March 1, 1507, he also published an *alvará* (royal decree) that stated that, from that time forward, the king would not make any ordinance against New Christians, but that they would always be treated as Old Christians. D. João III ratified this declaration in 1524.[4] All of these efforts aimed at the forced assimilation of the Jewish community into the Christian community. But they could not and did not propose to eliminate the already popular and widespread resentment against the New Christian population.[5]

In 1514, New Christians were excluded from holding public office. Formal exclusion from private institutions such as the religious and military orders and the *confrarias* (brotherhoods) began at least as early as 1546.[6] Papal decrees in 1558 and 1572 excluded New Christians from the Franciscan order and from the Order of Christ. In 1574, a royal edict prohibited New Christians from holding municipal offices in Vila Flor. Yet discriminatory laws became more common after 1581, with the assumption of the Portuguese throne by Philip I of Portugal (Philip II of Spain). Discriminatory laws and practices rapidly diffused into Portugal, where the population had already shown a marked tendency toward anti-Semitism.[7]

Pressured by Philip I, the papacy added to the legislation its famous brief, *De Puritate Sanguinis*, of 1598, which declared that some human blood could be originally impure, and it excluded New Christians from all ecclesiastical benefices. A brief in 1612 stated that New Christian priests could not become vicars or curates.[8] These new practices and laws imitated the manner in which Spanish anti-Semitism had manifested itself in Spain, but with their own Portuguese flavor.

Some have argued that the establishment of the Inquisition stalled out the process of assimilation and precipitated the legalization of anti-Jewish and anti-Moorish sentiments in Portugal.⁹ However, it can also be argued that political and social forces were far more important in deepening the already deep-seated tradition of discrimination in Portugal. That it existed before the establishment of the Inquisition and that it continued beyond the tenure of the Iberian union is indisputable and speaks to the enduring nature of ethnic-racial discrimination in the Luso-Brazilian world. Likewise, only a few discriminatory laws appeared before 1580, and they were only haphazardly enforced. The remainder all surfaced after Portugal became part of the Spanish Empire. Likewise, no requirement of pure blood (*limpeza de sangue*) appeared in any of the regulations or bylaws of the Inquisition until 1613, and even afterward some New Christians became familiares and at least one appears to have become an inquisitor.¹⁰

Simply because most of the legislation comes after the establishment of the Inquisition does not demonstrate that the Inquisition was, therefore, responsible for the rising tide of anti-Jewish sentiment in Portugal. The Inquisition did not create these attitudes any more than did the Spanish influence in Portugal. That sentiment already existed well before the sixteenth century, and the creation of the Inquisition was both a manifestation and an accelerator of it. But the fact that the Inquisition existed and functioned for nearly forty years before most of the discriminatory laws entered the codes and seventy-seven years before any discriminatory attitudes were codified in inquisitional *regimentos* suggests that legalized discrimination in Portugal cannot be simplistically explained by blaming the Inquisition. It received a heavy impetus from the increased Spanish influence in Portugal after 1581.

The first investigations into the cleanliness of blood of the candidates for inquisitional office occurred by the early 1590s. These investigations had already begun in Spain at least as early as the 1550s, and they appeared at the time when discriminatory laws and statutes were becoming more popular in Portugal.¹¹ But pure blood did not become a formal requirement until the 1613 Regimento.

These discriminatory laws and the popular sentiments from which they sprang migrated to Brazil in the minds and institutions of the Portuguese settlers, although they were somewhat attenuated initially by the demands of colonial life. Several factors contributed to a temporary softening (but certainly not the elimination) of ethnic-racial discrimination in the first century of the colonization of Brazil. Distance from Portugal, a lack of manpower to staff all of the necessary colonial institutions, and widespread miscegenation all contributed to this tendency.¹² Consequently, racial discrimination tended to be more legal than practical, and many New Christians gained considerable wealth and influence, acquired public office, and intermarried with the Old Christian population.¹³ Practical discrimination in Brazil began to increase toward the end of the sixteenth century with the inquisitional visits to Bahia and Pernambuco.

Likewise, the attempts at assimilation in the late fifteen and early sixteenth centuries had already worked to some extent. Despite the mid-sixteenth century declarations, the formal exclusion of New Christians from ecclesiastical offices and honorable institutions did not become widespread until the first decade of the seventeenth century. By that time, many New Christian families had already gained ecclesiastical offices, entered the military orders, and intermarried with Old Christian families. The economic possibilities for adventurous men and the shortage of Portuguese women in Pernambuco combined to make intermarriage with New Christian families commonplace, even desirable. During the years when the Episcopal seat was vacant in Pernambuco and the chapter of the Olinda See was in charge of ordinations to the priesthood, many New Christians managed to get ordained despite the restrictions. Likewise, bishops sometimes failed to be rigorous in their investigations, which also allowed many New Christian families to enter the priesthood.[14]

Yet families often chose to ignore or forget these circumstances, and the possession of one of these appointments within a family could be regarded as a proof of purity. But this tactic did not always work, and rumors of impurity could linger for many generations despite these outward signs of purity. The dream of wearing the inquisitional habit, whatever the motivation, could lead to disastrous results if a family impurity were found or if the family's efforts to cover it up were unsuccessful.

By the end of the seventeenth century, purity of blood had become fundamentally tied to family honor, which was something to be asserted and defended. The concept of honor remains difficult to define because it was based on complex codes of behavior that distinguished people from each other and reinforced social stratifications based on ethnic, cultural, or economic factors.[15] That said, the Portuguese word *honra* incorporated, though it did not clearly distinguish, the two concepts of virtue (personal behavior) and status (inherited or acquired reputation). Honor was weighed on the balance of public opinion—measured in terms of the jealousy or respect one could rouse in others.[16] It did not really matter whether one was truly of impure ancestry. What mattered was whether others thought that you were or, as the Inquisition put it, whether a person had "public fame" of impurity.

In colonial Brazil, these racial and cultural stigmas came to be attached not only to New Christians, but also to Africans, Indians, and mixed-race populations. Honor came to be associated with whiteness, with Old Christians, and with occupation. The so-called mechanical (*mecânico*) trades, low-level merchants, and fishermen were considered dishonorable, although over time the mechanical trades became less so. The Portuguese term *mecânico* referred to nonnoble groups and specifically to those professions engaged in manufacture, including shoemakers, tailors, hatmakers, and carpenters.[17]

Honor and purity of blood permitted access to positions of prestige, power, and privilege. The military and religious orders and many brotherhoods and guilds had pure-blood requirements in their statutes, and pure blood was also required for public office. Likewise, wealth and land did not necessarily grant social honor or status. Proof of family purity and outward signs of achieved status, such as public and military office, were also required.[18] These incentives stimulated most elite or upwardly mobile classes to assert their familial purity and honor. Thus honor provided the framework for self-assertion and the defense of social status and economic interests—hence, the infatuation with genealogies and record keeping that arose in the sixteenth century with the heightened concern over purity of blood.

The Inquisition served to confer honor, privilege, and status, and to preserve the collective memory of purity and impurity. It also provided one way of acquiring the status associated with purity of blood so necessary for entrance into a wide variety of institutions, including the prestigious military orders. Sometimes the Inquisition even granted certificates for purity of blood while still refusing to admit the applicant to work for the Inquisition.[19] The Inquisition became an important means of acquiring the "proof" of purity so essential to social mobility and the acquisition of status. But the desire to gain, reassert, or display one's family honor on the altar of inquisitional appointment opened up the very real possibility of losing it.

Problems in the Processo

Subjecting oneself to an inquiry that relied heavily on the testimony of one's peers and public opinion opened up the applicant to the possibility of accusations of impurity or poor behavior. These accusations, if not effectively refuted, could lead to indefinite delay in the inquiry or even outright rejection. They also led to public perceptions of a lack of honor on the part of the applicant. Because honor was not only based on ancestry but also on personal conduct, a rejection from the Inquisition, no matter what the reason, could signify a lack of honor, which could complicate one's attempts to promote oneself socially. Honor, once lost, could be regained, but only after considerable toil and expense. And if the Inquisition had reason to doubt one's purity, that doubt could place a nearly permanent stain on both personal and family honor.

By no means did a doubt about one's purity of blood or personal conduct result in automatic rejection.[20] The Inquisition investigated such rumors, and only if it found evidence that it considered conclusive did it formally reject the applicant. In fact, most applicants who encountered problems eventually overcame them. Of the 344 applicants from Pernambuco for whom we have information on problems of honor with their applications, only sixty-six were formally rejected. Seventy-two were simply left incomplete. The other 206 overcame the accusations. However, the mere suggestion of impurity could have lingering consequences for generations.

In Pernambuco, accusations of impurity (28.7% for men and 67.8% for women) occurred most frequently, followed by poor or dishonorable conduct (24.9% for men and 15.3% for women) and errors in the processo (23.4% for men and 13.6% for women). Accusations of mixed white and African ancestry also arose frequently (10.5% for men, but only 6.8% for women), as one would expect in colonial Pernambuco. But the most frequent accusation of impurity remained New Christian ancestry (15.2% for men and 45.8% for women). The fact that New Christian ancestry was the largest problem for women points to the difficulty familiares encountered when marrying into local Pernambucan families, many of whom had, or were rumored to have had, impure lineage.

Even though most of the problems dealt with issues of purity, more people were officially rejected in Pernambuco for poor or dishonorable conduct. This suggests that although witnesses considered purity of blood to be more significant and denounced it more frequently, the Inquisition cared at least as much about the conduct of its future officials as it did about their ancestry. So selecting the raw material from which to construct an inquisitional status group, the Inquisition investigated any matter that it believed might tarnish its image. After all, the honor and prestige of the Inquisition were also at stake.

Many of the difficulties arising from public rumor, which the Inquisition took seriously, were not as critical or as numerous as rumors of impurity, but they still represented outward signs of dishonor. One such minor impediment was poor dress.

Dressing poorly indicated a lack of dignity, decorum, and concern for social norms, as well as inadequate financial resources, and could, therefore, be an impediment to office. Although I have only encountered a few examples where poor dress became an issue for applicants, they illustrate the Inquisition's concern with respectable appearance and behavior from their officials. For example, João Pacheco Calheiros applied to become a familiar in 1712 but never received an appointment because he dressed poorly. The comissário Bartolomeu de Pilar, reported that he is not very becoming the occupation and degree of familiar because he ordinarily goes around in white leather shoes, white cotton socks, pants of fine silk, a black waistcoat without a dress coat, a truly miserable hat and a blue cloak. And thus he walks [about] during the week in this *praça*. On Sundays he wears baize clothing [a thick woolen cloth] with a sword. . . . He is miserable, because, according to what they tell me, he can appear even more extravagant.[21]

If we compare this account with the few existing descriptions that we have of familiares, we can see what the Inquisition considered appropriate. For example, a 1767 passport described the familiar Francisco José de Arantes as a single male, short, fat, and round faced, with dark eyes, and wearing a wig. He seems to have been the typical well-to-do gentlemen of the mid-eighteenth century. In addition, an 1800 passport described the familiar Vicente Ferreira Peixoto as a single white male with a tall, thin body, a small forehead with his hair tied back, thin eyebrows, brown eyes, a sharp nose, beard, and thin lips with all of his front teeth. This description gives a picture of a dignified looking man wearing his hair in the style popular during the last years of the eighteenth century. In each case, these men manifested what were the characteristics appreciated and accepted as attractive and fashionable in their times.[22] The Inquisition wanted their familiares to look good and to conform to the accepted standards of decorum and dignity. But of course what looked good and dignified changed over time.

A poor family reputation could also cause trouble for potential candidates. For example, Margarida Maria dos Prazeres, the wife of familiar Manuel de Rosa de Ávila, encountered problems with her habilitação because her family did not have a good public reputation. The comissário Francisco Fernandes de Souza reported in March 1769 that her father, Second Lieutenant João Ferreira Frazão, had acted the part of the *lacaio* (lackey: a man without dignity or a person protected by the king or other noble who served as a spy or informer) in public plays. The maternal grandfather died poor because he was a drunk, and her father had been imprisoned for stealing. Likewise, her mother and aunt had been accused of witchcraft.[23]

The Inquisition also developed a set of exclusionary tools that were specific to clerics and that limited the opportunities for inquisitional appointment for clerics in Brazil. Beyond the general requirements for all officials, the comissários, notários, and qualificadores had to be priests. The requirements for purity of blood were replaced in 1774 by requiring them to have good customs and no infamy on their part or the part of their ancestors. In addition, the notários had to be clerics who had taken the sacred orders and the qualificadores had to have a university degree. The 1774 Regimento stated that the qualificadores should be few in number, and doctors of the university in the faculty of sacred theology. The comissários had to be ecclesiastics of recognized prudence and virtue. In all cases, preference went to clerics who had university degrees.

These general principles were, of course, subject to interpretation and could be dispensed with or modified to suit the needs of the Inquisition and the disposition of the deputies. For example, the Inquisition rejected the Carmelite Gonçalo de São José, son of the familiar João Carneiro da Cunha, as qualificador in 1769 because he was not a *mestre* (master) in his religion, which some deputies thought was a necessary quality even though there are several examples of qualificadores who were only *pregadores* (preachers) or *homens de letras* (men of letters).24

The problems clerics encountered included all the variations of impure blood and poor behavior. Several had problems with concubinage, illegitimate children, lack of information, solicitation, and sodomy, and eight were rejected because they were regular clergy. For example, the Inquisition denied Manuel Bernardo Valente because of bad behavior. He had earned the nickname from the local boys of "father vicar of the capote" because he had been seen visiting the home of a woman in Olinda during the night hidden under a capote. They left together in a canoe, and it was public knowledge that their relations were sinful.25 Problems such as these sometimes only kept them from being appointed comissários, and the Inquisition granted them notário status instead.

For example, Antônio Dias da Conceição applied to become a comissário in 1768, but accusations of poor behavior and "incontinence of the tongue" surfaced. The general council wondered if the witnesses had been motivated by hatred. A second inquiry by the comissário Antônio Ribeiro Maio in 1771 revealed that some of the accusations had indeed been exaggerated. Nonetheless, the comissário stated:

> I know the difference that exists, and that should exist, between the offices of [comissário and notário]. About this [habilitação] I took particular information from some informants that could give me more individuation; and I found that the Reverend applicant could serve the Holy Office in the office of notário, but in no way in that of comissário. And the reason is, that even though he does not suffer from a grave note in his behavior, he is not a person of known prudence and virtue, as our regimento requires of the ministers of the Inquisition; and not even in his letters of which he has only studied [Latin] grammar, and some moral cases so that he could be ordained. I also found that he does not

respect his character or state of priest because he is very much inclined to speak frivolously and pass along news wherever he is, about whatever he knows and hears, which some attribute to the force of his temperament and others to the lack of consideration.

The deputies agreed with this assessment and only approved him for notário on August 4, 1771.[26]

Many regular clergy in Pernambuco sought appointment as comissários, notários, and qualificadores. But the existence of officials of the Inquisition who enjoyed inquisitional privileges caused turmoil in the convents. This turmoil combined with the opinion already held by the deputies of the General Council that regulars were not very well suited for such employment.[27] From the Inquisition's perspective, their lack of suitability had mostly to do with the fact that they could not be relied upon to stay in a given location because their prelate could send them somewhere else without notice. The Inquisition wanted to know to whom they could send commissions and inquiries, so they generally resisted appointing them, although they were happy to use them as *comissários delegados*.

For example, the Franciscan Jácome da Purificação applied for an appointment as a qualificador or a comissário in 1694 because, he said, the business of the Inquisition ended up going to the regular clergy anyway due to a lack of comissários in Pernambuco. He entered his petition on November 24, 1694. On April 25, 1695, the General Council accepted him for qualificador but not comissário because a regular was not suited for this occupation, so "for now it cannot be deferred." He petitioned again in November 1696, from Lisbon. In 1697, the General Council determined that he was qualified, but that it was not "convenient" to the ministry of the Holy Office for a comissário to be a regular because of the uncertainty of the place where he, as a regular, would reside. Also, the distance of Pernambuco from Lisbon meant that he would have little to do as a qualificador. So they denied him on both accounts.[28] The archbishop of Bahia likewise believed that Carmelites and other regular priests were unworthy and unsuited to be comissários.[29]

Internal conflict between the regular priests who did manage to get appointed as comissários and their prelates and provincials caused serious tensions and seemed to give good reason to doubt their suitability. For example, Rodrigo Gaiozo de São José, a Carmelite from Bahia, moved to Recife and applied to become a comissário in 1762. The mesa said that they did not normally appoint regular clergy to the position of comissário, but that this time they would do so. Later, Friar Rodrigo moved to the convent in Paraíba, where he entered into a conflict with his prelate. He wrote to the General Council in 1769 to complain that his new prelate would not accept his claim of exemption from the obligations of his order. The prelate argued that he could only be exempt when he was engaged in the work of the Holy Office and that he was required to give obedience to his prelate whenever he left the confines of the convent. The prior believed that Friar Rodrigo was going out to conduct business of his own under the pretense of having work to do for the Inquisition and that he was using it as a cloak to avoid the obligations of his office.[30] In 1770, the General Council ordered an investigation into the allegations, and the report came back that neither the prior nor the prelate sought to impede the functioning of the Inquisition and that neither the provincial in Bahia nor the prelate in Paraíba had ever ordered him to do so. They only wanted him to attend to his duties when he was not so engaged despite his assertion that he was exempt.[31]

These kinds of tensions eventually led to the formal exclusion of regular clergy from appointments to comissário. In 1783, the provincial of the Franciscans in Brazil requested that the religious of his order no longer be admitted as comissários of the Holy Office. He offered two main reasons for the request. First, he claimed that they used their office as a pretext for avoiding their responsibilities of obedience and to free themselves from the regular and monastic life they had professed. Second, the necessity of handling money to pay for their transportation to distant parts to perform inquiries and riding horses to do so when they were neither sick nor in manifest need forced them to break their vows of poverty and the rule of the order. He found this particularly irksome when secular comissários could perform the same inquiries without any difficulty. The Franciscan prelate's letter resonated with the growing attitude of the General Council, and in response to his letter, a verbal order went through the Inquisition that regular priests could not to be accepted as comissários.[32]

Despite the prohibition, regular clergy continued to apply. Some even had letters from their prelates in support of their applications. All too often, however, the only response was the ominous marginal note "*excuzado*" (useless or superfluous) or "*não deferir*" (reject or do not approve).[33]

Not all friars gave up easily, however. For example, Friar José de Santa Cruz applied for a position as a comissário in 1783. The General Council rejected him in 1785 because they had determined not to create any more comissários than were necessary in the colonies and because he was a regular cleric. In 1796, he wrote a letter to the General Council indicating that he had heard of the restriction on regular clergy. But, he argued, he had applied long before the restriction, and he had already been admitted to diligências and paid a deposit of 28$800 réis. The council accepted his argument and noted that a Carmelite from Bahia had presented a similar case and been granted the office. They concluded that Friar José had applied before the restriction and that he was worthy in every other way.[34] Even though the Inquisition accepted some who had applied before the prohibition, this did not thwart the vocal order, and the prohibition continued.[35] I have yet to discover when, or even if, the prohibition was ever lifted.

By far, the lack of a benefice remained the greatest impediment for secular clergy seeking the position of comissário. Thirty-nine of the 137 applicants for comissário ran into the problem of not having a benefice, and twenty-six were granted notário instead of comissário as a result. A benefice is an ecclesiastical office that gives the incumbent the right to collect a salary for his support. It also included certain obligations such as residence at the place of appointment (such as a cathedral or parish church). The real issue here was the applicants' abilities to provide for themselves, as well as the desire for the status that benefice holders enjoyed. Their salaries, called *congruas*, offered a regular source of support, but they were generally low, and the secular clergy often sought other sources of income, such as running sugar plantations, renting houses, and engaging in commerce.[36]

For the secular clergy, an appointment as an inquisitional official could offer another source of income, although this was not normally true for familiares. For example, the comissário Joaquim Marques de Araújo received more than 992$795 réis just for his work with the habilitações between 1770 and 1812, which amounted to about 5$000 for each extrajudicial or judicial that he performed, or 23$638 réis per year.

Even though the *regimentos* did not require a benefice for appointment, the deputies of the General Council usually did. For example, José de Andrade e Sousa applied for an appointment as comissário in 1751, but because he had not been invested in his benefice, the General Council investigated him for the position of notário even though they said they had a greater need for comissários in that area. José suspected that the issue was his benefice, so he sent a document showing that he had already been invested, and the council changed his appointment to comissário in 1755.[37]

Nonetheless, the lack of a benefice could be overcome in a variety of ways. The status of one's family, persistence, a little foresight and ingenuity, and a lot of luck could help. For example, Domingos de Araújo Lima acquired an appointment as a comissário even though he did not have a benefice. He received the appointment because he lived in Alagoas, where comissários were needed. He successfully justified his lack of a benefice by informing the council that he had given it up to "quiet his own conscience" and to live off his estate.[38]

Another avenue for becoming a comissário was to get accepted as a notário and then reapply. Francisco da Costa Bandeira failed in his application for appointment as a comissário in 1755 because he did not have a benefice, but he was appointed as a notário. Later in 1761, Francisco repetitioned to become a comissário. The Inquisition accepted him even though he still did not have a benefice because he owned some houses that he rented out by which he supported himself and because there were only two comissários in Olinda, each of whom was a simple clerk and not very capable.[39]

The Carmelite Antônio das Chagas took a more proactive approach. In a letter he wrote to the Inquisition regarding the delay of his habilitação, he offered to accept an appointment in any of the areas where the Carmelites had convents, such as Goiana, where there were no comissários at all. He even gave them a list of places with Carmelite convents and how far they were from Recife (Porto Calvo, Goiana, Paraíba, Nossa Senhora da Graça). He received an appointment as a comissário in Goiana in 1761.[40]

Another strategy that would-be clerical officials employed to improve their chances of being accepted included direct petitions to high-ranking officials in Lisbon or within the Inquisition.[41] For instance, the Carmelite friar Gregório Xavier de Almeida wrote directly to the inquisitional secretary. In September 1772, he applied to become a qualificador, and on January 3, 1773, he wrote to Manuel Francisco da Neves to ask for his help with his application. The first letter was never answered. In the second letter, he wrote, "I cannot understand the cause of this your tyranny against me."

> Even though I have not written to your grace before, I have experienced the honor of the favor and kindness that your grace, through your generosity, dispensed to my father and brother and I judged that its shadow should always cover me as well.

He requested that his diligência be sent to the comissário, Henrique Martins Gaio, not because he feared any bad information on the part of his own conduct, but because he knew of all the intrigue, jealousy, and vices of his brothers in the Carmelite convent and he feared that they might give false testimony that could impede his application and bring dishonor upon him. Henrique Martins, he believed, had experience dealing with the friars of the convent, and he knew that Gregório was honorable.

> If I were a secular, I would not fear. But in the monasteries of today we see divisive enmities, jealousies, and all kinds of vices. . . . God knows what it has cost me to become a Mestre—the opposition that I have experienced. For all

of this, I am afraid and I beg your grace that if some bad information is given about me that someone subject to the Holy Inquisition examine the certainty of it with trustworthy persons so that I am not injured.

He begged that the judicial be done in Lisbon, where many people knew him and had attended his lectures and classes. "Imagine that I am your son and what you would do for your son do so also for me. . . . I esteem you as a father." Apparently, unbeknownst to Friar Gregório, his letters had already elicited a response. Henrique Martins had already completed the extrajudicial on December 24, 1772, and the judicial was under way in Lisbon by May 27, 1773. He received his appointment on June 18, 1773.[42]

Limpeza de Sangue

The criteria for inquisitional appointment found particular resonance in colonial Pernambuco because of the very strong presence of New Christians early on in the conquest and colonization of Pernambuco and because it was a slave-based colonial society. Likewise, the Portuguese colonizers in Pernambuco who conquered the indigenous inhabitants tended to view them in negative ways. Hence we find persistent references to Indian, New Christian, and mulatto ancestry as dishonorable.

The most frequent difficulty encountered by all applicants was impurity of blood. Thirty-three percent of the problems raised in the inquiries and nearly 32 percent of those rejected in Pernambuco were related to issues of purity. Many of the stalled processos contained letters from the applicants complaining that their good names and reputations were being slandered by those who knew that they had applied for and not yet received appointments.

The Inquisition investigated rumors of impurity and attempted to discover the origins of those rumors. Both rumors of impurity and inquisitional explanations for them relied largely on public opinion. For that reason, both the rumors and the Inquisition's explanations are fallible and should be viewed critically. The fact that the Inquisition willingly conceded that rumors could and did arise from misinformation, personal conflicts, and superstition tells us that we need to be wary of reaching conclusions based solely on this type of evidence. Inquisitional investigations into rumors of impurity, however, reveal some of the social tensions that could result in accusations of impurity that could tarnish family honor.

Accusations of impurity often surfaced during personal conflict. For example, Antônio Araújo Lopes had been accused of New Christian ancestry, and the Inquisition reported that the rumor started with a conflict over an irrigation ditch. One of Antônio's ancestors had been called a Jew as an insult during the conflict, and the name calling turned into a rumor of impurity.[43] Rumors of impurity could also rest on accusation of having paid the Jewish tax (the *finta*).[44]

Sometimes the rumors sprang from ignorance and superstition. Padre Mestre, Friar Felipe da Madre de Deus, the prior of the Order of Carmo in Pernambuco, encountered a rumor of New Christian ancestry in his habilitação. The rumor reportedly had its origin in a banquet in which his maternal grandfather, Manuel da Costa Moura, ate and drank until he became ill and vomited up the uncured bacon or salted pork fat he had been eating. From this incident, he received the nickname *arremeça-toucinho* (bacon-launcher). His rivals raised up the rumor that he must be a Jew because he could not digest the uncured bacon. The subject came up in the applications of his relatives as well, and the General Council judged it to be ridiculous and irrational. Many of Felipe's relatives had been approved for various investigations, and he was reputed to be clean, so the deputies declared the rumor to be false, and he received the position of qualificador.[45]

Some rumors had truly bizarre origins. Paulo Carvalho da Cunha petitioned to become a familiar in 1729, but they found a rumor of New Christian ancestry. The comissário in Guimarães, Portugal, found that the rumor came from an ancestor of the Carvalho family who lived in the parish of São Clemente. The witnesses claimed that he had "*sangue mile.*" When asked what that meant, the witness replied that he had had many sores or ulcers all over his body from which he died. The parishioners of São Clemente had actually disinterred him, saying that they did not want his "bad blood" to leak out to their own dead. The term *bad blood* came to be associated with impurity of blood, which evolved into a public reputation of New Christian ancestry. This case went all the way to Braga before the parishioners were ordered to rebury the hapless corpse.[46]

Some accusations could simply be the product of xenophobia. In 1731, the Holy Office reported that there were doubts about one of the great-grandparents of Miguel Ferreira Souto. A neighbor had stated that those who came to marry from outside the village did not come for any good reason, and from there the rumor began that Miguel's family came from the "infected race."[47]

Sometimes the sources of rumors could be quite complicated and multifaceted. For example, the rumors of Manuel de Lemos Ribeiro's impurity reportedly came from four different sources. First, the abbot of the parish of Fontoura wanted to put the *Santíssimo* (the Blessed Sacrament) in the parish, but the parishioners opposed him. Ribeiros's family, who had the reputation of being New Christians, headed the opposition, so the priest said that the "Jews" did not want to take the Santíssimo Sacramento. Second, it came from the daughter of a man who had been banished from his own village and who married into the village. The third source was a woman who came from outside and married into the village. Fourth, a poor old mendicant had complained against a member of this family and called him a Jew. The mesa saw all of these origins as empty and so dismissed them and approved his petition to become a familiar in 1742.[48]

Next to accusations of New Christian ancestry, the second largest group of accusations regarding purity of blood were those regarding African descent (10.5% for men and 6.8% for women). When dealing with the question of African ancestry, the Inquisition tried to determine whether the ancestry came through a slave line. It goes without saying that, if one went back far enough, all blacks in Brazil probably had slave ancestors. The issue was slave ancestry within the fourth degree of consanguinity. For example, José Pedro dos Reis was accused of being a mulatto in 1736. The Inquisition decided that the ancestry was too ancient and that there was no rumor that it came from slavery.[49]

The General Council also sought information on physical characteristics associated with African ancestry. In the days before photographs, they had to rely on descriptions forwarded to them by their officials in the colony. For example, Lourenço Gonçalves Bastos's wife, Luísa da Paz do Nascimento, was reputed to be a mulatta and an Indian. The comissário, Francisco Fernandes de Souza, reported as evidence of African ancestry that Luísa's mother had *cabelo torcido* (twisted hair). Likewise, José Timóteo Pereira de Bastos was rumored to be a mulatto because his father had *cor tostada* (toasted color). And Manuel da Costa de Sá was accused of having *casta de negro* (negro race) by witnesses who said that it came from his sister, who married a man with the nickname *mano negro* (black brother).[50]

Nonetheless, mixed race did not necessarily impede appointment if the individual was a person of some means. In 1769, a deputy of the General Council stated that this "quality of defect [mulatto] your majesty has commanded to proceed to the judicial so that this should not impede the applicant who has sufficient riches from his business to live decently."[51] Only 9.3 percent of those rejected in the Portuguese Empire between 1739 and 1768 were rejected for African ancestry; and the figure was only 7.6 percent in Pernambuco. The last number is surprising given the very high number of Afro-Brazilians and the very high rate of miscegenation in the colony.

Accusations of impurity also included rumors of Indian descent. Of the problems encountered during inquiries, only 3.2 percent dealt with Indian descent (2.3% for men and 10.2% for women). But no one in Pernambuco was ever rejected for Indian descent, and only one in the Portuguese Empire between 1739 and 1768 was rejected for being a *caboclo* (either civilized Brazilian Indian of pure blood or a white-Indian mix). Indeed, Indian ancestry did not, at least technically, serve as an impediment for inquisitional appointment, but witnesses in Pernambuco continually demonstrated that they considered it a serious impurity. Their perception of Indian ancestry as impure and the Inquisition's position that it was not highlights the ongoing tension between local concepts of ethnic-racial honor and Portugal's attempts to alter those perceptions.

Throughout the colonial period, the indigenous population in Brazil held an ambiguous position. The colonists wished to exploit their labor, the clergy wanted to harvest their souls, and the crown wanted to turn them into tax-paying subjects. These desires were at once mutually compatible and inherently contradictory, and the Indians were trapped in the paradox. The laws promulgated throughout the colonial period vacillated between the extremes of granting absolute freedom to the Indians and legalizing their enslavement.[52] On April 4, 1755, D. José I published an *alvará* that stated that anyone who married an Indian did not retain any infamy either in themselves or in their descendants and that they were worthy of all honors and dignities. He also ordered that the term *caboclo* should no longer be used.[53] Similar laws promulgated about the same time for India and Africa attempted to create a group of intermediaries between the colonizing Portuguese and the indigenous societies. They also sought to further the royal policy of incorporating the indigenous population as vassals of the crown.[54] These laws need to be seen in the light of the later reforms regarding the pure-blood laws and New Christians. All of them attempted to rationalize Portuguese society and provide juridical equality for all Portuguese subjects.[55]

Sebastião José de Carvalho e Melo (later the Marquis of Pombal), the chief minister of the kingdom (1750–1777) under D. José I, was concerned with much larger matters than granting Indians juridical equality in Brazil, however. In the face of geopolitical conflict with Spain, the recently settled peace, and the Treaty of Madrid in 1749, Pombal hoped to secure Brazil's frontiers. He believed that the defense of those frontiers depended on a large population of loyal Portuguese, which could not possibly be sent from Portugal. So he concluded that it was essential to eliminate the distinction between Indians and Portuguese in the hopes of attracting the Indians away from the missions and the white Brazilians into marriages with them.[56] But to get the white Portuguese to marry Indians in large numbers, the entire social order had to be remade.

Because of earlier laws, which asserted more or less the same thing, Indian descent never posed a serious problem for those who applied to work for the Inquisition.[57] Even before the 1755 law, the Inquisition had ruled that Indian descent was not an impediment. For example, Francisco de Sá Peixoto's wife, Angela Teresa de Melo, had been accused by a single witness of being a *cabra* (mongrel, or of mixed Indian descent). In 1700, Deputy João Munis da Silva dismissed the accusation for two reasons. First, a single witness did not constitute a reliable foundation for such an accusation, and, second, Indian descent did not constitute an impediment to serving the Holy Office, as had been judged several times already. Her brothers Antônio Vieira de Melo and Manuel de Melo Bezerra applied together in 1701 and also received appointments.[58] The General Council usually dismissed such accusations with a brief note about how Indian descent was not an impediment or was beyond the fourth degree of consanguinity. Sometimes the council simply ignored these accusations.

Pernambucans consistently demonstrated, however, that they saw Indian ancestry as dishonorable, and they regularly reported it to the Inquisition as a defect.[59] In Brazilian society, ethnic-racial honor precluded Indian and New Christian descent despite the legislation that made discrimination against these groups technically illegal after 1773. The lingering accusations of New Christians and Indian ancestry highlight the continuing reality of inequality, discrimination, and concern for ancestral purity in the colony.

Yet some people appear to have been rejected after 1773, or at least their *processos* were left incomplete, for reasons of impurity of blood. References to impure blood continued to appear in the *processos* from Pernambuco into the nineteenth century and in the statutes for white brotherhoods in Brazil until at least 1839.[60] At the same time, others complained as late as 1800 that delays in the *processo* damaged their reputations as possessing cleanliness of blood.[61]

The persistent attempts to retain the now illegal distinction provoked an order from the crown on December 15, 1774, that declared that these "absurdities" should cease.[62] Yet the persistence of the concepts of impurity reveal an increasing tendency toward intolerance and discrimination, which eventually developed into full-blown racism. Tied as it was to individual status and honor, a simple legal prohibition could not erase the conflation of personal honor with ethnicity and race.

The perpetuation of concern over ancestral purity also appears in ecclesiastical investigations. In 1802, Joaquim Manuel Carneiro petitioned Prince Regent D. João to send a royal order instructing the prelate of the Madre de Deus Convent not to impede his entrance into the Congregation of São

Felipe Neri on the grounds that he had impure blood. The prelate had argued that he descended from a woman of mixed ancestry. Joaquim, of course, appealed to the law of 1773, and the prince regent responded with a letter ordering the prelate to observe the laws.[63]

The concept of the purity of blood and the honor and social prestige attached to it penetrated so deeply into Luso-Brazilian society that it lingered long after the legality of discrimination. Families used the Inquisition to prove the purity of their ancestry and to gain access to the honor and prestige that status provided. This mechanism for social advancement had become very popular during the eighteenth century. Even after the abolition of the pure-blood laws and statutes, individuals continued to denounce each other for impure ancestry and continued to decry the loss of honor due to delays in inquisitional procedures, which resulted in damaging challenges to the purity of their blood.

The 1773 pure-blood law did not immediately neutralize either the social importance of pure blood or the significance of the Inquisition as a purveyor of social prestige. Understanding this is essential to understanding the continuing rise in applications up to 1794. When combined with a wide variety of other political and economic factors, the elimination of pure blood as a legal tool for discrimination did contribute over the long run to a decline in the value of an inquisitional appointment. But the decline was not immediate and it took nearly half a century to ripen into full decay.

The risks and the costs of application were high, which meant that the payoff had to be high enough to warrant the risk. That payoff included the honor, prestige, status, and power that accompanied an appointment. The exclusionary tools that the Inquisition utilized (whether formal or informal) had the dual effect of enhancing the honor and prestige of inquisitional office, while at the same time they created problems for applicants who suffered from public rumors or accusations of impurity. An inquisitional investigation became a test of one's purity and honor, and even after ethnic-racial discrimination was made illegal, Pernambucans persisted in reporting rumors of impurity to the Inquisition. These challenges to personal and family honor had to be met. Genealogical fraud proved extremely useful for those who could not prove their purity through normal channels. And yet fraud could not hold off the increasing political pressure for legalized social reform.

Notes

1. Maria Luiza Tucci Carneiro, *Preconceito Racial no Brasil-Colônia: Os cristãos-novos* (São Paulo: Editora Brasiliense, 1983), 43–58.

2. For the history of legalized racism in the Luso-Brazilian world, see Carneiro, *Preconceito Racial*.

3. He also shipped many Jewish children to São Tomé to help colonize the island. See Stuart B. Schwartz, *Sugar Plantations in the Formation of Brazilian Society: Bahia, 1550–1835* (London: Cambridge University Press, 1985), 13.

4. These documents resurfaced in the royal order to consult on the topic of discrimination in 1771. ANTT, MNEJ, Livro 4, fols. 61–65.

5. Saraiva, *Inquisição*, 27–38.

6. Carneiro, *Preconceito Racial*, 57, 91, and Saraiva, *Inquisiçao*, 113–14.

7. A 1583 law stated that all Moors and Jews, whether captive or free, were required to wear an emblem so they could be identified. The Jews were required to wear a yellow cap and the Moors a "red cloth moon, four fingers [in size] sewn onto the right shoulder of the cape or the jerkin." Failure to do so resulted in a heavy fine or imprisonment. See Candido Mendes de Almeida, *Codigo Phillipino, ou Ordenações e leis do reino de Portugal, recopilados por mandado d'el Rey D. Phillipe I*, 5 vols. 14th ed. (Rio de Janeiro: 1870. Reprint, Lisbon: Fundação Calouste Gulbenkian, 1985), 1245 [Livro 5, Título XCIV]. This practice fell into disuse in the eighteenth century. In 1592, all New Christians and Moors from Granada, or those who descended from them, were forbidden to enter Portugal on pain of confiscation of their goods, imprisonment, and sentence to the galleys. See Almeida, *Codigo Phillipino*, 1217 [Livro 5, Título LXIX], Paragraph 2. In 1604, New Christians were officially excluded from military orders, and in 1621 and 1623 they were also excluded from the universities. See Azevedo, *História dos Cristãos-novos*, 151.

8. ANTT, MNEJ, Livro 4, fol. 63–63v.

9. Saraiva, *Inquisição*, 38.

10. ANTT, CGSO, m. 17, no. 28, and Saraiva, *Inquisição*, 117. See also Adriano Vasco Rodrigues, "'Inquisições' a pureza de sangue," in *Inquisição*, ed. Maria Helena Carvalho dos Santos (Lisbon: Universitária Editora, 1989), 2:745–54.

11. Azevedo Mea, *A Inquisição de Coimbra*, 180–81.

12. The first donatary captain, Duarte Coelho, implicitly encouraged miscegenation in Pernambuco by simply ignoring it, and important men such as Jerônimo de Albuquerque formed important tribal alliances by marrying Indian women. See Francis A. Dutra, "Duarte Coelho Pereira, First Lord-Proprietor of Pernambuco: The Beginning of a Dynasty," *Americas* 29, no. 4 (April 1973): 434.

13. Carneiro, *Preconceito Racial*, 195–96.

14. Evaldo Cabral e Mello, *O nome e o sangue: Um fraude genealógica no Pernambuco colonial* (São Paulo: Companhia das Letras), 53–54.

15. Ann Twinam, "Honor, Sexuality, and Illegitimacy in Colonial Spanish America," in *Sexuality and Marriage in Colonial Latin America*, ed. Asunción Lavrin (Lincoln: University of Nebraska Press, 1989), 123–25.

16. These notions of honor-virtue and honor-status have been described elsewhere in Latin America. See, for example, Lyman L. Johnson and Sonya Lipsett-Rivera, eds., *The Faces of Honor: Sex, Shame, and Violence in Colonial Latin America* (Albuquerque: University of New Mexico Press, 1998); Ramón A. Gutiérrez, *When*

Jesus Came, the Corn Mothers Went Away: Marriage, Sexuality, and Power in New Mexico, 1500–1846 (Stanford: Stanford University Press, 1991), and Patricia Seed, *To Love, Honor and Obey in Colonial Mexico: Conflicts over Marriage Choice, 1574–1821* (Stanford: Stanford University Press, 1988).

17. See Antônio de Morais e Silva, *Diccionario da lingua portugueza*, 2nd ed., (Lisbon: M. P. de Lacerda, 1823) s.v. "mecanico."

18. See Arno Wehling and Maria José Wehling, "O funcionário colonial foi parte significativa da burocracia absolutista," in *Revisão do Paraíso: Os brasileiros e o estado em 500 anos de história*, ed. Mary del Priore (Rio de Janeiro: Editora Campus, 2000), 141–59.

19. ANTT, CGSO, m. 27, no. 107.

20. Sonia Siqueira has argued that "doubts about cleanliness of blood implied rejection, which, of course, is not true." See Siqueira, *A Inquisição portuguesa*, 161.

21. ANTT, HSO, João, m. 177, no. 1572. See also ANTT, HSO, Jacinto, m. 6, no. 76; HSO, Raimundo, m. 1, no. 8; and HSO, Manuel, m. 220, no. 1306.

22. AHU, Pernambuco, cx. 105, doc. 8123; AHU, Pernambuco, cx. 215, doc. 14548.

23. ANTT, HSO, Manuel, m. 220, no. 1306.

24. Siqueira, "Os Regimentos da Inquisição," 615–18, 672–75, 693–96, 729–33, 738–41, 885–88, 894, 899 (1613 Regimento, Book I, Titles I and VIII; 1640 Regimento, Book I, Titles I, VII, X, and XI; 1774 Regimento, Book I Titles I, V, VII, VIII). See also Luiz Mott, *Regimento dos Comissários e Escrivães do seu cargo, Dos Qualificadores e dos Familiares do Santo Ofício* (Salvador: Universidade Federal da Bahia, 1990).

25. ANTT, HI, m. 23, no. 71.

26. ANTT, HSO, Antônio, m. 176, no. 2658.

27. ANTT, HSO, José, m. 42, no, 688.

28. ANTT, HI, m. 30, no. 13.

29. AHU, Bahia, Castro e Almeida, 12003. See ANTT, NH, cx. 58.

30. ANTT, CGSO, m. 59; IL, NT 2133.

31. ANTT, IL, NT 2132.

32. ANTT, NH, cx. 37. Fr. Gaspar da Soledade Matos from São Paulo was denied his petition for comissário in 1786. ANTT, IL, NT 2129.

33. Manuel da Encarnação Freitas had a letter from his prelate Zacharias de Jesus e Maria, a comissário, in support of his application. See ANTT, HI, m. 36, no. 91. Manuel da Ressurreição had two brothers who were both comissários, but he was still rejected. See ANTT, HI, m. 36, no. 81. José de Santa Margarida de Cortona was also rejected outright, and he requested a refund of what was left of his deposit. See ANTT, HSO, José, m. 176, no. 4196. See also ANTT, HSO, Luís, m. 41, no. 682 and Estanislão, m. 1, no. 5.

34. ANTT, HSO, José, m. 168, no. 4103. See also ANTT, HSO, Manuel, m. 198, no. 1106; CGSO, NT 4146; HSO, Francisco, m. 128, no. 1918; and CGSO, cx. no number.

35. ANTT, HSO, Manuel, m. 198, no. 1106.
36. Canons of the cathedral chapter, some of the highest-ranking ecclesiastical officials in Pernambuco, received an annual congrua of 160$000 réis. See ANTT, OC, PB, m. 12.
37. ANTT, HSO, José, m. 78, no. 1158. See also ANTT, HSO, José, m. 78, no. 1163; Antônio, m. 136, no. 2256; Carlos, m. 5, no. 65; and Leandro, m. 1, no, 5.
38. ANTT, HSO, Domingos, m. 19, no. 391. See also ANTT, HSO, Matias, m. 6, no. 84.
39. ANTT, HSO, Francisco, m. 88, no. 1497.
40. ANTT, HSO, Antônio, m. 52, no. 1137.
41. For this general practice, see A. J. R. Russell-Wood "'Acts of Grace': Portuguese Monarchs and Their Subjects of African Descent in Eighteenth-Century Brazil," *JLAS* 32 (2000): 307–32.
42. ANTT, IL, m. 33; HSO, Gregorio, m. 4, no. 70. See also ANTT, CGSO, NT 4181; NT 2133; ANTT, HSO, Manuel, m. 176, no. 1868, and HSO, José, m. 162, no. 3997.
43. ANTT, HSO, Antônio, m. 79, no. 1523. See also ANTT, HSO, João, m. 147, no. 2179.
44. The finta referred to fees periodically paid by the Jews in order to obtain a suspension of inquisitional activity. ANTT, NH, cx. 58.
45. ANTT, HSO, Felipe, m. 1, no. 24.
46. ANTT, HI, m. 34, no. 76 and no. 276.
47. ANTT, HSO, Miguel, m. 9, no. 159.
48. ANTT, HSO, Manuel, m. 122, no. 2181.
49. ANTT, HSO João, m. 40, no. 647.
50. ANTT, HSO, Lourenço, m. 9, no. 138; HSO, José, m. 132, no. 2717; HSO, Antônio, m. 83, no. 1586.
51. ANTT, NH, cx. 44.
52. See Ângela Domingues, *Quando os índios eram vassalos: Colonização e relações de poder no Norte do Brasil na segunda metade do século XVIII* (Lisbon: Comissão Nacional para as comemorações dos descobrimentos Portugueses, 2000), 25–62.
53. ANTT, Leis, m. 4, no. 160.
54. Domingues, *Quando os índios eram vassalos*, 39–40.
55. Linda Lewin, *Surprise Heirs: Illegitimacy, Patrimonial Rights, and Legal Nationalism in Luso-Brazilian Inheritance, 1750–1821*, vol. 1 (Stanford: Stanford University Press, 2003).
56. Kenneth Maxwell, *Pombal: Paradox of the Enlightenment* (Cambridge: Cambridge University Press, 1995), 53.
57. For a detailed review of the legal status of Brazilian Indians during the colonial period, see Beatriz Perrone-Moisés, "Índios livres e índios escravos: os princípios da legislação indigenista do período colonial (século XVI a XVIII)," in *História dos índios do Brasil*, ed. Manuela Carneiro da Cunha (São Paulo: Companhia das Letras, 1992), 115–32, and José Vicente César, "Situação legal do índio durante o periódo colonial (1500–1822)," *América Indígena* 45, no. 2 (April–June 1985): 391–425.

58. ANTT, HSO, Francisco, m. 136, no. 2044 and Antônio, m. 42, no. 990. See also HSO, João, m. 143, no. 2149 in 1768; HSO, Manuel, m. 220, no. 1306 in 1769; and HSO, Francisco, m. 117, no. 1765 in 1772. See also ANTT, HSO, Felipe, m. 4, no. 60.

59. Descent from a "noble" Indian line was considered honorable in eighteenth-century Pernambuco. See José Antônio Gonsalves de Mello, *Estudos Pernambucanos: Crítica e problemas de algumas fontes da história de Pernambuco*, 2nd. ed. (Recife: Fundação do Patrimônio Histórico e Artístico de Pernambuco, 1986), 193. Indian women could be "upgraded to the status of Indian princesses" if their desendants entered the upper class. See Dutra, "Duarte Coelho Pereira," 419. Genealogists for the elite families often constructed such genealogical myths. But these Indians were "noble savages" of the distant past and thus safely neutralized and could now be freely re-created as honorable and noble. See Antônio Cândido, "Literature and the Rise of Brazilian National Self-Identity," *LBR* 5, no. 1 (June 1968): 36–37. Still "non-noble" Indian descent was generally considered undesirable. For example, in 1768, the priest Manuel Garcia Velho do Amaral failed to get ordained two Indian boys he had trained to read and write Latin, because the bishop believed it would cause serious controversy in Pernambuco. See AHU, Pernambuco, cx. 105, doc. 8159 and cx. 105, doc. 8176.

60. João José Reis, *Death Is a Festival: Funeral Rites and Rebellion in Nineteenth-Century Brazil* (Chapel Hill: University of North Carolina Press, 2003), 44.

61. ANTT, HI, m. 7, no. 58.

62. ANTT, Serie Preta, 2242.

63. AHU, Pernambuco, cx. 234, doc. 15769.

CHAPTER SIX

Genealogical Fraud and Political Reform

As we have seen, the Inquisition's criteria for the selection of its officials resonated deeply within colonial Pernambucan society and culture. Rumors of impurity and the attempts to overcome them often surfaced during local conflicts within Pernambuco, and inquisitional appointment became a tool for individuals and families to assert their own purity and, therefore, their own position in society. One of the most interesting strategies to overcome rumors of impurity was genealogical fraud.

Cases of genealogical fraud show not only that the Inquisition's techniques of exclusion and criteria for selection reflected Pernambucan ideals of honorable ancestry and behavior, but also that these criteria had very real applicability and importance in that society. It is for that reason that the Pombaline reforms of the mid-eighteenth century, which sought to transform the status of "dishonorable" groups such as New Christians, Indians, and mixed-race populations, were so significant. Those reforms paradoxically forced open the ranks of the Inquisition to a broader section of society at the same time that they failed to transform local, racially based notions of honor and status. The contradiction proved too great. The persistence of these notions and the Inquisition's declining ability to reflect those attitudes and to offer the proofs of purity necessary in a society based on the perpetuation of social, ethnic, and economic inequality led to a cheapening of the symbolic value of the carta. Over time, the progressive cheapening of inquisitional appointment led to the declining relevance of the Inquisition in Pernambucan society.

Fraud and Manipulation

Genealogy in colonial Brazil was not the harmless pastime that it is today. It was vital to individual and family standing in society. It classified individuals and groups within the system of unequal privileges and shoved the ancestrally "impure" to the social, political, and economic margins. During the colonial period, the study of genealogy could not be separated from questions of purity of blood. Ancestry identified individuals and families in the eyes of their contemporaries and acted as a foundation for, and proof of, honor, reputation, and prestige. It also served as a mechanism for the reproduction and perpetuation of systems of domination and of unequally privileged groups. The intense interest in genealogy, then, responded to the basic need to situate oneself and one's family with some precision within the social strata. Genealogical wars frequently arose over succession disputes for all kinds of inheritance, patrimonies, and privileges.

Indeed, one's ancestry was so important that falsifying it, or at least manipulating it to publicly display one's purity, was not only a real temptation, but also a frequent pastime of noble and wealthy families. It is common to find that the genealogies of prominent families have been altered to provide the new elite with ancestors appropriate to their own social position.[1] Indeed, the genealogical histories produced in Brazil at various times and in various places attempted to compensate for the social deficiencies of the local elite.[2] Despite the importance of ancestry, genealogical research was difficult because of the inefficient or non-existent system of public records. Most genealogical information was drawn from oral memory passed on from parents to children, although some information could also be gleaned from parochial records. Combined with the early mixing of the New Christian population with Old Christians, even within the noblest families in Portugal and Brazil, this problem of records rendered the genealogical system unreliable and susceptible to fraud.

The temptation to manipulate one's genealogy became particularly acute in late-seventeenth- and early-eighteenth-century Pernambuco when the tension between the planter-dominated municipal council of Olinda and the merchant-dominated residents of Recife exploded into civil war. The growing importance of Recife and its merchant population after the restoration from the Dutch in 1654 led to a movement in Recife to separate it from the jurisdiction of the planter-dominated Olinda municipal council and to elevate Recife to the category of a town with its own municipal council. D. Pedro II had denied the request in 1700, but D. João V authorized it in 1709. The municipal council of Olinda refused to accept the royal decision and pressured the governor, Sebastião Castro e Caldas, not to implement the order. The governor sided with Recife, which resulted in an attempt on his life in 1710 and his flight to Bahia. An insurrection ensued known as the Guerra dos Mascates (Peddlers War), based on the rural militias that were under the command of the planters and their extended families.[3] The situation remained critical until the new governor, Félix José Machado, arrived in 1711 with orders to put down the uprising. He rounded up the principal leaders and shipped them to Portugal.[4]

These tensions between Olinda and Recife were also tied to genealogy. Most of the wealthy planter families either had New Christian or Indian ancestry, or were suspected of having it, while the merchants of Recife frequently came from lower-class families who needed to assert their own purity. Because many planters were immigrants, and because they generally came from undistinguished origins, they were especially "sensitive to any deprecation of their social position and desirous of the traditional insignia and accoutrements of nobility and gentle birth."[5] Even though merchants may not have suffered from specific rumors of impurity, they were often stereotyped as Jews, crypto-Jews, foreigners, or New Christians.[6] For that reason, they also had a vested interest in obtaining proofs of purity. Consequently, purity of blood became a tool of the rising merchant class to gain access to positions of power and to exclude their "tainted" planter adversaries. After the 1710 crisis, the planters and the merchants settled into hotly contested campaigns of genealogical warfare.

In this environment, it is not surprising that genealogies came to be manipulated either to discredit a rival, to camouflage an unsightly ancestry, or to rid oneself of accusations of impurity. The Inquisition became an important weapon in these genealogical battles. Even though a place in one of the military orders conferred more prestige than an appointment to the Inquisition, an inquisitional inquiry was generally thought to be more rigorous and, therefore, more reliable.[7]

New Christians came early to colonial Brazil before the practices of exclusion had become thoroughly entrenched in Luso-Brazilian society. The low numbers of Portuguese women also made New Christian women more acceptable as spouses for the early colonizing families. Consequently, most of the old rich and "noble" families in Pernambuco had some New Christian ancestry.[8] As anti-Semitic sentiment increased, so too did the desire to be free of the New Christian taint. Despite attempts to bury these increasingly embarrassing relations in the genealogical past, they could be unearthed by opponents and enemies to discredit rival families. The New Christian lines that became the focus of genealogical warfare in Pernambuco—battles often fought within the inquisitional system—were those of Duarte de Sá Matias, Branca Dias, Beatriz Mendes, Arcângela da Silveira, and Guiomar Nunes.

Duarte de Sá Matias and Arcângela da Silveira

The attempts to cover up ancestral impurity in Duarte de Sá Matias's line began with Duarte de Sá himself. He presented himself to the inquisitor Heitor Furtado de Mendonça when he arrived in Pernambuco in 1593 as an Old Christian with some New Christian ancestry on his mother's side, but claimed that he did not know the origin of the rumor. Duarte de Sá was too astute to attempt a complete cover-up because it was known that he was really one-half New Christian from Barcelos. By 1590, Duarte owned an *engenho* (sugar plantation) and was serving in the prestigious position as alderman of the municipal council. His descendants attempted to wipe out his New Christian background by claiming that there were actually two Duartes de Sá, and that their Duarte de Sá really descended from a noble family in Portugal, not a New Christian family.

To complicate matters, Duarte de Sá married a New Christian. Their son, Antônio de Sá Matias, married the sister-in-law of the famous Jerônimo de Albuquerque, the brother-in-law of the donatary captain of Pernambuco Duarte Coelho. Antônio de Sá was also accused of paying the finta imposed on all New Christians during the Dutch occupation, which was seen as proof of New Christian ancestry. Indeed, some said that he was a well-known Judaizer.[9] Antônio de Sá's daughter, D. Britis de Albuquerque, married Felipe Pais Barreto. Antônio de Sá's son married his cousin, the daughter of Felipe Pais Barreto. Felipe was one of the sons of João Pais Barreto Velho, who had arrived in Pernambuco at age thirteen in 1557, became one of the wealthiest men in Pernambuco, and created a dynasty of wealthy plantation owners who were active in the municipal council of Olinda. João Pais Barreto Velho had married Inês Guardes, the daughter of another *senhor de engenho* who had Indian ancestry.[10] The Pais Barreto family intermarried extensively with the Sá Matias, Rego Barros, and Albuquerque families, mingling their New Christian and Indian blood with that already present in these prominent families.

The Rego Barros family descended from Luís do Rego Barros from Viana, who married D. Maria de Holanda. Their son, Francisco de Rego Barros, married D. Arcângela da Silveira, who was rumored to be a *parda* (mixed race of African descent). Another son, Arnão de Holanda Barreto, married Inês de Góes, a daughter of Arnão de Holanda and Beatriz Mendes. Arnão was a Dutchman and Beatriz was rumored to have come banished to Pernambuco by the Holy Office in the entourage of D. Britis de Albuquerque, the mother of Jerônimo. It was also rumored that the Inquisition had burned her mother.

The descendants of these families sought, with good reason, to distance themselves from these lines of impurity by intermarrying with impeccable Old Christian lines, entering the priesthood, and acquiring appointments to locally powerful positions, habits of the Order of Christ, and appointments to the Inquisition. The descendants of João Pais Barreto Velho frequently succeeded in their endeavors, but they still encountered serious problems. The succeeding heads of the Pais Barreto clan obtained the almost hereditary position as captain major of the town of Cabo, and several of them became *fidalgos* (nobles) of the crown. They were much less successful, however, in their attempts to obtain an inquisitional carta.

João Pais Barreto Velho's descendant, Felipe Pais Barreto, sought a habit of the Order of Christ. His application became intermingled with the ongoing conflict between the landed aristocracy of Olinda and the merchants of Recife, which was particularly intense in the late seventeenth and early eighteenth centuries. After the Dutch occupation, the commercial center of the colony had shifted from Olinda to Recife. But Olinda remained the political and religious center. The merchants of Recife sought to wrest political control from Olinda, or at least distance themselves from that control at the same time that the planters sought to strengthen their hold on Recife.[11] These merchants found an effective tool for challenging the planters' social status by accusing them of some taint of New Christian ancestry. Acquiring inquisitional appointments and positions in the military orders and the priesthood also allowed the merchants to flaunt their purported ancestral superiority in the face of planter families who sought to cover up their own disgrace.

Many planter families obtained habits of the military orders, and some even became titled nobles. By the end of the seventeenth century, however, merchants were also entering the military orders in larger numbers. But these outward signs of honor and purity did not eliminate the memory of impurity or rivals' abilities to use it to discredit their enemies.

One of those merchants, Miguel Correia Gomes, received the order to perform the investigation on Felipe Pais Barreto for the Order of Christ in 1704. He had only recently been appointed, and he used the opportunity to discredit his enemy. He sent the investigation back to the Board of Conscience and Orders, who rejected Felipe because he was rumored to be of New Christian descent. The descent came through his maternal grandmother, Britis de Albuquerque, the daughter of Antônio de Sá Matias, who was the son of Duarte de Sá. Proof of his New Christian ancestry rested on the claim that Antônio had paid the finta.

This was not, however, Felipe Pais Barreto's first attempt to obtain proof of purity. He had also applied to be admitted as a familiar of the Inquisition in the 1690s and had been rejected in 1697 for the same reason.[12] When Felipe Pais Barreto applied to the Order of Christ, he was certainly aware of the dangerous rumors circulating about his family, and he was probably seeking to remove the taint he had received from the Inquisition's rejection. In his defense to the board, Felipe tried to argue that it had all been a mistake and that he had descended from a different Duarte de Sá, who was clean. He also listed several members of the family who belonged to the Order of Christ or had been ordained to the priesthood as evidence of his own purity. He included his cousin Pedro de Melo e Albuquerque, who became a canon of the Olinda cathedral. Pedro de Melo e Albuquerque failed in his application to the Inquisition in 1731 for the same reason that Felipe Pais Barreto did.[13]

Felipe acquired a justification from the ouvidor geral of Pernambuco regarding the purity of his descent and his family and resubmitted it to the Order of Christ. The witnesses for the justification were taken from family members or friends, and they declared that the impurity was a matter of confusion between the New Christian Matias and the Old Christian Matias.[14] The crown ordered a new investigation in 1716, which was delayed until 1721, when a relative of Felipe's, Francisco de Souza, became the head of the government in Pernambuco during the absence of both the governor and the bishop. This time, the investigation was in the hands of Felipe's friends and relatives, and the witnesses all came from Cabo, where Felipe was the captain major. Predictably, they declared that he was an Old Christian with no taint of New Christian ancestry and that he was related to several members of the Order of Christ and several clerics. They also found that there was confusion over the finta. They claimed that Antônio de Sá Matias came to Pernambuco in 1635, too late to have contributed to the Dutch finta. The living informants from the first investigation were requestioned and recanted their former testimony, declaring that Felipe was from one of the most honorable families of the captaincy.[15] But the board remained unconvinced, and they sent the application back for a third and more comprehensive examination of Felipe's bloodlines in 1724; but it never took place.

During this ongoing struggle to cover up the Pais Barreto genealogy, Felipe's son, Antônio Pais Barreto, applied to become a familiar of the Inquisition—hoping, perhaps, that he would be outside the fourth degree of descent and, therefore, exempt from the exclusion. His attempt failed, and he was rejected in 1718 for the same reason as his father.[16] Likewise, in 1736 Felipe's nephew, João Pais Barreto, applied to become a familiar and was rejected for New Christian descent.[17] Only after 1775, with the pure-blood law, did the grand-nephew of

Felipe, Estêvão José Pais Barreto, finally acquire an appointment as a familiar. The family's trouble with the Inquisition caused them considerable embarrassment and difficulty, but as one of the most powerful clans in Pernambuco, they could not be so easily displaced from positions of power and prestige.

The Rego Barros family experienced similar problems with their attempts to become familiares. João do Rego Barros applied to be admitted as a familiar in 1744. The witnesses testified that his great-great-great-grandmother Arcângela da Silveira was a parda and his family had always been known as mulattos. His investigation was never completed, but that of his brother, Francisco do Rego Barros, was. He applied in 1772 and immediately encountered the same problems and rumors that João did, that he descended from Beatriz Mendes, a known New Christian said to have been punished by the Inquisition. He was indeed related, but only by marriage. The brother of his great-great-great-grandfather had married a daughter of Beatriz Mendes. His wife, D. Ana Maria José de Melo, however, encountered more serious problems. She was descended through her paternal grandmother from Duarte de Sá. In 1773, Comissário Francisco Fernandes de Souza reported the ancestry, but claimed that this Duarte de Sá was from Ponte de Lima, thus distancing him from the Barcelos New Christians.

This was essentially the same line of argument that the familiar Antônio José Victoriano Borges da Fonseca took in his famous genealogy of the nobility of Pernambuco written in the mid-eighteenth century.[18] But the entire family knew full well that Duarte de Sá was from Barcelos and of New Christian descent.[19] As proof of this pure-blood line, the comissário Francisco Fernandes de Souza cited the many fidalgos and priests in the family and particularly the fact that a great-granddaughter of José de Sá de Albuquerque, D. Josefa Francisca de Melo e Albuquerque, had married the familiar Francisco Antônio de Almeida and was, therefore, clean. But a rumor of New Christian ancestry also dogged Francisco, and the inquiry on Josefa revealed the rumor of New Christian ancestry through Duarte de Sá. The General Council concluded that the rumor was false and approved them in 1757.[20]

Despite all of these doubts and rumors, the cover-up had worked, and Francisco do Rego Barros became a familiar in October of 1773. Things had become so confused by that time that when Francisco's nephew, Pedro Velho Barreto, applied, he went through with only vague rumors of mulatto ancestry and Judaism, which no one could place.[21] By then, it technically would not have mattered, anyway, because the new pure-blood law was in place, and the Inquisition could not legally have excluded him.

The related line that connected, through Arnão de Holanda Barreto, a son of Luís do Rego Barros who married Inês de Góes, the daughter of Beatriz

Mendes, encountered similar problems. Beatriz Mendes was another very important ancestor of the Pernambucan nobility. Antônio Borges chose to ignore the rumors of her New Christian ancestry in his genealogy and fabricated a link between her husband, Arnão de Holanda, and Pope Adrian VI. The background of these two is rather vague. Beatriz apparently came with D. Britis de Albuquerque, the mother of Jerônimo, and both her and Arnão had reputations as Old Christians until the 1590s, when a rumor that she was New Christian arose during the inquisitional visita. The rumor kept appearing because of its utility in the ongoing contest between Recife and Olinda. Since many of the noble families of Pernambuco could be traced back to Beatriz, if she was a New Christian, then their reputations would be seriously compromised. For the merchants of Recife, throwing up the impurity of the noble families in their faces gave them at least a sense of ethnic-racial superiority and a certain edge in social, political, and economic disputes.[22] The confusion of these genealogies was only compounded by the existence of several women of the same name.

José Gomes de Melo was rejected in 1699 because he was the great-great-grandson of Beatriz Mendes. The witnesses claimed that she had been banished by the Inquisition and punished with the sanbenito and that the Inquisition had burned her mother.[23] José's son, João Gomes de Melo, applied in 1706 in an attempt to erase the rumor of New Christian descent. The extrajudicial in Pernambuco revealed the descent from Beatriz, but João died before the inquiry could be completed.[24]

The great-great-great-great-grandson of Beatriz Mendes, João Carlos de Araújo, was still haunted by the rumors of her impurity in 1746, when he applied. In this case, the rumor came from two directions. The first came through descent from one of the daughters of Beatriz Mendes. The other came through his maternal grandmother, Maria Pessoa. It was rumored that her father, Nuno Campelo, was New Christian and her mother, Inês de Pessoa, was descended from an Indian woman and a New Christian. The comissário judged that the rumors were false because several members of the family from the same generation had entered the priesthood. The deputy Nunes da Silva Teles explained that the real problem came from confusion over the name Beatriz Mendes. He claimed that there were really two women by this name. One was the Beatriz Mendes, married to Arnão de Holanda, who had always been reputed an Old Christian of clean ancestry. Her granddaughter, also named Beatriz Mendes, married Felipe Dias and was considered a New Christian not because of her paternal grandparents, Beatriz and Arnão, but because of her maternal grandmother, Britis de Paiva, who was the granddaughter of the well-known Judaizer, Branca Dias. So the descendants of the

Beatriz Mendes married to Felipe Dias were New Christians, but those descended from the Beatriz Mendes married to Arnão de Holanda were not.[25]

Father José Campelo Pessoa, knight of the Order of Christ, also descended through Nuno Campelo, who was his paternal grandfather. His line became confused with the line from Beatriz Mendes and caused a delay in his processo for comissário. His brother, the canon João Ribeiro Pessoa de Lacerda, wrote to the Inquisition and informed them that his brother was no longer in a position to become a comissário, but he wanted to pursue the issue for himself to clear his family of the rumor of impurity that had arisen because of José's failure to obtain an appointment. João blamed the confusion on someone in Bahia who had the same last name. The inquiry sought further clarification, including in Bahia, but in the end, it encountered much confusion and was left incomplete.[26]

Branca Dias

As we have seen, Branca Dias was one of the other main sources of genealogical contention in Pernambuco. Antônio José Victoriano Borges da Fonseca also misrepresented her genealogy by obstinately denying that she had left any descendants in Pernambuco.[27] He had good reason to do so, since his wife was related to the Carneiro Cunha family, who descended directly from Sebastião de Carvalho, who married one of Branca's granddaughters. The problem was that there were at least two and possibly three Brancas of legend and history. The historical Branca Dias was a New Christian from Viana who married Diogo Fernandes, also a New Christian. Diogo had come to Pernambuco before his wife and obtained a piece of land in Camaragibe from Duarte Coelho where he built an engenho. Branca was denounced and imprisoned by the Inquisition in 1543 and released in 1545 on the condition that she not leave Portugal. She fled to Pernambuco, nonetheless, to be with her husband. Indians destroyed his engenho in an uprising, so Branca opened up a school for children in Olinda to help meet their expenses. Some of these children, when they were grown, denounced Branca and Diogo as Judaizers to the inquisitor Heitor Furtado de Mendonça in 1593. One of Branca's daughters was imprisoned and sent to Lisbon, and Branca's bones were sent with her to be properly burned. Despite Antônio José's declaration that Branca did not leave any descendants in Pernambuco, she had at least seven children who intermarried with some of the most important families in the colony.[28]

A great-granddaughter of Branca Dias named Joanna de Góes married Sebastião de Carvalho. This is where Manuel de Carneiro da Cunha's troubles began. He applied to become a familiar in 1707 and was immediately accused of New Christian ancestry from Branca Dias. Over the course of the next twelve years, the investigation revealed that his maternal grandfather, Sebastião, had actually married three times. His first wife had been Joanna de Góes, with whom he had had two daughters. His second and third wives were reputed to have been Old Christians, and Manuel had descended from the third wife. But if Sebastião had been willing to take a New Christian as his first wife, maybe he had also been a New Christian. The deputy reviewing the case did not trust genealogists of the noble families because they often belonged to the same families. But the investigation did not offer any evidence that Sebastião was himself a New Christian and showed that his descendants had become confused with those of his brother. Also, it showed that Manuel had descended from Sebastião's third wife and so could not be a descendent of Branca Dias.[29] Manuel's brother, João Carneiro da Cunha, escaped without the intense inquiry because of Manuel's approval, but his wife's application ran into extended problems of the same type, which delayed his approval for eleven years, until 1737.[30]

Guiomar Nunes
The persecution of an extended New Christian family that took place in Paraíba between 1739 and 1741 also left residual problems for some applicants to the Inquisition. The Inquisition swept up almost an entire family network for Judaizing, and two of them—Guiomar Nunes and Fernando Henrique Alvares—were burned at the stake.

The problem surfaced in the application of the priest Marcos Soares de Oliveira, who applied for a position as a comissário in 1760. He carefully listed his ancestors and mentioned all the priests in the family. He provided information on his maternal line all the way to his great-grandparents, but he conveniently omitted any mention of his paternal great-grandparents. He had good reason for doing so. The investigation revealed that his paternal grandparents were directly related to Guiomar Nunes and Fernando Henrique.

Marcos protested that he was suffering great damage due to the delay in the processo, that the information they had received was incorrect, and that his enemies were plotting against him. He even provided a list of no less than thirty individuals whom he considered his enemies and whose testimony should not be trusted. Some of them had acted as witnesses, so the General Council sent another inquiry in 1773, but the general consensus among all the witnesses, even those he did not list as his enemies, was that the ancestry was correct and that he was related to Guiomar and her family.[31]

About the same time, Cipriano Lopes da Fonseca Galvão, canon of the Olinda chapter, applied to become a comissário and was also rejected because of his relation to Guiomar Nunes.³² This ancestry had caused both Manuel de Carneiro da Cunha and Cipriano trouble before. The Jesuits had rejected Manuel because of it, but later he became a secular priest. Cipriano could not get himself ordained until he went to Lisbon, where his ancestry was unknown. This exclusion of impure relatives in their original petitions was nothing less than an attempt to hoodwink the Inquisition and so overcome their own ancestral impurity. At least for them, it did not work.³³

The struggles to cover up or dispel rumors of impurity and the Inquisition's attempts to maintain control over the ancestral purity of its officials became intertwined with the mid-eighteenth-century reforms that forced open the ranks of the Inquisition to a broader section of society. The opening up of the Inquisition brought respite to some of the genealogically embattled families, but it also diminished the prestige value of an appointment.

Reform and the Opening of the Inquisition

The use of inquisitional investigations in local conflicts shows how profoundly the values and selection criteria of the Inquisition reverberated within colonial Pernambucan society. Because these criteria had real importance in colonial Pernambuco, attempts to eliminate the racially based distinctions upon which inquisitional exclusiveness rested resulted in paradoxical consequences. The legal elimination of racially based discrimination diminished the value of an appointment precisely because it was only a legal elimination and failed to transform the popular racially based notions of honor and status. From the mid-eighteenth century on, the Inquisition struggled to maintain its autonomy in the construction of its status group. However, it experienced a largely top-down opening up that stripped away much of the exclusiveness upon which the prestige and honor of appointment rested, thus forcing open its ranks and diminishing its ability to provide the proof of purity. This process had a long gestation, and the colonial time lag delayed serious fractures in the inquisitional fortress until the early nineteenth century.

Throughout the sixteenth, seventeenth, and eighteenth centuries, the Inquisition had struggled to maintain its autonomy from both papal and royal control, and the history of the Inquisition is marked by extended conflicts between the Inquisition and the pope and the Inquisition and the crown. Its unique position as both a royal and ecclesiastical tribunal contributed to its strength and to its weakness. Although the papacy's influence over the Portuguese Inquisition was never strong, it did suspend the Inquisition in 1544–1547 and again in 1679–1681. In contests with the papacy, the Inquisition had the support of the crown, which saw papal encroachments as threats to royal authority in Portugal.[34]

Yet the crown and the Inquisition were often at odds over special dispensations to New Christians, privileges, and jurisdiction. For example, between 1649 and 1657, D. João IV engaged in a running battle with the inquisitor general, D. Francisco de Castro, over the Inquisition's ability to confiscate the property of heretics and the king's authority to suspend that right.[35] In each of these cases, the Inquisition emerged with a renewed desire to assert its authority and resumed its activities with fresh vigor. Even though the Inquisition was never completely autonomous, it was generally successful in countering crown and papal attempts to seriously constrict its authority until at least the mid-eighteenth century.

Conflicts between the Portuguese crown and the papacy also weakened the Inquisition's position in its relations with the crown. The split between Portugal and Rome in 1760 occurred because of the papacy's interference in royal policy and Rome's assertion that inquisitors were papal officials, not royal officials. The conflict lasted until 1771, and during that time Portugal did not have an inquisitor general and the crown was free to act without papal interference and to firmly subordinate the Church.[36] Sebastião José de Carvalho e Melo (later the Marquis of Pombal), the chief minister of the kingdom under D. José I, exercised considerable power at the time. His brother, Paulo de Carvalho e Mendonça, one of the oldest deputies of the General Council, assumed much of the responsibility of administering the daily affairs of the Inquisition.[37] This extraordinary and, for Pombal, fortuitous turn of events played into his hands and cleared the way for the reform of the Inquisition.[38]

The period in which the Marquis of Pombal dominated the political and administrative affairs of the empire (1750–1777) was a period of reform and centralization. Pombal reformed the colonial administration and economy, and he sought to limit the power of the Church. His policies toward the Church and the Inquisition had less to do with anticlericalism or antagonism toward either institution than with a specific political agenda that was a combination of regalism, secularization, and economic nationalism. Yet "it was a policy of reform, disguised, when prudence dictated, by traditional institutions and language."[39]

The Inquisition was one of those institutions in which Pombal dressed up his reforms.[40] The Inquisition had never been independent of either crown or papal authority, although at times it exercised considerable autonomy. Pombal's attempt to make it a crown tribunal, likewise, did not make it entirely dependent on the crown, as some have asserted.[41] To do so would have radically altered its nature and deprived it of ecclesiastical legitimacy, which was a fundamental part of its identity. And, at any rate, that was never Pombal's intention.[42] Pombal was a familiar of the Inquisition, as were his father, his uncle, his grandfather, and his wife's uncle.[43] Although his reforms did place significant limits on inquisitional activity, they did not strip the Inquisition of power, authority, or autonomy. What he accomplished through his reform of the Inquisition, and other seemingly unrelated reforms, was to force open the ranks of the Inquisition to previously excluded groups as part of his larger geopolitical strategy. That opening-up contributed to its decline and, therefore, needs to be understood.

In 1768, he stripped the power of censorship from the Inquisition and invested it in a new institution called the Real Mesa Censória (Royal Board of Censorship), although he permitted one inquisitor to sit on the board.[44] In the same year, he began his campaign to eliminate the distinction between New and Old Christians by destroying all the lists of *fintados* (those who paid the finta) and by ordering that all references to infamy be erased from the books of genealogy.

On May 5, 1768, he sent an order throughout the empire to gather all of the lists, or rolls of the fintas paid by New Christians, and any other papers that might contain similar information and deliver them to the chief treasurer of the royal exchequer within three months. (Interestingly, inquisitional documents were not included in the order.) The rolls listed the names of the New Christians and their descendants who contributed to the funds that were used to pay for general pardons or other privileges periodically purchased from the king. For a very long time, these lists had served as one of the few reliable sources for identifying New Christians. Claims that a person's ancestors paid the finta often appear in the records of the Inquisition.[45] To eliminate these records would leave not only the Inquisition, but also all other military and religious orders, brotherhoods, and guilds that retained pure-blood requirements, without some of the most important documentary means for proving the ancestral inadequacy of applicants.

The Inquisition did not confront the apparent challenge openly, but still it found a way to circumvent it. In a curious action by an institution that was more or less dominated by Pombal, the Inquisition decided to do what it could to preserve these records. On May 25, 1768, it secretly ordered its comissários to make a diligent search at the end of the three-month period for any lists or memories remaining about the fintas in their districts. If found, the lists were to be sent to them in all secrecy and security.[46] In Olinda, Pernambuco, the comissário Friar Rodrigo Gaioso de São José received the order and searched all of the archives in the region, finding only one list of fintados from Bahia. In Ceará, the comissário claimed that there had never been any fintados in the area or, if they had, they were so ancient that they no longer existed.[47]

These reforms were preparatory to the 1773 elimination of the distinction between New and Old Christians and the creation of a new regimento to govern the Inquisition in 1774.[48] The elimination of the distinction between New and Old Christians forced the Inquisition to reconsider its procedures. In 1773, the General Council recommended, probably at the instigation of Pombal, the introduction of a new regimento intended to eliminate the pureblood requirements and restrict the practices of secrecy, torture, and execution. In its consultation on the matter, the Inquisition manifested a concern for the image of the Inquisition in the eyes of the other European nations and with demonstrating that the Inquisition was a royal, not an ecclesiastical, tribunal.[49] The new regimento was, in part, the result of a new mentality that emphasized greater religious tolerance and the assertion of civil authority over ecclesiastical power.[50] The crown sought to rein in inquisitional autonomy and to render the institution less offensive to late-eighteenth-century sensibilities. At the same time, the crown opened the Inquisition up to a broader range of social groups.

The royal confirmation of September 1, 1774, followed the general outline of the recommendations and declared that the current "estilo" was incompatible with natural reason and religion. The new regimento expunged everything from the regulations that was not consistent with what the Marquis of Pombal believed was the Inquisition's condition as a crown tribunal.[51] Ironically, and despite the argument that the 1640 Regimento was invalid, the 1774 Regimento retained much of the original wording of the 1640 Regimento. The 1774 Regimento also shortened the regulations, eliminated purity of blood as a requirement for inquisitional office by simply omitting any reference to it, and placed strict limits on the use of the autos-da-fé. Beyond these revisions, only minor changes were made in the responsibilities of the inquisitional officials. In this regard, at least, the 1774 Regimento was more an exercise in abridgment than in reformation. In 1774, Pombal also oversaw the extinction of the tribunal in Goa, India.[52] The Inquisition emerged from the period with considerably less power and autonomy in the prosecution of heretics.[53]

Certainly, these measures constricted inquisitional power, but secrecy, torture, and execution all remained legitimate activities for the Inquisition, if not practiced with as much vigor, until it was abolished in 1821. Indeed, it may be argued that the regimento actually helped rejuvenate the Inquisition for a time by bringing it up to date with current enlightened philosophical and political ideas, which gave it at least the façade of a more rationalized institution. Even though the Inquisition's ability to produce terror, orthodoxy, prestige, and power may have been restricted, it gained a forty-seven-year lease on life.

All of these reforms addressed Pombal's larger program of economic nationalism, in which he sought to reinvigorate the Portuguese economy by releasing it from the overpowering influence of foreign commercial interests. To do so, he believed that he had to resuscitate the New Christian business community and tap into its wealth and expertise. That meant diminishing legal or semilegal distinctions that put the New Christians in a weak and threatened position. The Inquisition was the most visible institution dedicated to maintaining those distinctions, and its power of confiscation could seriously threaten business enterprises. But did these reforms really open up inquisitional office to previously excluded groups?

It is difficult to assess how many previously excluded individuals managed to get accepted by the Inquisition because the issue of purity of blood was no longer legally acceptable to discuss, but some did. Several habilitações bridge the transitional period of 1773–1774 and provide us with a glimpse of how the new reforms affected candidates' applications.[54] For example, Antônio Pereira de Azevedo applied to become a familiar in 1772. The initial inquiry determined that his paternal grandmother was a mulatta and his maternal grandfather was a New Christian who had been sentenced to ten years' exile in Angola and public whipping through the streets with chains on his feet while a proclamation of his crimes was read. Fortunately for Antônio, the investigation lasted until 1775. When the deputies finally saw it, they determined that "the seditious distinction between New Christians and Old Christians as well as that of mulattos is happily extinct and abolished" so it could not impede his application. He was approved in February 27, 1776.[55] This case, and at least three others like it, demonstrate that what had been impediments to appointment prior to 1774 generally ceased to impede applications. This meant that previously "impure" individuals could and did gain access to the Inquisition and by implication to other positions of honor and prestige within Luso-Brazilian society.

Abandoned and Illegitimate Children

The ranks of the Inquisition opened further during the Pombaline years through the legitimation of abandoned and illegitimate children. Prior to 1768, abandoned and illegitimate children were not accepted as officials of the Inquisition. For example, in 1739, the *clerigo inminoribus* (minor clergy) Felipe Neri do Espírito Santo applied to work for the Holy Office. He had been abandoned as a child at the home of the chief treasurer, Antônio Alves Castro, in Pernambuco. At age eleven, he successfully petitioned to get himself accepted as a cleric by compiling a stack of papers with the commentary of many learned men who argued that abandonment could not be an impediment to entering the ministry because it was against all divine and human laws.

He used the same bunch of documents to apply for the Inquisition ten years later. His argument rested on a papal brief of March 2, 1591, issued by Pope Gregory XIV and the arguments of no less then ten scholars. They maintained that foundlings did not need a special dispensation to seek office because by right of their status as foundlings they enjoyed the status of legitimate children.[56] The papal brief permitted men who had been abandoned to enter the priesthood without proof of ancestry. Felipe Neri succeeded in entering the priesthood, but not the Inquisition. Pope Gregory's declaration was apparently sufficient for ecclesiastical offices, but not for inquisitional appointment.[57]

The topic of abandoned children came up frequently in colonial Brazil.[58] The problem revolved around their potential entrance into communities such as colleges, brotherhoods, military orders, the Church, and the Inquisition, which had statutes requiring purity of blood. The checks for purity rested on positive oral or documentary proof of parentage. Most abandoned children could not provide such proof and so were altogether excluded, at least in theory. The problem existed for the children of foundlings, as well.[59]

A widely held conception claimed that abandoned children often came from noble, or at least "pure," families, and their exclusion was seen as unfair punishment of the guiltless. Francisco Xavier argued, in 1767, that abandoned children had as difficult a time as descendants of the Indians from the interior in proving their descent, but they had long been allowed to enter communities with statutes of purity. He then followed the standard Pombaline argument for most political errors by arguing that those who advocated the exclusion of abandoned children had "drunk of the barbaric doctrine of the Jesuits who were the first to publish it."[60]

The crown finally acted on the problem with the royal resolution of March 3, 1768. The resolution legitimated all abandoned children, which allowed them to qualify for entrance into all honorary groups and secular offices requiring positive proof of parentage. The General Council responded by modifying the regimento to permit foundlings to be qualified for inquisitional office. The March 22, 1768, declaration from the General Council argued that the royal resolution had finally allowed foundlings to qualify for secular offices in the same way that Pope Gregory had permitted them to receive ecclesiastical positions. The General Council altered the regimento to permit abandoned children to be dispensed from the qualification of positive proof of ancestry.[61] It also approved several abandoned and illegitimate children after the 1768 law.[62]

When comissários performed a diligência on an abandoned child, the Inquisition instructed them to take special care to try to identify the parents if possible. If the parents of the abandoned children were known, then they did not fall under the new law and could be investigated in the normal fashion.[63] They often managed to find the parents. For example, a comissário discovered the father of Maria Joaquina, and since he was a Carmelite monk living in the monastery in Paraíba she was declared clean. Likewise, Joaquim Marques de Araújo discovered that Ana Francisca Carneiro de Cunha was really the daughter of the comissário João Manuel Carneiro da Cunha and D. Teresa Maria de Jesus.[64]

The problem of illegitimacy of either the applicant or any of his children differed from that of abandoned children.[65] The fact of illegitimacy did not necessarily serve as an impediment to office. The Inquisition wanted to know, at least before 1773, whether the children were "unclean." If they were the children of New Christians, or of mulattos through slavery unto the fourth degree, they could be denied. For example, the canon Manuel Garcia Velho do Amaral had an illegitimate son with a mulatta. Since no rumors existed to the effect that she was a slave or the recent descendent of a slave and because he was so deserving in every other way, the deputies approved him.[66]

Abandoned children also claimed ignorance of their real parents, particularly after 1768, so that they could avoid possible embarrassments and expensive inquiries. For example, João Pereira de Brito married Ana Francisca Carneiro da Cunha and applied in 1787 to be admitted as a familiar. When he applied, he indicated that her parents were unknown because she had been abandoned as a child. The comissário Joaquim Marques found that it was fairly well known that her father was really the comissário of the Holy Office, João Manuel Carneiro da Cunha.[67]

We will never know how many individuals from previously excluded groups managed to enter the ranks of the Inquisition after it was opened up, because the previous impediments were no longer legal and were, consequently, seldom mentioned or dealt with. But quantity is not the issue here. The mere possibility that some previously "impure" individuals could be accepted meant that the wall of exclusivity upon which much of the prestige of an inquisitional appointment rested had been seriously breached.

The Marquis of Pombal felt that the expulsion of the Jews and the continuing discrimination against New Christians had retarded the Portuguese economic enterprise, and he permitted it to become subordinate to foreign influences. His elevation of Indians to juridical equality with whites in 1755, his elimination of the distinction between New and Old Christians, and his permitting abandoned children access to positions of honor and privilege can all be seen as part of his program of opening up society. It created conditions amenable to social mobility and permitted previously excluded groups to enter more honorable and prestigious positions.[68] This opening up from above proved paradoxical. At the same time that the opening cheapened the value of an inquisitional appointment, it did not alter the deep-seated racial attitudes and beliefs regarding honor and status already in place.

Attempts at genealogical fraud took various forms, but they all had the same general purpose. Families and individuals sought to rid themselves of rumors of impurity or cover up known "defects" in their ancestral line. Not only did rumors of impurity affect their social standing, but they could also compromise a person's ability to contract good marriages and acquire public offices. The problem became particularly acute in colonial Pernambuco, where most of the wealthy planters had some New Christian or Indian ancestry. Potential impure ancestry became a weapon to use against one's opponents and was employed by the merchants of Recife in their contest against the wealthy planters. Some families fought against the rumors for many generations and attempted to use the Inquisition to remove the rumored taint. Even the powerful Pais Barreto family, which had already obtained titles of nobility and entrance into the Order of Christ, were rejected by the Inquisition until after the pure-blood law of 1773.

Sometimes the existence of ordained priests, fidalgos, or members of the military orders within the family could be accepted as proof of purity by the Inquisition, but the Inquisition did not automatically accept such proofs. If they found what they considered consistent evidence of impurity, despite other evidence of purity, they rejected the candidate. So, although these other signs could help, they did not guarantee acceptance, which contributed to the impression of inquisitional rigor in their investigations. It is, of course, impossible to know how many were successful in their attempts at genealogical fraud. With New Christian ancestors who were less well known, fraud would be a far simpler task.

Cases of genealogical fraud, nonetheless, demonstrate that the Inquisition's techniques of exclusion and criteria for selection had very real applicability and importance in Pernambucan colonial society. For that reason, the Pombaline reforms of the mid-eighteenth century became all the more significant. Those reforms paradoxically forced open the ranks of the Inquisition to a broader section of society at the same time that they failed to change locally held notions of honor and status that were based on race. The persistence of these beliefs, combined with the Inquisition's declining ability not only to reflect those attitudes and notions, but also to offer the proofs of purity so necessary in a society based on racial purity, led to a cheapening of the symbolic value of the carta. The value of an appointment declined precisely because the Inquisition could no longer offer those proofs.

Notes

1. See Dutra, "Duarte Coelho Pereira," 419, and Dwight E. Petersen, "Sweet Success: Some Notes on the Founding of a Brazilian Sugar Dynasty, the Pais Barreto Family," *Americas* 40, no. 3 (January 1984): 326–27.

2. See Schwartz, *Sugar Plantations*, 273. For the two most important genealogies from colonial Pernambuco, see Antônio José Victoriano Borges da Fonseca, *Nobiliarchia Pernambuco*, 2 vols. (Rio de Janeiro: Biblioteca Nacional, 1935), and Antônio De Santa Maria Jaboatão, *Catalogo genealogico das principais familias que procederam de Albuquerques, e Cavalcantes em Pernambuco, e Caramurus na Bahia* . . . (1768); reprint, *RIHGB* 3, no. 1 (1889): 5–489.

3. For a study of the uprising and the attendant genealogical feuds, see Cabral e Mello, *O nome e o sangue*, 57–60, and Cabral e Mello, *A fronda dos mazombos: Nobres contra mascates, Pernambuco, 1666-1715* (São Paulo: Editora Schwarcz, 1995).

4. One of the "martyrs" who died in Portugal, Cosme Bezerra Cavalcante, applied to become a familiar in 1703 and was rejected for New Christian ancestry. See ANTT, IL, Livro 136, and Nelson Barbalho, *1710, Recife versus Olinda, a guerra municipal do açucar, nobres x mascates: Subsídios para a história de três municípios, Recife, Olinda, e Vitória de Santo Antão* (Recife: Centro de Estudos de História Municipal, 1986), 449.

5. Schwartz, *Sugar Plantations*, 273.

6. This stereotype has proven more tenacious in Luso-Brazilian historiography than in almost any other. In the seventeenth century, the terms *gente da nação* and *cristão-novo* came to be used as synonyms for *homen de negócio*. See David Grant Smith, "Old Christian Merchants and the Foundation of the Brazil Company, 1649," *HAHR* 54, no. 2 (May 1974): 233–59.

7. Cabral e Mello, *O nome e o sangue*, 134.

8. Evaldo Cabral e Mello shows this in his book, *O nome e o sangue*, 112–16. Even the children of Jerônimo de Albuquerque married New Christians.

9. Petersen, "Sweet Success," 339–40.

10. João Pais Barreto probably also had covered up the fact that he had come to Pernambuco as an exile from Portugal. See Petersen, "Sweet Success," 326–27, for this accusation and 328–34 for estimates of his wealth.

11. Cabral e Mello, *A fronda dos mazombos*.

12. ANTT, HI, m. 29, no. 29.
13. ANTT, HI, m. 37, no. 14.
14. Cabral e Mello, *O nome e o sangue*, 64–66.
15. Cabral e Mello, *O nome e o sangue*, 80–81.
16. ANTT, HI, m. 15, no. 89.
17. ANTT, NH, m. 1, no. 30.
18. Fonseca, *Nobiliarchia Pernambuco*, 2:368–75.
19. Antônio has been accused of genealogical fraud in trying to erase the New Christian ancestry of the Pernambucan nobility. See Cabral e Mello, *O nome e o sangue*, 90–92. But José Antônio Gonsalves de Mello argues that Antônio José Victoriano Borges da Fonseca was remarkably advanced and accurate in his research. See *Estudos Pernambucanos*, 147–94.
20. ANTT, HSO, Francisco, m. 86, no. 1477.
21. ANTT, HSO, Pedro, m. 36, no. 620.
22. Cabral e Mello, *O nome e o sangue*, 103.
23. ANTT, HI, m. 30, no. 21; HI, m. 14, no. 33.
24. ANTT, HI, m. 19, no. 23.
25. ANTT, HSO, João, m. 98, no. 1643.
26. ANTT, NH, m. 18, no. 35; NH, cx. 34; HI, m. 32, no. 105.
27. Cabral e Mello, *O nome e o sangue*, 93. Cosme Bezerra Cavalcante was also denied because of his descent from Branca Dias, see ANTT, CGSO, NT 4164.
28. See José Antônio Gonsalves e Mello, *Gente de nação: Cristãos-novos e judeus em Pernambuco, 1542–1654* (Recife: Editora Massangana, 1989), 117–60, and Cabral e Mello, *O nome e o sangue*, 89–163.
29. ANTT, HSO, Manuel 84/1595. Cabral e Mello also dealt with this inquiry, *O nome e o sangue*, 93–163.
30. ANTT, HSO, João, m. 70, no. 1306.
31. ANTT, HSO, Marcos, m. 3, no. 44.
32. ANTT, HI, m. 6, no. 129; CGSO, NT 4191, 4194.
33. See also ANTT, NH, cx. 35; IL, Livro 376.
34. Both the 1544 and the 1679 suspensions had to do with papal concerns of the excessive zeal of the Portuguese Inquisition. See Herculano, *História da Origem*, 3:55–131; Azevedo, *História dos Cristãos-novos*," 312–26; and ANTT, Armário Jesuítico, m. 30, nos. 74, 76–80, 85.
35. See António Baião, "El-Rei D. João IV e a Inquisição," *Academia Portuguesa de História* 4 (1942): 10–70.
36. During the schism, all vassals of the Portuguese crown were forbidden to communicate directly with Rome. See AHU, Pernambuco, cx. 97, doc. 7650.
37. Miguel de Oliveira, *História Eclesiástica de Portugal* (Portugal: Publicações Europa-América, 1994), 198–99. Pombal's brother, Paulo de Carvalho, was perhaps the most powerful deputy at the time, but certainly not the inquisitor general. Unless Pombal was going to change the rules of the game entirely, which he later showed he was not, that nomination would have required papal approval, which was impossible

under the circumstances. Besides, Paulo de Carvalho passed away in January 1770, before the schism had been healed. See Pe. Ernesto Sales, "Inquisidores Gerais em Portugal," *RH* 10 (1921): 207; Maxwell, *Pombal*, 91.

38. Azevedo, *História dos Cristãos-novos*, 312–26; ANTT, Armário Jesuítico, m. 30, no. 74, fols. 76–80, 85; Miguel de Oliveira, *História Eclesiástica de Portugal* (Portugal: Publicações Europa-América, 1994), 198–99. This schism did not end until June 1771, when the pope finally removed offensive phrasing from his approval letters for the inquisitor general. See ANTT, MNEJ, Livro 4, fols. 74v, 80, and *Collecção dos negocios de Roma no reinado de El-Rey Dom José I: Ministério do Marqués de Pombal e pontifidaco de Clemente XIV, 1769–1774*, 3 vols. (Lisbon: Imprensa Nacional, 1874), 3:241–54. ANTT, MNEJ, Livro 4, fols. 69v-70.

39. Maxwell, *Pombal*, 9.

40. Some have resurrected the myth to explain Pombal's success. Marcus Cheke has stated that "the passive obedience to authority, the extinction of all liberty which had resulted from the long domination of the Inquisition, made his methods fatally easy." See Marcus Cheke, *Dictator of Portugal: A Life of the Marquis of Pombal, 1699–1782* (Freeport, NY: Books for Libraries, 1938; reprint 1969), 194.

41. Oliveira Marques claims that, as early as 1769, Pombal had destroyed the Inquisition "as an independent tribunal and converted the Inquisition into a royal court entirely dependent upon the government." See Oliveira Marques, *History of Portugal*, 2nd ed. (New York: Columbia University Press, 1976), 402.

42. See *Collecção dos negocios de Roma no reinado de El-Rey Dom José I*, 242, and ANTT, MNEJ, Livro 4, fols. 76v–78v.

43. Pombal received his appointment in 1738. See ANTT, HSO, Sebastião, m. 10, no. 179. His son, Henrique José de Carvalho e Mello, became a familiar in 1765. See also Jordão de Freitas, *O Marquez de Pombal e o Santo Officio da Inquisição: Memoria enriquecida com documentos inéditos e facsimiles de assignaturas do benemerito da cidade de Lisboa* (Lisbon, 1916), 9, 16–17.

44. Among the loose papers of box 33 of the *Novas Habilitações* is a letter from the Inquisition complaining that the Real Mesa Censória did not include an inquisitor of the Holy Office on the board as stipulated by law.

45. Elias Lipiner, *Terror e Linguagem: Um dicionário da Santa Inquisição* (Lisbon: Círculo de Leitores, 1999), 114.

46. ANTT, IL, NT 2158.

47. ANTT, IL, m. 24, no. 18. The fact that they ordered the search to begin only after the three-month period expired suggests that the Inquisition had no intention of delivering the lists they found to the chief treasurer. The Inquisition sought to retain a small cache of previously valuable information for its archives.

48. Azevedo, *História dos Cristãos-novos*, 351. This law reinstated a curious law that arose during the high pitch of discriminatory decrees in November 1601 and prohibited the use of the terms *New Christian, Jew, Converso,* and *Marrano* to describe anyone. See Almeida, *Codigo Phillipino*, 5:1218. This was one of many laws periodically promulgated to appease the crown's conscience and that then was ignored be-

cause it was not really in the crown's interest to eliminate the distinction. See Carneiro, *Preconceito Racial*, 126–30.

49. ANTT, MNEJ, Livro 4, fols. 90–115v.
50. Siqueira, "Os regimentos da Inquisição," 562.
51. See Bethencourt, *História das Inquisições*, 41.
52. For a study of the Goa Tribunal, see Ana Cannas da Cunha, *A Inquisição no Estado da Índia: Origens, 1539–1560* (Lisbon: ANTT, 1995); António Baião, *A Inquisição de Goa: Tentativa de história de sua origem, estabelecimento, evolução, e extinção*, 2 vols. (Lisbon: Academia das Ciências de Lisboa, 1949); and Célia Cristina da Silva Tavares, "A cristanidade insular: Jesuitas e inquisidores em Goa, 1540–1682" (Ph.D. dissertation, Universidade Federal Fluminense, 2002).
53. This was part of a general constriction of ecclesiastical privilege. See Siqueira, "Os regimentos da Inquisição," 567–68.
54. When the new 1774 Regimento was sent out, the officials were required to return all the old ones still in their possession. ANTT, IL, Livro 159, fol. 14.
55. ANTT, HSO, Antônio, m. 188, no. 2785. See also ANTT, HSO, Joaquim, m. 17, no. 199; NH, cx. 58; HSO, Henriques, m. 4, no. 52.
56. ANTT, HI, m. 32, no. 45. See also Josef Metzler, ed., *America Pontificia: Primi saeculi evangelizationis, 1493–1592* (Vatican: Libreria Editrice Vaticana, 1991), 1423–26.
57. ANTT, HI, m. 32, no. 45. See also ANTT, HI, m. 32, no. 75.
58. See Castro Faria, *A colônia em movimento*, 52–96. See also Maria Luiza Marcílio, "A Irmandade da Santa Casa de Misericórdia e a assistência à criança abandonada na história do Brasil," in *Família, mulher, sexualidade e Igreja na história do Brasil*, ed. Maria Luiza Marcílio (São Paulo: Edições Loyola, 1993), 148–61; Maria Luiza Marcílio, "Abandonados y expósitos en la história de Brasil. Un proyecto interdisciplinario de investigación," in *La Família en el mundo iberoamericano*, ed. Pilar Gonzalbo Aizpuru and Cecilia Rabell (Mexico: Universidad Nacional Autónoma de México, 1994), 311–26; Renato Pinto Venâncio, "Nos limites da sagrada família: Ilegitimidade e casamento no Brasil colonial," in *História e sexualidade no Brasil*, ed. Ronaldo Vainfas (Rio de Janeiro: Editores de Livros, 1986), 107–24; Maria Beatriz Nizza da Silva, "O problema dos expostos na capitania de São Paulo," *RHES* 5 (1980): 95–104; Miriam Lifchitz Moreira Leite, "O óbvio e o contraditório da roda," in *História da criança no Brasil*, ed. Mary del Priore (São Paulo: Editora Contexto, 1991), 98–111; and Lana Lage da Gama Lima and Renato Pinto Venâncio, "O abandono de crianças negras no Rio de Janeiro," in *História da criança no Brasil*, ed. Mary del Priore (São Paulo: Editora Contexto, 1991), 61–75.
59. ANTT, IL, 158, fol. 257.
60. ANTT, CGSO, m. 13, no. 21.
61. ANTT, CGSO, Livro 381, fols. 260–261v, and MNEJ, Livro 3 (call number from the Biblioteca Nacional 9915), fols. 29–30v.
62. See ANTT, HSO, Domingos, m. 34, no. 614; Antônio, m. 199, no. 2926; and Tomás, m. 7, no. 103.

63. In 1779, the Inquisition sent out a judicial inquiry on Miguel Loureiro de Mirando in which they stated that he appeared to be an abandoned child, but that if his parents were known he would not enjoy the benefits of the new law. See ANTT, HI, m. 14, no. 129.

64. ANTT, HSO, Francisco, m. 122, no. 1815; HSO, João. m. 178, no. 1575.

65. See Linda Lewin, "Natural and Spurious Children in Brazilian Inheritance Law from Colony to Empire: A Methodological Essay," *Americas* 48 (January 1992): 351–96.

66. ANTT, HSO, m. 236, no. 1395. Later, Manuel petitioned the crown to legitimate his son so that he could inherit Manuel's estate. See AHU, Pernambuco, cx. 127, doc. 9635 (Olinda). See also ANTT, HSO, Antônio, m. 195, no. 2916; HSO, Antônio, m. 211, no. 3142; HSO, Manuel, m. 122, no. 2184; and ANTT, HI, m. 9, no. 13.

67. ANTT, HSO, João, m. 178, no. 1575.

68. Maxwell, *Pombal*, 78.

CHAPTER SEVEN

Nobility of Blood

The proof of purity and the status provided by an inquisitional appointment helped create a type of nobility based on blood and behavior that was not necessarily connected to landed wealth or hereditary titles. But it *was* associated with certain professions and behaviors that were considered honorable and respectable. The Inquisition became one of the institutions that facilitated and supported the acquisition and assertion of noble status. That does not mean, however, that all officials of the Inquisition were considered noble. It does mean that an inquisitional appointment created an opening for the assertion of noble status and the conditions for social promotion. The occupational and social data for the officials of the Inquisition show that, as a group, they tended to belong to this broad social category that could assert noble status if all the other necessary factors also existed. The social and geographic distribution of inquisitional officials also demonstrates that, despite the highly urban concentration of the Inquisition in Brazil, it still had a significant presence in the colony.

Individuals and families used the Inquisition as a means of promoting themselves socially. Immigrants found in the cartas a public declaration of purity that permitted them to insert themselves into local society. These attempts to use the Inquisition for social promotion also resulted in large family networks that point to the social blending of merchants and planters and of immigrants and established local families.

Nobility in Pernambuco

The idea of nobility retained as much currency in Brazil as it did in Portugal. When combined with purity of blood, ennoblement could overcome all barriers to social mobility.[1] But nobility was not limited to the families with long genealogies and fancy titles. Indeed, no new titled nobility were ever created in colonial Brazil and those of recognized noble status (i.e., fidalgos) were few in number and held no titles.[2] In this sense, it is important to distinguish between the hereditary nobility and the civil or political nobility (i.e., the lower or lesser nobility). The hereditary nobility were those who bore titles that were passed on from father to son. The civil or political nobility included those who, despite humble birth, achieved a degree of ennoblement through courageous actions or energetic activity in some honorable employment. They also needed to have, or at least to be able to fabricate, pure ancestry and to live after the manner of nobility. That is, they had to show that they did not have any impurity in their blood, that they did not participate in any of the dishonorable occupations, including any manual labor and small-scale merchandising, and that they lived a more or less genteel life. Nobility in Brazil came to be associated with "the way one lived and what one did as much as a legal charter."[3]

The civil and political nobility usually came from the so-called *estado do meio* (middle estate), which occupied the professions between the titled nobility and the mechanical trades.[4] The priest Raphael Bluteau described the estado do meio in his 1712 *Vocabulario Portuguez e Latino* this way:

> Between the mechanicos and the nobles there is a class of people that cannot be truly called noble because they do not possess political nobility, civil nobility, nor hereditary [nobility]. Neither can they rightly be called mechanicos, because they are different from them whether in the comportment of the individual, the use of the horse, being waited upon by servants . . . by privilege, [and by] esteem for art, such as painters, surgeons, and pharmacists that in many [instances have been] excused from paying *jugadas* and other *encargos* that the mechanicos are subject to.

Bluteau throws in sculptors, gold- and silversmiths, printers, composers, and book dealers and then continues:

> These make up a distinct category or order that we call the estado do meio, and they enjoy a quasi-nobility by way of certain exemptions. Nonetheless, it is necessary that they ride on horseback, and comport themselves well, because the art in-and-of-itself is not sufficient to privilege them. But by custom it does not serve as an impediment.[5]

As Bluteau's definition demonstrates, a large population of potential nobles existed in the Portuguese Empire. These groups generally sought the visible expressions of nobility to consolidate or promote their own social status. By the eighteenth century, most public offices, liberal professions, and large-scale commercial endeavors were considered potentially ennobling. Even some individuals who participated in the mechanical trades, once they gained a certain degree of financial independence, could enter the ranks of the lower nobility.[6] It should be remembered that potential is just that—potential. All the requirements had to be met before the potential could be translated into reality.

There had been some debate in the seventeenth century about the advisability of permitting titled nobles to become familiares, and the crown strongly opposed their appointment, but they were never formally excluded from office. The Inquisition also preferred men of "lower condition" who had some wealth and who could be trusted, even if they participated in the mechanical trades.[7] These preferences only increased popular interest in inquisitional appointments.

This rather open approach to social mobility had its roots in the realities imposed by Portuguese expansion. After the devastating wars in late-sixteenth- and seventeenth-century Europe had effectively thinned the ranks of the Portuguese nobility, the Portuguese monarchy accelerated the process that began in the twelfth century of opening up the ranks of the lower nobility to these professional classes.[8] These new nobility possessed the bureaucratic, seafaring, medical, merchant, and soldiering skills the crown so desperately needed for its colonial enterprise.[9] Even though the crown proved more receptive to families with the wealth and experience it needed, claims to nobility had to be continuously reasserted and substantiated with tangible proofs. Members of noble families and would-be nobles customarily sought to secure, improve, and protect their position by service to the crown. That service was most frequently military, but it could also include other services, such as colonization.[10]

In 1730, the crown defined the Pernambucan nobility as those whose ancestors had been nobles in Portugal or whose ancestors had been the first families to colonize the region, so long as they maintained honorable occupations.[11] The definition was sufficiently vague to permit the descendants of New Christians who had married into those families to assert their own nobility. The honorable occupations included any profession associated with governance, such as positions in the municipal council, officerships in the regular military, physicians, and doctors of theology and of canon law. Nobility could even extend to those occupations in the estado do meio that dealt with "noble" things. These occupations included gold- and silversmithing, bookselling, artistry, ecclesiastical offices, and teaching Latin grammar.[12] As early as 1449, and again in 1500, the crown declared that pharmacists enjoyed the privileges of the nobility. The crown reaffirmed that decision in 1606 and again in 1791. In fact, the pharmacist Custodio Moreira dos Santos from Olinda received royal confirmation of these privileges in 1791, in which the king declared that there was no reason to doubt their authenticity.[13]

Those who owned large estates and many slaves held a high enough social position to make claims of nobility and "demonstrated their noble status by living a seigniorial life with a landed estate, many slaves and retainers, and a responsibility to provide for the region's defense."[14] Wealthy sugar planters in Pernambuco regarded themselves as the *nobreza da terra* (literally, nobility of the land). Large-scale merchants could also be considered noble, especially after a 1775 law stated that large-scale merchants who had been accepted into the Junta de Comércio (Board of Trade) should be considered nobles.[15] Those who fell within this broad category of nobility often called themselves the "principal men," "good men," and even the "nobility of Pernambuco."

Even if an individual participated in one of these "noble" occupations, he still had to acquire the other indicators of nobility, which included the demonstration of refined manners and customs. Once these conditions had been met, the next step in solidifying one's claim to noble status was to acquire formal recognition of it. Such formal recognition could be acquired from one of the military orders, any position that required royal nomination, or the Inquisition. Until 1773, the certification of pure blood was implicit in all these positions. And once noble status had been achieved, it was necessary to maintain it and, if possible, expand it. This far-reaching conception of nobility combined with the intense concern over individual and family honor and status to stimulate interest in inquisitional appointments as "proof" of purity, honor, status, and nobility.[16] Those who acquired this noble status and assumed noble values and patterns of behavior could then presume to participate in municipal governance, "to vaunt their purity of blood, prestige and public recognition, insignias, precedence, and pomp in the exercise of their functions."[17]

Social and Geographic Profile

It is often stated, or inferred, that the Inquisition "had a limited geographical as well as social range."[18] This may have been true in terms of both willing confessions and resident officials at the beginning of the seventeenth century. But a century later, it would be completely inaccurate. A social and geographic profile of the officials in Pernambuco makes this clear.

The occupations of the officials of the Inquisition generally fell within the broad category of the estado do meio, which is reflected in the geographic distribution of the officials (see figures 7.1 and 7.2). Of the 1,046 individuals who applied to work for the Inquisition in Pernambuco between 1613 and

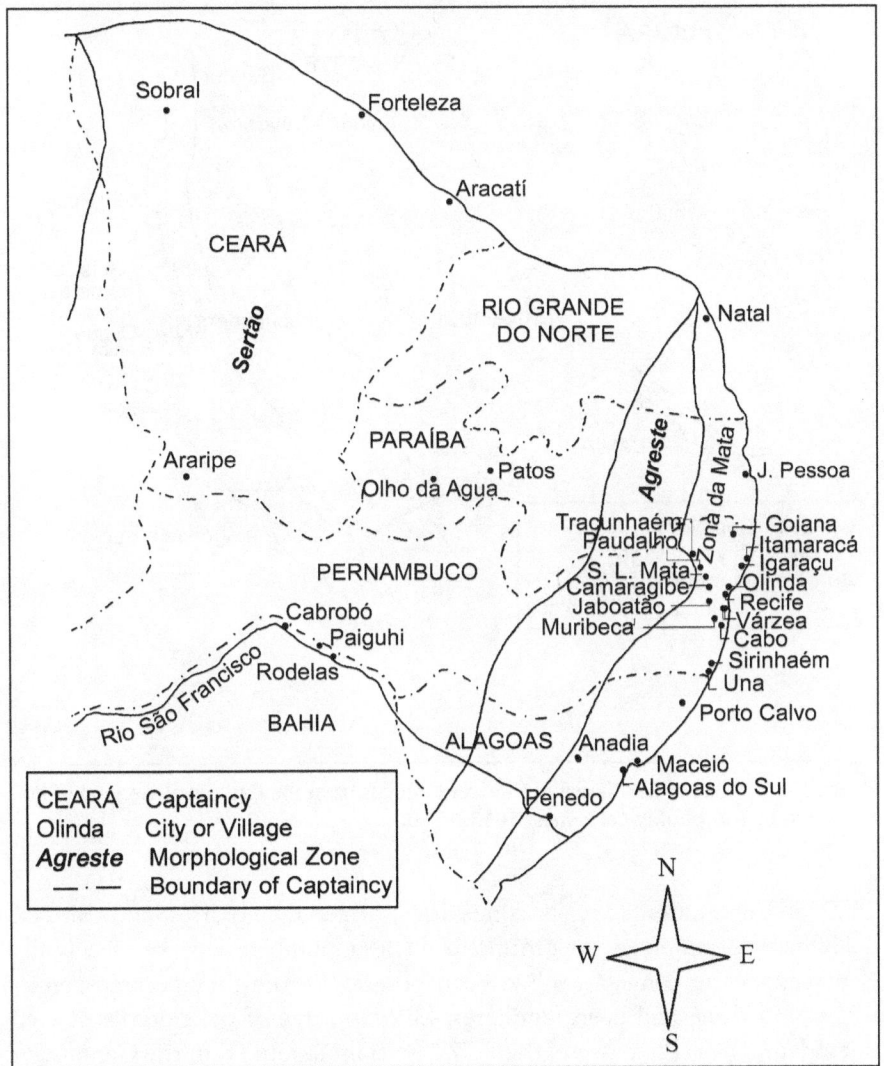

Figure 7.1. Place of Residence of Familiares in the Captaincy-General of Pernambuco by Morphological Zones, 1613–1820.

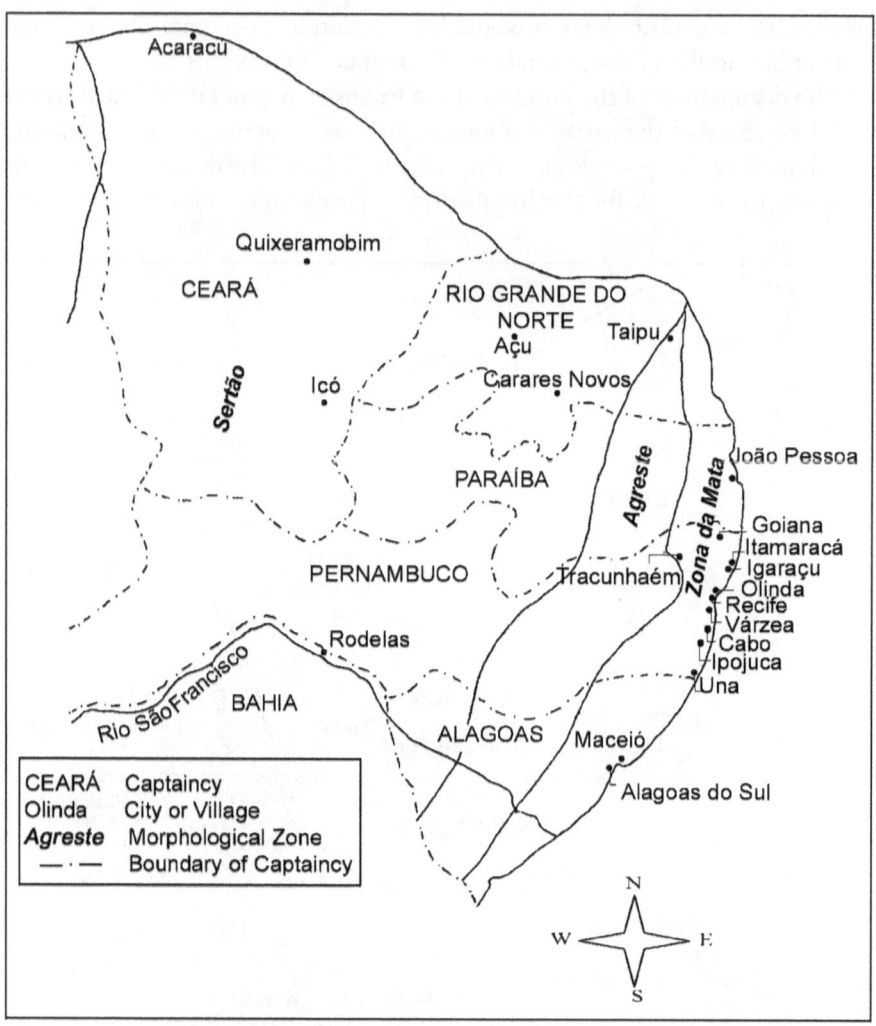

Figure 7.2. Place of Residence of Clerical Officials from the Captaincy-General of Pernambuco by Morphological Zones, 1613–1820.

1820, 663 familiares, sixty-six comissários, fifty-eight notários, and thirteen qualificadores received appointments. These numbers can be deceiving. Nineteen of the comissários had been notários before they became comissários, and three had been familiares. Likewise, five of the notários started out as familiares. There were, then, 773 officials appointed in the Captaincy-General of Pernambuco between 1613 and 1821. Most of these officials (91.1% of the familiares, 74.1% of the comissários, 91.5% of the notários, and 100.0% of the qualificadores) lived in the captaincy of Pernambuco. The rest were scattered unevenly throughout the other captaincies—although most of the principal settlements had a resident official at one time or another. Likewise, most of the officials lived in the Zona da Mata region (94.0% of the familiares, 80.3% of the comissários, 93.1% of the notários, and 100.0% of the qualificadores). Except for one notário who lived in the Agreste, the remaining officials lived in the Sertão, where pockets of inhabitants had settled along the main river and trade corridors. By far, the bulk of the officials lived in Recife and Olinda (81.3% of the familiares, 59.1% of the comissários, 65.5% of the notários, and 100.0% of the qualificadores). The highest concentration of both clerical and lay officials was in Recife itself (79.9% of the familiares, 39.4% of the comissários, 58.6% of the notários, and 61.5% of the qualificadores).

This pattern of residence for the ecclesiastical officials is, of course, to be expected. Most of the colonial population concentrated in the same coastal region, where they were, at least potentially, within reach of the Inquisition. The interior was sparsely inhabited, except for the Indians. Also, for work outside the coastal region, the Inquisition could always fall back on the old practice of using local secular and ecclesiastical authorities, which of course meant that there was not necessarily any pressing need for officials in most of the interior regions. Most of the clerical officials also resided in precisely the places where inquiries for qualification were in greatest demand (i.e., the populated regions within the Zona da Mata).

Likewise, these clerical officials generally came from the ranks of the upper ecclesiastical hierarchy and lived in the convents or near the cathedrals.[19] Those officials who lived in the less-populated regions tended to be curates, vicars, parish priests, or friars. The qualificadores were necessarily limited to the large population centers and port cities, where their power of censorship could find employment, however limited.

This urban bias of the Inquisition is not necessarily evidence of the weakness of the institution.[20] During the eighteenth century, the officials of the Inquisition increasingly represented a significant presence in the colony. It is impossible to know how many officials were alive at any given time, but we can estimate. In 1700, there were approximately 5.2 officials per 10,000 of the population (or one official for every 1,923 people). In 1777, there were 6.9 officials per 10,000 of the population (or one official for every 1,449 people). By 1794 there were 9.2 per 10,000 (or one official for every 1,087 people).[21]

It is useful to compare these ratios to those for public officials in Brazil during the nineteenth century. By the end of the nineteenth century, a proportion of fifty-four public employees in Brazil per 10,000 (one for every 185 people) was considered to be excessive, especially when the United States had only twenty-four per 10,000 (one for every 417 people) at about the same time. When only one branch of the ecclesiastical/royal establishment in Pernambuco with a jurisdiction restricted to a specific list of crimes against the faith could field 9.2 officials per 10,000, that is a significant presence. Certainly the ratios were not that high during the seventeenth century, but during the eighteenth century inquisitional officials represented a significant presence for the Inquisition in Pernambucan society.[22]

This presence should not deceive us, however, into making exaggerated claims of inquisitional strength. Ninety-four percent of the familiares and 65.8 percent of the clerical officials were concentrated in Recife and Olinda. To be sure, these were the largest urban centers in the captaincy-general, but by no means did most of the population live there. The economy was based on agricultural production, which meant that the bulk of the population was rural, although the late eighteenth century saw a shift toward the urban centers.

Likewise, we should not let this heavy urban bias mislead us into assuming that inquisitional activity was limited to the urban areas; the Inquisition had other ways of reaching the countryside. As we have seen, officials could and did travel to carry out inquiries in the interior. Ecclesiastical visitas also gathered information for the Inquisition, and local clergy frequently performed inquiries and carried out other inquisitional business.

Nonetheless, this urban bias does help explain the occupations of the officials of the Inquisition, and this also gives us a sense of their social standing. The occupations that the applicants reported fall generally within the estado do meio. Almost half of the comissários (43.1%) were secular priests, while 77.1 percent of the notários were secular priests. Nearly 14 percent (13.7%) of the comissários, 1.4 percent of the notários, and all but one of the qualificadores belonged to regular orders. The Inquisition favored the secular clergy for appointments as comissários, although fourteen comissários belonged to the regular clergy. Most of the secular clergy in Brazil belonged to the brotherhood known as the Clerics of St. Peter, who called themselves the "Presbyters of the Habit of St. Peter." These secular clergy appear most frequently as comissários and notários. Four of them were ex-Jesuits who took advantage of the king's offer to leave the Jesuit order when it was expelled from the Portuguese dominions in 1759.[23] Most of the qualificadores (nine of the thirteen), however, were Carmelites, and all but one were regular clergy. The higher education of the regulars combined with the general sense that regular clergy did not make good comissários contributed to the tendency to select regular clergy as qualificadores.

Nearly 16 percent of occupations comissários reported were high ecclesiastical offices. Many of the comissários also served in other respectable ecclesiastical positions, such as judges and vicars. Several of these clerics engaged in agriculture and commerce (6.9% of the comissários and 7.2% of the notários).

Of the 537 familiares (81%) for whom we have a known occupation, 55.1 percent were engaged in commerce, 11.7 percent held military posts, and 11.7 percent were students. The rest worked in a variety of occupations, including those in agriculture (3.6%), artisans (3.2%), bureaucrats and government officials (2.7%), pharmacists and physicians (2.1%), and ship pilots or captains (1.9%). The largest single group (164 or 25.9%) was that of the large-scale merchants, who called themselves *homens de negócio*.

We cannot know exactly what kind of business these men engaged in because they seem to use the term rather loosely. Both Raphael Bluteau (1712) and Antônio de Morais e Silva (1823) related the expression to the more generic term *negociante* (merchant).[24] Scholars generally accept that the homens de negócio of Brazil carried on large-scale commerce requiring capital and did not personally engage in retail trade. Indeed, retail trade carried the blemish of working with one's hands and was not considered honorable. An homen de negócio might own a retail shop, but his assistants actually sold the products. The homens de negócio also enjoyed high social status that permitted them entrance into prestigious brotherhoods and political offices.[25] They could also engage in trade with the interior, particularly after the opening of the mines in the 1690s, and in sugar and slaves. Sometimes the term also referred to a wide variety of commercial activities. For example, Agostinho Fernandes de Castro, who styled himself an homen de negócio, owned several houses that he rented, a ship that carried his trade, and a shop that sold cloth and leather.[26]

Consequently, the homens de negócio and negociantes often had other occupations, such as storeowner, ship captain, cane farmer, sugar planter, and livestock or tithing contractor. Likewise, some familiares (2.2%) reported working in both agriculture and commerce. Sometimes *senhores de engenho* called themselves negociantes or homens de negócio. It is quite possible that they used the term *homens de negócio* as a status indicator, but it is clear that the distinction between merchant and planter was not always rigid or meaningful. Indeed, for a planter to survive, he had to be a good businessman, while at the same time land and slaves were desirable investments for upwardly mobile merchants.[27] Likewise, at least eleven of those who reported occupations in commerce also listed appointments as officers in the military, and at least two of the sugar planters also served in the military. Military service was one of the outward manifestations of honor and prestige that helped fortify one's social position. The existence of multiple occupations points to the lack of a rigid division of labor within the colony and the ability, perhaps the necessity, of a single individual to function in multiple economic and potentially honorable activities.

The large number of merchants among the officials of the Inquisition challenges the long-held assumption that the Inquisition caused the economic stagnation of both Spain and Portugal.[28] The persecution of New Christian merchants certainly did little to strengthen the economy of the empire. But, unlike in Portugal, New Christians did not constitute a majority of merchants in Brazil. The New Christian minority experienced difficulty in social climbing because, among other things, they were barred from participation in the prestigious brotherhoods and from holding public office, but they did managed to rise socially; it just took them and their descendants more time than it did Old Christians.[29]

It appears that rather than suppressing economic activity, the Inquisition may actually have facilitated it, at least for a select group of individuals. The privileges that included exemption from certain kinds of taxation most certainly appealed to merchants. But, as we shall see, familiares could not always be certain that they would be able to take advantage of those privileges because of royal limitations. The suggestion that they used the Inquisition to eliminate their New Christian competitors is yet to be demonstrated.[30] The organizations of the Inquisition (discussed later) also provided networks that merchants could use to create and strengthen commercial relationships.

We should not, however, make too much of the fact that many familiares were engaged in commerce. It is tempting to generalize from this fact that "most" familiares were merchants, but that would oversimplify a very complex and heterogeneous group. We need to remember that 44.9% of them did not engaged in commercial activities.[31]

The other occupations of the familiares also fell generally within the estado do meio. Familiares were artisans, including a shoemaker, carpenters, and silver- and goldsmiths. Twenty-nine familiares owned slaves and twenty-three owned sugar mills. Ten familiares belonged to the Order of Christ and one was a fidalgo (lesser noble). Although nobility and prestigious military orders could be useful in an application, they by no means guaranteed acceptance. Two fidalgos and one knight of the Order of Christ were rejected. One of the fidalgos was rejected for New Christian ancestry.[32]

The extreme urban concentration, combined with the low numbers of sugar planters (3.6%) and weak distribution in the countryside, suggests that the Inquisition could not rely on the direct support of the rural wealthy, who generally had greater access to other positions of honor and prestige in the militia, military orders, and municipal councils. Rather, most of their support came from the urban groups involved in commerce, artisan trades, bureaucracy and government, and the regular clergy, as well as from young students in urban areas. These groups generally needed proof of purity but enjoyed only restricted access to those positions of honor and prestige enjoyed by the wealthy. The occupational spread within the ranks of the Inquisition also shows how well embedded it had become in the urban areas and that it was not simply a state-imposed institution. Likewise, the officials of the Inquisition belonged to those professions considered part of the estado do meio, which meant they could legitimately be considered "noble" if they met the other requirements. Social promotion could be more easily reached with an inquisitional declaration of purity.

The literacy and wealth requirements also contributed to the sense of noble status associated with an appointment and were consistent with inquisitional ideals of decent or respectable living.[33] The officials of the Inquisition demonstrated a remarkable degree of literacy and education. Some 45.8 percent of the occupations reported would have required a significant degree of education.[34] Access to better education suggests a relatively high social standing. The Inquisition's concern over wealth was closely tied to its concern that the applicants lived decently. The Inquisition never stipulated what it considered sufficient wealth. General estimates of the wealth of applicants were all that was offered, and statements that they lived decently were all that was required. Consequently, the reports of wealth are probably exaggerated and certainly inaccurate. They most likely reflect more how the witnesses perceived the applicants than what they actually possessed.

The disproportionate urban concentration also helps account for the strong presence of immigrants as inquisitional officials. Exactly 55.8 percent of the familiares were immigrants to Brazil, compared to 44.2 percent who were Brazilian born. Of the 55.1 percent commercial occupations for familiares, immigrants accounted for 78.5 percent, while native-born Brazilians represented 21.5 percent. Immigrants also accounted for 78.6 percent of the mixed merchant/agriculturist occupations. The immigrant planters and ranchers accounted for 52.2 percent of those involved in agriculture and ranching.

These findings are consistent with studies elsewhere in Brazil that show that the traditional view of the tensions between the planters and merchants and immigrants and native-born Brazilians, and the distinctiveness of these groups, although present, were not always meaningful.[35] These studies show that even poor Portuguese immigrants often became agents or apprentices of established merchants, married into established local mercantile or landed families, and used the wealth they accumulated to purchase land and establish a genteel life—particularly in a region where honor and status were closely associated with land and slave ownership.[36]

The strong immigrant presence among the familiares contrasts with the very strong native-born presence among the clerical officials (83.4% of the comissários, 93.1% of the notários, and 76.9% of the qualificadores). If we adjust the numbers to account for the twenty-seven officials who received second appointments as comissários or notários (all of whom were Brazilian born) we get 49.8 percent Brazilian born and 50.2 percent non-Brazilian born. This represents a nearly perfect half-and-half split. The slightly higher percentage of immigrants probably reflects a higher rate of application from this group. We cannot know whether the Inquisition preferred immigrants over native-born Brazilians because we do not know the ratio of immigrants versus native-born in the population. Nonetheless, these findings indicate that inquisitional office was a viable route to self-promotion for both groups.

Marriage and Family Strategies

The large contingent of immigrants in the ranks of the familiares helps explain the marriage patterns of the familiares. The 1640 Regimento required all familiares who were married to have their wives approved as well. All familiares who had accepted an appointment were required to receive the approval of the Inquisition before they could marry. If they married without the consent of the Inquisition, they could have their appointment suspended until the wife was approved, and if she was rejected they could lose it altogether. Of the familiares for whom we have marriage information, 383 (59%) were single when they applied, 206 (32%) were married, and eleven were widowers. Eventually, at least 289 (45%) of the familiares married and petitioned the Inquisition regarding those marriages. Of these, 280 were accepted, six were left incomplete, two were rejected, and one died during the processo. Seventeen familiares applied for a second marriage after the death of their first spouse. Seven of these women had already been married before and five of them had family members who worked for the Inquisition. The majority of the women who applied with familiares as their wives or applied to marry them (85.9%) were native to Pernambuco, and only 13.4 percent were immigrants.

As we have seen, 370 familiares (55.8%) were immigrants, and these were heavily involved in the merchant community in the colony. Of the 218 familiares who immigrated to Pernambuco before becoming familiares and who eventually married, 198 married women native to Pernambuco. In addition, at least eleven of those who were already familiares before they immigrated also married women from Pernambuco. Unfortunately, the investigations seldom mentioned the occupation of the women's fathers, which makes it impossible to know with any certainty the social standing of these women and their families; but research elsewhere in Brazil has shown that these kinds of marriages could be advantageous to both parties.[37]

Marrying into local families gave the newcomers greater access to lands, slaves, economic opportunities, elite organizations and positions, and local social networks, and gave them a modicum of respectability. Local families gained in return access to international commercial connections and capital. In this fashion, local merchant and landed families formed meaningful ties with newcomers and immigrants.[38] This was also true for many of the immigrant familiares in Pernambuco. For example, Antônio de Araújo Barbosa immigrated from northern Portugal to Alagoas, where he married Marianna de Araújo, the daughter of the wealthy planter Severino Correia de Paz and his wife Catarina de Araújo, who was also the sister of the comissário Antônio Correia da Paz. Severino owned several engenhos and large tracks of land in Alagoas, some of which passed on to Antônio de Araújo Barbosa's children.[39] Likewise, Brás Ferreira de Maciel came to Recife from Barcelos in the late 1730s and set himself up as an homen de negócio. He married the daughter of a lieutenant colonel and familiar of the Inquisition, João de Oliveira Gouvim, and succeeded in becoming a wealthy man.[40]

An appointment as a familiar proved useful in these endeavors because it served as a kind of letter of reference or introduction that affirmed one's quality and status in a new locality, thereby opening up the possibility of one's insertion into local society.[41] This was especially important for the immigrant community. Because these immigrants were seldom-known figures, those who wanted to become economically successful and insert themselves into the upper ranks of local society needed such a letter of reference to prove the purity of their family background.

Likewise, merchants frequently had to contend with the widespread perception that all merchants were New Christians and heretics. An appointment could be very useful in proving the unquestionable purity of their blood. It also helped them disassociate themselves from the assumption of heresy, because as familiares they were the new crusaders defending the faith against all heretical behavior.[42] It has been suggested that the men who left Portugal for Brazil rarely did so without first obtaining an appointment for this very purpose. That may be true, but only twenty-four familiares came to live in Pernambuco with appointments already in their pockets.[43] The rest obtained them while living in Pernambuco.

The established planter families may have sought cartas to combat negative rumors of their ancestry, but for them the carta was not as essential as it was for immigrants. The planters could rely on their locally established prestige to retain their social position, and therefore they felt less urgency to obtain a carta. We should recall that, despite difficulty in obtaining the outward proofs of purity and the attending embarrassment this could cause, the Pais Barreto family retained its social standing even after being rejected by the Inquisition and the Order of Christ.

These families held interests beyond their own social status. They also wanted some security in transferring their wealth and status from one generation to the next. Their capacity to do so rested on their ability to monopolize scarce and sought-after family resources. Colonial families tried to capture power resources within the kinship framework of their families, which often resulted in endogamous marriage patterns.[44]

The officials of the Inquisition also tended toward endogamy. Of the 663 familiares who received appointments, 412 (62.1%) of them had relatives who also held inquisitional appointments. At least fifty-three (8%) of them had more than four close relatives who held inquisitional appointments. One hundred twenty-nine (19.5%) of them were the sons of familiares. Of the 280 women who married familiares, 162 (24.4%) had close relatives who were inquisitional officials and sixty-six (10%) were the daughters of inquisitional officials.

The marriage patterns of familiares and of their children show a marked tendency to marry other inquisitional officials or into families already qualified by the Inquisition. Often, when the spouse of a familiar died, the familiar remarried a woman who had relatives who had already been qualified. The daughters of familiares also tended to marry familiares, and the widows of familiares often chose to remarry a familiar. For example, the familiar Inácio Joaquim da Costa married Caetana de Nascimento, who was the daughter of a familiar in Coimbra. When she passed away, he married Maria Joaquina, his first wife's cousin. When Inácio passed away, Maria married another familiar, Manuel Alves Monteiro.[45]

These intermarriages not only ranged across generations, but they also created extremely complex interfamily networks. The largest of these networks included more than 550 individuals, not including relatives not mentioned in the records. This family network accounted for 126 familiares (19.0%), seventeen comissários (25.0%), ten notários (16.1%), and one qualificador (7.1%). The family network also included inquisitional officials from Portugal, as well as many wealthy sugar planters, merchants, and high-ranking military officers. These networks also point to a certain amount of blending of immigrant, merchant, and planter families.[46]

On one level, the networks simply manifest the tendency of elite families to intermarry. On another, they resulted from the fact that inquisitional officials needed to marry women who were, or could be, qualified by the Inquisition in order to retain their cartas and avoid the loss of personal and family honor and prestige. This, of course, led them to a conscious effort to intermarry with families that already had members who had been approved in order to assure the potential spouse's acceptance by the Inquisition and decrease the chances of rejection.

Likewise, a marked tendency for multigenerational service to the Inquisition existed. For example, for four generations, the descendants of Jerônimo Dinis obtained appointments or, in the case of the daughters, married someone who had. Likewise, nearly all the grandchildren of Anastácia Gorjão received appointments. The tradition continued on to her great-grandchildren and her great-great-grandchildren. The four sons of Vicente Gorjão Sr. all received inquisitional appointments. Three of them became comissários, and Vicente Gorjão Jr. became a familiar. Two of Vicente Gorjão Jr.'s three daughters married familiares. The third married Domingos José da Silva Sampaio, who applied but was rejected for New Christian ancestry and lack of information. The six sons of Vicente's daughter, Maria José de Jesus Gorjão, all became familiares. Sometimes, as with the descendants of José de Freitas Sacoto, the tradition lasted four or five generations.[47]

This tendency for the sons of familiares to seek appointments partially accounts for the large numbers of minors who received appointments as familiares.[48] But inquisitional office had never been hereditary and had to be reobtained with each new generation. The regimentos never stipulated an age limitation for office, and consequently, of the 536 familiares (80.8%) for whom we have an age estimate, 209 (38.9%) were under the age of twenty-five (see figures 7.3 and 7.4). In most cases, the Inquisition did not allow them to perform any activities until they reached the age of majority. In other words, nearly one-third (31.5%) of the familiares in Pernambuco benefited from the prestige and potential privilege of the position without having to do any of the work it entailed. That also meant that the Inquisition had a reduced number of functioning officials, which suggests that the Inquisition was more concerned with increasing its popular support than with augmenting its repressive power at the same time that families sought to perpetuate the status and prestige of office within their families.

To do so, fathers sought to get their boys appointed at young ages. For example, the familiar Antônio Dantas Correia Góes tried to get his two very young sons appointed as familiares in 1801. The oldest boy, Antônio Dantas Correia Góes, was only three years old, and his brother, José Dantas Correia de Góes, was two years old. The General Council rejected Antônio because

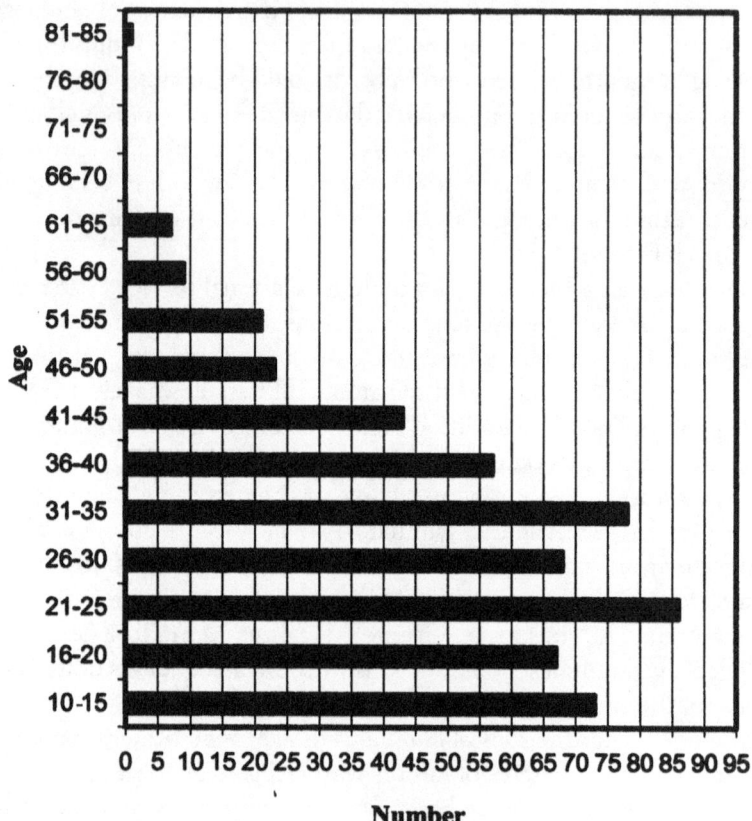

Figure 7.3. Ages of Familiares at Appointment in Pernambuco, 1613–1820.
Source: Processos de habilitação for Pernambuco, 1611-1820 [ANTT].

he was too young for the Inquisition to determine what his future behavior would be and because he was illiterate. It rejected José because it lacked any proof of what his future capacity would be.[49] The justification for their rejection was not that they were too young. Under the regimento, age could not be used as an impediment to office. But their young age did contribute to other impediments that excluded them.

The youngest familiares appointed in Pernambuco were ten years old.[50] Likewise, most inquisitional appointments were given to men under thirty-five years of age. These young men and their families were concerned with setting themselves up in society, thereby ensuring their position and future success.

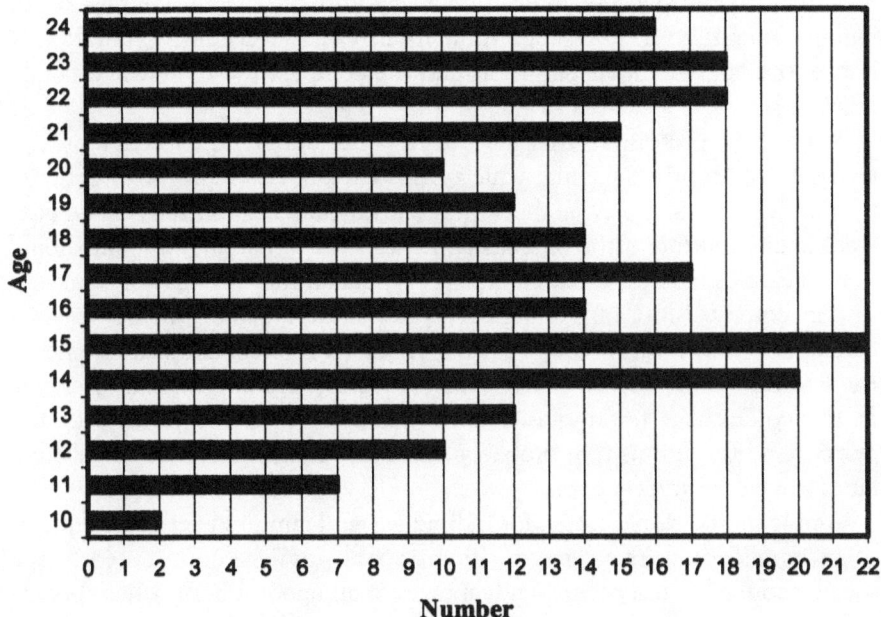

Figure 7.4. Minors Appointed as Familiares in Pernambuco, 1613–1820. *Source:* Processos de habilitação for Pernambuco, 1611-1820 [ANTT].

The minors, however, could not provide any immediate service to the Inquisition, and they were too young to gain immediate benefit from the appointments themselves. But the families could always hold up the appointment as proof of the family's purity.

Despite long-standing beliefs in the homogeneity of the officials of the Inquisition, the information for Pernambuco demonstrates that they were distinctly heterogeneous, at least in terms of personal background and occupation. The officials of the Inquisition generally belonged to the professions of the estado do meio, which were honorable occupations and could lead to noble status. But those occupations had to accompany the outward signs of nobility, which included demonstrations of respectable living and purity of blood. Another essential part of solidifying noble status, once the other conditions were met, were the "proofs" of status. The Inquisition acted as one of several institutions that could provide such proof. For this reason, some immigrants came to Pernambuco with cartas already in hand or soon acquired them, married into local families, and took up "honorable" occupations, most frequently in commerce. Families attempted to keep the proofs within the family by getting their sons appointed or marrying into families that already had such proofs. Because inquisitional appointments were not hereditary, families sought to acquire appointments in each succeeding generation—hence, the large numbers of minors and the complex interconnected family relationships.

Most of the professions that fell within the estado do meio were more appropriate to an urban setting, which helps explain the high urban concentration of officials in Pernambuco and within the Zona da Mata. The geographic distribution of the officials points to the high urban bias, but should not deceive us into exaggerated claims of inquisitional strength or weakness in the colony. Most of Pernambuco's population could still be reached through the Inquisition's use of secular and ecclesiastical authorities, and by the late eighteenth century these officials represented a significant presence in the colony. Yet few inquisitional officials lived in the Agreste or the Sertão, and the Inquisition probably could not count on the powerful rural landowners for direct support.

Ample motivations existed for individuals and families to risk the dangers of an inquisitional investigation. Inquisitional privilege contributed to the social, economic, and political advantages of an appointment. These potential benefits outweighed the potential costs even after the crown restricted the exercise of inquisitional privilege in the early eighteenth century.

Notes

1. Schwartz, *Sugar Plantations*, 248.
2. Schwartz, *Sugar Plantations*, 274.
3. Schwartz, *Sugar Plantations*, 273.
4. See Raphael Bluteau, *Vocabulario Portuguez e Latino* (Coimbra: Collegio das artes da Companhia de Jesus, 1712–1721), s.v. "estado," and Antonio de Morais e Silva, *Diccionario da lingua portugueza*, 2nd ed., s.v. "estado." For a good discussion of nobility in Brazil, see Maria Fernada Baptista Bicalho, "As câmaras ultramarinas e o governo do Império," in *O Antigo Regime nos trópicos: A dinâmica imperial portuguesa (séculos XVI–XVIII)*, ed. João Fragoso, Maria Fernanda Bicalho, and Maria de Fátima Gouvêa (Rio de Janeiro: Civilização Brasileira, 2001), 203–17.
5. Bluteau, *Vocabulario Portuguez e Latino*, s.v. "Estado," 302.
6. See Carlos da Silva Lopes, "Nobreza do século XVIII," in *Integralismo Lusitano* 1, no. 4 (September 1932): 313, 315.
7. See Azevedo Mea, *A Inquisição de Coimbra*, 186. For debates about the appointment of nobles as familiares, see Ajuda, 51-viii-16, no. 104, fol. 130; 51-viii-20, no. 35, fol. 46; 51-viii-5, nos. 99; 51-viii-11, nos. 90 105. See also Bethencourt, *História das Inquisições*, 128.

8. See Nuno Gonçalo Monteiro, "Poder senhorial, estatuto nobiliárquico e aristocracia," in *História de Portugal. O Antigo Regime*, ed. António Manuel Hespanha, vol. 4 (Lisbon: Editora Estampa, 1993), 337–38.

9. Francis A. Dutra, "The Maritime Profession and Membership in the Portuguese Military Orders in the Late Seventeenth and Early Eighteenth Centuries," in *Marginated Groups in Spanish and Portuguese History*, ed. William D. Phillips Jr. and Carla Rahn Phillips (Minneapolis: Society for Spanish and Portuguese Historical Studies, 1989), 89–109.

10. See, for example, Emilio Willems, "Social Differentiation in Colonial Brazil," *Comparative Studies in Society and History* 12, no. 1 (January 1970): 31–49; Schwartz, *Sugar Plantations*; and Castro Faria, *A colônia em movimento*.

11. Evaldo Cabral de Mello, *A ferida de narciso: Ensaio de história regional* (São Paulo: Editora SENAC, 2001), 52–53.

12. Guilherme Pereira das Neves, "Homens bons," in *Dicionário do Brasil colonial (1500–1808)*, ed. Ronaldo Vainfas (Rio de Janeiro: Editora Objectiva, 2000.), 284–86.

13. For the 1446, 1500, and 1791 confirmation, see APEJE, Diversos III, Cod. 2, Fol. 40v–41v. For 1606, see Candido Mendes de Almeida, *Auxiliar Juridico: Servindo de appendice a decima quarta edição do Codigo Philippino ou Ordenações do reino de Portugal, recopilados por mandado d'el Rey D. Phillipe I*, 2 vols. 24th ed. (Rio de Janeiro: 1869; reprint, Lisbon: Fundação Calouste Gulbenkian, 1985), 1:356 [Paragraph XCVIII].

14. Ownership of land was valued "because it was the most secure way to maintain the noble life." Despite a desire to acquire noble status, the sugar planters in Brazil really functioned as a kind of aristocracy that assumed the "traditional roles of the Portuguese nobility but never became an hereditary estate." Schwartz, *Sugar Plantations*, 249, 273.

15. Maria Beatriz Nizza da Silva, "Nobreza," in *Dicionário da história da colonização portuguesa no Brasil*, ed. Maria Beatriz Nizza da Silva (Lisbon: Editorial Verbo, 1994), 586.

16. Some officials complained that once Portuguese of humble origins crossed the Atlantic, they immediately acquired pretensions of nobility, asserting their equality with persons of higher distinction, and seeking honorable positions in the local government. See Bicalho, "As câmaras ultramarinas," 214.

17. Bicalho, "As câmaras ultramarinas," 204.

18. Aufderheide, "True Confessions," 219.

19. Both the secular and regular clergy in Bahia tended to concentrate in the urban areas and to have close ties to the privileged classes. See Eduardo Hoorneart, "As relações entre Igreja e Estado na Bahia colonial," *Revista eclesiastica brasileira* 32 (1972): 275–308. See also Eduardo Hoorneart, et al., *História da igreja no Brasil: Ensaio de interpretação a partir do povo: Primeira Época*, 2nd ed. (Petrópolis: Editora Vozes, 1979), 183–88, 274–90.

20. See Luiz Mott, "A Inquisição no Maranhão," *Revista Brasileira de História* 14, no. 28 (1994): 70; Siqueira, *A Inquisição portuguesa*; Robert Ricard, "Comparison of

Evangelization in Portuguese and Spanish America," *Americas* 14, no. 4 (April 1958): 444–53; and Almeida Figueiredo, *Barrocas famílias*.

21. These are only approximations. I took all the familiares (26) and clerical officials (4) appointed between 1691–1700 and added half of those appointed between 1671 and 1690 (5 familiares, no clerics) to get an estimate of those who would have been alive in 1700. I followed the same procedure for the next two estimates (i.e., appointments between 1767 to 1777 [155 familiares and 27 clerics] plus half of those appointed between 1747 and 1766 [113 familiares and 13 clerics] and appointments between 1784–1794 [177 familiares and 18 clerics] plus half of those from 1764–1783 [262 familiares and 25 clerics]). To calculate the per capita figure, I used the formula familiares divided by the population multiplied by 10,000. To estimate the population at 1794, I subtracted the population from Pernambuco in 1777 (226,254) from that of 1819 (368,465) and multiplied by the growth rate (142,211 x .013), which equaled 1,848.743, or a growth of nearly 2,000 per year. I multiplied this by 15 (the number of years between 1777 and 1794), which gave 27,731.145 population growth in Pernambuco during the fifteen-year hiatus. I cannot create estimates for the other captaincies because I do not have the data to construct growth rates or a second census to allow me to compute the population growth. I added the population increase to the 1777 population, which yielded 390,969.15. The other captaincies may have increased by half that of Pernambuco, hence the approximation 400,000 for 1794. These numbers are only approximations and cannot account for slave importation and European immigration. I calculated the growth rate from the deaths and births reported on the 1777 census. The census listed 13,435 births and 8,550 deaths. Divided by the population these numbers yield a birth rate of 37 and a death rate of 24. I used the equation % Growth Rate = (Birth Rate – Death Rate)/10 which gave 1.3 as the growth rate. For the 1700 population, see Feitler, *Inquisition*, 87. The 1777 census can be found in AHU, Pernambuco, cx. 127, doc. 9665. "Mapa, Que Mostra o Número dos Habitantes das Quatro Capitanias Deste Governo, a Saber, Pernambuco, Paraíba, Rio Grande, e Ceará, 30 Sept. 1777." See also Alden, "The Population of Brazil," 173–205.

22. See José Murilo de Carvalho, *A construção da ordem: A elite política imperial* (Rio de Janeiro: Editora Campus, 1980), 127–29.

23. ANTT, MNEJ, cx. 56, nos. 5–7.

24. Raphael Bluteau, *Vocabulario Portuguez e Latino* (1712), s.v. "negociante" and Antonio de Morais e Silva, *Diccionario da lingua portugueza*, 2nd ed., s.v. "negocio."

25. Rae Flory and David Grant Smith, "Bahian Merchants and Planters in the Seventeenth and Early Eighteenth Centuries," *HAHR* 58, no. 4 (1978): 573–74; Renato Pinto Venâncio and Júnia Ferreira Furtado, "Comerciantes, tratantes e mascates," in *Revisão do Paraíso: Os brasileiros e o estado em 500 anos de história*, ed. Mary del Priore (Rio de Janeiro: Editora Campus, 2000), 98–100; Antônio Carlos Jucá de Sampaio, "Os homens de negócio do Rio de Janeiro e sua atuação nos quadros do impéiro Português," in *O Antigo Regime nos trópicos: A dinâmica imperial portuguesa (séculos XVI–XVIII)*, eds. João Fragoso, Maria Fernanda Bicalho, and Maria de Fátima Gouvêa (Rio de Janeiro: Civilização Brasileira, 2001), 75–105; Rae Jean Dell Flory,

"Bahian Society in the Mid-Colonial Period: The Sugar Planters, Tobacco Growers, Merchants, and Artisans of Salvador and the Recôncavo, 1680–1725" (Ph.D. diss., University of Texas at Austin, 1978), 220–21; and Catherine Lugar, "The Merchant Community of Salvador, Bahia 1780–1830" (Ph.D. dissertation, State University of New York, Stony Brook, 1980), 32–34.

26. ANTT, HSO, Agostinho, m. 6, no. 92.

27. Stuart Schwartz appropriately entitled his chapter on the business end of running a plantation, "A Noble Business." See Schwartz, *Sugar Plantations*, 202–41, and João Luís Ribeiro Fragoso and Manolo Garcia Florentino, *O arcaísmo como projecto: Mercado atlântico sociedade agrária e elite mercantil no Rio de Janeiro, c. 1790–c. 1840* (Rio de Janeiro: Diadorim, 1993).

28. See, for example, Shaw, *Trade, Inquisition and the English Nation* and Fonseca, "Comércio e inquisição no Brasil."

29. Flory and Smith, "Bahian Merchants and Planters," 585–87.

30. Timothy Walker claims that physicians who received appointments as familiares in Portugal used their positions within the Inquisition to eliminate their competitors, the practitioners of folk medicine. Whether such a thing ever happened in the merchant community in either Portugal or Brazil remains to be investigated. David Grant Smith believes that no such thing occurred. Indeed, Old Christian merchants often appeared as character witnesses on the behalf of accused New Christians. See Timothy D. Walker, *Doctors, Folk Medicine, and the Inquisition: The Repression of Magical Healing in Portugal during the Enlightenment* (Leiden, Netherlands: Brill Academic Publishing, 2005), 211–62 and David Grant Smith, "The Merchant Class of Portugal and Brazil in the Seventeenth Century: A Socio-Economic Study of the Merchants of Lisbon and Bahia, 1620–1690," (Ph.D. dissertation, University of Texas at Austin, 1975), 259.

31. Such generalizations appear frequently. For example, see, Lugar, "Merchant Community," 215.

32. The two fidalgos were José Gomes e Melo and Manuel Carlos de Abreu e Lima. See ANTT, HI, m. 30, no. 2 and HSO, Manuel, m. 51, no. 161. The knight of the Order of Christ was Antônio Gonçalves Reis. See ANTT, NH, m. 25, no. 2.

33. Antônio de Morais e Silva associates decency with external manifestations such as clothing in *Diccionario da lingua portugueza*, 2nd ed., s.v. "decencia."

34. The occupations include bureaucrats and government officials (2.7% of the familiares occupations, 2.9% of the comissários, 4.3% of the notários), the legal officials (1.4% of the familiares, 3.9% of the comissários), the physicians and pharmacists (2.1% of the familiares), the priests (1.7% of the familiares, all of the comissários, notários, and qualificadores), those with university degrees (.5% of the familiares, 10.8% of the comissários, 7.1% of the notários, and 23.8% of the qualificadores), and the high number of students (11.7% of the familiares).

35. For studies dealing with this competition, see Manchester, "The Rise of the Brazilian Aristocracy"; Russell-Wood, *Fidalgos and Philanthropists*; Kennedy, "Bahian Elites"; Cabral de Mello, *A fronda dos mazombos*. Even the famous and powerful

planter João Pais Barreto Velho raised cattle and cotton and gave financial backing to merchants. See Petersen, "Sweet Success," 334–37.

36. See Flory and Smith, "Bahian Merchants and Planters"; Kennedy, "Bahian Elites"; and Elizabeth Anne Kuznesof, "The Role of the Merchants in the Economic Development of São Paulo, 1765–1850," HAHR 60, no. 4 (1980): 571–92; Fragoso and Florentino, O arcaísmo como projecto; and Castro Faria, A colônia em movimento, 175–76, 180–95.

37. The early literature on the family in Brazil focused on the patriarchal family while the revisionist literature has emphasized the non-elite family types and the regionality of family structures. The most influential study of the patriarchal family is Gilberto Freyre, Casa Grande e Senzala (Rio de Janeiro: Maia and Schmidt, 1933). For the revisionist literature, see Donald Ramos, "Marriage and the Family in Colonial Vila Rica," HAHR 55, no. 2 (May 1975): 200–225; Almeida Figueiredo, Barrocas Famílias; Elizabeth Anne Kuznesof, Household Economy and Urban Development: São Paulo, 1765–1836 (Boulder: Westview, 1986); Katia de Queiros Mattoso, Família e sociedade na Bahia do século XIX (São Paulo: Corrupio, 1988); Alida Metcalf, Family and Frontier in Colonial Brazil: Santana de Parnaíba, 1580–1822 (Berkeley: University of California Press, 1992); Dain Borges, The Family in Bahia, Brazil, 1870–1945 (Stanford, CA: Stanford University Press, 1992); Muriel Nazzari, Disappearance of the Dowry: Women, Families and Social Change in São Paulo, Brazil (1600–1900) (Stanford: Stanford University Press, 1991); Mariza Corrêa, "Repensando a Família Patriarcal Brasileira: Notas para o estudo das formas de organização familiar no Brasil," in Colcha de Retalhos: Estudos sobre a família no Brasil, ed. Maria Suely Kofes de Almeida (São Paulo: Editora Brasiliense, 1982), 13–38; Vainfas, Trópico dos pecados; and Castro Faria, A colônia em movimento.

38. For similar patterns elsewhere in colonial Brazil, see Stuart B. Schwartz, "Magistracy and Society in Colonial Brazil," HAHR 50, no. 4 (November 1970): 715–30; Flory and Smith, "Bahian Merchants and Planters," 585–87; Kuznesof, "Role of the Merchants," 571–92; Fragoso and Florentino, O arcaísmo como projecto; Metcalf, Family and Frontier, 90–94; and Castro Faria, A colônia em movimento, 189–218.

39. See ANTT, HSO, Antônio, m. 27, no. 744; AHU, Alagoas, cx. 1, docs. 16, 17; AHU, Alagoas, cx. 1, doc. 18; and AHU, Alagoas, cx. 3, doc. 209.

40. See ANTT, HSO, Brás, m. 4, no. 51. Antônio Pinheiro Salgado moved to Recife from Guimarães in the mid-eighteenth century, married the daughter of the influential José Vaz Salgado, and became an important contractor for collecting the tithe. See ANTT, HSO, Antônio, m. 146, no. 2367.

41. It was common for immigrants to take letters of reference to individuals already established in the colony. See Castro Faria, A colônia em movimento, 171.

42. See Smith, "The Mercantile Class," 258.

43. Eugénio Cunha e Freitas, Familiares do Santo Oficio no Porto (Porto, 1979), 6.

44. Kennedy, "Bahian Elites," 417.

45. See ANTT, HSO, Inácio, m. 9, no. 150, and HSO, Manuel, m. 162, no. 1693.

46. Recent studies have also found that the traditional conflict between merchants and planters has been overstated. See Flory and Smith, "Bahian Merchants and Planters"; Kennedy, "Bahian Elites"; Kuznesof, "Role of the Merchants," 571–92; Fragoso and Florentino, *O arcaísmo como projecto*; and Castro Faria, *A colônia em movimento*, 175–76, 180–95.

47. For these genealogies, see the website for this book, http://www.rowmanlittlefield.com/0742554465.

48. James E. Wadsworth, "Children of the Inquisition: Minors as Familiares of the Inquisition in Pernambuco, Brazil, 1613–1821," *LBR* 42, no. 1 (2005): 21–43.

49. ANTT, HSO, Antônio, m. 203, no. 3025; Antônio, m. 19, no. 124; and José HI, m. 19, no. 123.

50 ANTT, HSO, João, m. 161, no. 133; HSO, Tomé, m. 6, no. 87.

CHAPTER EIGHT

Corporate Privileges:
The Familiares do Número

As we have seen, the Inquisition was, at least by the beginning of the eighteenth century, a social institution as much as it was a royal or ecclesiastical tribunal, and it tied into the deeply held values of Luso-Brazilian society. Those men who chose to work for it expected some return for risking exposure to potential accusations of "impure blood" and for their monetary investment in paying for the inquiry. Beyond the possible benefit of acquiring useful social, political, and business acquaintances, these men expected much more. They expected to bolster their claims to honor, to enhance their personal and family prestige, to gain a certain amount of power over their neighbors, to acquire positive proofs of purity that would permit them to participate in a wide variety of religious and political institutions, and to enjoy inquisitional privilege.

But access to inquisitional privilege proved transitory. The privileges technically applied to all officials, both lay and clerical; but the question of privilege proved to be ambiguous and complex. Various and competing interpretations of what constituted inquisitional privileges and who should enjoy them surfaced continually. Royal restrictions on privileges only complicated the problem. The very complexity and ambiguity of the issue, however, left open the possibility that would-be candidates in Brazil might enjoy those restricted privileges. This ambiguity created an interesting paradox. The same ambivalence that allowed familiares room to maneuver in their conflicts with local ecclesiastical and secular authorities also provided those same authorities with the opportunity to constrain the power and privilege of inquisitional officials.

In the records of the Inquisition, frequent references exist to the *familiares do número* (familiares of the number).[1] And yet they are seldom mentioned in scholarly works of the Inquisition.[2] Indeed, few scholars understand the term and what it meant for the familiares of the Inquisition. It has generally been assumed that familiares were compensated for their service with privileges and that these privileges served as the primary motivation for seeking inquisitional appointments.[3] But, after 1693 in Portugal and 1720 in Brazil, most familiares could not be sure that they would enjoy the privileges that they supposedly received in compensation for their services. Yet far more familiares were appointed during the next one hundred years than had been appointed in the preceding 150 years. Familiares also found that they constantly had to defend and reassert their privilege and inquisitional authority in the face of powerful opposition. The fact that they defended them so persistently and so forcefully indicates how much they valued them.

The practice of granting privileges, such as benefices, land, and other concessions, in return for loyalty and dedication drew on ancient Roman practices and placed the sovereign in the position of a semipatriarchal figure. The Portuguese kings used this "moral economy of the gift" to grant privileges as rewards for services either to the king or to the faith, creating asymmetrical relations of exchange.[4] It also served the important task of differentiating the royal subjects into unequally privileged groups with sets of privileges granted, guaranteed, and controlled by the crown. These privileges not only distinguished groups, but they also provided individuals with a corporate framework that integrated them into society in a hierarchy of unequal associations. The military, the military orders, the clergy, the brotherhoods, the nobility, and other variously defined groups all received specific privileges from the crown. This system gave the crown effective monopoly over the regulation of these groups and permitted it to manipulate conflicts and competition between them for inclusion in the circle of privileged communities. At the same time, it legitimated the crown monopoly as well as the social and institutional structures of the empire.[5]

In the case of the Inquisition, both the crown and the papacy granted privileges.[6] In 1562, the king, D. Sebastião, granted the first privileges to the officials and familiares of the Inquisition. At the time, their numbers were small and nonthreatening. The privileges tended to be oriented toward economic exemptions and judicial prerogatives with the clear intention of differentiating them from the rest of the population. These privileges included exemption from paying extra taxes, tributes, loans, charges, or other requests for money by any council or tribunal. Inquisitional officials also could not be constrained to be guardians of children or compelled against their will to accept public offices. Nor could their homes and property be taken unless they were justly compensated. Inquisitional officials were exempt from being impressed into military service, either on land or on sea, while the king also permitted them to wear both offensive and defensive weapons. The officials and their wives and children were also permitted to wear silk, despite existing ordinances restricting its use. In 1566, D. Sebastião also excused them from contributing to a large service tax of 100,000 cruzados then being imposed.

In 1580, the king reaffirmed the privileges with a few modifications. He clarified that the officials and familiares did not have to pay the *aposentadoria* (property tax) except for those items that they purchased with the intention of reselling. He also gave them the *foro*, or the legal privilege of having their criminal and civil cases judged by the Inquisitors—with certain qualifications for familiares. Those crimes exempt from private adjudication included high treason, crimes against nature, mutiny or rebellion, violation of royal correspondence, disobedience to the orders of the king, disrespect to his officers, slander, rape, murder, robbery, forgery, burglary of houses, churches, or monasteries, arson of fields, fraud, and delinquency in public office. All these crimes were to be tried in secular courts.[7]

These privileges clearly offered inquisitional officials substantial freedom from existing laws and restrictions as well as protection from abuses of authority. They also provided visible signs of status. Consequently, inquisitional officials actively endeavored to maintain and wield them.

The first attempts at defining to whom the privileges applied and what they meant in real terms began almost immediately and intensified in the seventeenth and eighteenth centuries. Officials tried to extend the privilege to their servants and children. Although the Inquisition initially supported these attempts to make inquisitional privilege hereditary, the crown would not permit it.[8]

The privileges granted to inquisitional officials set them apart, creating a status group characterized by the exercise of certain prerogatives and exemptions, which contributed to the creation of social esteem. Nonetheless, despite the sweeping privileges granted to the familiares and other officials in the latter half of the sixteenth century, these privileges were not uniformly applicable. Their meaning and reach were constantly debated and eventually came to be limited to a very narrow grouping of familiares.

Despite the oft-repeated misconception, no limits were ever placed on the actual numbers of familiares permitted in the Portuguese Empire. Some very early and unsuccessful attempts did occur in the sixteenth century.[9] But the 1640 Regimento permitted the inquisitor general to determine how many familiares were necessary, as did the 1774 Regimento.[10] And yet, the crown could and did restrict the use of inquisitional privilege.

By 1682, D. Pedro II noted the growing number of familiares who enjoyed exemptions from several taxes and tributes. He claimed that these exemptions reduced royal revenues, and so in 1682 he limited the number of familiares who could enjoy exemption from taxes to two in each city or comârca (head village) in Portugal and the Algarve and one in each smaller village or place. Brazil was not included in the limitation.[11] This restriction was far from an arbitrary measure, given that the empire suffered from a whole series of difficulties: declining prices on its colonial imports, rising prices of its imports from northern Europe, a decline in the importation of silver bullion from Spain, a monetary crisis in Angola and Brazil, a smallpox epidemic in Angola, and the introduction of yellow fever to Brazil. All of these crises combined to create a very real drain on the royal pocketbook and provided ample motive for limiting the numbers of men who enjoyed fiscal privileges.[12]

The decree of 1682 did not specify exactly how these individuals were to be chosen, but it appears that up until 1744 they were selected by seniority. It is, as yet, unclear how this system of restriction on tax exemption articulated with the restrictions set in place in 1693, but it continued at least until 1744, apparently alongside the later restrictions, and set a precedent for limiting the privileges of familiares.[13] The king put a more sweeping restriction into place in 1693, which drew on this earlier attempt at limiting the number of familiares who enjoyed certain privileges. But its immediate impetus came from a different concern.

The concern arose over the issue of retirement. Familiares who had retired from active employment often sought to retain their privileges.[14] For example, in 1685 a retired familiar petitioned to continue enjoying the privileges. The chief pension officer (*aposentador-mor*) hesitated to recognize the privileges of retired familiares. The General Council appealed to the king, asking him to order the aposentador-mor to do so. The king complied, but noted that the aposentador-mor was correct in hesitating because of the excessive number of familiares and the damage that resulted to the king's vassals—probably referring to his own reduced revenues. So he ordered the inquisitor general to determine the number of familiares necessary to perform the work of the Holy Office, and only these would enjoy the privileges. To avoid accusations of inequality, those enjoying the privileges would be selected according to seniority in office.[15]

In 1693, D. Pedro II issued a decree that limited the number of privileged familiares in Portugal. In the decree, he declared that it was not his intention to take away the privileges of those who legitimately served, but that the number of familiares had grown so excessive that there were many superfluous familiares not necessary for the functioning of the Inquisition. The limitations were based on the recommendations of the inquisitor general in response to the previous order. The thirty-six largest towns and villages in Portugal were listed specifically, and the rest received one or two familiares, depending on their size. The cities that contained tribunals received the most familiares (Lisbon, 100; Coimbra, 50; Évora, 50) because they needed them to carry out inquisitorial duties. The familiares do número, as the privileged familiares came to be called, were selected by seniority. Familiares who wanted to enjoy the privileges had to apply to the Inquisition for a certificate designating them as familiares do número. All those who were in excess of the numbers retained the title of familiar but could not enjoy any of the privileges associated with the office, even though, if called upon, they were required to serve.[16]

These restrictions effectively meant that most of the familiares in Portugal would never enjoy the privileges. The list permitted 601 familiares for the places specifically mentioned. If we add to that the one or two permitted in the rest of the villages, the number of privileged familiares would probably have been a little more than one thousand. But between 1691 and 1700 alone, 1,434 familiares were appointed throughout the empire, and they continued to be appointed in large numbers and to concentrate in the urban centers. In other words, many familiares did not enjoy the privileges of the office immediately and many probably never did.[17]

The inadequacy of the royal decree became apparent early on. Conspicuously missing from the 1693 decree was any mention of the overseas territories, including Brazil. This omission and the practice of choosing by seniority led to problems for the Inquisition and for the familiares that were never fully worked out. Despite some debates and adjustments, it was fairly clear who belonged to those of the number and who did not in Portugal. But when it came to Brazil, the system was riddled with conflict and confusion.

Some familiares in Brazil found it necessary to seek certificates. For example, Simão Ribeiro Riba from Pernambuco argued in the early eighteenth century that, since all familiares in Brazil enjoyed the privilege, he was also one of the number, and he needed a certificate to prove it. His petition remained unanswered.[18] In 1709, Domingos de Oliveira Rosa, a familiar in Rio de Janeiro, complained that even though the familiares worked at great personal cost for the Inquisition, all they desired was to enjoy the privileges of their office. But they were continually denied those privileges by those who hated the Inquisition on the pretext that Rio did not have any privileged familiares according to the 1693 decree. He petitioned the crown to determine the number of privileged familiares for Rio and suggested that the number assigned to the city of Oporto (forty) would be sufficient.[19] These questions highlighted the weakness of the 1693 decree and threw into question its ultimate meaning. Did the omission of the overseas colonies mean that they could not have any privileged familiares? Did it mean that all the overseas familiares were privileged, or should their number be limited as well?

In response, the inquisitor general recommended that the system then functioning in Portugal be introduced into Brazil as a way of solving some of these difficulties. This included naming the ouvidor geral (superior magistrate) as the juiz do fisco (fiscal judge) to oversee sequestered and confiscated goods and, as the *juiz conservador dos familiares* (judge conservator of the familiares), to protect the privileges of the inquisitional officials and to hear civil cases brought against them. These cases could be appealed to the General Council.[20]

The inquisitor general also consulted the General Council regarding the question of whether the overseas familiares should enjoy their privileges. The council determined that they should continue to do so unless they were serving in the armed forces or as royal tax collectors.[21] The crown accepted the consultation and made these recommendations law in January 1711, with the exception of the recommendation regarding privileges, which he left undecided.

Consequently, the 1711 decree did not solve the problem, and local governmental officials in Brazil continued to refuse to recognize the privileges of the familiares. The comissário João Calmon from Bahia reported in 1718 that the familiares of Bahia complained that they were being forced to give slaves to soldiering duties and other jobs and also to house the prisoners of the Inquisition coming from Rio on their way to Lisbon while they waited for the next fleet to set sail. In response, the General Council recommended that the number of privileged familiares be restricted in Brazil in the same fashion that it had been in Portugal. At that time, the crown chose not to act on the recommendation, and still royal officials in Brazil demanded to see the certificates, which of course the familiares could not produce.[22]

The king ordered the inquisitor general to consult on the issue in 1720. The inquisitor general reasserted the Inquisition's position that all familiares in Brazil were privileged because they had been excluded from the 1693 list. But the crown had asked him to determine how many were needed, and so he produced a very short list.[23] It is unclear whether the inquisitor general really intended to limit the number of privileged familiares in the way that they eventually were, because his short list could not even begin to fill the needs of the Inquisition in Brazil, and there is no evidence that he consulted with anyone on the matter. Nonetheless, his recommendations became law.

In 1720, the king issued a decree limiting the number of privileged familiares in Brazil to three cities. Salvador, Bahia, received 30, Rio de Janeiro 20, and Olinda 10.[24] Consequently, in 1720, the Lisbon Tribunal ordered the comissários in these cities to forward to Lisbon a list of all the familiares with the dates they took their oaths so that they could determine who would enter the number of privileged familiares.[25] The instructions sent to the rector of the Jesuit College in Olinda, Father Luís de Morim, ordered him to make a list, based on seniority, of all the familiares who had received cartas in Olinda. He was specifically instructed, however, not to include any familiares who had received cartas in Portugal and later moved to Olinda, because their seniority related to the place where they had received the carta, not to the place they had moved to.[26]

It is interesting that in 1720, when Recife was already beginning to eclipse Olinda in size and power, that the inquisitor general and the king chose to grant privileged familiares to Olinda but not Recife. It seems probable that they did so because Olinda had been the political and religious center of the colony. It also seems probable that they had not yet perceived or understood the changes that were taking place in Pernambuco. In any event, the decision created more problems because the number of familiares in Recife soon far outstripped the number in Olinda. This meant that Recife possessed a growing number of familiares who were legally excluded from enjoying the privileges of office at the same time that Olinda had a higher percentage of familiares who did enjoy them. This situation did little to improve the tensions between the two cities and perhaps manifested the ignorance of the government in Lisbon of the conditions on the ground in their colonies.

None of the other captaincies were even mentioned in the 1720 decree. Nor was there any mention of whether the other towns and villages in Brazil should receive the one or two granted in Portugal. These omissions resulted in much later confusion. The distribution of the privileged familiares in Brazil indicates the relative economic importance of the captaincies at the time. But even then, such numbers were woefully inadequate for the huge expanse of territory occupied in colonial Brazil, which was rapidly expanding inward toward the mines in Minas Gerais. From 1711 to 1720, the Inquisition churned out 935 new familiares, twenty of whom were from Pernambuco. In the following decade, the Inquisition produced 1,108 new familiares, fourteen of whom were from Pernambuco.[27] The 1720 decree only complicated an already difficult and divisive situation, and the continually rising numbers of new familiares in Brazil and Portugal placed pressure on an inadequate and ill-conceived system.

By the 1730s, the system already manifested the signs of strain. For example, even though Minas Gerais had not been mentioned in either edict, the comissários in Minas were already complaining that nonprivileged familiares grumbled about having to do the work of the Inquisition. The local authorities did not respect inquisitional privilege, either. For example, during the festivities for the brotherhood of St. Peter Martyr in Vila Rica, Minas Gerais, in 1734, local cavalry pursuing an escaped criminal seized some of the familiares' horses.[28]

The comissário who reported on the incident used it as an opportunity to criticize the system. He argued that all the familiares in Minas should be privileged because they were so few for such a large area. If not, then at least one should be approved for each parish because any one of those parishes was larger than many villages in Portugal that possessed privileged officials. He also argued that the granting of privileges should not be based on seniority, because the older familiares were often less suitable than the younger ones. In addition, privileging them would not damage the royal treasury because the taxes from which they would be exempt were not even collected in Minas. His observations appear to be valid, but they received no response from Lisbon.

The familiares in Rio also struggled over the loss of the privilege of exemption from military service and refused to accept the new and more limiting restriction. In 1736, during the war with Spain over Uruguay (1735–1737), they would not obey the governor when he ordered them to present themselves for military service. The king chastised them for disobedience, particularly for coming in a time of war, and ordered them to regularize the familiares do número in Rio so that only those "of the number" could enjoy the privileges. Despite their initial resistance, the familiares of the city of Rio also began applying for certificates of privilege.[29]

The practice of selecting the officials based on seniority also added to the confusion and inefficiency of the system. It effectively meant that a man in Lisbon had to serve as a familiar for thirty-seven years before he could hope to be named a familiar do número. This meant that when he finally did receive the privileges, he was too old or too ill to actually do any work, and the Inquisition had to rely on the younger, nonprivileged familiares. Also, the workload had increased, due mostly to applications for inquisitional offices, and there were not enough privileged officials to do all the work. In response, the inquisitor general requested that the king permit an increase of another twenty familiares for Lisbon who would be selected, not by seniority, but by the quality of their service to the Inquisition. The king granted the request in November 1737 with the condition that if the new *familiares do vinte* ("familiares of the twenty," also *supranumerarios* or *extranumerarios*), as they were called, failed in their duty, they could be removed. He also stipulated that if one of the twenty reached the age where he could become one of the one hundred privileged, he had to do so and vacate his place in the twenty.[30]

Modification was not only necessary; it was possible. But the room for adjustment remained limited. Attempts to reform the inadequate allocations for Brazil failed, and royal officials in the colony remained intransigent and repeatedly refused to grant inquisitional privileges based on conflicting interpretations of the 1693 decree. Officials in Brazil continually found it necessary to reassert and defend their privileges against powerful royal officials who sought to check them. As a result, a continuous running battle ensued that was never fully resolved.

The 1720 decree, which limited the number of privileged familiares in Brazil, left the issue ambiguous at best. It is clear that many people either were unaware of the decree, chose to ignore it, or were simply confused by it. As a result, some argued that the omissions meant that in those places not listed all the familiares were privileged. Others argued that if a place was not mentioned then none of the familiares were privileged. The General Council did not help the matter by granting certificates in a very haphazard manner. They appear to have been just as confused as the officials in the colony on the ultimate meaning of the restriction.

The problem was widespread, and many familiares found it necessary to ask for certificates of privilege, even though they did not concede the legitimacy of the argument. For example, Antônio da Silva Coutinho, a familiar from Mato Grosso, deep in the interior of Brazil, petitioned to become one of the number in 1786, even though Mato Grosso had not been indicated in any royal orders. The terse *escuzado* (useless or superfluous) written at the top of the petition indicates that the Inquisition believed either that he was unworthy or that familiares do número were either not necessary or not permitted in Mato Grosso.[31] But in 1788, when Antônio da Silva Coutinho applied again to become one of the number in Mato Grosso because, as he said, a position had become vacant, he received a certificate.[32] Likewise, João Silvestre de Araújo e Souza was successful in arguing that the limitation of twenty privileged familiares for Rio referred only to the city of Rio and not to the surrounding region, where all familiares enjoyed their privileges. His petition for a certificate of privilege indicates, however, that he felt the need to assert his position.[33]

In 1761, the familiares of the captaincy of Grão Pará petitioned the General Council as a group for certificates of familiar do número. They argued that, since Pará, Maranhão, and their surrounding territories were not mentioned in the 1720 list, they were all privileged. The General Council agreed that they were not restricted and, therefore, they were all privileged, and they requested a list of the familiares ranked by seniority.³⁴ Despite this obvious assertion of the General Council that all the familiares in areas not listed in the 1720 list retained their privileges, problems continued to arise.

For example, in 1776, Domingos Antunes Pereira, resident of São Luís do Maranhão, petitioned the General Council to excuse him from an appointment to the municipal council. He had shown the council his certificate of privilege, and they still attempted to force him to take the position. The General Council sent an order to the ouvidor geral to give his reasons for not recognizing the privilege and ordered the municipal council to honor them as well. Even though the Inquisition was ready and willing to support the familiares, others did not agree. A marginal note on one of Domingos's petitions argued that his petition should be denied because the king did not want to grant privileges that would impede his royal service. It also asserted that the petitions for those of the number should be given only to the most noble people in each city and village, which of course was not stipulated in either the 1693 or 1720 decrees.³⁵

A more complicated case occurred two years earlier in 1774 in Maranhão. A man named João, the slave of the familiar Antônio Gomes Pires, sought to force his master to permit João's free wife to purchase his freedom. Gomes Pires attempted to block the sale by claiming that his inquisitional privileges protected him in the performance of his inquisitional duties from outside interference. He argued that he took his slave with him in the performance of these duties, which made the slave necessary for such duties and therefore protected his status as a slave under inquisitional privilege. Despite the fact that the argument stretched inquisitional privilege beyond the breaking point, the judge did not confront the privilege head-on. Instead, he argued that since the crown had limited the number of privileged familiares, and Maranhão did not appear on the list, Gomes Pires could not enjoy those privileges and was thus subject to civil law. Consequently, the judge ordered Gomes Pires to accept the offered payment and free the slave.³⁶ All of this occurred despite the ruling by the General Council thirteen years before that the familiares of Maranhão were privileged precisely because they did not appear on the lists.

Similar conflicts occurred in Bahia. In 1751, the familiares of Bahia complained that their privileges were not being honored. The comissário Bernardo Germano de Almeida wrote on their behalf that he had always found them to be prompt and well disposed to fulfill their obligations even at great risk and discomfort. He also noted that many familiares were being forced to work in public offices despite their privileges, which were denied them on the pretense that they were not of the number.[37] The same issue arose again in 1767 and in 1782.

The 1767 conflict arose because of a meeting of several members of the high court called by the *desembargador* (judge of the high court), Manuel Sarmento. They agreed that the familiares should no longer be allowed to submit their cases to the private judgment of the ouvidores gerais because the privileges of the office had only been granted to those in Portugal and all familiares in Brazil were exempt from enjoying those privileges.[38] In a unique and wholly unjustified interpretation of the 1693 decree, the ministers of the high court also argued that the familiares in Brazil belonged to the Lisbon Tribunal, and so they were counted with the familiares of Lisbon in selecting the one hundred privileged familiares granted to that city.

In 1768, the juiz conservador in Bahia argued that this attempt to extinguish the privileges of the familiares would not only eliminate that privilege, but also destroy the office of juiz conservador. Ten years later, the juiz conservador dos familiares complained that he had lost considerable revenue because the familiares ceased to bring cases for him to adjudicate. He did not receive any salary for the position, only compensation for each case.[39] His complaint echoed a similar complaint from 1738 in which the juiz conservador petitioned the crown to pass a law rendering null and void all judgments in civil and criminal cases against familiares that were not given from his office.[40]

The familiares of Bahia complained to the king and forwarded a large body of documents that demonstrated that familiares in Brazil were regularly exempt from paying the *sisa* (excise tax on immovable property) and holding public office against their will, and were generally allowed to submit their legal cases to the juiz conservador. They argued that, until the 1720 restriction, all familiares had enjoyed their privileges. The 1720 decree did not mention the other places in Brazil, and so they continued to enjoy the privileges without restriction. They offered a variety of cases in which royal officials interpreted the 1693 and 1720 decrees in this manner as proof of their case.

The king consulted with the General Council on the matter. The General Council concluded that the most important privilege the familiares enjoyed in Brazil was that of private adjudication of their civil and criminal cases by the juiz conservador. To take that privilege away from them not only made their task more irksome because they were not otherwise compensated for their work, but it also considerably reduced the income of the juiz conservador and his scribes. In addition, it had always been impractical to limit the number of privileged familiares in Brazil either because few of them were actually from Brazil or because those who went to Brazil either for business or commercial reasons did not have a permanent domicile. The 1720 restriction had only limited the numbers in Rio, Salvador, and Olinda. Consequently, either because they had not heard of the restriction or because it was impossible to put it into practice, the familiares in Brazil had continued to enjoy all of the privileges without restriction. They advised the king to remove all restrictions in Brazil based on the spirit of the 1693 decree, which had intentionally excluded Brazil because it was impractical and unnecessary to limit the numbers of privileged familiares in the colony.[41]

Despite all these efforts, the issue remained unresolved, and in 1782 the juízes ordinários and the desembargadores of the high court of Bahia again refused to accept the familiares' right to private adjudication with the juiz conservador in civil cases. The familiares complained, using the same arguments as before. This time, they offered a 1718 declaration by the juiz do fisco in Bahia and a 1743 ruling by the high court that made the same argument, as evidence that the 1693 decree had generally been interpreted in their favor. They did not, however, make any mention of the 1720 decree, either through ignorance or by design.[42] Likewise, the comissário, Antônio da Costa de Andrade, argued in 1775 that none of the familiares in Bahia could be said to be superfluous because of the large size of the captaincy. All of them were necessary and therefore privileged.[43] Again, the crown refused to offer any resolution to the problem.

Another point that the 1693 decree left unmentioned had to do with clerics who were also familiares. This issue came to the attention of the General Council in 1760. The issue of clerical officials and privileges usually revolved around individual cases and specific privileges, because the crown never limited the number of clerics who could enjoy the privileges.[44] But for those clerics who had become familiares before they took their vows and did not later become comissários, notários, or qualificadores, the limitations could be an issue. The 1760 case arose over a petition from a cleric to be received into the familiares do número because of his seniority. The General Council noted that the secretary of the council and his predecessor had never counted clerics when determining who should be accepted into the familiares do número because they believed that clerics were more privileged than familiares. But the council had granted a certificate to some clerics in the past, and with this new petition they determined to establish the status of familiares who were clerics, once and for all.

Friar Francisco de São Tomás consulted on the subject and determined that clerics should not be considered in determining the familiares do número and, that if any had been given certificates, they should be considered void. He based his argument on a comparison of the privileges granted to the familiares with the privileges enjoyed by clerics. Clerics were already exempt from paying the tributes and taxes that familiares did not have to pay. They could not carry arms, and they had no need for a privilege to allow their wives to wear silk. Likewise, they had no use for the privilege of having their cases tried by the Inquisition because they already had the privilege of being tried in ecclesiastical courts. Not only that, but the private adjudication of the familiares, which began with the juiz conservador, was secular in nature, and clerics could not be tried before a secular court.

He also argued, in tune with the current attitude of the Pombaline reform, that the inquisitors should be guided by secular not canon law in this matter, because they were royal, not pontifical, ministers. For these reasons, Friar Francisco determined that the exercise of the privileges of the familiar by clerics was both useless and repugnant to their office. Hence, clerics received certificates rarely, and after 1760 probably not at all.[45]

By the end of the eighteenth century, these tensions combined with other stresses being placed on the Inquisition and contributed to its decline.[46] In 1796, the comissário Joaquim Marques de Araújo, from Pernambuco, noted that the Inquisition ordered the comissários to employ those of the number first when executing an order from the Inquisition. If they refused, the comissários were to inform the Inquisition, take their cartas, and declare them incapable of enjoying their privileges.[47] But in 1797, Joaquim Marques wrote that they did not even know who the familiares do número were in Pernambuco and that the captain-general of the captaincy employed the familiares in the service of the king and did not respect their privileges. The captain-general and the magistrates argued in turn that there were no privileged familiares in Pernambuco, and that only the familiares in Portugal were privileged. For this reason, the familiares were reluctant to serve the Inquisition. They could not, as they said, "burn in two fires." Joaquim Marques requested that the Inquisition inform him as to which familiares were privileged so that they could serve the Inquisition and enjoy their privileges.[48]

The stresses appeared elsewhere in Brazil, as well. José Antônio Carvalho claimed that nineteen of the twenty positions of those of the number in Rio were vacant in 1794, and he claimed they had been vacant for years.[49] In 1770, the crown abolished the juiz do fisco in Rio de Janeiro because the position had fallen into disuse.[50] Despite all of the conflict and ambiguity, the system continued to function, more or less, right up to the end.[51]

The familiares represented one branch of an extensive bureaucracy created to increase the effective power of the crown and the Church. But the crown could not afford to pay them a salary or stipend. Instead, it created an arrangement where candidates paid for the opportunity to exercise inquisitional privileges and for a declaration of purity of blood. When the costs became too demanding, rather than eliminate the privilege, the crown sought to constrict it by creating the familiares do número. All in all, this system served both parties well. The benefits of an appointment could be socially very important and economically beneficial even when the privileges were limited. For the crown, it was a relatively risk-free system of acquiring a more extensive bureaucracy tied closely to the crown, while at the same time increasing revenues that could offset the costs of maintaining that bureaucracy.

Contrary to what has generally been believed, most familiares after 1693 could not be certain that they would ever fully enjoy the privileges of their office. Not only did they find that they had to constantly defend those privileges, but also, by the early eighteenth century, those privileges came to be legally limited to a narrowly defined group of familiares, even though in practice it was a much-debated point.

One of the motivations for seeking office was to gain some control over the often arbitrary political power that could limit economic and social opportunities and decisions. Inquisitional privilege served as a buffer to the power of the Church, the state, and their officials—hence, the ardent attempts by familiares in the colony to retain privileges and especially the privilege of private adjudication.

The ambiguity of the problem probably permitted most familiares in Brazil, at least until the mid-1700s, to enjoy the privileges to some degree. This room to maneuver also played into the hands of those who sought to restrict inquisitional power and privilege. The paradox created a space for conflict and contestation between the secular and ecclesiastical powers on the one hand and the officials of the Inquisition on the other.

This history contradicts the oft-unstated assumption that the main motivation for desiring an inquisitional appointment was the privileges that came with the office. Those privileges were supposed to be a man's only compensation for service.[52] The near fanatical paranoia with which the familiares sought to assert and defend their privileges indicates that they took them seriously and valued them highly. But the previous discussion demonstrates that these could not have been the only, or even the most important, motivations for seeking inquisitional office. If those privileges were effectively limited to a small number of individuals, or at least widely contested, and it was questionable whether a familiar would ever be able to exercise them with any consistency, then it seems unlikely that the privileges would be the primary motivation for seeking appointments.

Any well-informed applicant would have been aware of the restriction or at least the ongoing debate. Because that was the case, the continued interest in inquisitional appointments must be explained elsewhere. Social honor, prestige, and mobility could motivate as effectively as transient and unstable privilege and in the end remained far more important. The Inquisition also established corporate institutions that provided new avenues for honor and prestige and the opportunity to regain lost or fleeting privilege.

Notes

1. The term *familiar do número* was borrowed from an old Portuguese term that referred to a limited number of laymen and laywomen associated with a monastery who received special privileges from the monastery, such as clothing, food, and burial in the monastery's cemetery in return for land or wealth given to the monastery. See Viterbo, *Elucidario das palavras*, s.v. "Familiares," 305–6.

2. James E. Wadsworth, "Os familiares do número e o problema dos privilégios," in *A Inquisição em Xeque: temas, controvérsias, estudos de caso*, ed. R. Vainfas, L. Lage, and B. Feitler (Rio de Janeiro: Editora Universidade do Estado do Rio de Janeiro, 2006), 97–112.

3. See Bethencourt, *História das Inquisições*, 263.

4. Ângela Barreto Xavier and António Manuel Hespanha, "As redes clientelares," in *História de Portugal. O Antigo Regime*, ed. António Manuel Hespanha, vol. 4 (Lisbon: Editora Estampa, 1993), 382, and Maria Fernada Baptista Bicalho, "As câmaras ultramarinas e o governo do Império," in *O Antigo Regime nos trópicos: A dinâmica imperial portuguesa (séculos XVI–XVIII)*, ed. João Fragoso, Maria Fernanda Bicalho, and Maria de Fátima Gouvêa (Rio de Janeiro: Civilização Brasileira, 2001), 206.

5. Bicalho, "As câmaras ultramarinas," 206.

6. *Traslado autentico de todos os Privilegios Concedidos pelos Reis destes Reinos, e Senhorios de Portugal aos officiaes, e Familiares do Santo Officio da Inquisição*. Several copies can be found in BNLL, Cod. 867, including those published in 1685, 1691, and 1787. A manuscript copy can be found in the Biblioteca da Ajuda, 44-xiii-57, fol. 113. BNLL, Res. 105A, F221. *Collectorio das Bullas e breves apostolicos. . .* (Lisboa nos Estaôs por Lourenço Craesbeeck Impressor del Rey Anno 1634). See also ANTT, MNEJ, Livro 4, fols. 69v.

7. In 1596, D. Philip I (Philip II of Spain) confirmed all the previous royal decrees. See BNL, Res. 105A, F221, fols. 152v–153v, 159–163.

8. See BNL, Res. 105A, F221, fols. 164v–165v, 166v; "Sobre os filhos dos familiares serem excusos de ir as companhias de guerra," May 15, 1625, ANTT, CGSO, NT 4165; "Sobre os filhos dos familiares serem excusos de ir as companhias de guerra," May 15, 1625, ANTT, CGSO, NT 4165; IL, NT 2146; IL, Livro 151, fols. 80–82; Ajuda, 51-vi-12, fol. 336; BNL, Cod. 867, fols. 150–157b. For debates and rulings regarding taxes and public offices, see BNL, Cod. 1537, fol. 46; ANTT, CGSO,

NT 4155; CGSO, Livro 97, fols. 105–105v; CGSO, m. 30 and m. 24, nos. 36, 37; IL, Livro 154, fol. 85; CGSO, NT 4155; and AHU, Rio de Janeiro, cx. 15, doc. 75.

9. Citing Joaquim Verríssimo Serrão's *História de Portugal*, William Michael Donovan mistakenly claims that Lisbon had a limited number of familiares, which barred individuals from serving the Inquisition. Donovan, "Commercial Enterprise and Luso-Brazilian Society during the Brazilian Gold Rush: The Mercantile House of Francisco Pinheiro and the Lisbon to Brazil Trade, 1695–1750" (Ph.D. dissertation, Johns Hopkins University, 1991), 62. The crown tried unsuccessfully in 1620 to limit the familiares the way they had been limited in Spain. See ANTT, CGSO, Livro 213, fols. 310–312v, and CGSO, m. 22, no. 34.

10. See Siqueira, "Os Regimentos da Inquisição," 616, 694, 885–86 (1613 Regimento, Book I, Title I, Paragraph II; 1640 Regimento, Book I, Title I, Paragraph 1; 1774 Regimento, Book I, Title I, Paragraph 1).

11. ANTT, CGSO, Livro 381, fols. 1–1v.

12. C. R. Boxer, *The Golden Age of Brazil, 1695–1750: Growing Pains of a Colonial Society* (Berkeley: University of California Press, 1964), 28–29.

13. A notation on page 1v of Livro 381 of the CGSO notes that the General Council voted on the issue in 1744 and determined that it should not be regulated by seniority any longer, but should be left to the determination of the council.

14. ANTT, CGSO, Livro 213, fols. 391–395v, 450v–451v.

15. ANTT, ML 168, fols. 333–333v.

16. ANTT, CGSO, Livro 381, fols. 1–3; BNL, Mss., cx. 75, nos. 3, 9. This decree was often reprinted and used as evidence in the various disputes that arose over privileges. It is also found in ANTT, MNEJ, Livro 5. For faults in the system, see ANTT, CGSO, NT 4146, and ANTT, CGSO, NT 4174.

17. Ajuda, 44-xiii-32, 116a. The crown issued the same decree again on April 30, 1699, hence the various references to either 1693 or 1699 as the date of the decree in the literature.

18. ANTT, CGSO, m. 22, no. 51.

19. ANTT, CGSO, Livro 38, fols. 3–3v.

20. *Regimento do Juizo das Confiscaçoens pelo crime de Heresia, & Apostasia*, published in 1695, can be found in the BNL, Cod. 867.

21. See ANTT, CGSO, Livro 381, fols. 5v–6, and ANTT, MNEJ, Livro 5, fols. 23v. In 1733, Pernambuco received an additional officer called the *depositario dos bens do fisco* who received a salary of 40$000 réis and 2 percent of the money the fisco sent to Lisbon. See CGSO, Livro 381, fol. 110v.

22. ANTT, IL, Livro 154, fols. 450–450v, 461–461v.

23. ANTT, CGSO, Livro 381, fols. 64–65.

24. ANTT, CGSO, Livro 381, fols. 64–66v. A copy of the same document found in the Ministerio do Reino, m. 362 lists Bahia as 20.

25. ANTT, IL, Livro 153, fols. 525.

26. ANTT, IL, Livro 21, fols. 1v–2v.

27. Torres, "Da repressão religiosa," 130.

28. ANTT, CGSO, m. 4, no. 12.
29. See ANTT, CGSO, NT 4156; CGSO, m. 28, nos. 98, 99.
30. ANTT, CGSO, Livro 381, fols. 126–27, 161. The crown reasserted this decision in 1744. See ANTT, CGSO, NT 4185. In the loose papers of the boxes of the Novas Habilitações, many petitions to enter either the familiares do número or the extranumerarios appear. Those who wanted to serve as extranumerarios had to go through another extrajudicial review to determine their worthiness. See ANTT, NH, cxs. 33, 47, and m. 73, no. 1. See also ANTT, CGSO, NT 4146, 4156, 4174, 4175, 4185, 4188; CGSO, m. 13., no. 17, m. 8, no. 2873, m. 52, 53; IL, Livro 158, fol. 115; and IL Livro 123, fol. 216v.
31. ANTT, CGSO, NT 4146.
32. ANTT, CGSO, NT 4180.
33. ANTT, CGSO, NT 4188.
34. ANTT, NT 4156 and CGSO, m. 53. See also ANTT, CGSO, NT 4188.
35. ANTT, CGSO, m. 58. See also ANTT, IL, m. 23, no. 51.
36. Colin M. MacLachlan, "Slavery, Ideology, and Institutional Change: The Impact of the Enlightenment on Slavery in Late-Eighteenth Century Maranhão," *JLAS* 11, no. 1 (May 1979): 8–9.
37. ANTT, CGSO, m. 17, no. 3 and IL, NT 2133.
38. ANTT, MR, m. 362.
39. AHU, Bahia, cx. 52, docs. 10021–27.
40. AHU, Bahia, cx. 64, doc. 18.
41. This entire bundle of papers can be found in the ANTT, MR, m. 362.
42. ANTT, CGSO, m. 22, no. 50.
43. AHU, Bahia, cx. 48, nos. 8901 and 8865.
44. For a comissário who sought to utilize his privileges, see AHU, Pernambuco, cx. 67, doc. 5677.
45. ANTT, CGSO, m. 17, no. 2.
46. The decline also occurred in brotherhoods of New Spain during the eighteenth century. See María Águeda Méndez, "La fiesta de San Pedro Mártir: Preparativos y vicisitudes de la Inquisición novohispana dieciochesca," *CMHLB Caravelle* 73 (1999): 66–70.
47. ANTT, IL, Livro 24, fol. 284.
48. ANTT, IL, m. 40.
49. ANTT, CGSO, m. 22, no. 65, and CGSO, Livro 352, fol. 65.
50. ANTT, CGSO, Livro 381, fol. 291–297.
51. ANTT, MNEJ, Livro 123, fol. 216v.
52. Siqueira, "Os Regimentos da Inquisição," 521–22.

CHAPTER NINE

Corporate Institutions: Brotherhoods and Militias

At the end of the seventeenth century and the beginning of the eighteenth century, the Inquisition created corporate institutions that mediated inquisitional relationships in Brazil. These institutions, a brotherhood and a militia company, embodied the only more or less frequent public and political rituals of the Inquisition in the colonies. Their rites of power served as pedagogical displays that promoted the Inquisition's self-image as a unified and autonomous institution of great power and prestige that defended the Church and society from all forms of spiritual deviance.[1] Where they occurred, the public displays of the brotherhood (e.g., the celebration of the saint's day and the burial processions) and the monthly drills of the militia company put the familiares and other officials of the Inquisition very much into the public eye.

These institutions filled an important historical niche, arriving in Brazil at about the same time that royal limitations on inquisitional privilege were being put in place. Because they were established in the late seventeenth and early eighteenth centuries, they helped offset a potential decline in interest for inquisitional appointments by permitting at least some familiares to recoup those lost privileges. In a society where group membership mediated relationships, these inquisitional organizations facilitated the creation and maintenance of group identity. They also represented the image-conscious Inquisition to society in a positive light and attempted to create and maintain inquisitional power, prestige, and status.

Both the brotherhood and the militia company enhanced status and honor by creating distance and exclusiveness through granting such opportunities as participation in public rituals and military displays, the wearing of special uniforms, the use of rich and forceful symbolism, and the carrying of weapons. Likewise, these organizations brought the disparate group of familiares together and re-created social relationships in which the wealthy and powerful served in the positions of command and leadership over familiares of lesser social status. This is particularly true of the militia company, which was generally organized as other military companies and suffered from the same strengths and weaknesses.

Celebrating St. Peter Martyr

As with the other brotherhoods in Brazil, the brotherhood of St. Peter Martyr was organized around the cult of a saint.[2] Frequently, these brotherhoods organized around the patron saint of a specific trade or profession, such as blacksmiths, locksmiths, barbers, and bleeders, who celebrated the cult of St. George. The officials of the Inquisition celebrated the cult of St. Peter of Verona, the patron saint of the Inquisition and, therefore, of the inquisitional confraternity.

Peter of Verona was a Dominican who had been named inquisitor general of the Milanese Inquisition in 1234 by Pope Gregory IX. His zealous activities won him enemies, some of whom finally assassinated him while he was traveling from Como to Milan in 1252. Tradition states that he had been born into a family of Catharist heretics but had zealously defended the faith even against his own family. His zeal was so great that, with the last flicker of life, he reportedly wrote on the ground (or on his robe—the accounts differ) with his own blood "Credo in Deum" (I believe in God). Pope Innocent IV canonized him a year after his death, and he became the symbol of inquisitional zeal and sacrifice for the faith. His feast day is celebrated on April 29.[3]

Thirteen years after his martyrdom, the cult of St. Peter of Verona arrived in Portugal. In 1266, Pope Clement IV admonished the prelates of Portugal to hold the celebration of St. Peter of Verona on April 29, which they apparently did. These early celebrations, however, took place on one among many holy days dedicated to Christian saints and were not associated with any confraternity. The Iberian Inquisitions, established in the fifteenth and sixteenth centuries, selected St. Peter of Verona as their patron saint and protector and eventually appropriated his cult as a central aspect of their devotion.

The brotherhood first appeared in Italy in 1569 and in Spain in 1604.[4] From Spain, it spread to Portugal, where the Inquisition had been established in 1536. The papal bull of Paul V, *Cum inter caeteras* ("together among the others"), of June 29, 1611, stressed that the brothers of St. Peter Martyr should be considered servants of the Inquisition, and he encouraged faithful Christians to seek membership.[5]

The inquisitor general of Portugal, Pedro de Castilo, approved the organization of the brotherhood, and it first appeared in Lisbon and Goa in 1615 and in Coimbra and Oporto in 1620. The brotherhood eventually spread to Évora, Funchal, Madeira, and Brazil, and possibly other areas under Portuguese dominion.[6] Until 1632, the brotherhood lacked any formal and certified regulations in Portugal. In that year, the inquisitor general, D. Francisco de Castro, and the General Council approved the *compromisso* (statutes or bylaws). The compromisso stated that the purpose of the brotherhood was to keep the memory of St. Peter Martyr alive and to encourage the officials of the Inquisition to emulate his qualities of zeal and sacrifice.

The brotherhood did not come to Brazil until at least the end of the seventeenth century, although considerable uncertainly still persists regarding the origin and extent of the brotherhoods in Brazil.[7] The familiares of Bahia held their first celebration in 1697. The familiares of Olinda and Recife soon followed suit in 1698. Minas Gerais held its first celebration in Ouro Preto in 1733.[8]

Unlike the confraternities in Spain and Mexico, and despite the 1611 papal bull, the brotherhoods of St. Peter Martyr in Brazil and Portugal normally admitted only officials of the Inquisition.[9] This practice helped solidify the group's identity and the exclusiveness of inquisitional office.

All inquisitional officials were instantly admitted into the brotherhood and were required to pay the entrance fee of 2$400 réis.[10] These fees entered the coffers of the brotherhood and were to be used to cover expenses. During the eighteenth century, the Lisbon Tribunal dipped into these coffers to help cover their own operating costs as their proceeds from confiscated property decreased.[11]

The compromisso also stated that any minister or familiar from the jurisdiction of a different tribunal could be allowed to participate in the activities of the brotherhood upon presenting his letter of appointment to the Inquisition. Likewise, a brother could be expelled only by the order of the Inquisition. Unlike the Spanish brotherhoods, however, the Portuguese brotherhood did not permit the wives of members to belong.[12]

In Pernambuco, the senior comissário acted as the judge of the brotherhood.[13] In Recife, the brothers elected two majordomos, one treasurer, and four procurators (two from Recife and two from Santo Antônio). The treasurer reported directly to the comissário then serving as the judge. The elections occurred in the afternoon of the Sunday before the festival, with all the brothers present.[14]

These brotherhoods served as mutual aid societies. The leaders held responsibility for overseeing these and other activities of the brotherhood, such as pious devotions, providing for the welfare of their members, and organizing the annual celebration of the saint. In addition to the entrance fee, the brothers paid yearly dues and intermittent donations to pay for masses, funeral processions, yearly religious services, and financial assistance to needy brothers.[15]

If the fees and donations did not cover the expenses of the brotherhood that year, then the majordomos and the scribe had to make up the difference from their own pockets. Any extra funds raised during the year could either be used to buy candles or other things the brotherhood needed or be retained and delivered to the incoming officers.[16] In Recife, the brotherhood collected these dues and contributions, although they were a bit higher than elsewhere at 2$000 réis each.[17]

Any property bequeathed to the brotherhood in wills could be used for expenses or to purchase necessary materials, such as oil for the lamps of the saint, ornaments, and silver. Any real estate it received had to be sold at public auction because "experience has shown very great inconveniences in communities administering estates of this type." Chapter 19 of the compromisso states that the sale of this property should be used to support the costs of the festivals and other expenses of the brotherhood. This requirement in the compromisso effectively prevented the Portuguese brotherhoods from gaining the kind of wealth that their counterpart in Mexico City accumulated. It also kept them from becoming a significant financial institution.[18] In doing so, the Inquisition prevented the familiares and other inquisitional officials as a group from developing corporate sources of wealth and prestige independent of the tribunals.

The most important day of the year for the brotherhood was the day it celebrated the festival of St. Peter Martyr.[19] This was the crowning showpiece of inquisitional dignity, honor, prestige, and power in the colony. The familiares and other officials paraded through the streets arrayed in their finest habits, with the crusader's cross over their breasts and their medallions of office gleaming in the sun, bearing the standard of the Inquisition before them. This festival also provided a type of psychological conditioning for the participants and observers. In Brazil, where no autos-da-fé were held except during the infrequent visitas, these celebrations were probably the most visible and ostentatious displays of inquisitional power and prestige.[20]

The festival of St. Peter Martyr took place on the evenings of April 28 and April 29. The compromisso stated that, where possible, the celebrations should be held at churches dedicated to St. Dominic, which should be decorated with "all possible decency."

The judge took care of the music and the furnishings, and the majordomos handled everything else. The scribe ensured that they did not overspend. The spending limit existed so that no one would refuse to serve as majordomo because of the expense, and to prevent unholy "excess and vain glory."

The compromisso attempted to keep the celebrations solemn and pious occasions. In keeping with this desire, all dances, comedies, and extravagance were forbidden. Only a procession at vespers, a sermon, ornamenting of the church, and a procession on the saint's day were permitted. Nonetheless, the inquisitional brotherhoods of Brazil adopted the more ostentatious displays of the other brotherhoods, such as the ringing of bells, music, food, and flowers, in the ongoing competition among the religious brotherhoods for public prestige.[21] The senior comissário approved the preacher of the sermon, and the brothers' donations paid for new wax candles at each festival. In Recife, the celebrations were held at the parish church of Corpo Santo (see figures 9.1 and 9.2).[22] The officials lined up and paraded with lighted candles to the chapel, where the sermon was given.

The next morning, they gathered again and marched to the church, where they heard the Mass of the Holy Spirit and listened to colorful discourses on

Figure 9.1. The Igreja do Corpo Santo. *Source:* Museu do Recife, Liv. 12, Photo 08617. *Note:* This is the church where the brotherhood of St. Peter Martyr in Pernambuco held their celebrations and had their chapel. It was destroyed in the early twentieth century when the center of Recife was torn down to modernize the city.

Figure 9.2. The Corpo Santo Just Prior to Its Demolition. *Source:* **Museu do Recife, Livro 12, Photo 08553.**

the life and accomplishments of St. Peter Martyr that employed all the imagery and symbolism of the Inquisition. These sermons were lessons in inquisitional symbolism and mythology and recitations of baroque Christian iconography, designed to instruct the listeners, to justify the existence of the Inquisition and the brotherhood, and to promote an ideal of inquisitional zeal for all to follow. They reveal the crusading spirit of militant Christianity and the rhetoric the Inquisition used to justify its activities and continued existence.[23]

The sermons employed the rich symbolic repertoire, both visual and verbal, to instruct and edify. The insignia of the brotherhood combined the coat of arms of the Inquisition with the iconography of the Dominicans and of St. Peter Martyr (see figure 9.3). The insignia of the brotherhood consisted of a cross with an olive branch on one side and a sword on the other, both placed within a black border shaped like a shield. Several of the fleurs-de-lis of St. Dominic framed the border.[24] The standard of the brotherhood had this insignia on one side and the image of St. Peter Martyr, within a similar black border, on the other.[25] On the right-hand side of St. Peter Martyr was the coat of arms of the Church, and on the left was the royal coat of arms in the same manner as the Tribunal of Lisbon. St. Peter Martyr was, and is, usually portrayed in a Dominican cape and robe. His right hand rests on his breast, holding a palm branch bearing three crowns of gold (the symbols of victory and martyrdom), while his left hand holds a book. He is also represented variously with a knife in or splitting his head, a knife in his hand, or a sword in his breast. Sometimes a man behind him stabs a knife into his head.[26]

Figure 9.3. Coat of Arms of the Inquisition, Évora, Portugal. *Source:* Photo taken by James E. Wadsworth, 1998.

The cross that the familiares wore on their habits also had fleurs-de-lis on each end. This was the crusader cross that the inquisitional assistants were first permitted to wear in 1254. At the same time, they received the same indulgences and privileges given to the crusaders who went to the Holy Land. The association of the Inquisition with crusading was intentional and demonstrates how the early Inquisition perceived itself. The association was not lost on later inquisitional officials, who often portrayed themselves as modern crusaders against heresy.[27]

The fleur-de-lis that appears on the 1632 Portuguese compromisso of the brotherhood is divided: one half is shaded black and the other white. The opposition of black and white (Dominican colors) contrasted the guilt and suffering of heretics with the hope and peace the Inquisition offered. The fleur-de-lis itself represented purity and light and was commonly used in representations of St. Dominic. The cross, sword, and olive branch represented the death of Christ and the redemption of humanity, mercy and peace, and punishment and death. The sword was also one of the symbols associated with St. Peter Martyr as the instrument of his martyrdom.

The use of the iconography of St. Dominic and of St. Peter Martyr provided a legitimation of the Inquisition by drawing on the prestige of such holy and renowned saints. This symbolism made it clear that the brotherhood was part of the religious, social, and political mission of the Inquisition. It also provided a symbolic universe that tied the officials of the Inquisition to each other.[28] The 1640 and 1774 regimentos limited the use of these symbols and the wearing of the habit to special occasions. They could be worn only at the celebrations of the brotherhood, the autos-da-fé, and when the officials were sent to imprison heretics.[29] All of these occasions were public demonstrations of inquisitional prestige and power and served to reinforce the social honor of inquisitional service and group identity.

A surviving sermon from Recife illustrates the kind of language and rhetoric employed in the sermons.[30] Friar Antônio de Santa Maria Jaboatão, famous for his genealogy of Pernambucan families and his *orbe serafico*, offered the sermon at the 1750 celebration in Recife.[31] He used the sword, blood, and war as his central themes. His swords were the sword of doctrine and the sword of rigor—doctrine to destroy the errors of heretics and rigor to punish the obstinate apostates. For him, heretics were the dry branches that scripture commanded to be cast into the fire and burned.

Friar Jaboatão also created a unique metaphor. He declared that St. Peter Martyr had been permitted to drink the milk of a heretic mother so that he would imbibe hatred and abhorrence of heresy. "The milk that babies drink originates in the mother's blood," he said. And since St. Peter Martyr was the greatest enemy of all heretics, he did not drink his mother's milk as milk. He drank it as blood. "In drinking the blood of the enemy, one shows the greatest hatred that it is possible to have," he declared. "St. Peter Martyr drank the blood of heretics when he drank the milk of a Manichean. And in drinking the milk as blood and not as milk, he did not drink love and an inclination [to heresy], but he drank hatred and abhorrence."

Then Friar Jaboatão compared St. Peter Martyr to Christ, but in a way that portrayed the martyr as the superior of Christ in the battle against heresy. Christ, he said, was afraid to enter the battle against heresy, and that explains why he sought to avoid the suffering in the garden of Gethsemane. He lacked strength of body. From childhood, and even until his death, Christ had fled from heresy—not so St. Peter Martyr. Not only had St. Peter sought out and battled heresy his entire life, but he had also converted heretics to the faith. For Jaboatão, St. Peter Martyr was holier than any other because he was a holy martyr, a holy doctor, a holy virgin, and a holy inquisitor.

Jaboatão wiggled out of this potentially heretical and blasphemous speech by claiming that the three crowns that St. Peter Martyr wore were all for Christ because the battles he had fought had been for the mysteries of Christ.[32]

It is impossible to tell, and is perhaps irrelevant, whether the members of the brotherhood understood the intricacies and manipulations of symbol, or even believed these discourses. We know, however, that they ingested a steady diet of religious symbolism in both public and private life in colonial Brazil. The annual festivities of the brotherhood instructed them at least once a year in inquisitional symbolism and ideals. In fact, the officials themselves were symbolic of inquisitional ideals and advertised these ideals to the community each time they participated in a public ceremony or went out on inquisitional business. Some, such as the indomitable ex-Jesuit Joaquim Marques de Araújo, appear to have imbibed the symbolism with gusto.[33]

During the celebrations, the familiares prayed for peace among Christian rulers, the extirpation of heresy, and the exaltation of the Holy Office. To persuade those who might be inclined to worship in their own oratories, all those who participated in the celebrations and took communion at the end of the mass received a plenary indulgence (forgiveness of all temporal punishments for sin, usually granted to crusaders and in jubilee years) and remission of all their sins.[34]

Because of the lower number of familiares paying the entrance fee, the Brazilian brotherhoods functioned with considerably fewer financial resources than did those in Portugal. After 1790, the new brothers in Recife paid 4$000 réis, which was the only income the brotherhood had except for what they received from selling the candle wax left over after the celebration.[35] The candles had to be sold because the compromisso expressly required that all the candles had to be new each year.[36] As the numbers of new members declined in the last decade of the eighteenth century (from 156 between 1781 and 1790 to fifty-six between 1791 and 1800 in Pernambuco), the resources of the brotherhood also declined. These restricted resources caused the Recife brotherhood to limit their celebrations to the vespers procession, the mass, and the sermon.[37]

The celebrations provided opportunities for interaction and the construction of a common identity, but they could also cause strife and exacerbate personal rivalries. For example, in 1702, the comissário Manuel da Costa Ribeiro in Recife reported that the majordomo of the festival had asked a cleric who had the public reputation of being a New Christian to preach the sermon during the celebrations. The comissário refused to permit the priest to preach on such a holy occasion and told the majordomo to select another preacher to give the sermon, to avoid scandal and to maintain the dignity of the celebration.[38]

The celebrations could also reveal internal strife between inquisitional officials, as well as the territoriality some comissários developed. For instance, in 1763, the Carmelite comissário Antônio das Chagas, who had received his appointment to serve in the town of Goiana in 1761, happened to be in Recife in April during the celebration for St. Peter Martyr. He went to the senior comissário, Antônio Alves Guerra, to request permission to participate in the celebration. Antônio Alves refused to permit it on the grounds that Chagas had been appointed as a comissário in Goiana and not in Recife. His refusal was in direct violation of the fifth chapter of the compromisso. Antônio das Chagas knew this and shot off a letter to the Lisbon Tribunal in which he argued that as a comissário his jurisdiction was not limited to his place of residence. The tribunal agreed and ordered Antônio Alves to desist. The next year, Antônio das Chagas made a point to be in Recife during the festivities and to participate in them. Antônio Alves saw this as a display of arrogance and called the act "sinister." He bowed to the will of the tribunal, but indicated that he now perceived Antônio das Chagas as an enemy.[39]

By the end of the eighteenth century, the inquisitional brotherhood had entered into decline. The cult of St. Peter Martyr had fallen into decay in Rio de Janeiro in the late eighteenth century and in Madeira by 1779.[40] Familiares became increasingly unwilling to assume the financial burdens of participation in the brotherhood, and the numbers of new familiares declined, decreasing the revenue for the brotherhood.

The decline in the brotherhoods was common to all of them during this period, including that of the powerful and prestigious Third Orders in the colony. By the end of the eighteenth century, they experienced recruiting difficulties, which they blamed on the sagging economy.[41]

The decline of the brotherhood of St. Peter Martyr cannot, however, be blamed solely on economic difficulty, although this was clearly a contributing factor. The decline was also symptomatic of the general malaise that had spread throughout the Inquisition by the beginning of the nineteenth century.

One of the primary reasons for the decline of the brotherhood of St. Peter Martyr was the rising cost of participation, which, coupled with the economic downturn of the late eighteenth century squeezed the familiares' financial resources at both ends. The brotherhoods often ignored the limit that the compromisso placed on the cost of the celebrations. As a result, by the end of the eighteenth century, the expense had become so restrictive that familiares in Brazil and Portugal refused to serve as majordomos. The diminishing numbers of new brothers in the late eighteenth century also decreased the annual income of the brotherhoods, which placed serious strains on their resources.[42]

In Recife in 1790, many familiares had begun to refuse to join the brotherhood and participate in its activities, and local religious authorities attempted to exert control over the brotherhood. In 1790, the *juiz de capelas* (judge of chapels or shrines) notified the treasurer of the brotherhood to give an account of the finances of the brotherhood. This was completely without precedent, and the treasurer appealed to the senior comissário, Henrique Martins Gaio, who petitioned the Lisbon Tribunal for advice. The members of the tribunal, of course, instructed him not to give an account to anyone but them.[43]

Companhia dos Familiares

The debates over privilege also branched out to include the militia company of the Inquisition, known as the Companhia dos Familiares. These militia companies represent the only inquisitional institutions in colonial Brazil that were not closely tied to and controlled by the tribunal in Lisbon. The inquisitional militia companies also provided a forum for the familiares to publicly display their identity and status and thus became a part of the debates and conflicts over privilege.

The Companhia dos Familiares was created in 1640, but did not come to Brazil until 1713—only seven years before the 1720 limitations. This eighty-year time lag reflects the lack of a sufficient number of familiares anywhere in Brazil to make such a company possible. The initial creation of the company in Portugal and its later establishment in Brazil both responded to larger crises in the Portuguese Empire and came at a time when Portugal could not afford to allow privileged groups to completely avoid military service.

In November 1640, the Duke of Bragança became D. João IV, king of Portugal, after a conspiracy of nobles declared Portuguese independence from Spain. When D. João IV assumed the throne, Portugal was in a poor state to carry on the war for independence that ensued. Portugal lacked a modern army. She suffered from weak fortifications, and her best military leaders were off fighting for the Spanish elsewhere in Europe. In response to the crisis, the crown ordered every royal tribunal in Lisbon to create and finance its own company composed of at least 150 men.[44]

The Inquisition obeyed the command and ordered all of its officials and their servants to join the Companhia dos Familiares (company of familiares).[45] The Inquisition believed that its privileges prevented the new company from being subject to the colonels and captains of the regular army—a position that the familiares in Brazil continually reasserted.[46] The crown acquiesced and dismissed the Companhia dos Familiares from the jurisdiction of regular army officers and permitted them to accompany his royal person in the same manner as the knights of the military orders and required them to drill once a month.[47] After the wars of restoration, the auxiliary companies fell into disuse for half a century.

The new conflict over the Spanish succession (1701–1714) erupted in the first years of the eighteenth century and suddenly rendered the auxiliary companies significant once again. It also stimulated considerable discussion about how the Companhia dos Familiares was to be organized and how it was supposed to function. Also, by this time, the familiares do número had been created, and it was necessary to clarify which familiares were required to serve. In 1701, the inquisitor general made it clear that all the familiares, not just the familiares do número, had to serve; otherwise there would not be enough men to form a company.[48]

The crisis of the Spanish succession also forced the crown to retract the privilege of exemption from service in the militia from all privileged groups. In 1699, and again in 1709, the crown determined that none of the privileged groups in Portugal or Brazil, including the familiares, could be exempt any longer from military service, and he ordered them to organize companies.[49] But in 1704, in response to a conflict in Rio de Janeiro, D. Catarina ordered that the familiares should not be forced to serve in the militia except in times of war or when some unexpected emergency required it.[50]

To stimulate interest in the companies when they were first created, the crown granted privileges to the new auxiliary troops, including the Companhia dos Familiares. In 1645, D. João IV granted them exemption from a variety of forced taxation, monetary contributions, and property exactions. He granted them all the privileges of the full-time paid soldiers, and the captains and officers enjoyed the privileges of their counterparts in the full-time military, which included the *foro militar* (the right to be tried in a military court). He also exempted them from being impressed into the militia.[51] In 1751, the crown also granted them exemption from forced employment in public offices.[52] These were many of the same privileges being limited to a small minority of familiares from the 1680s on. This opened the possibility that familiares could recoup lost privileges by participating in the Companhia dos Familiares.

The Company in Brazil

When the company was finally established in Brazil in 1713, it was integrated into the complex military organization the crown had already created in Brazil by the eighteenth century. The military organization consisted of full-time professionals called the *tropas da linha* ("first line," or *tropa paga*) and the part-time, unpaid units called *milícia* ("second line," or militia) and the *ordenanças* ("third line," or *terços*). The first-line troops represented the permanent troops of Portugal (where these were stationed) or paid full-time regulars raised from the local population. The second-line auxiliary units enlisted all healthy free adult males between eighteen and forty and were organized by parish and segregated by social status and ethnicity.[53] For example, the company of Henrique Dias, organized in Pernambuco in the seventeenth century, limited its enlistees to free blacks only. The third line consisted of all free adult males eighteen to sixty years of age who had not been enlisted in the other two groups for reasons of age or health. These corps divided themselves into *terços* or regimentos (regiments), which were further divided into companies.[54] The auxiliary troops of the second line drilled once a month and often participated in public displays on special occasions and holy days. The third line drilled only four times a year, and the drills took place only on Sundays, which made service in the second and third lines compatible with earning a living.[55]

Those who belonged to privileged groups, such as the titled nobility, the familiares, and the *moedeiros* (coiners), did not have to serve in the tropas pagas and the ordenanças so long as they had their own militia units. These groups organized militia companies of their own or joined the *regimento dos nobres* (nobles), the *regimento dos privilegiados* (privileged), or later the *regimento dos úteis* (useful), all of which were considered second-line auxiliaries.[56] The familiares studiously resisted incorporation into the other privileged militia groups and struggled to maintain their sense of exclusiveness.

The first Companhia dos Familiares appeared in Bahia in 1713 under captain Sebastião de Brás de Araújo.[57] This company formed the prototype for all the later companies established in Brazil. The royal confirmation of Sebastião's appointment followed the precedent set in Portugal and excused the company from the jurisdiction of the colonels. As with other militia companies, the officers of the Companhia dos Familiares did not receive a salary, but the crown granted them all of the privileges, honors, exemptions, and liberties inherent in their offices. The companies usually contained a full complement of officers, including lieutenants, ensigns, sergeants, and corporals.

The Companhia dos Familiares also sported a distinctive uniform (see figure 9.4). It adhered generally to the other styles of the times, but their colors were green, red, and white. In 1774, the familiares of Bahia wore a red jacket with green cuffs and a green vest.[58] In 1800, the familiares of Pernambuco dressed in a manner very similar to the company of nobles. They probably

Figure 9.4. Companhia dos Familiares Uniforms, c. 1800. *Source:* Gustavo Barroso and J. Wasth Rodrigues, eds. *Uniformes do exército brasileiro* (Rio de Janeiro, 1922), plates 26 and 29. *Note:* The familiar on the left is from Bahia c. 1798, and the one on the right is from Pernambuco c. 1800.

wore a black top hat with a gold band and a white feather, and a red taper-cut jacket with a green collar, green cuffs, and green lapels studded with brass buttons. The epaulets were red with green and gold trim. White pants, white gaiters, and black boots completed the outfit.[59] The uniform was distinguished and the colors and style distinct enough to set them apart from all of the other companies. It also conformed to the styles of the time and contributed to the Inquisition's desire for respectability and exclusiveness. For many familiares, their militia uniforms represented their most expensive set of clothing. Together with the medallion of office, the uniforms represented a significant outlay of financial resources.

The companies created in Rio and Pernambuco came into being because the familiares refused to be subordinated to regular military officers or to be combined in units with other privileged groups. For example, in the 1720s, the familiares in Rio continued to resist the attempts to enlist them in the companhia dos privilegiados with the "nobility" of Rio on the pretense that they were excused from all military service because of their privileges (which, of course, was no longer true).[60] In response, the governor of Rio in 1724 proposed the creation of a Companhia dos Familiares (with sixty individuals). In 1725, the king ordered the creation of the company and reprimanded the familiares for causing such a scandal when they knew that it was against the law for anyone to be exempt from military service, particularly in times of crisis.[61] As late as 1736, they still debated whether the company should be incorporated into the regimento dos privilegiados or not, which was a frequent cause for conflict in both Portugal and Brazil.[62]

Pernambuco did not establish a company until 1734, when the number of familiares was sufficient to warrant its creation. The primary stimulus for its creation, however, came from the fact that the familiares did not like being subordinated to the colonels of the third-line troops. As with the other companies, the new company remained directly subordinated to the governor, and it was allowed to gather at the gubernatorial palace to await his orders when the company was called into service.[63]

The 1713 order creating the company in Bahia, and a 1743 letter confirming its creation, formed the basis for the organization of the companies in Brazil. These letters were frequently cited by those trying to defend inquisitional privilege.[64] The familiares repeatedly called on these declarations to assert their independence from the regular military, and the crown affirmed this privilege every time it passed a patent of office to a new official in the company.[65]

Governors and military leaders periodically challenged familiares' independence from regular military authority because they wanted to force the familiares to serve in the regular or third-line units. For example, in 1745, the familiares of Olinda and Recife complained that Governor Henrique Luis Pereira Freire forced them to serve in the ordenanças on the pretext that before they were familiares they had been auxiliary soldiers. To make matters worse, he forced them to serve in the same companies as mulattos, mestizos, and other "vile people"(*gente vil*). The crown ordered the governor to respect previous orders relating to the Companhia dos Familiares in Brazil.[66]

Similar problems occurred in Bahia. When soldiers in the ordenança in Bahia became familiares, they wanted to leave the militia and enter the Companhia dos Familiares, arguing that their privileges exempted them from service in the ordenança. The governor, however, would not honor the privilege and ordered them to remain in the militia.[67] The General Council responded to one of these complaints in 1787 and sent a comissário to investigate.[68] The familiar Francisco Pedro Cardoso da Silva made the same complaint in a petition to the overseas council in 1806, but his petition was denied.[69] By that time, inquisitional privilege was becoming increasingly difficult to uphold.

As with the familiares do número, a certain amount of confusion surrounded the companies. For example, in 1746, the governor of Pernambuco tried to re-create a company for privileged men, including the knights of the Order of Christ and other retired officers, that would be subject only to the governor. The overseas council denied his petition because, they said, Recife already had the Companhia dos Familiares, which was a privileged company, and privileged men should join it.[70] This was not strictly in accordance with the previous royal orders and, since we do not have any lists of this company, it is impossible to tell if they were ever included in the Companhia dos Familiares. It seems unlikely, however, because we find references to the regiment of nobles later on, and all of the fifteen officers I have identified of the Companhia dos Familiares were, in fact, familiares.[71]

It is impossible to tell whether all of the familiares actually participated in the company or how many usually served at any one time because we have no lists of the company for Pernambuco; but in 1744, when Roque Antunes Correia was named captain, there were forty familiares enlisted in the company.[72] We also know that, in 1724, sixty familiares served in the company in Rio.[73] The two existing lists for Bahia, however, give us some sense of how large the companies could be and what they did. In 1762, the Companhia dos Familiares in Bahia contained seventy-five familiares and forty-eight adjuncts (*caixeiros* or clerks) of the familiares—eight of the familiares were absent, one was blind, and the caixeiro of the widow of the familiar José Ferreira Bandeira had been ordered by the governor to serve.[74] It is unclear whether the caixeiros normally served in the company or not.

In 1775, the governor of Bahia had the comissário Antônio da Costa de Andrade send a description of each privileged company and the privileges they exercised to the overseas council. In response, Antônio listed all of the privileges the familiares do número enjoyed as if they were not restricted.[75] He then declared that when the company in Bahia had been ordered to prepare for war, they were the first to present themselves for service. They had equipped themselves at their own cost with flags, drums, fifes, and uniforms with red vests and green cuffs. The Companhia dos Familiares in Bahia was also the first to form up for the disembarkation of the bishop of Pernambuco and the first to present itself for guard duties, drills, and marches. Domingos da Costa Braga served in Bahia when the city prepared for an expected Spanish invasion. While still a lieutenant, he enlisted the soldiers, equipped them at his own cost, and drilled them. When the captain was sick for two years, he effectively mounted guard duty while the regular army was dispatched to Rio.[76]

When asked to comment on the usefulness of the familiar company, the comissário claimed that the company was very necessary because of the "infected nation of Negros" and the "gentiles from the coast of Guinea" who abounded in America and who practiced their "barbarous dogmas" full of "abominable deviltries, and witchcraft" and who only respected the Inquisition and their familiares.[77] This declaration came after the elimination of the pure-blood statutes, so the absence of New Christians in the declaration is to be expected. But it also reveals the changing concern of inquisitional officials in the colony toward other forms of religious unorthodoxy as well as the need to justify their own existence.

Questioning the need for the company was tantamount to challenging the necessity of the Inquisition, which could not be justified in military terms—hence, the argument that the company's main purpose was to ensure religious orthodoxy in a heterodox and interracial society.[78] This, of course, was not true because the company in Brazil was never at the disposal of the Inquisition to be used for military purposes but was always subject to the governor. The list of the company from 1775 shows that there were 101 familiares in Salvador—sixty-six of whom served in the company. The others were exempt because they were either ill, serving in one of the other tribunals, or in the regimento dos úteis by choice.[79]

Like the other military organizations in colonial Brazil, the officerships in the company generally went to individuals from high social backgrounds. Of the seven known captains in Pernambuco, one was a knight of the Order of Christ, four were wealthy businessmen, one was a *capitão-mor* (captain major), and one held a bachelor of arts from Coimbra. At least two of the others were considerably wealthy.[80]

The company also resembled other militia companies in their practice of promoting Portuguese immigrants as officers, which sometimes resulted in conflicts. These conflicts show that even though the company provided outward signs of prestige, compensated for lost privileges, and provided a framework for joint action and public manifestations of group identity, the company was not immune from internal conflicts.[81] As we might expect, promotions served as one of the arenas for conflicts within the Companhia dos Familiares. Promotion by seniority was the ideal, but a mixture of "professional and class criteria" frequently came into play.[82]

For example, José Lopes Viana became a familiar in 1780. He was appointed *alferes* (ensign) of the company in Pernambuco in 1795, but had to wait nine years for the formal confirmation. In the meantime, the captain of the company, Manuel Francisco Maciel Monteiro, had been promoted, leaving the position vacant. José expected to be promoted and was offended when the interim governing junta named Joaquim Gomes da Silva e Azevedo. José requested that Joaquim's nomination be annulled because he was not in the direct line of promotion and Joaquim was a "filho de Europa" (a child of Europe) only recently established in Recife with no military experience or service in the company. Joaquim had also served only as the *capitão agregado* (associated captain). These supernumerary captains were appointed, even when no vacancies were available, as prestige titles with no responsibilities, to powerful individuals at a time when military promotions were slow and infrequent. The practice created large numbers of men with military titles who did virtually nothing of a military nature—hence, José argued that Joaquim was not the legitimate successor.

The ex-captain Manuel Francisco Maciel Monteiro wrote in support of José's petition to the overseas council. The overseas council requested the opinion of the interim governors of Pernambuco on the matter. The governors argued that José's petition was "destitute of all purity" (*destituido de toda pureza*), but they studiously avoided engaging his arguments. They simply stated, as they had in their nomination, that Joaquim was a wealthy merchant who had contributed an enormous loan to the royal treasury and supported various charities. As José pointed out, none of that qualified Joaquim to serve as captain of the company, but the overseas council rejected José's petition.[83] They made it clear that promotion was not simply a matter of merit or seniority and that wealthy Portuguese immigrants who willingly contributed funds to local and royal treasuries would continue to be favored by the colonial government to the detriment of native-born Brazilians.[84]

These corporate bodies arrived at a crucial time for the officials of the Inquisition in Brazil. Just as inquisitional privilege came to be limited, the brotherhood and the militia company provided access to lost privileges and an arena for the assertion of prestige and status.

The Inquisition in Brazil could not rely on the autos-da-fé to excite public interest and fear of inquisitional power and to bolster public esteem, because they were held in Lisbon. Yet the monthly drills of the Companhia dos Familiares, the weekly masses, frequent burial services, and yearly celebrations of the brotherhood placed the Inquisition continuously before the public eye and manifested its power and prestige. Together with the whole repertoire of rich symbolism and flamboyant costumes, these organizations allowed the Inquisition to sink deep roots into the urban sectors of Brazilian society where the brotherhoods and militias functioned and to reproduce its power and prestige. They also created the opportunity for inquisitional officials to manifest in public their common identity and dependence on the Inquisition for their status.

The organization of the brotherhood and the militia also permitted a sort of vertical integration that reinforced social hierarchies. Portuguese-born familiares were promoted over native-born familiares in the militia companies. The wealthy and powerful generally held the positions of power and influence in both organizations.

The brotherhood and the militia also provided frequent opportunities for corporate action and a foundation for group identity, which tied each brother's status and prestige to that of his fellows. Participation in the brotherhood could also be very demanding in time and resources—particularly for the elected officials. The rising cost of the celebrations in the late eighteenth century contributed to the growing reluctance of familiares to spend their time and resources in the service of the Inquisition and to the growing lack of interest in appointments.

There was clearly much more to the Inquisition as an institution than the prosecution of accused heretics. We can no longer see the Inquisition only from the perspective of those caught in its clutches. That perspective is certainly valid and important, but it is also one sided. We need to shift our perspective to the men who were, in fact, the Inquisition. Only then can we really see how the Inquisition articulated with the values and interests of Portuguese society and created a symbiotic relationship with individuals and families, giving it the broad social base it needed to withstand reform and challenge for almost three hundred years. When that relationship began to weaken, so did the Inquisition as an institution.

We should also see the transfer of the brotherhood and the militia company to Brazil in the context of the larger European world. The brotherhood arrived in Portugal from Spain when Portugal was subordinate to the Spanish crown (1580–1640). That union permitted a kind of institutional cross-breeding or cross-pollination in which Spanish institutions and forms were adopted by Portugal and remolded to fit Portuguese interests and realities. Many of those institutions, once they had proven their value in Portugal, were later transferred to Brazil, where their form and organization had to be remolded once again to fit a different set of social and historical realities. In that sense, then, the creation and development of the brotherhood of St. Peter Martyr and of the Companhia dos Familiares become, as yet unnoticed, chapters in Portuguese overseas expansion.

The near continuous wrangling over inquisitional privilege also highlights one of the most enduring myths of the Inquisition. Claims are regularly made that the familiares were universally feared—that their very presence struck fear into the hearts of their associates. Often these claims rest on the shaky foundation of accused imposters pleading their case before an inquisitional court.[85] How else does one justify the usurpation of inquisitional power and prestige other than to say that one craved the honor and esteem of the Holy Office? Such accounts should be viewed with guarded skepticism. The ongoing combat to preserve inquisitional privilege and the history of the abuse and falsification of inquisitional authority represent two sides of the same coin. Together they demonstrate that inquisitional officials were feared only in certain contexts. In others, they could be, and were, attacked, challenged, threatened, and ignored as we have already seen. But inquisitional power was real, and it could be appropriated, abused, and subverted.

Notes

1. Irene Silverblatt, *Modern Inquisitions: Peru and the Colonial Origins of the Civilized World*. (Durham: Duke University Press, 2004), 80–81.

2. See A. J. R. Russell-Wood, "Black and Mulatto Brotherhoods in Colonial Brazil: A Study in Collective Behavior," *HAHR* 54, no. 4 (November 1974): 567–602; Julita Scarano, "Black Brotherhoods: Integration or Contradiction?" *LBR* 16, no. 1 (Summer 1979): 1–17; Scarano, *Devoção e escravidão: A Irmandade de Nossa Senhora do Rosário dos pretos no distrito diamantino no século XVIII* (São Paulo: Editora Nacional, 1978); Elizabeth W. Kiddy, "Ethnic and Racial Identity in the Brotherhoods of the Rosary of Minas Gerais, 1700–1830," *Americas* 56, no. 2 (October, 1999): 221–52; Patricia A. Mulvey, "Black Brothers and Sisters: Membership in the Black Lay Brotherhoods of Colonial Brazil," *LBR* 17, no. 2 (Winter 1980): 253–79; Reis, *Death Is a Festival*, 39–65; and Patricia A. Mulvey, "Slave Confraternities in Brazil: Their Role in Colonial Society," *Americas* 39, no. 1 (July 1982): 39–68. See Manoel S. Cardozo, "The Lay Brotherhoods of Colonial Bahia," *Catholic Historical Review* 33, no. 1 (April 1947): 23; Kiddy, "Ethnic and Racial Identity," 231. See also Russell-Wood, *Fidalgos and Philanthropists*; A. J. R. Russell-Wood, "Prestige, Power,

and Piety in Colonial Brazil: The Third Orders of Salvador," *HAHR* 69, no. 1 (February 1989): 61–89; and Caio César Boschi, *Os leigos e o poder: Irmandades leigas e política colonizadora em Minas Gerais* (São Paulo: Editora Ática, 1986).

3. See Herbert Thurston and Donal Attwater, eds. *Butler's Lives of the Saints: Complete Edition*, 4 vols. (New York: Kenedy and Sons, 1956), 2:186–87; Bethencourt, *História das Inquisições*, 93–94; Thurston and Attwater, *Butler's Lives of the Saints*, 3:586–87; ANTT, IL, Livro 155, fols. 444–445; and Thurston and Attwater, *Butler's Lives of the Saints*, 4:693–94. See also ANTT, CGSO, m. 22, no. 65; CGSO, Livro 352, fol. 65, and ANTT, IL, NT 2126.

4. Lea, *History of the Inquisition of Spain*, 2:282–84. The privilege to create a brotherhood was apparently granted in 1530 by Pope Clement VII. See ANTT, CGSO, m. 59.

5. See Bethencourt, *História das Inquisições*, 90.

6. Bethencourt, *História das Inquisições*, 90. For the establishment of the brotherhood in Goa, see ANTT, CGSO, Livro 96, fols. 209–218v, 258–259v. For the Coimbra brotherhood, see BNL, Res., Cod. 1497.

7. I have dealt with this debate elsewhere in James E. Wadsworth, "Celebrating St. Peter Martyr: The Inquisitional Brotherhood in Colonial Brazil," *Colonial Latin American Historical Review* 12, no. 2 (Spring 2003): 173–227.

8. For Bahia, see BNL, Res. 9335. For Olinda and Recife, see ANTT, IL, Livro 154, fol. 26, and Ajuda 5-IV-46, 225–248. For Ouro Preto, Minas Gerais, see ANTT, CGSO, m. 4, no. 12.

9. The only exception to this pattern was the tribunal in Coimbra. See BNL, Cod. 668, F 543, fol. 181. The incomplete records of the Coimbra brotherhood can be found in the ANTT, IC, Livros 94–96, and BNL, Cod. 1497. See José Enrique Pasamar Lázaro, "Inquisición en Aragón: La cofradía de San Pedro Mártir de Verona," *Revista de la Inquisición* 5 (1996): 303–16; Pasamar Lázaro, *La cofradía de San Pedro Mártir de Verona: En el distrito inquisitorial de Aragón* (Zaragoza: Institución Fernando el Católico, 1997); Richard E. Greenleaf, "The Inquisition Brotherhood: Cofradía de San Pedro Mártir of Colonial Mexico," *Americas* 40, no. 2 (October 1983): 171–207.

10. The Lisbon Tribunal used the resources of the Lisbon brotherhood as a reserve account from which it borrowed to meet its own operating costs. See ANTT, IL, Livro 154, fol. 113. Some financial records can be found in ANTT, CGSO, m. 63, and m. 64; IL, NT 2126, 2142–2144, 2148, 2157, 2159, and several of the unnumbered boxes; IL, Livro 158, fols. 158, 161, 169, 219, 226, 233; and IL, m. 1, 6, 7, 11, 14, 29, 35, 41, 42.

11. See ANTT, IL, Livro 154, fol. 113. Some financial records can be found in ANTT, CGSO, m. 63, and m. 64; IL, NT 2126, 2142–2144, 2148, 2157, 2159, and several of the unnumbered boxes; IL, Livro 158, fols. 158, 161, 169, 219, 226, 233; and IL, m. 1, 6, 7, 11, 14, 29, 35, 41, 42.

12. Galende Díaz, "Una aproximación," 64. This is from the 1781 *compromisso* of the brotherhood of the Tribunal of the Corte in Spain.

13. See ANTT, IL, Livro 160, fols. 88–89. When dealing with the brotherhood of Salvador, Bahia, the Tribunal of Lisbon sent correspondence to the senior comissário. See ANTT, IL, Livro 157, fols. 36–37. The comissário from Minas, Manuel Freire Batalho, who wrote about the brotherhood to the Lisbon Tribunal, was also probably the senior comissário in Ouro Preto. See ANTT, CGSO, m. 4, fol. 12. He received his appointment as comissário in 1730. See ANTT, HSO, Manuel, m. 98, no. 1820. The same system was also used in Madeira. Madeira clearly had a brotherhood before 1779, when a comissário requested to be appointed as the president so that he could reorganize the celebrations of the cult and have the two familiares that used to organize it be elected in the old manner. See ANTT, CGSO, m. 66.

14. The Tribunal of Coimbra held its elections on the first Friday in March. See BNL, Cod. 1497, fols. 2–2v.

15. ANTT, CGSO, m. 59.

16. See ANTT, CGSO, m. 59, and ANTT, IC, Livro 94.

17. ANTT, IL, Livro 160, fols. 87–89.

18. Greenleaf, "Inquisition Brotherhood," shows that the brotherhood in Mexico accumulated vast amounts of wealth.

19. Reis, *Death Is a Festival*, 53–54.

20. See Francisco Bethencourt, "Inquisição e controle social," *História e crítica* 14 (1987): 13.

21. ANTT, IL, Livro 157, fols. 36–37; ANTT, IL, Livro 160, fols. 87–89, 102–104.

22. Ajuda 5-iv-46. In Bahia, they held the celebrations in the church of the convent of St. Benedict until 1792, when they moved to the church of the Third Order of St. Dominic. See ANTT, IL, Livro 160, fols. 102–104.

23. Only four sermons given at these festivals survive—two from Portugal and two from Brazil: Oporto, 1620, see BNL, Res. 3024, 18p; Lisbon, 1686, see BNL, Res. 3024, 18p; Bahia, 1697, see BNL, Res. 9335; Pernambuco, 1758, see Ajuda, 5-IV-46.

24. See George Ferguson, *Signs and Symbols in Christian Art* (London: Oxford University Press, 1961), 115.

25. Ferguson, *Signs and Symbols*, 139.

26. ANTT, CGSO, m. 59. The triple crown with a cross on the top (called the tiara) is worn only by the pope. But the triple crown without the cross is used by other saints. When used with a martyr, it indicates victory over sin and death. See Ferguson, *Signs and Symbols*, 160, 166.

27. ANTT, CGSO, m. 59.

28. For a discussion of inquisitional iconography, see Bethencourt, *História das Inquisições*, 78–89.

29. See Siqueira, "Os Regimentos da Inquisição, 758, 899 (1640 Regimento, Book I, Title XXI, Paragraph 3; 1774 Regimento, Book I, Title IX, Paragraph 3).

30. One also survives from Bahia. See BNL, Res. 9335, *Sermam do Glorioso S. Pedro Martyr* . . . (Lisbon: António Pedrozo Galrão, 1697).

31. Antônio de Santa Maria Jaboatão, *Orbe Serafico novo Brasilico Descoberto* . . . (Lisbon: António Vicente da Silva, 1761). A copy of the orbe serafica can be found in ANTT, Serie Preta 907. Jaboatão, *Catalogo genealogico*.

32. Ajuda, 5-IV-46, *Jaboataõ Mystico em correntes sacras dividido* . . . (Lisbon: António Vicente da Silva, 1758).

33. See Higgs, "Á recepção da revolução francesa," and James E. Wadsworth, "Joaquim Marques de Araújo: O poder da inquisição em Pernambuco no fim do período colonial," in *De Cabral a Pedro I: Aspectos da colonização Portuguesa no Brasil*, ed. Maria Beatriz Nizza da Silva (Porto: Humbertipo, 2001), 309–28.

34. For a description of the 1615 celebration in Goa, see ANTT, CGSO, Livro 96, fols. 213v–214v. For the 1624 celebration in Goa, see ANTT, CGSO, Livro 96, fols. 258–259v.

35. ANTT, IL, Livro 160, fols. 87–89.

36. This requirement is found at the end of chapter 10 of the *Compromisso*, which dealt with the festival of St. Peter Martyr. See ANTT, CGSO, m. 59.

37. ANTT, IL, Livro 154, fol. 26.

38. ANTT, IL, Livro 323 and Livro 124.

39. ANTT, IL, Livro 158, fols. 152–154.

40. ANTT, CGSO, m. 22, no. 65, and CGSO, Livro 352, fol. 65; See also ANTT, CGSO, m. 66.

41. Russell-Wood, "Prestige, Power, and Piety," 66.

42. ANTT, IL, Livro 160, fols. 117–118. See also ANTT, IL, NT 2127.

43. ANTT, IL, Livro 160, fols. 87–89. Men still applied to serve St. Peter Martyr. See ANTT, HSO, Jacinto, m. 6, no. 76; José, m. 103, no. 1465; Manuel, m. 227, no. 1362; NH, cx. 39.

44. ANTT, CGSO, NT 4147. It is possible that something along these lines had occurred in 1639, but it is not clear. See ANTT, IL, Livro, 151, fol. 340. The crown also exacted a levy on horses at the same time. See AHM, 1st division, 2nd section, "Companhas da Guerra da Restauração," Azul 76, no. 20, cx. 1.

45. ANTT, IL, Livro 151, fol. 533. Pope Pius V issued a bull entitled *Sacrosantae romanae et universali Ecclesiae* in 1570, which noted that the familiares (called *crocesignati* in Italy) had been formed into a company to act as inquisitional auxiliaries. See Bethencourt, *História das Inquisições*, 90. The companies never served that purpose in Portugal or Brazil.

46. ANTT, CGSO, NT 4147; ANTT, IL, Livro 151, fol. 521.

47. BNL, Cod. 641, fols. 521, 533; ANTT, CGSO, NT 4147. The inquisitor general described how the company functioned in Lisbon in the early eighteenth century. See ANTT, CGSO, NT 4151 and 4147; BNL, Cod. 749, fols. 20–20v; ANTT, MNEJ, Livro 5, fols. 14v–15v; and AHM, 1st division, 2nd section, cx. 2, no. 58.

48. ANTT, CGSO, NT 4147. They also discussed the possibility of creating two companies, one for the old and sick and another for those capable of service. See ANTT, CGSO, NT 4147; ANTT, MNEJ, Livro 5, fol. 13v.

49. AHU, Rio de Janeiro, cx. 15, doc. 75.

50. ANTT, CGSO, Livro 381, fol. 30v, and AHU, Bahia, cx. 48, doc. 8869, 8905.

51. These privileges were ratified periodically by royal declarations. See AHM, 1st division, 2nd section, cx. 2, no. 58.

52. AHM, 1st division, 2nd section, cx. 2, no. 58.

53. This is a constant theme in Hendrik Kraay's work. See Kraay, *Race, State, and Armed Forces in Independence-Era Brazil: Bahia, 1790s–1840s* (Stanford: Stanford University Press, 2001).

54. See Caio Prado Jr., *Formação do Brasil contemporâneo: Colônia* (São Paulo: Livraria Martins Editora, 1942), 308–11; F. W. O. Morton, "The Military and Society in Bahia, 1800–1821," *JLAS* 7, no. 2 (1975): 250; Gustavo Barroso and J. Wasth Rodrigues, eds., *Uniformes do exército brasileiro* (Rio de Janeiro: n.p., 1922), 5–8; Aliatar Loreto, *Capítulos de história militar do Brasil (Colônia-Reino)* (Rio de Janeiro: Edifício do Ministério da Guerra, 1945), 11–19; Cecília Maria Westphalen, "A milícia da comarca de Paranaguá e Curitiba," in *De Cabral a Pedro I: Aspectos da colonização portuguesa no Brasil*, ed. Maria Beatriz Nizza da Silva (Porto: Humbertipo, 2001), 329–36.

55. AHM, 1st division, 2nd section, cx. 2, no. 58.

56. Catherine Lugar mistakenly assumes that the Companhia dos Familiares is incorporated into the regimento dos úteis. See Lugar, "Merchant Community," 218.

57. AHU, Pernambuco, cx. 48, doc. 4303. I thank Luiz Mott for providing some of the initial leads on the company in Brazil. See Mott, "A Companhia dos Familiares do Santo Ofício no Brasil (notas preliminares)" (unpublished manuscript; Salvador, 1989).

58. AHU, Bahia, cx. 48, doc. 8870/8906. See Barroso and Rodrigues, *Uniformes do exército brasileiro*, 29.

59. This description is based on an artist's rendition from Barroso and Rodrigues, *Uniformes do exército brasileiro*, plate 25. The style of coat without tails and the top hat may come from a later period, but the colors and style are generally accurate.

60. AHU, Rio de Janeiro, cx. 13, doc. 146.

61. AHU, Rio de Janeiro, cx. 15, doc. 75.

62. AHU, Rio de Janeiro cx. 32, doc. 104.

63. AHU, Pernambuco, cx. 48, doc. 4303.

64. AHU, Bahia, cx. 179, doc. 19.

65. There are several examples of these patents in the AHU. See AHU, Bahia, cx. 161, doc. 22; AHU, Pernambuco, cx. 105, doc. 8122; AHU, Pernambuco, cx. 106, doc. 8203. Several can also be found in the APEJE. See APEJE, P.p., Codice 8, fol. 23v; P.p., Cod. 8, fol. 45v; P.p., Cod. 8, fol. 178v; P.p., Cod. 8, fol. 179; P.p., Cod. 10, fol. 20v; P.p., Cod. 10, fol. 150; P.p. Cod. 12, fol. 113.

66. ANTT, CGSO, Livro 381, fol. 168.

67. ANTT, CGSO, NT 4152.

68. ANTT, CGSO, NT 4152.

69. AHU, Bahia, cx. 238, doc. 70.

70. AHU, Pernambuco, cx. 62, doc. 5347.

71. See AHU, Pernambuco, cx. 105, doc. 8165; cx. 107, doc. 8298; and cx. 109, doc. 8467.

72. ANTT, Mercês, D. João V, Livro 34, fol. 446.

73. AHU, Rio de Janeiro, cx. 15, doc. 75.
74. AHU, Bahia, cx. 32, docs. 5954–5963.
75. AHU, Bahia, cx. 48, docs. 8863–8899 and 8901–8911.
76. ANTT, Mercês, D. Maria I, Livro 16, fol. 93, and AHU, Bahia, cx. 182, doc. 19.
77. AHU, Bahia, cx. 48, docs. 8865 and 8875.
78. The discussion in these documents apparently led Catherine Lugar to conclude, incorrectly, that "by the end of the eighteenth century . . . it [the company] was little more than an antiquated honor society." Lugar, "Merchant Community," 218.
79. AHU, Bahia, cx. 48, docs. 8875 and 8911.
80. See AHU, Pernambuco, cx. 48, doc. 4303; ANTT Mercês, D. José I, Livro 23, fol. 419; ANTT Mercês, D. Maria I, Livro 16, fol. 78v; AHU Pernambuco, cx. 210, doc. 14307.
81. Promotion based on merit became an issue in Bahia as well. See AHU, Bahia cx. 152, doc. 66.
82. Kraay, *Race, State, and Armed Forces*, 84–87.
83. AHU, Pernambuco, cx. 191, doc. 13211; Pernambuco, cx. 215, doc. 14547; Pernambuco, cx. 239, doc. 16077; Pernambuco, cx. 249, doc. 16702; Pernambuco, cx. 210, doc. 14307.
84. These conflicts were frequent in the colonial military. See Morton, "Military and Society," 254–57, 264–66.
85. Calainho, "En Nome do Santo Ofício," 149.

CHAPTER TEN

~

Impostors, Abusers, and Obstructers

In March or April 1593, Belquior Mendes de Azevedo visited the home of the New Christian Tomás Lopes and made him swear never to reveal the secret he would tell him. Belquior had just returned from Bahia, where the inquisitor Heitor Furtado de Mendonça was holding an inquisitional court and where Belquior had denounced the New Christians of Recife for Judaizing. Belquior informed Tomás that the inquisitor had given him orders to take Tomás prisoner for crimes against the Inquisition. But, if Tomás would give him a barrel of wine and ten cruzados, he would tear up the orders right away.

When Tomás asked what the crimes were, Belquior said he was accused of Judaizing and traveling through the village with one bare foot tied with a dishrag to signal the Jews to gather and to give him the money to pay for the Jewish lamps. Tomás replied that he had neither wine, money, nor guilt, and Belquior went away, but returned two more times with the same declaration. When he discovered that Tomás would not give in to his demands, he threatened to take him to Bahia in chains. In desperation, Tomás went to the Jesuit college and told the rector, Henrique Mendes, that he would hang himself with a rope if Belquior returned to his home, and he begged the rector to get Belquior to leave him alone. The Jesuit did so, and Belquior did not return.

But the damage had been done. When the inquisitor arrived in Pernambuco in 1593, Tomás denounced Belquior, who at first denied the accusation, but eventually admitted what he had done. Belquior was punished in the auto-da-fé held in Olinda on September 9, 1595. His sentence included confessions once a month for a year in which he had to recite the penitential psalm of David three times, fasting every Wednesday, on which day he had to hear mass, and paying the costs of his trial.[1]

This is the first known case of a fake official in Pernambuco. Not all unwitting victims were as fortunate as Tomás; nor did all impostors get off so easy as Belquior. But the general dynamics remained the same. The mechanisms that the Inquisition put in place to attract the highest quality individuals and provide them with the prestige, honor, and status necessary to retain their continued support and reproduce their own power and prestige often backfired. The potential prestige, status, honor, and power of inquisitional office attracted impostors and abusers of inquisitional authority drawn by a desire for the personal advantages such power offered. Inquisitional power and prestige were real, and they could be subverted. The potential power of inquisitional authority in personal affairs proved too tempting for both officials and non-officials alike. But most frequently, the abuse or falsification of inquisitional authority had very limited objectives, such as gaining advantage in a personal conflict, obtaining protection from arrest or prosecution, or extorting money. Most cases involved a single event, and few impostors or abusers of inquisitional authority possessed the wherewithal to maintain the fraud for long periods of time.

In all cases, the Inquisition could not countenance abuse, fraud, or interference in the inquisitional process and sought to restrict such activity. These cases reveal both the extent and the limits of inquisitional power. That it could be used for temporary personal advantage in cases where people feared to challenge the false authority, even though they may have perceived it as such, shows how very real and powerful that authority could be. While at the same time, the fact that these abuses were denounced, prosecuted, and punished by the Inquisition demonstrates that the Inquisition was serious about controlling the use of inquisitional power. The fine line between the zealous official and the corrupt or fake official, however, was not always distinguishable to those caught up in inquisitional or pseudo-inquisitional activity. And the existence of abuse and false authority only contributed to the sense of the arbitrary and destructive nature of inquisitional power. It also provided much of the fodder for the myth of the universally powerful and feared familiar of the Inquisition. This chapter demonstrates the paradox of inquisitional power as wielded by its agents. This power was indeed real and could be threatening, but it was also banked and constrained by both internal and external forces.

Far from being untouchables, officials were denounced for a variety of crimes. Most frequently, these crimes included some form of abuse of their authority or obstructing the work of the Inquisition, but they were also denounced for heretical propositions, solicitation, freemasonry, and homicide.

Inquisitional Regulations for the Control of Impostors, Abusers, and Obstructers

From the Inquisition's perspective, all those who abused its authority, obstructed its work, or impersonated its officials diminished the authority, power, prestige, and good name of the Inquisition. The problem began soon after the creation of the Inquisition in Portugal and continued to grow as the number and popularity of inquisitional appointments increased.[2] The 1613 Regimento attempted to deal with the problem and declared that the misbehavior of officials should be reported to the Inquisition; but it did not discuss the matter in any detail.[3] The 1640 Regimento, however, rectified that problem. The regimento broke down offenders into two main categories—those who obstructed or disturbed the ministry of the Inquisition and those who impersonated ministers and officials of the Inquisition.

Obstructing or disturbing the ministry included insulting or offending inquisitional officials, threatening or intimidating witnesses, stealing and destroying inquisitional documents, helping prisoners escape, prohibiting officials from carrying weapons or carrying out diligências, refusing to obey orders of the Inquisition, revealing inquisitional secrets, and bribing inquisitional officials. The penalties for these behaviors were harsh. Besides excommunication *ipso facto*, they were to be whipped, banished to the galleys, and given any other punishments the inquisitors saw fit. Officials who engaged in any of these practices could lose their office and suffer any of the above penalties, unless they were clerics.

Impersonating an official included falsifying an order from the Inquisition, pretending to have some secret pertaining to the Holy Office, taking prisoners in the name of the Holy Office without orders, and pretending to have some crime to denounce to the Inquisition. If the criminal was a commoner, he would be whipped and banished. If he was a person of "quality," then he would only be banished. Both had to pay back anything they had extorted, and in some cases double what they had taken.[4] The 1774 Regimento abridged the discussion of crimes and their punishments somewhat but did not change the essential intent or meaning. It added a warning to bishops who created regulations that disturbed the ministry of the Holy Office, and it diminished the harshness of the punishments. The crimes, however, remained essentially the same.[5]

Abuse of Authority

Abuse of inquisitional authority manifested itself in a variety of ways. Most often, it involved officials who attempted to use their authority for personal gain or for protection from other powerful individuals. Officials were accused of revealing inquisitional secrets, falsifying orders, taking prisoners without orders, mistreating prisoners, extorting money, and a variety of other crimes.

As might be expected, one of the greatest temptations for someone who possessed the power to imprison and confiscate property was to extort money from persons who had reason to fear the Inquisition. For example, in Portugal in 1709, Francisco Lopes Sarafana accepted money from people he had been sent to imprison for the purpose of keeping it safe and dividing it up between himself and the prisoners later on. He even diverted some of the confiscated goods to his own pocket during the taking of the inventory. As a consequence, he lost his carta and never got it back.[6] In 1736, the guard of the inquisitional prison in Évora was whipped and sent to the galleys for ten years for taking money to help prisoners communicate with their families.[7] In Pernambuco, Francisco de Sales Gorjão was accused of selling inquisitional secrets to Friar José Maria de Jesus.[8] Sometimes officials took advantage of the vulnerable position of their prisoners. For instance, in 1706, José do Vale was reprimanded for mistreating a female prisoner by pinching and whipping her.[9]

Comissários could also use their authority to strong-arm potential witnesses into providing the denunciations they desired. For example, Francisco Inácio da Cunha, second lieutenant of the artillery company of Recife, complained to the Inquisition in 1787 that the comissário Henrique Martins Gaio had extorted his denunciation of Bernardo Luís Ferreira Portugal. He claimed that Henrique came to his quarters and asked him if he knew that Bernardo Luís had made heretical statements. Francisco at first denied that he had, then finally admitted that he had heard some vague rumors about the matter, but he did not remember to whom they referred. The comissário insisted that he write them down right then, even though Henrique did not have his scribe with him. Francisco mentioned this lapse to Henrique, who replied that he had authority to perform extrajudicial inquiries and that Francisco's only duty was to obey.

Without further argument, Francisco took up the pen; and Henrique began to dictate to him what to write. The first words, "I denounce" caused Francisco to pause, and he told Henrique that he could not denounce the priest because he had nothing to denounce. Henrique replied with great anger that he was not really denouncing but only informing and that it was necessary to begin in this way. Francisco informed the Lisbon Tribunal that, at the time, he could not believe that such a venerable comissário would work evil in a matter of such consequence, so he set aside his scruples and wrote what Henrique dictated to him. Although, as far as I know, Henrique was never formally reprimanded for this behavior, the diligência against Bernardo Luís was eventually discontinued.[10]

Abuse of inquisitional authority could be even more overt. For example, in 1710, Second Lieutenant Luís Barradas de Sá denounced the comissário Antônio Correia Paz from Alagoas for abuse of authority. A small group had gathered at some property that the local judge was going to turn over to Antônio Correia Paz. Antônio had a long-standing conflict with some members of the group who contested the land possession, and a heated debate arose between Antônio and Luís. During the argument, Luís raised his cane and gesticulated, saying that if Antônio took the land in this manner there would be an effusion of "blood and entrails." This declaration sent Antônio into a frenzy of anger. He cried in a loud voice for the judge to arrest Luís Barradas de Sá for crimes against the Inquisition—presumably for threatening an official of the Inquisition. The judge ordered two of his men to take Luís prisoner, and they did so, grabbing hold of his reins and saddle. Antônio then produced his letter of appointment and read it to the crowd in a loud voice. Luís, who was still on horseback, shouted that he had not committed any crimes against the Inquisition and, jerking himself free, fled. The officials pursued but could not catch him. Later, Antônio obtained a warrant for his arrest, called witnesses, and began an inquiry of his own accord.[11]

The Inquisition sent the comissário Bartolomeu de Pilar to investigate the accusation of abuse of authority in 1717. He indicated that some of the witnesses stumbled over their words and feigned having forgotten so as not to incriminate themselves. Unfortunately, we do not know how far Antônio went with his inquiry against Luís; nor do we know whether Antônio was ever reprimanded or punished by the Inquisition. Nonetheless, this case shows that some officials were willing to employ inquisitional power in their personal conflicts. Whether they managed to do so over the long term or not, they were successful in the short run in disarming potential opponents and complicating personal rivalries.

False orders from the Inquisition could also be used as a protection in personal conflicts. For example, the familiar Antônio Raposo Cordeiro had taken his oath in 1783 from Joaquim Marques de Araújo at the age of eleven. He later fled to Lisbon from Recife without a passport because he had mistreated his wife and his in-laws. In the spring of 1797, Antônio Raposo encountered an impressment gang in Lisbon who wanted to impress him into military service. He told them that he was a familiar and showed them his carta, telling them that he was engaged in the work of the Inquisition and ordered them to accompany him. They followed him to Manuel Ferreira da Silva's confectioner's shop, where they arrived at 10:00 p.m. Antônio flashed a folded piece of paper he said was his carta and ordered Manuel to put on his cloak and accompany him on an errand for the Inquisition. When Manuel asked to see the orders from the Inquisition, Antônio told him that he would show him in his own due time. The soldiers, seeing that he was recognized as a familiar by another familiar, let him go and went their own way. Antônio then told Manuel that he was no longer needed and left the shop.

Antônio claimed to have realized that what he had done was wrong, and so he went to the inquisitional palace the next day to confess his crimes. The doorkeeper turned him away because he was not dressed appropriately to see the inquisitors and told him to come back the next day dressed more appropriately. Antônio did not return because he took ill and spent a long time in the hospital.

The inquisitors did not think that his confession was complete, and they gave him several opportunities to make it so. He insisted that he did not have anything else to confess, and the inquisitors determined that he had failed to indicate his real intention. They declared that he had purposely disturbed the good order of the Inquisition and used its authority for his own personal interests. So they stripped him of his carta and banished him from Portugal.[12]

Antônio's case not only demonstrates the limits of the legitimate use of inquisitional authority, but it also reveals one of the problems with appointing young boys as familiares. During his trial, Antônio told the inquisitors that he was only eleven at the time he had taken his oath, and he could not remember anything it contained. Since he was not permitted to carry out diligências until he reached his majority, he had had little opportunity to learn how to use that authority properly. These cases show that the misuse of inquisitional authority could be either a premeditated, deliberate act or a random knee-jerk response to threatening situations in which the official reached out to the most powerful authority at his command to protect himself or to further his own interests.

Impostors

Those who impersonated inquisitional officials, usurped inquisitional authority, or disturbed the ministry of the Inquisition also came in a variety of forms. There were the extortionists, such as Belquior Mendes (mentioned previously) and the parish priest in Recife who took two people prisoner in the name of the Holy Office and released them after they gave him money.[13] And there were also the small-time usurpers, such as the slave owner José Valeiro de Magalhães, who imprisoned his own slave Francisco Chamba for witchcraft, which he said the slave confessed to after "rigorous punishment."[14]

Sometimes the crimes could be quite sinister. For example, Baltasar Coelho took two prisoners from Pernambuco in 1611 in the name of the Inquisition, placed them in irons, confiscated their property, and took them to Lisbon. The prisoners claimed to have received irreparable damage to their persons and their property, and Baltasar received two years in the galleys and fifty lashes throughout the streets of Lisbon.[15]

The Inquisition could also be used as a cloak for attempted murder and revenge. For example, somewhere in the interior of Pernambuco near Minas Gerais, a man appeared at the home of Captain Major Garcia Rodrigues Pais on March 21, 1724, to ask for assistance as a familiar of the Holy Office in carrying out orders to imprison some criminals who had committed crimes against the Inquisition. The captain major gave the man seven slaves and some armed Carijó Indians to help him, but ordered them not to kill anyone, only to take them prisoner. They hid themselves along the caminho das minas (path to the mines) and waited. Eventually, Antônio de Araújo and his wife Rosa Maria came along. The false familiar ordered the men to kill Antônio and all his slaves, but to bring Rosa to him.

The slaves refused to kill the travelers and instead took them prisoner and led them back to their owner. When the captain major and his son heard their slaves' story, the son, Fernando Dias Paes, asked to see the medallion of office and the orders of imprisonment. The fake familiar tried to avoid the difficulty by claiming that he had not brought them with him. But he finally confessed, and Fernando learned that the fake familiar was none other than the priest Dionísio de Almeida da Costa, who had once robbed Rosa Maria and was now seeking revenge because Antônio owed him money but would not pay. Antônio and Rosa were released, and Dionísio spent twenty-two months in prison in Rio before going to Lisbon, where he was sentenced to five years' banishment to the Algarve in 1728.[16]

Few impostors managed to maintain the façade for very long, but Januário de São Pedro was a special case.[17] Januário began his career as an impostor in Quito (in modern Ecuador) in 1736. He was a professed lay brother of the Dominican order in the convent of Qualquil and wanted to become a priest. So he forged a letter from his prelate stating that any bishop could ordain him. He then fled to Lima and stayed in the convent São João Baptista, where he was treated as a priest for several months. Finally, he took his forged letter and presented it to the archbishop of Lima. When he realized that the archbishop was indisposed to ordain him, he fled to Chile, fearful that his fraud had been discovered.

In Santiago, he roomed with Friar José Iguareta for several months. When José left the convent for a time, leaving his papers of ordination and several letters of recommendation behind, Januário took advantage of the opportunity, stole the papers, and fled across the Andes to Tucumán. When he arrived in Tucumán, he found that the bishop had already heard of his forgery and had been ordered to punish him and return him to his convent. So Januário kept on moving until he reached Buenos Aires. Then he crossed the Río de la Plata to the Portuguese settlement of Nova Colônia do Sacramento, where he assumed the name Friar José Iguareta and falsified an order from Rome that he was to be the procurator general of the Dominican order. He stayed in Nova Colônia, saying mass, hearing confession, and baptizing until he finally took a ship for Bahia as a chaplain.

When he reached Bahia, he presented himself to the archbishop, who, assuming that he was the José Iguareta of the letters, gave him leave to execute all the functions of a priest in the archbishopric. After four months, Januário left Bahia on the pretext of going to Recife, where he hoped to catch a ship to Lisbon. His ship stopped in Sergipe, where he spent several months traveling around to all the parishes with a portable altar, performing all the sacraments, and collecting alms for a hospice that he said would be built.

While traveling in the interior of Sergipe on the border of Alagoas, he heard about the use of an amulet, called *breve da marea*, that had been distributed by Italian Capuchin monks in large numbers and was supposed to protect the wearer from any kind of weapon. These amulets were being sold for very high prices in the interior. On one occasion, Januário came upon a crowd of people surrounding a dog that had one of these amulets tied around his neck. The people in the crowd were arguing about whether or not they should shoot the dog to see if the amulet really worked. Januário saw the opportunity and declared to the crowd that he was a comissário of the Inquisition and that he had been sent to collect all of the amulets. The people gave him the amulets, which he turned around and resold for a profit.

After passing through several Indian villages in Minas Gerais and the interior of Pernambuco, Januário decided to go to Olinda to ask the bishop to send more priests to instruct the Indians. The bishop refused to meet with him, however, because he had heard of his escapades. Januário then turned toward Bahia again, and he stopped at an engenho whose owner gave him the habit of a familiar and the medallion of gold, both of which had belonged to the familiar João de Aguiar, as alms. He began wearing the medallion around his neck, acting alternatively as a comissário, a qualificador, and a familiar.

While he was in Pernambuco, the priest Francisco Ferreira received orders from the bishop to take Januário prisoner, but Januário had already escaped to Bahia. Despite these attempts to stop him, it became widely believed among the residents of the Sertão that he was a comissário, and he began taking denunciations, swearing in witnesses, and acting as if he were investigating crimes against the Inquisition.

While carrying on in this manner in the border regions of Pernambuco and Bahia, he received a denunciation that a man named João de Souza Pereira had whipped an image of Christ. He ordered a large crowd to follow him in the name of the Holy Office and went to arrest João. Januário took him, confiscated all of his goods, and made an inventory, which revealed a large quantity of money, slaves, pigs, cloth, and gold. Januário started moving toward Salvador, Bahia, to deliver João to a real comissário, using the confiscated goods to pay for the trip. A cousin of João de Souza Pereira tried to liberate him with the help of a cavalry lieutenant, but when they saw the twenty-five to thirty people who accompanied Januário, they desisted.

En route, Januário ordered several people to accompany him in the name of the Holy Office, one of whom was a local schoolteacher. The schoolteacher hid, and Januário went after him with his crowd of followers. They captured him and forced him to accompany them; but after another three leagues, the schoolteacher escaped and Januário pursued him again. They recaptured him and took him to a nearby engenho and held an "inquisitional" court. Januário formally excommunicated the man and condemned him to stand nude in the local church in front of the entire congregation for three consecutive Holy Days. He then let him go with the provision that the parish priest would inform him when the man had completed his sentence. He also sent out various orders of excommunication in the name of the Inquisition to be posted on the doors of the churches.

Januário continued on with his prisoner toward Bahia, but realizing that he did not have much of a case against him, he fabricated evidence and made people sign a sworn statement in support of the false evidence. When Januário finally arrived at a port where he could take ship to Bahia, then seven leagues distant, he found that the boats were not ready to leave. He ordered some boatmen in the name of the Holy Office to take him and his company to Bahia, which they immediately did.

Upon arriving in Salvador at 11:00 p.m., Januário delivered the prisoner, what money there was left from what he had confiscated, and the several sworn statements, including the falsified one, to the comissário Antônio

Rodrigues. The comissário sent him to deliver the prisoner to the prison in the Jesuit College. Two days later, the governor sent soldiers to arrest Januário and put him in the same prison with the man he had brought in from the interior. Januário apparently confessed to the archbishop and then decided to escape. He leapt from a window of the college and broke an arm and a leg in the fall.

His luck having run out for the time being, he was shipped to Lisbon, where he was condemned to ten years in the king's galleys—which amounted to a death sentence—and was prohibited from ever becoming a priest. After three years of galley service, he petitioned to have his sentence considered fulfilled because his health was so poor that he could no longer row in the galleys. Two physicians certified that he had a high fever, a bloated belly, a dislocated shoulder, and a broken leg. The Lisbon Tribunal relented and sent him to a convent in Elvas, Portugal, until it could decide his case. On October 23, 1745, the tribunal decreed that he was to be banished from all the Portuguese dominions, anywhere in the world, forever. On October 25, however, the abbot of the Elvas convent wrote a letter to the Lisbon Tribunal stating that Januário had fled the convent, and they had no idea where he might have gone. The ever-resourceful Januário made good his escape, and as far as can be told was never heard from again—although it seems likely that he probably slipped across the border to Spain and continued his career as a fake priest.

Januário's case paradoxically reveals both the strength and weaknesses of the Inquisition in colonial Brazil. In the interior, the population was accustomed to wandering priests and pious men and women who filled the void left by a thin force of priests who often had responsibility for more than one parish. Januário found his escapades more readily accepted in this milieu of popular religiosity and uneducated, "prattling storytellers"—as one priest put it. Those who tried to resist him were either confounded by the fear that he might just be what he said he was or by the fear of the followers he had gathered. The vast interior gave him ample opportunity to avoid those officials with authority to check him. He was also a novelty to the inhabitants of the interior, who seldom if ever saw a minister of the Holy Office, who readily denounced all that they knew to him, and who for the most part submitted to his false authority. Paradoxically, the fact that he was able to impersonate an inquisitional official for so long speaks to the sparseness of ecclesiastical and of royal authority in the vast, thinly populated interior. At the same time, the fact that he was obeyed by so many, even those who suspected his falsehood, for fear of offending the Inquisition shows that the Inquisition held real power over the hearts and minds of men and women, even in the remote interior.

The tribunal in Lisbon determined that Januário's real purpose had been to embarrass the Inquisition and to cause others to engage in heresy. It is more likely, however, that he was simply an opportunist who found that, once he had crossed the line of legal and legitimate behavior, there was no turning back. By faking not only ecclesiastical but also inquisitional authority, he was able to roam the interior, where few individuals had the influence or power to oppose him.

Not all impostors were so bold or so long lived. The vicar general of the bishopric of Pernambuco, Francisco da Fonseca, found inquisitional power useful in carrying out his designs, and the protection of the bishop could be sufficient to defer punishment for so doing. The case involved the imprisonment of the priest Isidro de Casio in 1698.[18] Isidro had fallen afoul of the bishop for some unknown reason, and when he arrived in Olinda from the Sertão, the bishop ordered him incarcerated in the public prison. When Isidro appeared before the bishop and the bishop ordered him back to the public prison, Isidro protested that as a priest he should be held in the prison of one of the convents in the city and not in the public prison. The bishop replied that there were no convents of his order and sent him back to the public prison. When Isidro and his guards reached the last step of the bishop's palace, Isidro broke away and fled to the cathedral, but he found the doors shut. The bishop's guard caught Isidro, and they began to struggle. The scribe Antônio de Amorim de Lima, who had gone to tell the bishop, arrived with the bishop while the men still struggled at the doors of the cathedral. The bishop ordered Isidro to deliver himself up, but Isidro declared that he would not recognize the bishop's authority and punched the guard with great force. At this point, the scribe moved to help the guard, and they managed to throw Isidro to the ground. The scribe sat on top of him and tried to tie his hands. Isidro drew a hidden knife and stabbed the scribe in the thigh, and then, leaping to his feet, he fled to the convent of São Francisco with the knife still in his hand. Seeing the bloody knife in his hands, no one tried to stop him.

The acting prelate of the convent, Friar Gabriel da Anunciação, placed Isidro in prison for safekeeping. A little while later, Vicar General Francisco da Fonseca, the vicar Antônio da Silva, and several other servants of the bishop of Pernambuco burst into the convent, brandishing naked swords and yelling that Friar Gabriel should deliver Isidro to them. A company of soldiers encircled the convent. The acting prelate refused the demand, claiming that he could not do so until the real prelate returned. The vicar general then demanded that he deliver Friar Isidro to him because he had committed crimes against the Inquisition. When the prelate heard this, he called for

Isidro and told him what the vicar general had said. When Isidro had heard that the Inquisition wanted him, he freely delivered himself up.

These actions were denounced to the Inquisition, which sent the Jesuit rector Felipe Coelho to perform an investigation. Felipe Coelho found that some of the Franciscans he had questioned informed the vicar general of the inquiry, and the bishop sent an agent to keep track of his activities. Consequently, Felipe had to postpone the investigation until a more appropriate time. He finally sent what he managed to gather to the Inquisition, and the inquisitional prosecutor recommended that the vicar general be called to Lisbon and punished in accordance with the regimento. In the meantime, the bishop had sent a letter in support of the vicar general to the Inquisition, and the inquisitors decided not to prosecute. Not only had an ecclesiastical official falsely claimed inquisitional jurisdiction, but also the bishop had successfully intervened in an investigation.

Interference and Obstruction of Authority and Privilege

As in the case of Friar Isidro, ecclesiastical officials sometimes forcefully interfered in the inquisitional investigations. Most frequently, their interference was tied to disputes over privilege and jurisdiction. Conflicts with bishops were frequent. As each new bishop sought to establish his authority, the existing inquisitional officials found that they had to defend their privileges against attacks. Some bishops caused more trouble than others. For example, in 1760 the recently appointed bishop of Pernambuco, Francisco Xavier Aranha, ordered the notário Inácio Ribeiro Maio to assume the office of parish priest of the newly created parish of Nova Vila de Soure.[19] Soure was one of the old Jesuit missions that had recently been abandoned when the Jesuits were expelled in 1759. Inácio excused himself "with all due submission" because "curing souls" was "repugnant" to him and because he was an officer of the Inquisition and could not be forced to accept any position against his will. Indeed, he had never sought a position as a parish priest, even though many had come open where he lived, and there were many priests in the area who wanted to serve as parish priests. Seeing that the bishop had no intention of excusing him from the service, Inácio sent him a petition together with his letter of appointment and a copy of the privileges.

The bishop replied to the petition that the privileges did not mention priests, but only the secular officials (which was, of course, false). Inácio then appealed to the Inquisition through the juiz conservador to mediate on his behalf. But the juiz, who was also the ouvidor geral, delayed his petition for five days. When Inácio went to the bishop to report on the state of his appeal, the bishop took the opportunity to throw him into the public prison in Olinda for disobedience.

Finding himself without any further options, Inácio requested an audience with the bishop to submit to his will. The bishop replied that he had already declared his intent and, if he had anything else to say, he should say it in writing. After writing the bishop again and declaring his willingness to submit since he had no other recourse, the bishop set him free, and he traveled the 230 leagues to the Vila de Soure. From there, he sent another petition to the Inquisition seeking redress, but apparently he found none.[20]

Sometimes the inquisitional officials found that they had to act in concert to protect their interests and privileges from Episcopal interference. For example, on November 1, 1768, Bishop Francisco Xavier Aranha ordered that all ecclesiastics within two leagues of their respective parish churches should attend all of the celebrations held at the parish church. He did not specifically mention the comissários, notários, and qualificadores, but the parish priest of Recife declared that inquisitional officials were not exempt from attendance and ordered them to attend. The comissário Francisco Fernandes de Souza immediately wrote to the bishop justifying his position that comissários were exempt from attendance at such celebrations when engaged in the work of the Holy Office. Francisco challenged the parish priest's assertion that comissários were not privileged, citing his own letter of appointment as proof. He also pointed out that their attendance was not necessary in a parish where there were so many clerics, and if he were required to attend, the diligências that he then possessed would be unnecessarily delayed, to the detriment of the Inquisition and the Church. In April 1769, the bishop asked the comissários to show why they believed they were exempt. After they made an effort to do so, the vicar general publicly stated that they had failed to make a case. In response, the comissários and notários of the Inquisition in Recife presented a long commentary in June 1769, replete with citations of papal bulls and learned authors to prove their case.

The comissários did not attempt to challenge the bishop's right to order the ecclesiastics under his jurisdiction to attend to the services of the parish, nor their obligation to attend. Such an argument would not have helped their cause. Instead, they tried to show that their work as inquisitional officials was special; and even though the services of the parish were important they were not more important than the work of the Inquisition. The comissários demonstrated that both the crown and the papacy had granted the officials of the Inquisition certain privileges that excluded them from coerced participation in church services, celebrations, and processions when they were engaged in the work of the Inquisition. Then they went on to argue that, as comissários and notários, they had "their hands in the same dough" as the inquisitors, and as their assistants they enjoyed the same privileges. This, of course, meant that they could not be forced to participate, nor could they be punished by the bishop for refusing to do so. The comissários concluded that, even though all of this was true, it was not necessary to debate the issue because the bishop already knew it all. That is why, in his wisdom, they said, the bishop had not included the comissários and notários in his decree.[21]

Sometimes these conflicts over privileges involved heated disputes among inquisitional officials themselves, which eventually involved the interference of bishops and the highest courts in the empire in inquisitional activities. Such a conflict occurred in late-eighteenth- and early-nineteenth-century Pernambuco between two comissários, Joaquim Marques de Araújo and Bernardo Luís Ferreira Portugal.[22] This dispute eventually merged with a long and heated dispute with the cathedral chapter.

The conflict began in the late 1780s when Bernardo Luís Ferreira Portugal returned from his studies at the University of Coimbra, where he had earned degrees in law, philosophy, mathematics, and canon law in 1784. Shortly after returning to Pernambuco, Bernardo Luís entered into conflict with Henrique Martins Gaio, comissário of the Inquisition since 1765. Henrique Martins, the same who had extracted a forced denunciation on this very matter, denounced Bernardo to the Inquisition for stating that baptism did not erase original sin and that baptism was not necessary for salvation. He also accused him of reading forbidden material, such as the writings of Jean-Jacques Rousseau.[23] Despite these denunciations, Bernardo Luís received an appointment as comissário of the Inquisition in 1788. Ironically, Joaquim Marques performed the investigation in Pernambuco and found that Bernardo Luís was a man of great confidence and sufficient secrecy, decency, gravity, and good public opinion to serve the Inquisition as a comissário.[24]

Joaquim Marques soon changed his opinion, however, with the 1794 clandestine wedding of Manuel José Viana and Isabel Maria dos Reis. The wedding, which was carried out with a forged letter of authorization, ignited a general conflict between the ecclesiastical authorities and the civil authorities in Pernambuco. Bernardo Luís had been the primary legal counsel for the groom, and he was immediately suspect.[25] Eventually, the crown ordered the governor, Tomás José de Melo, to imprison the principal actors in the wedding and to banish Bernardo Luís to Pará as a disturber of the peace. Bernardo was forbidden to return to Pernambuco without royal license upon pain of banishment to Angola for life.[26]

He eventually obtained a royal license, however, and on October 5, 1798, he returned to Pernambuco on the same ship that brought the newly appointed Bishop D. José Joaquim da Cunha de Azeredo Coutinho. Bishop Azeredo Coutinho and Bernardo Luís had both studied at Coimbra after Pombal had imposed his enlightened reforms. Consequently, both were more open to the new ideas gaining force in Europe in the late eighteenth century than were many of their ecclesiastical colleagues in Pernambuco. Both came under scrutiny for their views.[27] We have no way of knowing what occurred on the ship, but the two apparently formed a friendship, because soon after Bernardo's return the bishop publicly declared Bernardo's innocence, appointed him *promotor e defensor dos matrimônios* (prosecutor and defender of marriages), and nominated him for a seat on the cathedral chapter.[28]

The clandestine wedding proved to be the springboard for a new conflict between Bernardo Luís and Joaquim Marques that evolved into a contest between the cathedral chapter of Olinda and one of its members. Joaquim Marques had sided with those who opposed Bernardo Luís in the clandestine wedding, and he assisted D. Anna Ferreira Maciel, the mother of the bride, to draw up her petition to the overseas council. In her petition, she fulminated against Bernardo Luís as a diabolical heretic and "the declared enemy of the laws of the Church."[29]

In 1796, the Lisbon Tribunal sent a diligência to Joaquim Marques to investigate Bernardo Luís and his activities in the clandestine wedding. Joaquim Marques completed the diligência and sent it to Lisbon on December 13, 1796, but it never reached the tribunal because the French took the ship that carried it.[30]

On January 8, 1801, the Lisbon Tribunal sent another order to Joaquim Marques to carry out a diligência against Bernardo Luís. This order came in response to the 1796 denunciations by the secular priest and professor of Latin grammar Friar Elias Francisco Xavier da Cunha, who had been one of the most outspoken critics of Bernardo Luís in the clandestine wedding. Friar Elias Francisco denounced Bernardo Luís for several heretical propositions he claimed Bernardo Luís made in his presence.[31]

Joaquim Marques began the inquiry on April 8, 1801, in the Convento dos Religiosos do Carmo da Reforma. Soon after he began, however, bishop D. José Joaquim da Cunha de Azeredo Coutinho (1798–1804) summoned him to his presence. The bishop had been a deputy of the Lisbon Tribunal and was also acting as one of the interim governors of Pernambuco, and as such was a very powerful man in Pernambuco. He later became the last inquisitor general of the Portuguese Inquisition (1818–1821).

In a series of interviews, the bishop made it clear that he supported Bernardo Luís and that he wanted Joaquim Marques to desist from carrying out the diligência.[32] He claimed that it was his prerogative as the prelate to be involved in any matters that concerned those under his jurisdiction. Joaquim Marques saw the bishop's interference as a direct affront to the Inquisition and its comissários. He also understood that the bishop had a vested interest in seeing that Bernardo Luís was not publicly humiliated, because it would reflect on him and his judgment in appointing Bernardo Luís as promotor and in nominating him for a seat on the chapter.

At the same time, Bernardo Luís prepared a letter for the Lisbon Tribunal in which he attacked Joaquim Marques as an evil and irreligious man inspired only by hatred and vengeance, just as Henrique Martins Gaio had been. He also argued that Friar Elias Francisco Xavier da Cunha, the Latin teacher whose denunciation had resulted in the current diligência, was nothing more than a crazy cleric and little worthy of trust or confidence, while Bernardo Luís was a pious priest who stood falsely accused. Bernardo sent the letter to Joaquim Marques in an obvious attempt to intimidate him into discontinuing the inquiry. But Joaquim Marques refused to accept the letter because he felt it would compromise his position as the comissário charged with the execution of the diligência. Bernardo then turned to the bishop, who called Joaquim Marques to his presence once again.

The bishop read Joaquim the letter and tried to convince him to stop the diligência. Not at all pleased by this turn of events, Joaquim reminded the bishop, in forceful terms, that he should uphold the honor and dignity of the Inquisition and not meddle in its affairs. The bishop responded with equal acidity that the tribunal was very far away and that he had the jurisdiction to do what he needed to do in his diocese without depending on the inquisitors, who were merely his coadjutors. His reply seemed surprising for an ex-deputy and his behavior clearly shocked Joaquim Marques.

His apparent antipathy toward the Inquisition may reflect his general attitude for reforming what he saw as outmoded institutions, or it may have stemmed from some underlying conflict with the Lisbon Tribunal that may have influenced his decision to impede the diligência and humiliate Joaquim Marques. Although the bishop's motives are not entirely clear, there can be little doubt that Bernardo Luís sought to derail the investigation and strike back at Joaquim Marques and that the bishop was an active partner in the conflict.

After this encounter, the bishop forwarded Bernardo's letter to the tribunal in Lisbon, and Joaquim Marques penned a long letter on September 20, 1801, in response to the pressure he was receiving from the bishop and Bernardo Luís to end the inquiry. In the letter, he bewailed the declining respect for the Inquisition and its officials, and he dramatically requested that he be dismissed from the diligência, and from all others, if at any time his honor, faith, and zeal had been lacking or unworthy of his office. The General Council responded to this letter and the June 27 letter of Bernardo Luís on December 9, 1801, by closing the diligência and ordering the papers to be forwarded to the Lisbon Tribunal.[33]

Joaquim Marques had taken testimonies throughout April and March 1801, but he did not write his concluding statements until November 6, 1802. His conclusions on this occasion were considerably different from those he had issued in 1788. He now found Bernardo Luís to be a man of "loose and infernal morality whose conduct is so horrible that there is no vice that he does not pursue to the great damage and scandal of his neighbors, and by the disobedience he has toward his own mother." (Several witnesses had testified that Bernardo Luís had thrown his own mother into the street because she had complained about a female slave whom he kept as a concubine.) Joaquim Marques concluded that Bernardo Luís was "an irreligious man, . . . a great libertine, and a famous heretic."[34]

Despite Joaquim Marques's harsh assessment, the inquisitional prosecutor in Lisbon declared that he could find nothing in the report that justified legal action. He noted that Bernardo Luís, in his 1801 letter, had indicated that Joaquim Marques was his capital enemy and that this defect probably influenced his selection of witnesses. He also noted that the testimony of the bad reputation and poor public opinion of Bernardo Luís was really a matter of hearsay and not of personal experience. The inquisitional prosecutor, therefore, dismissed the charges pending further evidence.

This conflict eventually evolved into a conflict between Joaquim Marques and the cathedral chapter of the See of Olinda, which sought to remove him from his canon chair in 1801.[35] Bernardo Luís, who eventually joined the chapter, used the conflict to attack Joaquim Marques in an attempt to stop the investigation.[36] The chapter accused Joaquim Marques of failing to fulfill his obligations as a canon and of being more interested in his financial ventures.[37] He countered their position by arguing that his health prevented him from fulfilling his obligations and that he was engaged in the work of the Inquisition and, therefore, exempt from service.[38] The conflict eventually went to the Board of Conscience and Orders, which ruled in Joaquim's favor and ordered the chapter to keep him in his position and pay him the back stipend he was due.

The chapter refused to pay him, despite several royal orders to do so, and he continued to petition for redress. The Overseas Council asked the previous governor, Caetano Pinto de Miranda Montenegro, to offer his opinion on the conflict. In his June 11, 1806, reply, the governor indicated that he found it astonishing that an ecclesiastic who had seventy to eighty thousand cruzados in interest from the fifty houses he owned in Recife, besides his other wealth, would make such a fuss "over the wretched crumbs of a half-prebendary."[39] He noted that Bernardo Luís did not have the best character or public opinion, but he was not the great irreligious libertine he was made out to be. Montenegro concluded that Joaquim Marques was the more irreligious of the two, carrying on, as he supposed, the old Jesuit machinations. He believed that Joaquim Marques should also have been punished if he were not an old sick man who would soon be consumed by his own avarice.[40]

The governor was correct in one sense at least. It would be astonishing that Joaquim Marques would make such a fuss over the small stipend if all that was at stake was a mere 60$000 réis. Even though Joaquim Marques was clearly interested in money, this was not the most important issue for him. He was very concerned that inquisitional authority, and thus his own authority, was being defied and thwarted by the very men who should have upheld it. He had become a comissário in 1770, and for over thirty years he had given faithful, some might say fanatical, service to the Inquisition. He witnessed the decline in inquisitional power and lashed out in helpless anguish at a decline he could neither avoid nor prevent.

The documentary sources leave us hanging. We do not know whether the chapter continued to resist or capitulated and paid the stipend. Any resolution that may have been in motion in Lisbon was, no doubt, interrupted by the Napoleonic invasion of Portugal and the flight of the royal court to Rio de Janeiro in 1807–1808. In any case, the bishop successfully intervened in an inquisitional investigation and intentionally obstructed the normal functioning of the Inquisition for personal ends.[41] At the same time, both Bernardo Luís and Joaquim Marques used the authority of the Inquisition for personal advantage in an ongoing conflict.

The abuse of inquisitional authority in this case was more premeditated and sustained than most, but the purposes were essentially the same—the use and subversion of inquisitional authority for personal advantage. In the end, the Inquisition never punished Bernardo Luís, and he continued to be promoted within the ecclesiastical hierarchy in Pernambuco. He became involved in the 1817 revolt in Pernambuco, and after four years in prison he returned to occupy various positions in the ecclesiastical and governmental leadership of the newly independent Brazil.[42] Joaquim Marques also continued his devoted and zealous work for the Inquisition, taking every opportunity to remind the Holy Office of Bernardo Luís and his libertine disciples.

The inquisitional system for appointing officials and creating the honor, prestige, status, and power necessary for attracting high-quality officials and forwarding its own larger program was susceptible to sabotage and hijacking by the unscrupulous. The Inquisition found that, at least in the short run, its authority could be very useful in its officials' own personal conflicts. Officials and non-officials alike sought to manipulate inquisitional authority for their own ends and found that it was temporarily possible to do so. But the Inquisition could not countenance such abuse and vigorously prosecuted those who breached the boundaries of the legitimate use of authority—when they could catch them. They constructed limits and constraints in an attempt to safeguard the reputation and authority of the Inquisition and its officials.

By the end of the eighteenth century, however, high ecclesiastical officials, such as Bishop Azeredo Coutinho, were willing to interfere in inquisitional proceedings when it suited their interests and they could do so with impunity, which demonstrates that the boundaries between legitimate use and abuse were crumbling, or could at least be stretched by powerful men. The crumbling of inquisitional authority in late colonial Brazil had serious repercussions for inquisitional officials. The social, political, and economic stresses of the period placed heavy strains on the sinews of inquisitional power, which began to rupture from within. The late-eighteenth- and early-nineteenth-century ruptures occurred over a long period and can be understood only by studying the men who benefited from their inquisitional appointments for so long and who began to turn against the source of the status and prestige they so desired.

Notes

1. ANTT, IL, Processo 7956.
2. ANTT, IL, Processos 2160 and 5555.
3. Siqueira, "Os Regimentos da Inquisição," 667 (1613 Regimento, Title VI, Paragraphs II, III).
4. Siqueira, "Os Regimentos da Inquisição," 865–68 (1640 Regimento, Book III, Title, XXI–XXII).
5. Siqueira, "Os Regimentos da Inquisição," 961–63 (1774 Regimento, Book III, Title XVIII–XIX).
6. ANTT, IL, Processo. See also Calainho, "En nome do Santo Ofício," 140–44, and Novinsky, "A igreja no Brasil colonial," 25.
7. ANTT, IL, Processo 2243.
8. ANTT, IL, Processo 17392.
9. ANTT, IL, Livro 154, fol. 145.
10. ANTT, IL, Processo 14218.
11. ANTT, IL, Livro 271, fols. 376–378; Livro 280, fols. 340–364. See also ANTT, IL, Livro 319, fols. 315–315v.
12. ANTT, IL, Processo 12945.

13. ANTT, IL, Livro 277, fol. 226.
14. ANTT, IL, Livro 23, fol. 325; IL, NT 2132 and 2133.
15. ANTT, IL, Processo 9492.
16. ANTT, IL, Processo 9128.
17. The following account has been taken from ANTT, IL, Processo 3693.
18. The following account is taken from ANTT, IL, Livro 265, fols. 184–198.
19. Bishop Francisco Xavier Aranha was appointed in 1753 to replace Friar Luís de Santa Teresa, who had been recalled to Lisbon. See Ajuda, 49-ix-4, no. 178.
20. ANTT, IL, NT 3135.
21. ANTT, CGSO, NT 4159.
22. For a more detailed account of this conflict, see Wadsworth, "Joaquim Marques de Araújo," 309–20.
23. David Higgs, "Os perigos da francesia no Brasil no período da revolução francesa," in *Actas do colóquio A recepção da revolução francesa em Portugal e no Brasil II em 2 a 9 de Novembro de 1989* (Porto: Universidade de Porto, 1992), 229–30; ANTT, IL, Processos 14985, 14971.
24. ANTT, MCO, OC, PB, BPE, m. 12.
25. AHU, Pernambuco, cx. 223, doc. 15074, Letter of Bishop, May 4, 1795; ANTT, IL, Processo 7058. ANTT, IL, Processo 7058, fol. 4–9. See also Higgs, "Os perigos da francesia no Brasil," 237–42.
26. AHU, Pernambuco, cx. 223, doc. 15074, Letter from Queen to Governor, November 18, 1795; also in ANTT, IL, m. 25, no. 17, copied by Joaquim Marques and sent to the Inquisition in Lisbon.
27. See David Higgs and Guilherme P. Neves, "O oportunismo da historiografia: O Padre Bernardo Luís Ferreira Portugal e o movimento de 1817 em Pernambuco," in *Sociedade Brasileira de Pesquisa Histórica* (São Paulo, 1989), 179–84. Azeredo Coutinho has been credited with mentally preparing Brazilians for independence. See Apolônio Nóbrega, "Dioceses e Bispos do Brasil," in *Revista do Instituto Histórico e Geográfico Brasileiro* 22 (January–March 1954), 100–113; E. Bradford Burns, "The Role of Azeredo Coutinho in the Enlightenment of Brazil," *HAHR* 44, no. 2 (May 1964): 145–60; Manoel Cardozo, "Azeredo Coutinho and the Intellectual Ferment of His Times," in *Conflict and Continuity in Brazilian Society*, ed. Henry H. Keith and S. F. Edwards (Columbia: University of South Carolina Press, 1969), 72–103.
28. Bernardo Luís could have received his appointment as canon as early as 1790, but it may not have been until 1802. See ANTT, IL, m. 13, no. 44.
29. One wonders who was responsible for the language of the document, since similar phrasing appears in Joaquim's letters to the Inquisition. See AHU, Pernambuco, cx. 223, doc. 15074.
30. ANTT, IL, m. 40, documents unnumbered.
31. Bernardo Luís supposedly stated that the Holy Sacrament should not be worshipped; that God created the world but did not govern it nor heaven nor hell because everything is governed by the laws of this world; that Christ was not present in

the sacrament of the Eucharist; and that "everything is false." See ANTT, IL, Processo 7058. See also Higgs, "Os perigos da francesia no Brasil," 232.

32. ANTT, IL, Processo 7058. See Higgs, "Os perigos da francesia no Brasil," 232.

33. A marginal note ordered the end of the diligência and its return to Lisbon. ANTT, IL, m. 53.

34. ANTT, IL, Processo 7058.

35. ANTT, MCO, OC, PB, BPE, September 30, 1801.

36. Bernardo Luís had been nominated in 1787 for a seat on the chapter. See ANTT, MCO, OC, PB, BPE, m. 12. The nomination can be found in the fifty-fourth set of documents. See also AHU, Pernambuco, cx. 159, doc. 11459, for a series of documents supporting his nomination, including the letter he sent to be attached to any petitions of those who opposed his appointment.

37. AHU, Pernambuco, cx. 260, doc. 17465, a document produced by the chapter on May 13, 1805. See also ANTT, MCO, OC, PB, BPE, m. 13, documents unnumbered.

38. Joaquim Marques laid out these arguments in successive letters to the overseas council. See AHU, Pernambuco, cx. 232, doc. 15691; AHU, Pernambuco, cx. 260, doc. 17465; ANTT, MCO, OC, PB, BPE, m. 13; and ANTT, IL, m. 30.

39. A half-prebendary received 60$000 réis at the time.

40. AHU, Pernambuco, cx. 260, doc. 17465.

41. Bishop Azeredo Coutinho was reprimanded by the crown for misappropriation of funds and was eventually recalled from Pernambuco. See ANTT, MCO, OC, PB, BPE, m. 13, documents unnumbered; AHU, Pernambuco, cx. 218, doc. 14785; and AHU, cod. 585, fols. 159–160. For a heated debate with the Board of Conscience and Orders and the bishop over the congrua, see ANTT, MCO, OC, PB, BPE, m. 12, second to last set of unnumbered documents and maço 13; AHU, Pernambuco, cx. 263, doc. 17594 ; Pernambuco, cx. 264, doc. 17688. See also Neves, "A suposta conspiração de 1801 em Pernmbuco."

42. Higgs, "Os perigos da francesia no Brasil," 228. See also Higgs and Neves, "O oportunismo da historiografia."

CHAPTER ELEVEN

Decay and Decline

The slow collapse of the Inquisition between 1770 and 1821 rested on the Inquisition's decreasing ability to produce the honor and prestige it had once provided. The symbolic capital used to purchase prestige, honor, and power began to lose its social value. The Inquisition as an institution came under increasing scrutiny. Applications for appointment plummeted after 1770 in Portugal and after 1794 in Pernambuco; inquisitional officials at all levels began refusing to serve and defend the Inquisition. Finally, in early 1821, the Inquisition was abolished by a political act.

Explanations for the decline and abolition of the Portuguese Inquisition hinge upon the increasing political and cultural irrelevance of the institution.[1] The cultural changes brought about by the Enlightenment created an atmosphere in which the Inquisition came to be seen, paradoxically, as an important regulator of social tensions, but also as a threat to individual liberties.[2] For this reason, the enlightened absolutists of Portugal chose to reform the tribunal and subordinate it to the will of the crown rather than disrupt the balance of institutional power within Portugal. This occurred at a time when new forms of social control, such as the civil police, were being developed.[3]

Over time, the Inquisition became simply another privileged institution—"one more chess piece on the institutional game board, a capital of privilege that permitted the enlargement of the social space of noble families and local oligarchies." As a result, the Inquisition began to lose its power to intervene actively in institutional conflicts. That is to say, the "dynamic equilibrium with other powers . . . based on the capacity to strategically persuade, inverted itself and the Inquisition became increasingly involved in the plays of local interests, and even at the center, it [was] increasingly used by other powers." The loss of jurisdiction over certain crimes and the decrease in repressive activity signaled the declining utility of the institution. According to this line of reasoning, the initial abolition of the tribunal of Goa in 1774—it was reestablished in 1779—was more than simply a rationalization of inquisitional activity by the inquisitor general. It was an attempt to recuperate the deteriorating political, military, and economic situation in late-eighteenth-century Portugal. The final abolition of the tribunal in Goa in 1812 was the result of English pressure on the Portuguese crown.[4]

A study of the officials in Pernambuco demonstrates that this argument is accurate as far as it goes. But it also shows that it is incomplete. These arguments focus on the external forces that brought about inquisitional decline. Although those forces were very real and powerful, the decline was most strikingly internal. All of the various currents of historical change in the late eighteenth century could not help but influence the men who ran the Inquisition.

All these changes also reflected the fact that the Inquisition had itself changed dramatically. That change is most clearly seen in the choices and behaviors of the men who worked for the Inquisition. By the end of the eighteenth century, we can see serious stress on the inquisitional system in Brazil. But the collapse of the Inquisition was as much a result of the internal decline as manifested by its own officials' response to the changing social, political, and intellectual climate of the colony as it was a result of the exterior battering away at the inquisitional edifice. And as the internal and external decline progressed, the prestige and honor value of an appointment declined as well, creating a vicious downward spiral that could end only in the abolition or disintegration of the institution.

The Enlightenment in Portugal and Brazil

The myth of the Inquisition had always been part of a larger program to discredit Spanish and Portuguese royal power, as well as the power of the Catholic Church in Europe, after the Protestant reformation. During the eighteenth century, the Inquisition became the whipping boy of the Enlightenment and a favorite example of Iberian despotism and Catholic oppression. It seemed to represent all that the Enlightenment rejected—ecclesiasticism and obscurantism. It was seen as the bulwark of irrationality and the rejection of individual rights and freedoms. To a certain extent, the growing opposition to or disinterest in the Inquisition, even within the Iberian peninsula, was also an outgrowth of the decline in the political power of the Church and the growing irrelevance of religious purity to the political scene in Europe.

As the philosophical and ideological underpinnings of the Inquisition gradually gave way before the enlightened onslaught, the Inquisition adopted various responses to deal with the threat. As we have seen, the Inquisition first sought to create a broader social base of support by bringing in ever-larger numbers of officials from an ever-broader social base. By the mid-eighteenth century, the political and philosophical climate demanded more radical change. The Inquisition managed to survive this period by initiating a series of reforms that tried to bring it more in line with enlightened ideas. Yet, in doing so, it chipped away at its own ideological underpinnings. By 1821, the room for ideological and philosophical maneuvers had become so constricted that the Inquisition was simply voted out of existence by the liberal junta then governing Portugal.

The Enlightenment came late to Portugal and Brazil, and as in other ancien régime societies the implementation of its ideas proved selective.[5] The Portuguese monarchy and administrators chose those ideas and practices oriented toward strengthening and rationalizing the state. The Enlightenment came to Portugal first in the minds and practices of the *estrangeirados*, those men who had lived and studied in France, England, Germany, and Italy and returned to Portugal with new political, social, religious, and scientific ideas.[6]

The introduction of the Enlightenment was part of a broader revolution that was occurring in the Luso-Brazilian world. During the seventeenth century, Spanish influence began to decline, and French, English, Italian, and German influences took over. Spanish as the second language of Portugal gave way to French. Spanish literature and theater became old fashioned. Baroque art gave way to French and Italian classicism. Backroom amateur and intelligentsia societies and intellectual academies sprang up, including the Royal Academy of Science in 1779, which incorporated the doctrines of the Enlightenment. Educational reform replaced Jesuit-dominated teaching and methods with Cartesian mathematics, experimentation, and reason. In 1772, Pombal imposed his reforms of the University of Coimbra, which included the creation of colleges of mathematics and natural philosophy. Indeed, Pombal declared that all laws should be based on "good reason" in order to be valid. The rising generation of Portuguese intellectuals, clergymen, educators, physicians, administrators, and governors imbibed these new ideas and methods. The implementation of reforms in the mid-to-late-eighteenth century represented a one-hundred-year time lag behind what was already being done in northern Europe; but for Portugal, they also represented major innovations. It should not be supposed, however, that the eighteenth-century enlightened reforms were coupled with intellectual freedom. Censorship continued even though it could be avoided.[7] The Enlightenment in Portugal and Brazil was not an exercise in expanding individual freedoms. Rather, it was an attempt to rationalize and enhance state power.[8]

These ideas and practices entered Brazil in much the same way as they had Portugal. The ideas came in migrating heads and libraries, through the international book trade, through students returning from Coimbra, in literary societies, in Masonic lodges, in the visits of scientific missions from Europe, with visitors, with traders, with contrabandists, with foreign-born and foreign-trained priests, through friendly correspondence, through the sharing of books, and through word of mouth. Academies also sprang up in Brazil in the eighteenth century, and the libraries of learned men and clerics overflowed with enlightened literature. The academy set up by Bishop Azeredo Coutinho in Pernambuco in 1800 brought the methods being employed in Coimbra to Pernambuco.[9] Because clerics were often trained in Coimbra and had access to the "subversive" works of Voltaire and others, they often assumed leadership roles in promoting enlightened ideas in Brazil.[10]

Judges also reflected the influence of the Enlightenment during their deliberations on cases in Brazil. Judges in Maranhão used the enlightened ideas of the natural rights of the individual to liberty and freedom in cases of slave manumission in 1774.[11] The doctrines of the Enlightenment also surfaced in several rebellions that erupted in the last several decades before Brazilian independence.

Participants in the Inconfidência Mineira in 1789 in Minas Gerais had libraries filled with works by French and English writers of the Enlightenment. The ideas of the French and American revolutions also spread and found expression on the tongues and pens of revolutionaries and conspirators in Rio (1794), Bahia (1798), and Pernambuco (1801 and 1817).[12]

In the 1798 "Revolt of the Tailors" or the "Tailors Conspiracy," handwritten manifestos appeared throughout the city of Salvador, Bahia, affixed to public buildings. They were addressed to the "Republican Bahian people," who were encouraged to support an armed revolt "claiming to include 676 persons—soldiers, ecclesiastics, merchants, even agents (i.e. familiares) of the Holy Office—whose purpose was to overthrow 'the detestable metropolitan yoke of Portugal' and to install a French-style republic."[13]

Revolutionary tendencies arose in Pernambuco around the turn of the century that were tied to broader social and economic changes. The rise of cotton production allowed many small-time dirt farmers to abandon subsistence agriculture for the new cash crop. The new wealth provided new opportunities for social, economic, and political mobility that ruptured the centuries-old dominance of sugar and reinvigorated the mercantile interests of Recife. England remained the primary market for Brazilian cotton. These stronger economic ties coincided with a strengthening of political ties between England and Portugal, which contributed to a new rise in nativist feelings in certain parts of Pernambuco. The merchants of Recife and the cotton growers began to move in the direction of independence from Portugal and the old sugar planter aristocracy, while the sugar planters remained predominantly counterrevolutionary.[14]

The supposed conspirators of the 1801 Suassunas conspiracy in Pernambuco reportedly used the language of revolution. They were denounced for espousing revolutionary ideas, such as freedom for their *patria*, seeking French help, and sabotaging any future efforts by the crown to collect loans in the region.[15] The accusation caused a sensation, but the inquiry determined that the allegations were false.[16] Nonetheless, these nativist and separatist tendencies were in the air, and they reemerged in the short-lived 1817 rebellion. This was a rebellion against Portugal and against the crown then ensconced in Rio. The revolutionaries sought to establish a representative republic, and they used the language of liberty.[17] These dramatic shifts in thinking all contributed to a decrease in the influence of the Inquisition, which still represented the ideals of the ancien régime.

The French invasion of Portugal in 1807 also decreased the effectiveness of inquisitional operations. The system was interrupted by the French control of Lisbon, the flight of the crown to Brazil, the increasing Portuguese reliance on English shipping and protection, and the absence of the inquisitor general, who spent the next six years in Bayonne, France.[18] The most common problem was the inability of the Inquisition to continue the processos that they already had initiated because of a breakdown in communication with Brazil. For example, Pascoal Martins da Costa Cunha Souto Maior applied for an appointment as a comissário in 1806. His judicial was done in 1807, but he did not receive the appointment until 1812. The Bastos brothers applied in 1802, and their diligências were stalled out until 1818.[19]

Father Gabriel José Pereira de Sampaio's application further illustrates these difficulties. He was in Lisbon taking care of some business when he applied to become a comissário in 1807. His diligência was completed in 1808, and he was approved because of the extreme lack of comissários and notários in Alagoas, where he lived. A note on the front of his processo stated: "This Provisão was not sent to America because the government there was of His Highness. The French stamps [we had to use] were not accepted in America. As soon as the kingdom was returned to its legitimate government a new provision was passed and sent on October 29, 1808."[20] Nothing in his diligência was sent to Brazil, probably for the same reason. For Lourenço Pereira de Carvalho e Gama, the General Council waited for four years for the judicial to come back from Brazil. The council realized that to request baptismal certificates, which were missing, from Brazil would merely delay his processo further; so under the circumstances, it simply approved him for comissário.[21] This disruption from the war also caused some to discontinue the process all together.

In July 1807, three brothers applied together for appointments as familiares, José de Souza Barroso, João de Santa Ana de Souza Barroso, and Manuel Pereira de Souza Barroso. They were all sons of the familiar Antônio de Souza Barroso. In 1810, the diligências were pronounced incomplete because the judicial from Recife had ended up in England—probably because they had been sent on an English ship. The General Council had sent another letter in May 1809 to Joaquim Marques de Araújo to ask him to redo the judicial, but in August 1810, their father, Antônio, wrote a letter to Cipriano José de Amorim, the secretary of the Lisbon Tribunal, stating that he no longer wanted to continue the diligências and asking that they discount what they had spent from his deposit of 100$000 réis and return the rest. He stated that he did not want to spend any more money; nor did he want his sons to become familiares any longer.[22] Although Antônio does not state his reasons, his decision was probably symptomatic of the increasing animosity toward the Inquisition and the Portuguese crown in the early decades of the nineteenth century as much as it was of the disruption of war, which only increased the difficulty and cost of the process.

Treaties with foreign powers also affected the functioning of the Inquisition in Brazil. In 1641, with the independence movement in Portugal, the Portuguese signed a peace treaty with the Dutch in which they allowed Dutch nationals to be exempt from inquisitional jurisdiction. The 1654 treaty with England went further and declared that no tribunal in the Portuguese Empire could molest English nationals. It also permitted them to use English Bibles and to practice their religion in their homes and on board their ships without interference. They were also granted land where they could bury their dead. Essentially the same guarantees were granted the Dutch in the treaty of 1661.[23]

The Napoleonic wars also brought Portugal and England closer together to oppose Napoleon and his Spanish allies, resulting in a series of treaties. The treaty of 1810 dealt explicitly with the Inquisition. Article IX of the Treaty of Alliance and Friendship with Great Britain, signed in Rio de Janeiro in 1810, has prompted some confusion about the state of the Inquisition in Brazil in the last decade before independence. The wording of the article is sufficiently ambiguous to leave its ultimate meaning obscure to those not familiar with the organization of the Inquisition:

> The Inquisition or Tribunal of the Holy Office, not having been hitherto established, or recognized in Brazil. His Royal Highness the Prince Regent of Portugal, guided by an enlightened and liberal policy, takes the opportunity afforded by the present treaty to declare spontaneously in His own name, and in that of his heirs and successors, that the Inquisition shall not hereafter be established in the South American dominions of the Crown of Portugal.
>
> And His Britannic Majesty in consequence of this declaration on the Part of his royal Highness the Prince Regent of Portugal, does on His part engage and declare that the Fifth Article of the Treaty of 1654, in virtue of which certain exemptions from the authority of the Inquisition are exclusively granted to British subjects shall be considered as null and having no effect in the South American dominions of the Crown of Portugal.
>
> And His Britannic Majesty consents that this abrogation of the fifth Article of the Treaty of 1654 shall also extend to Portugal upon the abolition of the Inquisition in that Country, by the Command of his Royal Highness the Prince Regent, and generally to all other parts of his Royal Highness's Dominions where he may hereafter abolish that Tribunal.[24]

Some scholars have suggested that this article suppressed the Inquisition in Brazil, insinuating that it ceased to function there.[25] The fact that denunciations from Brazil continued to be received and acted upon and that officials continued to apply for and receive appointments all over Brazil up until 1820 demonstrates that inquisitorial activity was certainly not suppressed. The wording of the article is technically correct, however. A tribunal of the Holy Office had not been established in Brazil, and all the Prince Regent (later D. João VI) did was declare that no such tribunal would be established. He did not state that the Tribunal in Lisbon, which continued to have jurisdiction over Brazil, would cease its operations in the colony. D. João knew that the Inquisition functioned in Brazil, and most Portuguese certainly knew it. The English, however, apparently misunderstood the nature of inquisitorial organization and assumed that without a tribunal in Brazil their subjects would be free of any inquisitorial oversight. By declaring Article V of the 1654 treaty null in Brazil, they unwittingly removed the veil of protection their subjects had enjoyed in Brazil, and the Portuguese managed to give the appearance of granting a concession without really granting anything. This treaty is reminiscent of the 1830 law abolishing the transatlantic slave trade, which was only *uma lei para a inglês ver* (a law for the English to see).

Nonetheless, the Prince Regent clearly demonstrated that it was not only possible to abolish the Inquisition, but that he had entertained the idea, even anticipated it. Incidentally, when the Prince Regent set up the royal court in Rio de Janeiro after fleeing the French invasion of Portugal, he set up a full complement of state institutions, but not the Inquisition. No tribunal was ever established in Brazil, and it remained under the jurisdiction of the Lisbon Tribunal. Apparently, the Prince Regent and his advisers did not feel that they needed an inquisitional tribunal to govern from Brazil. This omen of abolition came true in 1821, but not by royal decree.

In August 1820, while D. João VI was still in Brazil, a constitutionalist revolution broke out in Portugal. The new government formed a council and proceeded to write a liberal constitution. Early in 1821, a proposal to abolish the Inquisition was presented to the council, and on April 5, 1821, the Inquisition was abolished.

Inquisitional Decline in Pernambuco

The case of Joaquim Marques, Bernardo Luís, and Bishop Azeredo Coutinho, discussed in the last chapter, highlights the decline of inquisitional authority in Pernambuco and shows how the changes of the eighteenth century contributed to its decline. Bernardo Luís and Bishop Azeredo Coutinho had both studied at Coimbra and were, consequently, more open to the ideas of the Enlightenment. They both showed a certain amount of disrespect and contempt for inquisitional authority and ideals.[26] The ex-Jesuit Joaquim Marques had no such openness and perceived the new ideas of the eighteenth century and those who espoused them as threats and enemies of the good order of society and religion. He became the prophet of doom for the Inquisition, the Catholic religion, and Luso-Brazilian society.

For example, in 1810, Joaquim Marques complained that the English were influencing even the powerful and respected leaders in Pernambuco to eat meat on the fast days during Lent and to participate in Protestant rituals so that practically no one kept Lent any longer.[27] The sacred processions of Lent had been transformed, he claimed, into irreligious theatrical performances that ridiculed Christ and the Holy Sacraments. He also claimed that the English ridiculed the participants in the procession of the Lord's Passion, calling them Jews, and that in a procession of children, the English made a great mockery of some small saints by taking the images of the devil and of death and making them dance together. Joaquim Marques reported that when the clergy reprimanded the people for these disorders during the services of Lent, the ouvidor railed against them, calling them ignorant and fit only to instruct the rude Indians and not the king's magistrates.

The traveler Henry Koster also noticed the changes occurring in Recife and the growing English influence. Ladies began strolling in the evening in the English fashion, and both men and women began assuming English styles of dress. "The time of advancement was come," he said, "and men, who had for many years gone on without making any change either in the interior or exterior of their houses, were now painting and glazing on the outside, and new furnishings within; modernizing themselves, their families, and their dwellings."[28]

Where Koster saw these changes as positive signs of modernization, Joaquim Marques saw them as evidence of social, political, and religious degeneration. He attributed these disorders to the "stupid [cathedral] chapter . . . and the great heretic Bernardo Luís Ferreira Portugal, who is also the vicar general of the bishopric, a man so libertine . . . that he had already been judged an enemy of religion . . . and as the chief of the libertines; . . . he has permitted all of the abuses that have been introduced into the good order of the Church and the purity of our Holy Faith."[29] In his denunciation, Joaquim Marques highlighted two related developments that had been gathering strength throughout the eighteenth century—the growing influence of the ideas of the Enlightenment in the Luso-Brazilian world and the increasing subordination of Portugal to the political and economic power of England.

The Inquisition had also experienced repeated challenges to its power and suffered a similar diminution of autonomy in the eighteenth century. From its inception in the sixteenth century, the Inquisition had struggled to increase its autonomy from both the crown and the papacy. During the periods of conflict with the crown and the papacy, the Inquisition found that its autonomy was more restricted than it might have preferred. The eighteenth century witnessed the most serious challenge to inquisitional autonomy when the state sought to reign it in. This loss of autonomy contributed to the late-eighteenth-century decline, not only in power, but also in the ability to produce status and prestige.

The decline of inquisitional power in the last quarter of the eighteenth century, due in part to the Pombaline reforms, decreased the value of the symbolic capital represented by a letter of appointment to the Inquisition. The revocation of pure-blood requirements, which effectively eliminated the Inquisition's ability to provide proof of purity in a society highly attuned to such public declarations, could only diminish the value of inquisitional appointment.

218 ~ Chapter Eleven

This loss combined with the increasing constriction of privilege starting in the late seventeenth century. The most important losses of privilege were the restriction of the foro (private adjudication) and the exemption from military service. The frequent and continuous challenges to inquisitional privilege and the continuing ambiguity of the question also contributed to its diminishing desirability.

In addition, the inquisitional institutions that had counterbalanced the constrictions by providing opportunities for privilege, status, social welfare, camaraderie, and honor also experienced decline in the last quarter of the eighteenth century. The brotherhood of St. Peter Martyr suffered from rising disinterest on the part of the familiares and an unwillingness to accept the increasingly oppressive financial burdens of participation. By the end of the eighteenth century, the brotherhoods of St. Peter Martyr everywhere in the empire had entered into decline. The governors of Pernambuco also began to apply the same practices they used in the militia companies to the Companhia dos Familiares by promoting Portuguese immigrants over native Brazilians, which only further constricted the pathways to privilege.

Although this decline appears to be general, it was not complete and total. Despite growing opposition to the Inquisition, it remained relevant to local power struggles and could not be ignored with impunity. It continued to attract applicants up to 1821, although in much smaller numbers, and royal courts were still willing to uphold inquisitional privilege in the face of serious challenges from powerful opponents—as in the case of Joaquim Marques. The Inquisition also received the ability to issue orders in the name of the crown in the late 1760s, which was intended to make it a crown tribunal. Clearly, the crown did not consider the institution completely irrelevant in the 1770s. But the increasing influence of Enlightenment ideas in Portugal and Brazil and within the Inquisition combined with the disruption of the French Revolution, the Napoleonic wars, and the growing English influence in Portuguese foreign and domestic policy to create a very difficult situation for the Inquisition.

All of these foreign influences, and particularly the ideas of the Enlightenment, were summed up by Joaquim Marques in the term *libertino*. When Joaquim Marques used the terms *libertino* and *libertinagem*, he had something specific in mind. Today these terms have lost some of their original meaning. Today, *libertine* generally refers to an unbelieving, wicked, or depraved individual who is free from all moral pricks of conscience. This is a diminution of the original eighteenth-century meaning, which referred to "He who shakes off the yoke of revelation and presumes that reason alone can guide with certainty with respect to God, life, etc."[30] This definition, proffered by

Antônio de Morais e Silva, who twice was denounced to the Inquisition and once was prosecuted by it, suggests the author's libertine persuasion in the matter.[31] Those who had been "tainted" by any variety of enlightened thought were so labeled, including Bernardo Luís Ferreira Portugal, Bishop Azeredo Coutinho, and many other Brazilian intellectuals who had been educated at Coimbra after 1772. Those who still adhered to the ideas of scholasticism and were dedicated to the preservation of the current religious, political, social, and economic status quo feared those ideas and the men who espoused them. Joaquim Marques was the most outspoken of the Pernambucan officials against the libertines, but his colleague Henrique Martins Gaio was equally acerbic in his denunciations of French ideas and those clerics who had been trained in them.[32] This was one of the underlying causes of the conflicts, which engulfed Bernardo Luís, Joaquim Marques, and Azeredo Coutinho in the late eighteenth and early nineteenth centuries. Bernardo Luís and Azeredo Coutinho got along so well partly because they had both been trained at Coimbra after 1772 and shared a common set of enlightened beliefs.

The fear of social and religious dissolution caused Joaquim Marques to decry the growing influence of French ideas in late-eighteenth-century Pernambuco. He labeled Bernardo Luís a libertine, and in 1798 he declared that if it had not been for the Inquisition, Pernambuco would have become "worse than France."[33] He accused Antônio de Morais e Silva, the author of a Portuguese language dictionary, of disregarding all religious fasts and holy days and obliging his slaves to do likewise. Antônio, he said, was reputed by all faithful people as a great libertine.[34] In 1803, Joaquim Marques was beginning to despair. Despite all of his efforts, the libertines were growing in number and sagacity because, he said, they realized that they were never going to be punished, or that at least their punishment would be delayed.[35] Likewise, by 1810, he had become so preoccupied with the increasing English influence in Pernambuco that he claimed that, if corrective measures were not taken, Brazil would become a "new England."[36]

In 1812, Joaquim Marques claimed that an epidemic had struck Brazil.[37] He asserted that it was most virulent in Rio, where more than two thousand people supposedly died in fifteen days. Joaquim Marques did not hesitate to attribute the epidemic to divine retribution and a sign that the end of the world was near. What was the cause? Of course, it was the libertines, who trod upon holy religion and spread every form of heresy.[38] Had Joaquim Marques lived to witness the 1817 movement for independence in Pernambuco and Brazilian independence in 1822, he would have felt mortified and justified at the same moment, for the dissolution he had prophesied appeared to have occurred. He would have found even more evidence to support his prophecies of doom in the fact that thirteen of the 1817 conspirators were officials of the Inquisition, including his old nemesis, Bernardo Luís Ferreira Portugal.[39]

Perhaps the most important signs of decline were the behavior of the officials of the Inquisition and the attitude of local authorities to the institution. For example, in 1747, the notário Leandro Ferreira de Azevedo, from Goiana, complained that when he went to the vicar Antônio Gonçalves Lima to ask for the baptismal and marriage records to extract the needed certificates, the vicar denied his request. The vicar used the pretext that the constitution of the archbishopric of Bahia said that the baptismal records could not be given to anyone to extract entries without an order from the bishop. Leandro reported this to the comissário, Antônio Alves Guerra, who obtained an order from the bishop, and the vicar gave them up. A deputy of the General Council noted that similar incidents had occurred in Évora and that they should do something about it.[40]

In this case, the priest's opposition was not a blatant attack on the Inquisition. It was, at least, thinly veiled by recourse to a standing order in the archbishopric. Toward the end of the eighteenth century, however, those who opposed the Inquisition were often quite open and direct in their opposition. In 1784, Comissário Friar José de Jesus Maria Souza reported the "deplorable state of the Holy Office" in Pernambuco, where so many sought appointments in hopes of acquiring the privileges. Once they discovered the very real limitation on those privileges, they became less inclined and less willing to serve.

His concern arose over a case he was involved in. He had requested the marriage records of the parish church of Corpo Santo in Recife from the priest Manuel de Mendonça. When José asked Mendonça about it, the priest replied that if he wanted to see the books he had to go to the church. When José said that his convent was only a short distance away and that it was customary to deliver the books directly to the comissário, the priest responded with belligerence, "Tell the Holy Office that I do not want to give the books."

Later, when José sent the familiar, Antonio José Sedrim, to collect the books, the priest responded impetuously, "Tell him that I do not want to send them and tell him to tell the Inquisition." José sent the familiar back to call Manuel to testify because he had been named in a commission he had received from Lisbon. This time Manuel responded, "I do not want to go and I will not, and he can report it to the queen and the Holy Office. But the book the comissário asked for, I will give it to him."

Likewise, when the familiar Antônio José Sedrim went to ask another familiar, Manuel Antônio Duarte, to help him with some diligências related to this case, he found Manuel in a small shop passing his time. In response to the summons, Manuel yelled at Antônio and publicly insulted him, claiming to have other things to do. Antônio knew that he was lying, because the business Manuel claimed to have would not take place for another four days. Then Antônio wrote this revealing sentence to the comissário, Friar José de Jesus Maria Souza: "I beg your reverence, for the love of God, that you dispense me from notifying anyone for the service of the holy tribunal so that I do not suffer these impolitic discomfitures which have happened to me so many times . . . principally from the familiares."

At least three things stand out here. A parish priest had openly and brazenly refused to obey the order of a comissário. A familiar had likewise openly and brazenly refused to fulfill his duty, giving a very weak excuse in his defense. And a familiar had begged to be excused from serving the Inquisition because of the abuse he received not only from non-inquisitional personnel, but also, and more importantly, from his own colleagues.

Friar José informed the Lisbon Tribunal that from this experience they could see the sorry state to which the respect due the Inquisition had been reduced. If a parish priest, who was obliged to set the example, could so easily ignore his duty in such a delicate matter, then what could they expect of his flock, who would follow his example. He also bewailed the "deplorable slothfulness, indolence, and lack of devotion" of the familiares regarding the things of the Holy Office in Pernambuco.[41]

This behavior became widespread by the end of the eighteenth century. For example, in Portugal, the treasurer of the General Council reported that, in 1792, the familiar Manuel Gaspar da Boiça faked illness so that he would not have to perform a diligência.[42] In 1796, Joaquim Marques reported that the ship captains of Pernambuco refused to write receipts, as was the custom, for the bags of letters or for the prisoners being sent to the Inquisition in Lisbon.[43] Familiares also began to seek permission to carry pistols as defensive weapons to protect themselves not only from bandits[44] but also from personal enemies they had acquired while serving the Inquisition.[45]

Even the habilitação was in decline. After 1794, applications and appointments in Pernambuco declined precipitously. In hindsight, some have concluded that the removal of the pure-blood laws diminished the appeal of the carta, but such a conclusion was probably not immediately obvious to contemporaries. It seems more likely that most people in Pernambuco were not aware of the effect that the changes of the 1770s would have on inquisitional practice and prestige, if they were even aware of the changes at all. And only after those changes became apparent and combined with the transformations just mentioned did the prestige value of inquisitional cartas decrease. This helps explain the time lag between the decline of the Inquisition in Portugal and that in Pernambuco.

Likewise, the Inquisition became increasingly lax in its requirement that investigations be carried out in the place of residence of the applicant and permitted more inquiries in Lisbon. And in 1820 the inquisitor general, Azeredo Coutinho, simply dismissed the applicant Francisco José Alves de Barros from Alagoas from all diligências and gave him a carta.[46] This is the only case I have ever seen where the processo was completely ignored. This mentality of disinterest and even hostility seems to have pervaded the upper echelons of the Inquisition as well as the lower.

For example, the General Council consulted on the pure-blood law of 1773 and gave its hearty approval. Also, it was the inquisitor general who suggested the abolition of the tribunal in Goa and the reformation of the regimento in 1774. Even though Pombal may have been behind these activities, and despite the fact that we cannot know the General Council's true feelings in the matter, its willingness to use the language of the Enlightenment in the reformation of the Inquisition is an indication of the shift already under way within the Inquisition. The Inquisition had already made the transition from an institution primarily oriented toward repression to one focused on promotion. That shift permitted a continuing transformation that reached its fruition in the debates held in the constitutional convention of 1821 in Lisbon.

Already in October 1820, the provisional junta required all the officials of the General Council and the tribunals to swear an oath of loyalty and obedience to the new government and the future constitution.[47] In the eighth session of the liberal court, on February 8, 1821, Francisco Simões Margiocchi proposed the abolition of the Inquisition. His proposal was not opposed, even though at least one member of the General Council of the Inquisition was present as a deputy. The vote finally came after a lively debate on March 24, 1821. Of course, the debate included long discourses about the barbarism and monstrosities of the Inquisition. The inquisitor present at the debate argued that the establishment of the Inquisition was a result of the intolerance of the age and that it persisted because of "the moral causes that retarded the progress of human understanding." This was not the language of the Inquisition. It was the language of the Enlightenment, and it came from the mouth one of the highest officials of the Inquisition.

Whatever desires the officials of the Inquisition may have had to resist were doubtless pacified by the promise of a pension for all of the officials of the Inquisition—excepting, of course, the familiares, comissários, notários, and qualificadores. On March 29, the members of the General Council were present at the Catholic mass where all the civil and military authorities swore allegiance to the new constitution.

On April 5, 1821, the order abolishing the Inquisition was formally published. It abolished the entire inquisitional bureaucracy, reverted all spiritual crimes to the bishops and the rest to the civil authorities, abolished all the regulations, laws, or orders pertaining to the Inquisition, and confiscated all inquisitional property and all inquisitional documents. The property went to the national treasury, and the documents went to the national library to be inventoried. In symbolic representation of the Inquisition's demise, the doors of the inquisitional palace were thrown open and the sacred precinct was desecrated by the public, who were permitted to wander throughout the entire edifice, including the secret prisons.

These are all signs of a deep internal decline at all levels within the Inquisition. Had the inquisitional officials been as dedicated to defending their position, privileges, power, and institution as they had been in the seventeenth century, it is unlikely that the abolition would have been so undramatic. The fact is that the Inquisition had changed. The shift that began in the seventeenth century turn away from repression and toward promotion had altered the inquisitional identity. The Inquisition could no longer repress as effectively, and by the end of the eighteenth century it could no longer promote socially. Indeed, it appears that its own officials were not entirely dedicated to either course of action.

Not everyone was pleased to see the Inquisition go, however. We have already mentioned Joaquim Marques, and there is every reason to believe that there were many others like him. The ideas and values that the Inquisition had fostered did not die with the liberal revolution. They persisted. In the late 1820s, the cathedral chapter of Vizeu in Portugal begged the crown to reestablish the Inquisition. They complained somewhat dramatically that since the Inquisition had been abolished, the holy Catholic faith had almost become extinguished in Portugal.[48] For those still tied to the old order, the Inquisition continued to resonate deeply with the values and beliefs that they cherished, particularly in the accelerating transformation of Luso-Brazilian society in the nineteenth century. The roots of the Inquisition remained, even though the tree had been chopped down.

The decline of the Inquisition was not so much an indication that the Inquisition was paralyzed, moribund, or in ruins as it was that it had changed. It had changed politically, institutionally, and socially. Politically, it had effectively become a royal tribunal with power to order in the name of the king. It had thus lost its autonomy and much of its distinctiveness as an institution. Inquisitional privilege had also been sharply cut back during the course of the eighteenth century. Its repressive role had been in decline since the end of the seventeenth century, but it was by no means paralyzed. Socially, it remained an important tool in local politics, but its potential for legitimizing and promoting social status had been sharply curtailed by the ongoing political and social transformations within the Luso-Brazilian world.

The signs of internal deterioration demonstrate that the Inquisition was complicit in its own decline. The great transformations of the late eighteenth century limited its ability to promote socially, and the changing attitudes toward the Inquisition and within the Inquisition all signaled a drastic need for reform if it were to survive the early-nineteenth-century political and cultural transformations.

The Inquisition had faced similar challenges in the shifting political and social context of the seventeenth century and the mid-eighteenth century and successfully weathered the storms. That it did not do so in the early nineteenth century testifies, first of all, to the depth of the social, political, and cultural metamorphoses of Luso-Brazilian society and, secondly, to the fact that the officials of the Inquisition were simply not interested in reforming the institution. It should be remembered that the inquisitor general in 1821 was none other than Bishop Azeredo Coutinho. He had not only interfered with an inquisitional inquiry, but had also manifest a less than positive opinion of the Inquisition while in Pernambuco. He was an unlikely candidate to support a drive to save the Inquisition from extinction.

In the end, the purposes for which the Inquisition had been created and continued to exist no longer resonated in the altered social, political, and intellectual climate of the early nineteenth century. The Inquisition was inconsistent with the new order that the liberal council was trying to establish and with the political ideals prevalent in Pernambuco. The council could not erect a state with a constitution that contained the language of rights and freedom and retain an institution founded on privilege and censorship that did not, and perhaps could not, concede those rights.

Notes

1. Francisco Bethencourt, "Declínio e estinção do Santo Ofício," *RHES* (1987): 77–85; Maria Helena Carvalho dos Santos, "A abolição da Inquisição em Portugal: Um acto de poder," in *Inquisição*, ed. Maria Helena Carvalho dos Santos, 3 vols. (Lisbon: Universitária Editora, 1989), 3:1381–86.

2. There is no generally accepted term for the Enlightenment in Portuguese. Frequently used terms include *illuminismo*, *illustração*, and *época das luzes*. See E. Bradford

Burns, "The Intellectuals as Agents of Change and the Independence of Brazil, 1724–1822," in *From Colony to Nation: Essays on the Independence of Brazil*, ed. A. J. R. Russell-Wood (Baltimore: Johns Hopkins University Press, 1975), 211.

3. Bethencourt, *Histórias das Inquisições*, 355–59.

4. Bethencourt, *Histórias das Inquisições*, 285.

5. A. H. de Oliveira Marques, *History of Portugal*, 2nd ed. (New York: Columbia University Press, 1976), 406–17; Kenneth Maxwell, *Pombal*, 87–109, 159–61; Alexander Marchant, "Aspects of the Enlightenment in Brazil," in *Latin America and the Enlightenment*, ed. Arthur P. Whitaker, 2nd ed. (Ithaca: Cornell University Press, 1961), 95–118; Cardozo, "Azeredo Coutinho," 104–12; Burns, "Role of Azeredo Coutinho"; Guilherme Pereira das Neves, "De 1789–1798: Percurso da francesia na Bahia," in *De Cabral a Pedro I: Aspectos da colonização portuguesa no Brasil*, ed. Maria Beatriz Nizza da Silva (Porto: Humbertipo, 2001), 334–37; Jane Herrick, "The Reluctant Revolutionist: A Study of the Political Ideas of Hipólito da Costa (1774–1823)," *Americas* 7, no. 2 (October 1950): 171–81; and Guilherme Pereira das Neves, "Ilustração," in *Dicionário do Brasil colonial (1500–1808)*, ed. Ronaldo Vainfas (Rio de Janeiro: Editora Objectiva, 2000), 296–99.

6. Ana Carneiro, Ana Simões, and Maria Paula Diogo, "Enlightenment Science in Portugal: The Estrangeirados and Their Communication Networks," *Social Studies of Science* 30, no. 4 (August 2000): 591–619.

7. The censorship board granted many licenses to read prohibited books. See Luiz Carlos Villalta, "As licenças para posse e leitura de livros proibidos," in *De Cabral a Pedro I: Aspectos da colonização portuguesa no Brasil*, ed. Maria Beatriz Nizza da Silva (Porto: Humbertipo, 2001), 235–45. Booksellers avoided inquisitional censure by importing forbidden books in false covers. See Burns, "Intellectuals as Agents of Change," 219–20. The printing presses in Brazil after 1808 did not publish "dangerous" liberal materials. Most liberal publications circulating in Brazil were contraband. See Maria Beatriz Nizza da Silva, *Cultura no Brasil Colônia* (Petrópolis: Vozes, 1981), 144–60.

8. Maxwell, *Pombal*, 160.

9. See Burns, "Role of Azeredo Coutinho."

10. See Ney de Souza, "A formação do clero no Brasil colonial e a influência do iluminismo," *Revista eclesiástica brasileira* 231 (September 1998): 618–33, and Burns, "Intellectuals as Agents of Change," 211–46.

11. MacLachlan "Slavery, Ideology, and Institutional Change."

12. See Burns, "Intellectuals as Agents of Change," 220–21, 235–36, 245–46. For a summary of the major rebellions of the eighteenth century in Brazil, see Dauril Alden, "Late Colonial Brazil, 1750–1808," in *Colonial Brazil*, ed. Leslie Bethell (Cambridge: Cambridge University Press, 1991), 336–43. For a good study of the movements inspired by liberal ideas in Brazil during the late colonial period, see Kenneth R. Maxwell, *Conflicts and Conspiracies: Brazil and Portugal, 1750–1808* (Cambridge: Cambridge University Press, 1973).

13. Alden, "Late Colonial Brazil," 339.

14. Evaldo Cabral e Mello, *A ferida de narciso: Ensaio de história regional* (São Paulo: Editora SENAC, 2001), 69–76.

15. AHU, Pernambuco, cx. 228, doc. 15440, September 25, 1801, Recife.

16. Guilherme Pereira das Neves, "A suposta conspiração de 1801 em Pernmbuco: Idéias ilustradas ou conflitos tradicionais?" *Revista Portuguesa de História* 32, no. 2 (1999): 439–81.

17. Franklin Tavora, "Os patriotas de 1817," in *A república em Pernambuco*, ed. Leonardo Dantas Silva (Recife: FUNDAJ, Editora Massangana, 1990), 1–28.

18. The invasion also created irritating problems for familiares. When the French sacked Lisbon in 1807, they stole the cartas of familiares such as José Belém Lima, who had to request new ones. See ANTT, CGSO, m. 15.

19. ANTT, HSO, Pascoal, m. 2, no. 35; HSO, Joaquim, m. 21, no. 262; HSO, João, m. 128, no. 2007; HI, m. 8, no. 107.

20. ANTT, HSO, Gabriel, m. 4, no. 40.

21. ANTT, HSO, Lourenço, m. 10, no. 150.

22. ANTT, HI, m. 27, no. 131.

23. ANTT, Gaveta 18, m. 13, no. 2. "Artigos do Tratado de Paz entre o protector de Inglaterra e o senhor Rei D. João IV feitos a 10 de Julho de 1654. E confirmados em 29 de Fev. de 1655." ANTT, IL, Livro 154, fol. 354.

24. ANTT, Tratados: Inglaterra, cx. 5, nos. 1–2.

25. Nanci Leonzo, "As instituições," in *O império Luso-Brasileiro, 1750–1822*, ed. Maria Beatriz Nizza da Silva. Nova história da expansão Portuguesa, vol. 8 (Lisbon: Editorial Estampa, 1986), 314; Bethencourt, "Declínio e estinção do Santo Ofício," 81.

26. Bishop Azeredo Coutinho published several works that drew upon the ideas of the Enlightenment. See Guilherme Pereira das Neves, "Pálida e oblíquias luzes: J. J. da C. de Azeredo Coutinho e a análise sobre a justiça do comércio do resgate dos escravos," in *Brasil: Colonização e escravidão*, ed. Maria Beatriz Nizza da Silva (Rio de Janeiro: Nova Fronteira, 2000): 341–70.

27. Burns, "Intellectuals as Agents of Change."

28. Henry Koster, *Travels in Brazil*, ed. C. Harvey Gardiner (Carbondale: Southern Illinois University Press, 1966), 88–89.

29. ANTT, IL, m. 40. See also ANTT, IL, Processo 16460.

30. See Morais e Silva, *Diccionario da lingua portugueza*, s.v. "libertino."

31. António Baião has published the proceedings of António's trial in *Episódicos dramáticos da Inquisição Portuguesa*, vol. 2, *Homens de letras e de ciência por ela condenados—vária* (Lisbon: Seara Nova, 1973), 113–27.

32. For libertines in Maranhão around this same time, see Mott, "A Inquisição no Maranhão," 51–54.

33. ANTT, IL, Processo 13817.

34. ANTT, IL, Processo 14321.

35. ANTT, IL, Processo 16460.

36. ANTT, HI, Manuel, m. 27, no. 132.

37. I have been unable to find evidence for an epidemic in 1812.
38. ANTT, IL, NT 2126.
39. IAHGPE, Estante B, Gaveta 28.
40. ANTT, HSO, José, m. 57, no. 885.
41. ANTT IL, 319 and 320.
42. ANTT, CGSO, m. 6, no. 27.
43. ANTT, HI, Luís, m. 26, no. 130.
44. See "A Capitania de Pernambuco no governo de José César de Menezes (1774–1787)," *RIHGB* (1918): 558–60.
45. AHU, Pernambuco, cx. 204, doc. 13951; AHU, Pernambuco, cx. 148, doc. 10778; and AHU, Pernambuco, cx. 184, doc. 12793. Bento Furtado de Mendonça obtained permission to arm two of his slaves with pistols, muskets, or carbines. AHU, Pernambuco, cx. 191, doc. 13168; AHU, Pernambuco, cx. 242, doc. 16226. Antônio Marques da Costa Soares also gained permission to arm a slave with a pistol. AHU, Pernambuco, cx. 209, doc. 14211. Antônio Baptista Coelho gained permission to use a musket. AHU, Pernambuco, cx. 62, doc. 5284. For other examples, see AHU, Pernambuco, cx. 246, doc. 16473; AHU, Pernambuco, cx. 244, doc. 16367; AHU, Pernambuco, cx. 178, doc. 12482; AHU, Pernambuco, cx. 188, doc. 12995; AHU, Pernambuco, cx. 212, doc. 14407; AHU, Pernambuco, cx. 187, doc. 12977.
46. ANTT, HSO, Francisco, m. 95, no. 1572.
47. See Bethencourt, *História das Inquisições*, 349–50. António Baião published a facsimile of the order abolishing the Inquisition in A *Inquisição de Goa*, 1:370–71.
48. ANTT, MNEJ, m. 693, no. 5.

CHAPTER TWELVE

Conclusion

The characterization of the officials of the Inquisition as evil-minded religious fanatics, as ruthless spies, and as unprincipled bandits imposed upon an unsuspecting and impotent society has far outlived its usefulness. Where that characterization once served to justify Protestant opposition to Catholic dominance and to explain the demise of Iberian power on the world stage, it now obscures the Inquisition's larger program and distorts our view of the men who ran it and the societies that upheld it. The inquisitional beast has lurked for too long in historical hyperbole devoid of shape and substance. To call the monster from the shadows, clothe it in flesh, and face it squarely permits us to comprehend the larger inquisitional program and understand how profoundly the Inquisition sunk its roots into the Luso-Brazilian society that embraced it with open arms.

The extension of inquisitional authority to Brazil late in the sixteenth century required the institution to adapt to the demands of colonial Brazilian society and geography. Initially, it relied on local secular and ecclesiastical authorities. The bishops of Brazil also retained inquisitional jurisdiction and alternately worked with and fought against the tribunal in Lisbon, which sought to extend inquisitional control over the colony. The Inquisition developed this system early on, permitting it to extend its reach deep into colonial Pernambuco, both geographically and socially.

The Inquisition did not permit permanent resident officials in Brazil until after 1613, but even then applications for appointments in Pernambuco only trickled in. The Dutch occupation contributed to the slow development of a network in the seventeenth century, but the ongoing conflict between planters and merchants and Olinda and Recife in the late seventeenth and early eighteenth centuries contributed to an increased interest in inquisitional appointments. Purity of blood became a weapon in the ongoing conflicts where merchants and planters utilized the Inquisition to discredit their rivals.

In this sense, a metropolitan and imperial institution came to be appropriated by Pernambucan colonials and redeployed in local conflicts. Indeed, the large numbers of applicants suggests not only their active but also their willing participation in the institutions of colonial rule. Like other colonial institutions, the Inquisition was the product of an intercontinental monarchy engaged in a broad program of colonization, which required innovative adaptations. Seeing colonial Brazil from this perspective has recently become the focus of research on the colony.[1] The Inquisition in colonial Pernambuco, then, was not simply an outside imposition, but an important institution closely tied to the production and retention of honor, prestige, and social promotion in the captaincy.

Social mobility was also a reality in colonial Brazil. The Inquisition became one more tool in a much larger tool kit that socially mobile families and individuals used to assert and maintain their status and prestige. Inquisitional records provide numerous examples of men and families who started out with relatively little and came from comparatively humble backgrounds, but who nevertheless managed to acquire wealth, land, slaves, and status in the colonies.

The evidence for upward social mobility found in the Inquisition's records directly challenges the older, but still widely held, view of colonial Brazil as a rigidly hierarchical society dominated by a narrow and closed elite of wealthy planters. In this way, this study contributes to a growing body of literature that has begun to reevaluate that older view.[2] But much of that more-recent literature focuses on southeastern Brazil and on frontier areas or other regions where plantation agriculture did not fully develop until after 1700. By contrast, this research deals with the northeastern Captaincy-General of Pernambuco, a region where, already by the end of the sixteenth century, a slaved-based plantation economy had been firmly established. In other words, it deals with an area of colonial Brazil where, according to the older literature, social hierarchies should have been the most rigid.

The very real possibility of social mobility did not, by any means, translate into a completely open society. On the contrary, as many of the examples presented in this study demonstrate, wealth, land, and slaves did not by themselves guarantee access to political power, social honor, or prestige. These men and their families needed proof that they were "honorable."

In Pernambuco, honor, status, and nobility were tied to pure blood, honorable occupations, and a respectable lifestyle. These were ideals to be asserted and defended because they could have a very real bearing on individual and family access to economic, political, and social opportunities. But honor, status, and nobility were tried in the court of public opinion, so external "proofs" were necessary to solidify and legitimate claims to honor and nobility. The Inquisition became an important provider of such proof because other means of acquiring it were fairly limited. No new titles of nobility were ever created for Brazil, and the few fidalgos (lesser nobles) in colonial Pernambuco held no titles. Likewise, entrance into the military orders, though more frequent, still required military experience and was limited by the resources the crown had at its disposal. Other honorable positions, such as seats on the municipal council and officerships in the militia, were also finite and costly endeavors.

The procedures the Inquisition developed to select its own officials were meant to exclude those groups who had dishonorable ancestry, behavior, or occupations. These exclusionary practices contributed to the appeal of an appointment because it could grant status along with formal proof of purity. For this reason, when problems occurred in the application process, regardless of their source, complaints of loss of honor and status resulted. Consequently, some families and individuals engaged in genealogical fraud to cover up unsightly ancestries or to combat accusations of impurity. In Pernambuco, the production and defense of genealogies became a sort of protonativism. The old established families who had participated in the conquest of Pernambuco and the expulsion of the Dutch sought to retain their social position against challenges by more recent arrivals, who tended to be more heavily involved in commerce.

But these new arrivals could also utilize the Inquisition in their rivalry with the landed elite. Most of the officials of the Inquisition tended to belong to the so-called middle estate, which meant that their occupations were generally considered to be potentially honorable, and therefore they possessed the potential to exert honor and to become nobles if they could meet all the other requirements. To accomplish this, they often engaged in marriage strategies that reinforced their claims to purity and honor. Immigrant familiares tended to marry into local families and create mutually beneficial economic, political, and social relationships.

These findings challenge the scholarly literature, which emphasizes competition and rivalry between planters and merchants and between Portuguese immigrants and native-born Brazilians.[3] Such competition and rivalry did indeed exist and appears in the inquisitional documentation. Planters and merchants often found themselves at odds over issues such as prices and credit. Likewise, Portuguese immigrants tended to regard native-born Brazilians with disdain precisely because they were colonials; their "whiteness" and "purity" were, therefore, suspect. In turn, the well-established planters in Pernambuco, who saw themselves as the *nobreza da terra*, often regarded the immigrants as upstarts and usurpers.

Yet, as has been shown, the narrow focus on rivalry and competition that characterizes much of the historiography ultimately results in a distorted image of colonial society. As officials of the Inquisition, planters, merchants, immigrants, and native-born Brazilians all found within the Inquisition an institutional framework that encouraged collaboration, cooperation, and social interaction. In fact, quite frequently, immigrant merchants found that appointments to inquisitional office facilitated social acceptance and marriage into locally powerful merchant and planter families. Despite internal squabbling, intermarriage, economic relationships, and participation in inquisitional institutions provided different segments of the colonial elite with an arena for political solidarity and for a common social identity.

This broad-based intermingling and cooperation helps to explain the surprising convergence of interest and the enduring strength of the Pernambucan elite during the colonial period and beyond.[4] Despite all their differences, both planters and merchants, whether native-born Brazilians or immigrants, all shared a common interest in fostering the growth of the export economy, maintaining a slave-based society, and obtaining social honor within the Portuguese imperial system. They proved, over time, remarkably successful in defending that common interest not only against external challenges (such as the Dutch invasion of 1630–1654 and French, Dutch, and English piracy), but also, and perhaps more importantly, against frequent and serious internal challenges from both slaves and the growing free poor population.

Along with the "proofs" of purity came a series of inquisitional privileges that could also be beneficial. But early in the eighteenth century, those privileges were technically limited to clerical officials and a very small number of familiares in Brazil. This limitation of privilege resulted in ongoing conflict and confusion in colonial Brazil, which paradoxically permitted familiares, who otherwise would have been excluded, to enjoy some of the inquisitional privileges. At the same time, it provided leverage for local secular and ecclesiastical authorities who sought to constrict inquisitional power.

The ongoing confusion regarding inquisitional privilege and the continuing conflict with ecclesiastical and secular authorities suggests that ambiguity was a regular feature of colonial rule. It was part of the structure of unequally privileged groups who vied with one another for space within the privileged ranks and legitimated the crown's monopoly on privilege and the institutions of colonial rule. The creation of the brotherhood of St. Peter Martyr and the company of familiares in the late seventeenth and early eighteenth centuries permitted some officials to regain lost privileges. These organizations also contributed to the construction and maintenance of inquisitional power and authority by providing a rich and powerful symbolic repertoire that reinforced the philosophical underpinnings of the institution and that could be displayed in the public celebrations of St. Peter Martyr and the monthly drills of the company. These displays provided for the outward expression of group identity and the reproduction of social prestige and honor. They also offered some very real social welfare benefits for their members.

The regional concentration of inquisitional officials in the Zona da Mata and the occupational makeup of the officials of the Inquisition points to the paradox of inquisitional power in Pernambuco—it was both strong and weak. Geographically, the Inquisition had very little penetration into the interior, but its use of local secular and ecclesiastical authorities permitted it to reach more broadly than is generally assumed.

Socially, the Inquisition included officials from the highest levels of Pernambucan society and many of the important professions within the economic and political establishment. It was well entrenched in the upper levels of urban society. But the cost of an appointment and the exclusionary requirements limited the accessibility of an appointment, which meant that day laborers, low-level merchants, and poor farmers could not acquire an appointment even if they wanted one.

Despite the fact that inquisitional officials could and did travel outside the urban centers and that the Inquisition could and did use bishops and other ecclesiastical and secular authorities to assist in its work, inquisitional reach was neither pervasive nor all powerful. It was continuously held in check by local power figures who could, and did, interfere. It also struggled with its inability to count on the support of the powerful rural landholders, who joined the inquisitional ranks only in small numbers. These findings, together with the argument that the Inquisition shifted its focus from social control to social promotion in the late sixteenth century, may help explain similar dynamics found elsewhere in Latin America, where the Inquisition persisted even when limited geographic reach and increasingly limited repressive capacity no longer seemed to justify its continued existence.

The mechanisms that the Inquisition created to attract the highest-quality individuals and provide them with the prestige, honor, and status necessary to retain their continued support could and did backfire. The potential prestige, status, honor, and power of inquisitional office attracted impostors and abusers of inquisitional authority who hijacked it for personal advantage. Most frequently, the abuse or falsification of inquisitional authority had very limited objectives, such as gaining advantage in personal conflicts, obtaining protection from arrest or prosecution, or extorting money. But some impostors managed to maintain the charade for long periods of time, and ecclesiastical and secular authorities frequently obstructed the inquisitional process and challenged inquisitional privilege to assert their own authority or to protect their personal interests.

The Pombaline reforms of the mid-eighteenth century contributed to the growing decline of inquisitional power and prestige. The extension of inquisitional office to previously excluded groups effectively diminished the Inquisition's ability to provide proof of ethnic-racial purity in a society highly attuned to such public declarations. The restriction of privilege combined with the declining interest in the inquisitional brotherhood and militia, whose participants began to conclude that the social and economic costs of participation exceeded the potential payoff. The old forms of exclusion and integration based on race, behavior, and orthodoxy ceased to function, and the Inquisition ceased to occupy a prominent place on the institutional game board. The prestige value of an inquisitional appointment began to decline, and fewer people sought inquisitional appointments after 1794 in Pernambuco. The growing influence of enlightened ideas and the political transformations within the Luso-Brazilian world chipped away at the inquisitional edifice and infiltrated the ranks of inquisitional officials. The external pressures, combined with this internal rot, finally brought the edifice down.

The men who ran the Inquisition in colonial Pernambuco were not necessarily the sadistic social misfits of the myth. The Inquisition and its officials in Pernambuco filled important social and economic roles in a symbiotic relationship in which they each drew power and prestige from one another. This relationship was mediated by the institutional structures and organization of the Inquisition and was supported by the social and religious values it promoted. The Inquisition was an integral part of Luso-Brazilian society. Its institutional and ideological tentacles of power intertwined comfortably, even pleasantly, with the deep-seated values of honor, prestige, and status that were fed by a society based on exclusion and intolerance. These conclusions not only challenge the perceptions of the Inquisition in Pernambuco and Brazil as weak and largely irrelevant, but they also challenge the larger perceptions about the construction, application, and decline of inquisitional power and authority in the Portuguese Empire and the myths that continue to obscure our understanding of Luso-Brazilian society.

As we peer at the monster we have called from the shadows, we see a many-headed hydra. But it does not simply possess the sinister visage of Julio Dantas's sensual and corrupt inquisitor general. It also has the determined and slightly fanatical face of Joaquim Marques de Araújo as he writes in his impeccable hand to denounce the rampant libertines who threaten to destroy the ancien régime to which he so desperately clings. It has the hopeful and aspiring face of the Portuguese immigrant Antônio de Araújo Barbosa, who successfully used his inquisitional appointment to arrange a marriage into an established planter family. It has the confident and assured face of the sugar planter Antônio Alves Gorjão, the son and grandson of familiares. It even has the anxious, concerned, and perhaps angry faces of Antônio Gonçalves Carneiro and Felipe Pais Barreto as they struggle to get their applications approved and to put down embarrassing rumors of personal impurity. These many and changing faces warn us to be cautious in applying inaccurate and rigid stereotypical labels and clichés as blanket descriptions of the Inquisition as an institution and of its officials. They also warn us to beware viewing regimes of intolerance only through the lens of repression. Repression of any kind cannot occur without the acquiescence of those who support repressive and intolerant institutions and ideologies and, in many cases, benefit from them. A study of the men who worked for the Portuguese Inquisition in colonial Pernambuco reveals that institutions of intolerance are inherently parasitic. They appropriate widely held social norms and values and manipulate social tensions to reproduce themselves.

The techniques, practices, ideologies, rituals, and institutions utilized by the Portuguese Inquisition developed over a long period of time, paralleling the creation of systematized governance and jurisprudence during the medieval and early modern periods, and coincided with the rise of the European nation-state, race-based nationalism, rationality, and bureaucratic rule.[5] Indeed, the inquisitional technology of power continues to resonate in today's world precisely because it forms the heart of the modern bureaucratic state, which suffers from both its strengths and its defects.

Notes

1. See, for example, João Fragoso, Maria Fernanda Bicalho, and Maria de Fátima Gouvêa, eds., *O Antigo Regime nos trópicos: A dinâmica imperial portuguesa (séculos XVI–XVIII)* (Rio de Janeiro: Civilização Brasileira, 2001).

2. See, for example, Willems, "Social Differentiation"; Schwartz, *Sugar Plantations*; and Castro Faria, *A colônia em movimento*.

3. See, for example, Manchester, "Rise of the Brazilian Aristocracy"; Russell-Wood, *Fidalgos and Philanthropists*; Kennedy, "Bahian Elites"; Cabral de Mello, *A fronda dos mazombos*.

4. Emilio Willems noted this convergence of interest in "Social Differentiation in Colonial Brazil."

5. See Given's *Inquisitional and Medieval Society* for the medieval origins of modern forms of governance and jurisprudence. Irene Silverblatt demonstrates that the Inquisition epitomizes the central characteristics of the modern nation-state, in *Modern Inquisitions: Peru and the Colonial Origins of the Civilized World* (Durham: Duke University Press, 2004).

Bibliography

Archives and Manuscript Collections

Arquivo Histórico Militar, Portugal
Arquivo Histórico Ultramarino, Portugal
Arquivo Nacional/Torre do Tombo, Portugal
    Armário Jesuítico
    Autos Forenses
    Bulas e Breves
    Conselho Geral do Santo Ofício
    Habilitações do Santo Ofício
    Habilitações Incompletas
    Inquisição de Coimbra
    Inquisição de Évora
    Inquisição de Lisboa
    Leis
    Manuscritos da Livraria
    Manuscritos do Brasil
    Mesa da Consciência e Ordens
    Mercês
Arquivo Público Estadual Jordão Emerenciano, Pernambuco, Brazil
Biblioteca da Ajuda, Portugal
Biblioteca Nacional, Portugal
Instituto Archeológico Histórico e Geográphico Pernambucano, Brazil
Ministerio dos Negócios Eclesiásticos e da Justiça
    Ministerio do Reino
    Novas Habilitações

Serie Preta
Tratados

Primary Published Sources

Almeida, Candido Mendes de. *Auxiliar Juridico: Servindo de appendice a decima quarta edição do Codigo Philippino ou Ordenações do reino de Portugal, recopilados por mandado d'el Rey D. Phillipe I.* 2 vols. 24th ed. Rio de Janeiro, 1869. Reprint ed.; Lisbon: Fundação Calouste Gulbenkian, 1985.

———. *Codigo Phillipino, ou Ordenações e leis do reino de Portugal, recopilados por mandado d'el Rey D. Phillipe I.* 5 vols. 14th ed. Rio de Janeiro, 1870. Reprint ed.; Lisbon: Fundação Calouste Gulbenkian, 1985.

Baião, António. "El-Rei D. João IV e a Inquisição." *Academia Portuguesa de História* 4 (1942): 10–70.

———. "Tentativa de estabelecimento duma Inquisição privativa no Brasil." *Brotéria* 22 (1936): 477–82.

Bluteau, Rafael. *Vocabulario portuguez e latino, aulico, anatomico, architectonico, botanico . . . autorizado com exemplos dos melhores escritores Portuguezes e Latinos e offerecido a El Rey de Portugal D. João V.* 8 vols. Coimbra: Collegio das Artes da Companhia de Jesus, 1712–1721.

Collecção dos negocios de Roma no reinado de El-Rey Dom José I: Ministério do Marqués de Pombal e pontifidaco de Clemente XIV, 1769–1774. 3 vols. Lisboa: Imprensa Nacional, 1874.

Constituiçoens primeiras do arcebispado da Bahia feitas, e ordenadas pelo illustrissimo, e reverendissmo senhor D. Sebastião Monteiro da Vide Arcebispo do dito Arcebispado, e do conselho de Sua Magestade, propostas, e aceitas em o synodo diecesano, que o dito senhor celeberou em 12 de Junho do anno de 1707. Lisboa: Na officina de Miguel Rodrigues, impressor do Eminentissimo Senhor Cardeial Patriarca, 1765.

Dellon, Charles. *Narração da Inquisição de Goa.* Translated by Miguel Vicente de Abreu. Lisbon: Edições Antígona, 1996.

Documentos para a história da Inquisição em Portugal. Porto: Arquivo Histórico Dominicano Português, 1984.

Fonseca, Antônio José Victoriano Borges da. *Nobiliarchia Pernambuco.* 2 vols. Rio de Janeiro: Biblioteca Nacional, 1935.

França, Eduardo d'Oliveira and Sonia Siqueira, eds. *Segunda Visitação do Santo Officio às partes do Brasil pelo inquisidor e visitador o licenciado Marcos Teixeira: Livro das confissões e ratificações da Bahia.* Vol. 17, Anais do Museu Paulista. 123–547.

Freitas, Jordão de. *O Marquez de Pombal e o Santo Officio da Inquisição: Memoria enriquecida com documentos inéditos e facsimiles de assignaturas do benemerito da cidade de Lisboa.* Lisbon, 1916.

Furtado e Mendonça, Hippolyto Joseph da Costa Pereira. *Narrativa da perseguição de Hippolyto Joseph da Costa Pereira Furtado de Mendonça, natural da Colonia do Sacramento, no Rio-da-Prata. Prezo e processado em Lisboa pelo pretenso crime de Fra-maçon ou pereiro livre.* 2 vols. London: W. Lewis, 1811.

Jaboatão, Antônio de Santa Maria. *Catalogo genealogico das principais familias que procederam de Albuquerques, e Cavalcantes em Pernambuco, e Caramurus na Bahia, tiradas de memorias, manuscritos antigos e fidedignos, autorizados por alguns escritores, e em especial o Theatro Genealogico de D. Livisco de Nazáo Zarco e Colona, aliás Manuel de Carvalho de Atahide, e acrescentado o mais moderno, e confirmado tudo, assim moderno, como antigo com assentos dos livros de baptizados, casamentos, e enterros, que se quardam na camara eccleziastica da Bahia*. 1768. Reprint; *RIHGB* 3, no. 1 (1889): 5–489.

———. *Orbe Serafico novo Brasilico Descoberto, estabelicido, e cultivado a Influxos da nova luz de Italia, estrella brilhante de Hespanha, Luzido sol de Padua, Astro Mayor do Ceu de Francisco, o thaumaturgo Portuguez Sto. Antonio, a quem vay consagrado, como Theatro glorioso, e parte primeira da Chronica dos Frades menores da mais estreita, e regular observancia da provincia do Brasil*. Lisboa: António Vicente da Silva, 1761.

Jaboataõ Mystico em correntes sacras dividido. Corrente primeira Panegyrica, e moral, offerecida, debaixo da Protecçaõ da milagrosa imagem do Senhor Santo Amaro, Venerada na sua Igreja Matriz do Jaboataõ, Ao Illustrissimo E Excellentissimo S.nhor Luiz José Correa de Sá, Governador de Pernambuco, por Fr. Antonio de S.ta Maria Jaboatam, Filho da Provincia de Santo Antonio do Brasil. Lisboa: António Vicente da Silva, 1758 (Biblioteca da Ajuda, 5-IV-46).

Koster, Henry. *Travels in Brazil*. Edited by C. Harvey Gardiner. Carbondale: Southern Illinois University Press, 1966.

Livro da Visitação do Santo Oficio da Inquisição ao Estado do Grão-Pará (1763–1769). Petrópolis: Vozes, 1978.

Livros das Denunciações que se fizeram no Visitação do Santo Ofício à Cidade de Salvador da Bahia de Todos os Santos do Estado do Brasil, no ano de 1618. Vol. 49, Anais da Biblioteca Nacional. 1927.

Mello, José Antônio Gonçalves de, ed. *Primeira Visitação do Santo Ofício às partes do Brasil. Confissões de Pernambuco, 1594–1595*. Recife: Universidade Federal de Pernambuco, 1970.

Morais e Silva, Antonio de. *Diccionario da lingua portugueza*. 2 vols. Lisbon: M. P. de Lacerda, 1823.

Mott, Luiz. *Regimento dos Comissários e Escrivães do seu cargo, dos Qualificadores e dos Familiares do Santo Oficio*. Salvador: Universidade Federal da Bahia, 1990.

Nieto, David. *Noticias Reconditas del procedimiento de las Inquisiciones de España y Portugal con sus Presos; Dividas en dos Partes, la primeira en Idioma Portuguez, la Segunda en Castellano; Deduzidas de Autores Catholicos Apostolicos Romanos, Eminentes por Dignidad, o por Letras Obra tan curiosa como Instructiva, Compilada, por un Autor Anonimo En Villa Franca. 1720*. London, 1720.

Pereira, Isaías da Rosa, ed. *Documentos para a história da Inquisição em Portugal*. Porto: Arquivo Histórico Dominicano Português, 1984.

———. *A Inquisição em Portugal: Séculos XVI–XVII-Período Filipino*. Lisbon: Vega, 1993.

Primeira Visitação do Santo Ofício às partes do Brasil. Confissões da Bahia, 1591–1592. Preface by João Capistrano de Abreu. Rio de Janeiro: Briguet, 1935.

Primeira Visitação do Santo Ofício às partes do Brasil. Denunciações da Bahia, 1591–1593. Introduction by João Capistrano de Abreu. São Paulo: Paulo Prado, 1925.

Primeira Visitação do Santo Ofício às partes do Brasil. Denunciações de Pernambuco, 1593–1595. Introduction by Rodolfo Garcia. São Paulo: Paulo Prado, 1929.

"Segunda visitação do Santo Ofício às partes do Brasil. Livro das Confissões e Ratificações da Bahia, 1618–1620." Introduction by Eduardo d'Oliveira França and Sônia Siqueira. Vol. 17, *Anais do Museu Paulista*, (São Paulo: 1963), 123–547.

Sermam do Glorioso S. Pedro Martyr, O primeiro Inquisidor martyrizado, ou o primeiro que deo a vida em defensa da Fé, que defende o Santo Tribunal da Inquisição; Mandado imprimir pelos Familiares do Santo Officio da Cidade da Bahia na occasião, em que celebrarão a sua primeira Festa com uma procissão solemníssima, trazendo o Santo da Sé para o Mosteyro do Patriarcha S. Bento. Pregou-o Muito Reverendo Padre Mestre O Doutor Fr. Ruperto de Jesus, Lente Jubilado em Theologia, Qualificador, e Revedor do S. Officio, Monge Benedictino, da Provincia do Brasil, na era de 1697. Lisboa: António Pedrozo Galrão, 1697 (BNL, Res 9335).

Sermam do invicto Martyr e protector da Fe, Pedro de Verona. Impresso por ordem do Il.mo S.nr Inquisidor Geral e pregado no convento de S. Domingos desta cidade. M. R. P. fr. Manuel Guilherme. Leitor de Vespera do Real Collegio de N. S. da escada no anno de 1686. Lisboa: Miguel Manescal, 1686 (BNL, Res 3024, 18p).

Sermao feito em S. Domingos do Porto anno do Senhor, 1620 na festa de S. Pedro Martyr Padroeiro da Santa Inquisição, na instituição da Irmandade dos familiares do Santo Officio, por mandado, & authoridade do senhor Inquisidor Geral dom Fernão Martinz Mascarenhas. Porto: Nicolao Carvalho, 1620 (BNL, Res 3024, 18p).

Siqueira, Sonia A. "Os Regimentos da Inquisição." *Revista do Instituto Histórico e Geográfico Brasileiro* 157, no. 392 (July–September 1996): 495–1020.

Viterbo, Joaquim de Santa Rosa de. *Elucidario das palavras, termos e frases que em Portugal antigamente se usaram e que hoje regularmente se ignoram.* 2nd. ed. Edited by A. J. Fernandes Lopes. Lisbon: Em casa do Editor A. J. Fernandes Lopes, 1865.

Published and Unpublished Secondary Sources

Alden, Dauril. "Late Colonial Brazil, 1750–1808." In *Colonial Brazil*, ed. Leslie Bethell, 284–343. Cambridge: Cambridge University Press, 1991.

——— . "The Population of Brazil in the Late Eighteenth Century: A Preliminary Survey." *HAHR* 43, no. 2 (May 1963): 173–205.

——— . "Price Movements in Brazil Before, During, and After the Gold Boom, with Special Reference to the Salvador Market, 1670–1769." In *Essays on the Price History of Eighteenth-Century Latin America*, ed. Lyman L. Johnson and Enrique Tandeter, 173–205. Albuquerque: University of New Mexico Press, 1990.

——— . *Royal Government in Colonial Brazil: With Special Reference to the Administration of the Marquis of Lavradio, Viceroy, 1769–1779.* Berkeley: University of California Press, 1968.

Almeida, Fortunato de. *História da Igreja em Portugal.* 4 vols. Porto: Livraria Civilização, 1971.
Andrade, Manuel Correia de. *The Land and People of Northeast Brazil.* Translated by Dennis V. Johnson. Albuquerque: University of New Mexico Press, 1980.
Athayde, Johildo Lopes de. "Filhos ilegítimos e crianças expostas (Nota para o estudo da família)." *Revista da Academia de Letras da Bahia* 27 (1980): 9–25.
Aufderheide, Patricia. "True Confessions: The Inquisition and Social Attitudes in Brazil at the Turn of the XVII Century." *Luso-Brazilian Review* 20, no. 2 (December 1973): 208–40.
Azevedo, J. Lúcio de. *História dos Cristãos-Novos Portugueses*, 3rd ed. Lisbon: Clássica Editora, 1989.
Baião, António. *Episódicos dramáticos da Inquisição Portuguesa.* 3 vols. Lisbon: Seara Nova, 1973.
———. *A Inquisição de Goa: Tentativa de história de sua origem, estabelecimento, evolução, e extinção* 2 vols. Lisbon: Academia das Ciências de Lisboa, 1949.
———. *A Inquisição em Portugal e no Brasil: Subsidios para a sua história: A Inquisição no século XVI.* Lisbon: Arquivo Histórico Portuguese, 1920.
Baigent, Michael, and Richard Leigh. *The Inquisition.* London: Viking, 1999.
Barata, Manuel. "Apontamentos para a história eclesiastica de Pernambuco." *Revista do Instituto Archeológico, Histórico e Geográphico Pernambucano* 24 (1922): 319–428.
Barickman, Bert. *Bahian Counterpoint: Sugar, Tobacco, Cassava, and Slavery in the Recôncavo, 1780–1860.* Stanford: Stanford University Press, 1998.
Barman, Roderick, and Jean Barman. "The Prosopography of the Brazilian Empire." *LARR* 13, no. 2 (1978): 78–97.
Barroso, Gustavo, and J. Wasth Rodrigues, eds. *Uniformes do exército brasileiro.* Rio de Janeiro, 1922.
Beattie, Peter M. "The House, the Street, and the Barracks: Reform and Honorable Masculine Social Space in Brazil, 1864–1945." *HAHR* 76, no. 3 (1996): 439–73.
Bethencourt, Francisco. "Declínio e estinção do Santo Ofício." *Revista de História Económica e Social* (1987): 77–85.
———. *História das Inquisições: Portugal, Espanha, e Itália.* Lisbon: Temas e Debates, 1996.
———. "Inquisição e controle social." *História e crítica* 14 (1987): 5–18.
Bicalho, Maria Fernada Baptista. "As câmaras ultramarinas e o governo do Império." In *O Antigo Regime nos trópicos: A dinâmica imperial portuguesa (séculos XVI–XVIII)*, ed. João Fragoso, Maria Fernanda Bicalho, and Maria de Fátima Gouvêa, 191–221. Rio de Janeiro: Civilização Brasileira, 2001.
Borges, Dain. *The Family in Bahia, Brazil, 1870–1945.* Stanford: Stanford University Press, 1992.
Boschi, Caio C. "As visitas diocesanas e a Inquisição na colônia." *Revista Brasileira de História* 7, no. 14 (March/August 1987): 151–84.

———. *Os leigos e o poder: Irmandades leigas e política colonizadora em Minas Gerais.* São Paulo: Editora Ática, 1986.

Boxer, C. R. *The Golden Age of Brazil, 1695–1750: Growing Pains of a Colonial Society.* Berkeley: University of California Press, 1964.

Burns, E. Bradford. "The Intellectuals as Agents of Change and the Independence of Brazil, 1724–1822." In *From Colony to Nation: Essays on the Independence of Brazil,* ed. A. J. R. Russell-Wood, 211–46. Baltimore: Johns Hopkins University Press, 1975.

———. "The Role of Azeredo Coutinho in the Enlightenment of Brazil." *HAHR* 44, no. 2 (May 1964): 145–60.

Calainho, Daniela. "Em nome do Santo Ofício: Familiares da Inquisição portuguesa no Brasil colonial." Master's thesis, Universidade Federal do Rio de Janeiro, 1992.

Cândido, Antônio. "Literature and the Rise of Brazilian National Self-Identity." *Luso-Brazilian Review* 5, no. 1 (June 1968): 27–43.

Cardozo, Manoel S. "The Lay Brotherhoods of Colonial Bahia." *Catholic Historical Review* 33, no. 1 (April 1947), 12–30.

Cardozo, Manoel. "Azeredo Coutinho and the Intellectual Ferment of His Times." In *Conflict and Continuity in Brazilian Society,* ed. Henry H. Keith and S. F. Edwards, 72–103. Columbia: University of South Carolina Press, 1969.

Carneiro, Ana, Ana Simões, and Maria Paula Diogo. "Enlightenment Science in Portugal: The Estrangeirados and Their Communication Networks." *Social Studies of Science* 30, no. 4 (August 2000): 591–619.

Carneiro, Maria Luiza Tucci. *Preconceito Racial no Brasil-Colônia: Os cristãos-novos.* São Paulo: Editora Brasiliense, 1983.

Carvalho, Augusto da Silva. "Dois processos da Inquisição interesantes para a história da propaganda contra êste tribunal." *Anais da Academia Portuguesa da História* 9 (1945): 47–91.

Carvalho, José Murilo de. *A construção da ordem: A elite política imperial.* Rio de Janeiro: Editora Campus, 1980.

Caulfield, Sueann. *In Defense of Honor: Sexual Morality, Modernity, and Nation in Early-Twentieth Century Brazil.* Durham: Duke University Press, 2000.

Caulfield, Sueann, and Martha de Abreu Esteves. "Fifty Years of Virginity in Rio Janeiro: Sexual Roles in Juridical and Popular Discourse, 1890–1940." *Luso-Brazilian Review* 30, no. 1 (1993): 47–74.

César, José Vicente. "Situação legal do índio durante o periódo colonial (1500–1822)." *América Indígena* 45, no. 2 (April–June 1985): 391–425.

Cheke, Marcus. *Dictator of Portugal: A Life of the Marquis of Pombal, 1699–1782.* Freeport, NY: Books for Libraries, 1938. Reprint ed., 1969.

Codeceira, José Domingues Codeceira. "Expozição de factos históricos que comprovam a prioridae de Pernambuco na independência e liberdade nacional." *RIHGB* 53 (1890): 327–42.

Contreras, Jaime. *El Santo Oficio de la Inquisición en Galicia, 1560–1700: Poder, sociedade y cultura.* Madrid: Akal Editor, 1982.

Corrêa, Mariza. "Repensando a Família Patriarchal Brasileira: Notas para o estudo das formas de organização familiar no Brasil." In *Colcha de Retalhos: Estudos sobre a família no Brasil*, ed. Maria Suely Kofes de Almeida et al., 13–38. São Paulo: Editora Brasiliense, 1982.

Cunha, Ana Cannas da. *A Inquisição no Estado da Índia: Origens, 1539–1560.* Lisbon: ANTT, 1995.

Dantas, Júlio. *Santa Inquisição.* Lisbon: Arthur Brandão, 1909.

Domingues, Ângela. *Quando os índios eram vassalos: Colonização e relações de poder no Norte do Brasil na segunda metade do século XVIII.* Lisbon: Comissão Nacional para as comemorações dos descobrimentos Portugueses, 2000.

Donovan, William Michael. "Commercial Enterprise and Luso-Brazilian Society during the Brazilian Gold Rush: The Mercantile House of Francisco Pinheiro and the Lisbon to Brazil Trade, 1695–1750." Ph.D. dissertation, Johns Hopkins University, 1991.

Dutra, Francis A. "Duarte Coelho Pereira, First Lord-Proprietor of Pernambuco: The Beginning of a Dynasty." *Americas* 29, no. 4 (April 1973): 415–41.

——— . "The Maritime Profession and Membership in the Portuguese Military Orders in the Late Seventeenth and Early Eighteenth Centuries." In *Marginated Groups in Spanish and Portuguese History*, ed. William D. Phillips Jr. and Carla Rahn Phillips, 89–109. Minneapolis: Society for Spanish and Portuguese Historical Studies, 1989.

Eisenberg, Peter L. *The Sugar Industry in Pernambuco: Modernization without Change, 1840–1910.* Berkeley: University of California Press, 1974.

Faria, Sheila de Castro. *A colônia em movimento: Fortuna e família no cotidiano colonial.* Rio de Janeiro: Editora Nova Fronteira, 1998.

Feitler, Bruno. *Inquisition, Juifs et Nouveaux-Chrétiens au Brésil: le Nordeste XVIIe et XVIIIe Siecles.* Louvain, Belgium: Leuven University Press, 2003.

Ferguson, George. *Signs and Symbols in Christian Art.* London: Oxford University Press, 1961.

Figueiredo, Luciano Raposo de Almeida. *Barrocas famílias: Vida familiar em Minas Gerais no século XVIII.* São Paulo: Editora Hucitec, 1997.

Flory, Rae Jean Dell. "Bahian Society in the Mid-Colonial Period: The Sugar Planters, Tobacco Growers, Merchants, and Artisans of Salvador and the Recôncavo, 1680–1725." Ph.D. dissertation, University of Texas at Austin, 1978.

Flory, Rae, and David Grant Smith. "Bahian Merchants and Planters in the Seventeenth and Early Eighteenth Centuries." *HAHR* 58, no. 4 (1978): 571–94.

Fonseca, Célia Freire A. "Comércio e Inquisição no Brasil do século XVIII." In *Inquisição: Ensaios sobre mentalidade, heresias e arte*, ed. Anita Novinsky and M. Luiza Tucci Carneiro, 195–207. Rio de Janeiro: Expressão e Cultura, 1992.

Foucault, Michel. *Power/Knowledge: Selected Interviews and Other Writings 1972–1977.* Edited by Colin Goerdon. New York: Pantheon, 1980.

Fragoso, João Luís Ribeiro, and Manolo Garcia Florentino. *O arcaísmo como projecto: Mercado atlântico sociedade agrária e elite mercantil no Rio de Janeiro, c. 1790–c. 1840.* Rio de Janeiro: Diadorim, 1993.

Fragoso, João, Maria Fernanda Bicalho, and Maria de Fátima Gouvêa, eds. *O Antigo Regime nos trópicos: A dinâmica imperial portuguesa (séculos XVI–XVIII).* Rio de Janeiro: Civilização Brasileira, 2001.
Freitas, Eugénio Cunha e. *Familiares do Santo Oficio no Porto.* Porto, 1979.
Freyre, Gilberto. *Casa Grande e Senzala.* Rio de Janeiro: Maia and Schmidt, 1933.
Galende Díaz, Juan C. "Una aproximación a la hermandad inquisitorial de San Pedro Mártir." *Cuadernos de Investigación Histórica* 14 (1991): 45–86.
Given, James. *Inquisitional and Medieval Society: Power, Discipline, and Resistance in Languedoc.* Ithaca: Cornell University Press, 1997.
———. "The Inquisitors of Languedoc and the Medieval Technology of Power." *AHR* 94, no. 2 (April 1989): 336–59.
Gomes, Alfredo Dais. *O Santo Inquérito.* 1966.
Greenleaf, Richard E. "The Inquisition Brotherhood: Cofradía de San Pedro Mártir of Colonial Mexico." *Americas* 40, no. 2 (October 1983): 171–207.
Haliczer, Stephen. *Inquisition and Society in the Kingdom of Valencia, 1478–1834.* Berkeley: University of California Press, 1990.
Hassig, Ross. *Mexico and the Spanish Conquest.* London: Longman, 1994.
Herculano, Alexandre. *História da Origem e estabelecimento da inquisição em Portugal.* 3 vols. Lisbon: Editora Livraria Bertrand, 1975.
———. *History of the Origin and Establishment of the Inquisition in Portugal.* Translated by John C. Branner. Stanford University Press, 1926.
Herrick, Jane. "The Reluctant Revolutionist: A Study of the Political Ideas of Hipólito da Costa (1774–1823)." *Americas* 7, no. 2 (October 1950): 171–81.
Higgs, David. "Á recepção da revolução francesa em Portugal e no Brasil." In *Actas do Colóquio A recepção da revolução francesa em Portugal e no Brasil II em 2 a 9 Novembro de 1989*, 227–46. Porto: Universidade do Porto, 1992.
———. "Comissários e familiares da Inquisição no Brasil ao fim do período colonial." In *Inquisição: Ensaios sobre mentalidade, heresias e arte*, ed. Anita Novinsky and M. Luiza Tucci Carneiro, 374–88. Rio de Janeiro: Expressão e Cultura, 1992.
———. "Os perigos da francesia no Brasil no período da revolução francesa." In *Actas do colóquio A recepção da revolução francesa em Portugal e no Brasil II em 2 a 9 de Novembro de 1989*, 227–46 Porto: Universidade de Porto, 1992.
———. "Sacred and Secular Law in Late Colonial Brazil." Paper presented at the Latin American Studies Association, Chicago, 1998.
Higgs, David, and Guilherme P. Neves, "O oportunismo da historiografia: O Padre Bernardo Luís Ferreira Portugal e o movimento de 1817 em Pernambuco." In *Sociedade Brasileira de Pesquisa Histórica*, 179–84. São Paulo, 1989.
Hoorneart, Eduardo. "As relações entre Igreja e Estado na Bahia colonial." *Revista eclesiastica brasileira* 32 (1972): 275–308.
———, et al. *História da igreja no Brasil: Ensaio de interpretação a partir do povo: Primeira Época.* 2nd ed. Petrópolis: Editora Vozes, 1979.
Johnson, Lyman L., and Sonya Lipsett-Rivera, eds. *The Faces of Honor: Sex, Shame, and Violence in Colonial Latin America.* Albuquerque: University of New Mexico, 1998.

Kamen, Henry. *The Spanish Inquisition: An Historical Revision*. London: Weidenfeld, 1997.
Kennedy, John Norman. "Bahian Elites, 1750–1822." *HAHR* 53, no. 3 (August 1973): 415–39.
Kiddy, Elizabeth W. "Ethnic and Racial Identity in the Brotherhoods of the Rosary of Minas Gerais, 1700–1830." *Americas* 56, no. 2 (October 1999): 221–52.
Kraay, Hendrik. *Race, State, and Armed Forces in Independence-Era Brazil: Bahia, 1790s–1840s*. Stanford: Stanford University Press, 2001.
Kuznesof, Elizabeth Anne. *Household Economy and Urban Development: São Paulo, 1765–1836*. Boulder: Westview, 1986.
———. "The Role of the Merchants in the Economic Development of São Paulo, 1765–1850." *HAHR* 60, no. 4 (1980): 571–92.
———. "Sexual Politics, Race and Bastard-Bearing in Nineteenth-Century Brazil: A Question of Culture or Power?" *Journal of Family History: Studies in Family, Kinship and Demography* 16, no. 3, (1991): 241–60.
Lea, Henry Charles. *A History of the Inquisition of Spain*. 4 vols. New York: MacMillan, 1922.
———. *A History of the Inquisition of the Middle Ages*. 3 vols. New York: MacMillan, 1922.
Leite, Miriam Lifchitz Moreira. "O óbvio e o contraditório da roda." In *História da criança no Brasil*, ed. Mary del Priore, 98–111. São Paulo: Editora Contexto, 1991.
Leite, Serafim. *História da Companhia de Jesus no Brasil*. 5 vols. Rio de Janeiro: Civilização Brasileira, 1938.
Leonzo, Nanci. "As instituições." In *O império Luso-Brasileiro, 1750–1822*, ed. Maria Beatriz Nizza da Silva, 302–31. Nova história da expansão Portuguesa. Lisbon: Editorial Estampa, 1986.
Levine, Robert M. *Pernambuco in the Brazilian Federation, 1889–1937*. Stanford: Stanford University Press, 1978.
Lewin, Linda. "Natural and Spurious Children in Brazilian Inheritance Law from Colony to Empire: A Methodological Essay." *Americas* 48 (January 1992): 351–96.
———. *Surprise Heirs: Illegitimacy, Patrimonial Rights, and Legal Nationalism in Luso-Brazilian Inheritance, 1750–1821*, vol. 1. Stanford: Stanford University Press, 2003.
Lima, Lana Lage da Gama. "O Santo Ofício e a moralização do clero no Brasil colonial." *Vozes* 83, no. 6 (November–December 1989): 693–703.
Lima, Lana Lage da Gama, and Renato Pinto Venâncio. "O abandono de crianças negras no Rio de Janeiro." In *História da criança no Brasil*, ed. Mary del Priore, 61–75. São Paulo: Editora Contexto, 1991.
Lipiner, Elias. *Terror e Linguagem: Um dicionário da Santa Inquisição*. Lisbon: Círculo de Leitores, 1999.
Lopes, Carlos da Silva. "Nobreza do século XVIII." *Integralismo Lusitano* 1, no. 4 (September 1932): 312–17.
Loreto, Aliatar. *Capítulos de história militar do Brasil (Colônia-Reino)*. Rio de Janeiro: Edifício do Ministério da Guerra, 1945.
Love, Joseph L. *São Paulo in the Brazilian Federation, 1889–1937*. Stanford: Stanford University Press, 1980.

Lugar, Catherine. "The Merchant Community of Salvador, Bahia 1780–1830." Ph.D. dissertation, State University of New York, Stony Brook, 1980.

Lustosa, Fernanda Mayer. "Raízes judaicas na Paraíba colonial: Séculos VXI–XVIII." Master's thesis, University of São Paulo, 2000.

MacLachlan, Colin M. "Slavery, Ideology, and Institutional Change: The Impact of the Enlightenment on Slavery in Late-Eighteenth Century Maranhão." *JLAS* 11, no. 1 (May 1979): 1–17.

Manchester, Alan K. "The Rise of the Brazilian Aristocracy." *HAHR* 11, no. 2 (May 1931): 145–68.

Marchant, Alexander. "Aspects of the Enlightenment in Brazil." In *Latin America and the Enlightenment*, ed. Arthur P. Whitaker, 95–118. 2nd ed. Ithaca: Cornell University Press, 1961.

Marcílio, Maria Luiza. "A Irmandade da Santa Casa de Misericórdia e a assistência à criança abandonada na história do Brasil." In *Família, mulher, sexualidade e Igreja na história do Brasil*, ed. Maria Luiza Marcílio, 148–61. São Paulo: Edições Loyola, 1993.

———. "Abandonados y expósitos en la história de Brasil. Un proyecto interdisciplinario de investigación." In *La Família en el mundo iberoamericano*, ed. Pilar Gonzalbo Aizpuru and Cecilia Rabell, 311–26. Mexico: Universidad Nacional Autónoma de México, 1994.

Marques, A. H. de Oliveira. *History of Portugal*. 2nd ed. New York: Columbia University Press, 1976.

Mattoso, Katia de Queiros. *Família e sociedade na Bahia do século XIX*. São Paulo: Corrupio, 1988.

Max, Frédéric. *Prisioneiros da Inquisição: Relato de vítimas das inquisições espanhola, portuguesa e romana transcritos e traduzidos com anotações e precedidos por um levantamento histórico*. Translated by Jusmar Gomes and Susie Fercik Staudt. Porto Alegre: L&PM, 1991.

Maxwell, Kenneth R. *Conflicts and Conspiracies: Brazil and Portugal, 1750–1808*. Cambridge: Cambridge University Press, 1973.

———. *Pombal: Paradox of the Enlightenment*. Cambridge: Cambridge University Press, 1995.

Mea, Elvira Cunha de Azevedo. *A Inquisição de Coimbra no século XVI: A instituição, os homens, e a sociedade*. Porto: Fundação Eng. António de Almeida, 1997.

Meihy, José Carlos Sebe Bom. "Antônio José da Silva: O teatro judaizante. História ou Literatura?" In *Inquisição: Ensaios sobre mentalidade, heresias e arte*, ed. Anita Novinsky and M. Luiza Tucci Carneiro, 583–607. Rio de Janeiro: Expressão e Cultura, 1992.

Mello, Evaldo Cabral de. *A ferida de narciso: Ensaio de história regional*. São Paulo: Editora SENAC, 2001.

———. *A fronda dos mazombos: Nobres contra mascates, Pernambuco, 1666–1715*. São Paulo: Editora Schwarcz, 1995.

———. *Imagens do Brasil holandês 1630–1654*. Rio de Janeiro: Ministerio da Cultura, Fundação Nacional ProMemoria, 1987.

———. *O Nome e o sangue: Uma fraude genealógica no Pernambuco colonial*. São Paulo: Editora Schwarz, 1989.
———. *Olinda restaurada: Guerra e açucar no Nordeste, 1630–1654*. São Paulo: Editora Forense-Universitária, 1975.
———. *Rubro veio: O imaginário da restaurção Pernambucana*. Rio de Janeiro: Editora Nova Fronteira, 1986.
Mello, José Antônio Gonsalves de. *Estudos Pernambucanos: Crítica e problemas de algumas fontes da história de Pernambuco*. 2nd. ed. Recife: Fundação do Patrimônio Histórico e Artístico de Pernambuco, 1986.
———. *Gente da nação. Cristãos novos e judeus em Pernambuco, 1542–1654*. Recife: Editora Massangana, 1989.
———. *Restauradores de Pernambuco: Biografias de figuras do século XVII que defenderam e consolidaram a unidade brasileira*. Recife: Imprensa Universitaria, 1967.
———. *Tempo dos flamengos: Influência da ocupação holandesa na vida e na cultura do Norte do Brasil*. Rio de Janeiro: Livraria José Olympio Editora, 1947.
———. "Um Tribunal da Inquisição em Olinda, Pernambuco (1594–1595)." *Revista da Universidade de Coimbra* 36 (September 1991): 369–74.
Méndez, María Águeda. "La fiesta de San Pedro Mártir: Preparativos y vicisitudes de la Inquisición novohispana dieciochesca." *CMHLB Caravelle* 73 (1999): 61–70.
Metcalf, Alida. *Family and Frontier in Colonial Brazil: Santana de Parnaíba, 1580–1822*. Berkeley: University of California Press, 1992.
Metzler, Josef, ed. *America Pontificia: Primi saeculi evangelizationis, 1493–1592*. Vatican: Libreria Editrice Vaticana, 1991.
Meyers, Albert. "Religious Brotherhoods in Latin America: A Sketch of Two Peruvian Case Studies." In *Manipulating the Saints: Religious Brotherhoods and Social Integration in Postconquest Latin America*, ed. Albert Meyers and Diane Elizabeth Hopkins, 1–21. Hamburg: Wayasbah, 1988.
Mier, E. *El conflicto del poder y el poder del conflicto. El familiar de la Inquisición, Toribio Sánchez de Quijano de Cortés*. Spain: Santander, 1992.
Monteiro, Nuno Gonçalo. "Poder senhorial, estatuto nobiliárquico e aristocracia." In *História de Portugal. O Antigo Regime*, ed. António Manuel Hespanha, 333–79. Vol. 4. Lisbon: Editora Estampa, 1993.
Morton, F. W. O. "The Military and Society in Bahia, 1800–1821." *JLAS* 7, no. 2 (1975): 249–69.
Mott, Luiz. "A Companhia dos Familiares do Santo Ofício no Brasil (notas preliminares)." Unpublished manuscript. Salvador, 1989.
———. *A Inquisição em Sergipe*. Aracajú: Editora Fundesc, 1989.
———. "A Inquisição no Maranhão." *Revista Brasileira de História* 14, no. 28 (1994): 45–73.
———. *Homosexuais da Bahia: Dicionário Biográfico (Séculos XVI–XIX)*. Salvador: Editora Grupo Gay da Bahia, 1999.
———. "Um nome . . . em nome do Santo Ofício: O Cônego João Calmon, comissário da Inquisição na Bahia setecentista." *Universitas, Cultura* 37 (July–September 1986): 15–31.

Mulvey, Patricia A. "Black Brothers and Sisters: Membership in the Black Lay Brotherhoods of Colonial Brazil." *Luso-Brazilian Review* 17, no. 2 (Winter 1980): 253–79.

Nazzari, Muriel. *Disappearance of the Dowry: Women, Families and Social Change in São Paulo, Brazil (1600–1900)*. Stanford: Stanford University Press, 1991.

Neves, Guilherme Pereira das. "A suposta conspiração de 1801 em Pernmbuco: Idéias ilustradas ou conflitos tradicionais?" *Revista Portuguesa de História* 32, no. 2 (1999): 439–81.

———. "De 1789–1798: Percurso da francesia na Bahia." In *De Cabral a Pedro I: Aspectos da colonização portuguesa no Brasil*, ed. Maria Beatriz Nizza da Silva, 337–46. Porto: Humbertipo, 2001.

———. "Pálida e oblíquias luzes: J. J. da C. de Azeredo Coutinho e a análise sobre a justiça do comércio do resgate dos escravos." In *Brasil: Colonização e escravidão*, ed. Maria Beatriz Nizza da Silva, 341–70. Rio de Janeiro: Nova Fronteira, 2000.

Nóbrega, Apolônio. "Dioceses e Bispos do Brasil." *RIHGB* 22 (January–March 1954): 3–355.

Novinsky, Anita. *Cristãos novos na Bahia: A Inquisição*. 2nd ed. São Paulo: Editora Perspectiva, 1992.

———. "A Igreja no Brasil colonial. Agentes da Inquisição." *Anais do Museu Paulista* 33 (1984): 17–34.

———. *A Inquisição*. São Paulo: Brasiliense, 1982.

———. *Inquisição: Prisioneiros do Brasil, Séculos XVI–XIX*. Rio de Janeiro: Expressao e Cultura, 2002.

———. "A Inquisição: Uma revisão histórica." In *Inquisição: Ensaios sobre mentalidade, heresias e arte*, ed. Anita Novinsky and M. Luiza Tucci Carneiro, 3–10. Rio de Janeiro: Expressão e Cultura, 1992.

———. *Rol dos Culpados: Fontes para a história do Brasil, século XVIII*. Rio de Janeiro: Expressão e Cultura, 1992.

Novinsky, Anita, and M. Luiza Tucci Carneiro, eds. *Inquisição: Ensaios sobre mentalidade, heresias e arte*. Rio de Janeiro: Expressão e Cultura, 1992.

Oliveira, Miguel de. *História Eclesiástica de Portugal*. Portugal: Publicações Europa-América, 1994.

Oliveira Ramos, Luís A. de. "A Inquisição pombalina." *Brotéria* 115, no. 2–4 (August–October 1982): 170–80.

Palacios, Guillermo. *Cultividores libres, estado y crisis de la esclavitud en Brasil en la época da la Revolución Industrial*. Mexico City: Fondo de Cultura Economica, 1998.

Pang, Eul-Soo. *In Pursuit of Honor and Power: Noblemen of the Southern Cross in Nineteenth-Century Brazil*. Tuscaloosa: University of Alabama Press, 1988.

Pasamar Lázaro, José Enrique. "El comisario del Santo Oficio en el distrito inquisitorial de Aragón." *Revista de la Inquisición* 6 (1997): 191–238.

———. "Inquisición en Aragón: La cofradía de San Pedro Mártir de Verona." *Revista de la Inquisición* 5 (1996): 303–16.

———. *La cofradía de San Pedro Mártir de Verona: En el distrito inquisitorial de Aragón*. Zaragoza: Institución "Fernando el Católico," 1997.
———. *Los familiares del Santo Oficio en el distrito inquisitorial de Aragón*. Zaragoza: Ebro Composición, 1999.
Pereira, Paulo. "O riso libertador em Antonio José da Silva, 'o judeu'." In *Inquisição: Ensaios sobre mentalidade, heresias e arte*, ed. Anita Novinsky and M. Luiza Tucci Carneiro, 608–20. Rio de Janeiro: Expressão e Cultura, 1992.
Perrone-Moisés, Beatriz. "Índios livres e índios escravos: Os princípios da legislação indigenista do período colonial (século XVI a XVIII)." In *História dos índios do Brasil*, ed. Manuela Carneiro da Cunha, 115–32. São Paulo: Editora Schwarcz, 1992.
Peters, Edward. *Inquisition*. Berkeley: University of California Press, 1988.
Petersen, Dwight E. "Sweet Success: Some Notes on the Founding of a Brazilian Sugar Dynasty, the Pais Barreto Family." *Americas* 40, no. 3 (January 1984): 325–48.
Pieroni, Geraldo. *Banidos: A Inquisição e a lista dos Cristãos-Novos condenados a viver no Brasil*. Rio de Janeiro: Bertrand Brasil, 2003.
———. *Os excluídos do reino: A inquisição portuguesa e o degredo para o Brasil colonial*. Brasília: Editora Universidade de Brasília, 2000.
———. *Vadios e ciganos, heréticos e bruxas*. Rio de Janeiro: Bertrand Brasil, 2000.
Prado, Caio, Jr. *Formação do Brasil contemporâneo: Colônia*. São Paulo: Livraria Martins Editora, 1942.
Ramos, Donald. "Marriage and the Family in Colonial Vila Rica." *HAHR* 55, no. 2 (May 1975): 200–225.
Reis, João José. *Death Is a Festival: Funeral Rites and Rebellion in Nineteenth-Century Brazil*. Chapel Hill: University of North Carolina Press, 2003.
Ricard, Robert. "Comparison of Evangelization in Portuguese and Spanish America." *Americas* 14, no. 4 (April 1958): 444–53.
Rodrigues, Adriano Vasco. "'Inquisições' a pureza de sangue." In *Inquisição*, ed. Maria Helena Carvalho dos Santos, 745–54. Vol. 3. Lisbon: Universitária Editora, 1989.
Rowland, Ronald. "Inquisição, intolerância e exclusão." *Ler História* 33 (1997): 9–22.
Russell-Wood, A. J. R. "'Acts of Grace': Portuguese Monarchs and Their Subjects of African Descent in Eighteenth-Century Brazil." *JLAS* 32 (2000): 307–32.
———. "Black and Mulatto Brotherhoods in Colonial Brazil: A Study of Collective Behavior." *HAHR* 54, no. 4 (November 1974): 567–602.
———. *Fidalgos and Philanthropists: The Santa Casa de Misericórdia of Bahia, 1550–1755*. Berkeley: University of California Press, 1968.
———. "Prestige, Power, and Piety in Colonial Brazil: The Third Orders of Salvador." *HAHR* 69, no. 1 (February 1989): 61–89.
Sales, Ernesto. "Inquisidores Gerais em Portugal." *Revista da História* 10 (1921): 202–8.
Sampaio, Antônio Carlos Jucá de. "Os homens de negócio do Rio de Janeiro e sua atuação nos quadros do impéiro Português." In *O Antigo Regime nos trópicos: A*

dinâmica imperial portuguesa (séculos XVI–XVIII), ed. João Fragoso, Maria Fernanda Bicalho, and Maria de Fátima Gouvêa, 75–105. Rio de Janeiro: Civilização Brasileira, 2001.

Santareno, Bernardo. *O judeu.* 1996.

Santos, Maria Helena Carvalho dos. "A abolição da Inquisição em Portugal: Um acto de poder." In *Inquisição*, ed. Maria Helena Carvalho dos Santos, 1381–86. Vol. 3. Lisbon: Universitária Editora, 1989.

Santos, Maria Helena Carvalho dos, ed. *Inquisição.* 3 vols. Lisbon: Universitária Editora, 1989.

Saraiva, António José. *Inquisição e Cristãos-Novos.* 6th ed. Lisbon: Editora Estampa, 1994.

———. *The Marrano Factory: The Portuguese Inquisition and Its New Christians, 1536–1765.* Translated by Hp. Salomon and I. S. D. Sassoon. Boston: Brill, 2001.

Scarano, Julita. "Black Brotherhoods: Integration or Contradiction?" *Luso-Brazilian Review* 16, no. 1 (Summer 1979): 1–17.

———. *Devoção e escravidão: A Irmandade de Nossa Senhora do Rosário dos pretos no distrito diamantino no século XVIII.* São Paulo: Editora Nacional, 1978.

Schwartz, Stuart B. "Magistracy and Society in Colonial Brazil." *HAHR* 50, no. 4 (November 1970): 715–30.

———. "Plantations and Peripheries, c. 1580–c. 1750." In *Colonial Brazil*, ed. Leslie Bethell, 67–144. Cambridge. Reprint ed., 1991.

———. "The Plantations of St. Benedict: The Benedictine Sugar Mills of Colonial Brazil." *Americas* 39, no. 1 (July 1982): 1–22.

———. "Somebodies and Nobodies in the Body Politic: Mentalities and Social Structures in Colonial Brazil." *LARR* 31, no. 1 (1996): 113–34.

———. *Sovereignty and Society in Colonial Brazil: The High Court of Bahia and Its Judges, 1609–1751.* Berkeley: University of California, 1973.

———. "State and Society in Colonial Spanish America: An Opportunity for Prosopography." In *New Approaches to Latin American History*, ed. Richard Graham and Peter H. Smith, 3–35. Austin: University of Texas Press, 1974.

———. *Sugar Plantations in the Formation of Brazilian Society: Bahia, 1550–1835.* London: Cambridge University Press, 1985.

Shaw, L. M. E. *Trade, Inquisition and the English Nation in Portugal, 1650–1690.* Manchester: Carcanet, 1989.

Silva, Lina Gorenstein Ferreira da. *Herético e impuros: A Inquisição e os cristãos-novos no Rio de Janeiro século XVIII.* Rio de Janeiro: Secretaria Municipal de Cultura, Departamento Geral de Documentação e Informação Cultural, Divisão de Editoração, 1995.

Silva, Maria Beatriz Nizza da. *Cultura no Brasil Colônia.* Petrópolis: Vozes, 1981.

———. "O problema dos expostos na capitania de São Paulo." *Revista de História Econômica e Social* 5 (1980): 95–104.

Silveira, Francisco Maciel. "*O Judeu*, de Bernardo Santareno: O poder das trevas e o santo ofício da ficção." In *Inquisição: Ensaios sobre mentalidade, heresias e arte*, ed.

Anita Novinsky and M. Luiza Tucci Carneiro, 638–45. Rio de Janeiro: Expressão e Cultura, 1992.

Silverblatt, Irene. *Modern Inquisitions: Peru and the Colonial Origins of the Civilized World*. Durham: Duke University Press, 2004.

Siqueira, Sonia A. *A Inquisição portuguesa e a sociedade colonial*. São Paulo: Editora Ática, 1978.

———. "A Inquisição portuguêsa e os confiscos." *Revista de História* 40, no. 82 (April–June 1970): 323–40.

———. "O momento de inquisição (I)." *Revista de História* 42, no. 85 (January–March 1971): 49–73.

———. "O momento de inquisição (II)." *Revista de História* 43, no. 87 (July–September 1971): 43–85.

Smith, David Grant. "Old Christian Merchants and the Foundation of the Brazil Company, 1649." *HAHR* 54, no. 2 (May 1974): 233–59.

———. "The Merchant Class of Portugal and Brazil in the Seventeenth Century: A Socio-Economic Study of the Merchants of Lisbon and Bahia, 1620–1690." Ph.D. dissertation, University of Texas at Austin, 1975.

Souza, Laura de Mello e. *Inferno atlântico: Demonologia e colonização séculos XVI–XVIII*. São Paulo: Companhia das Letras, 1993.

———. *O diabo e a terra de Santa Cruz: Feitiçaria e religiosidade popular no Brasil colonial*. 2nd ed. São Paulo: Companhia das Letras, 1994.

Souza, Ney de. "A formação do clero no Brasil colonial e a influência do iluminismo." *Revista eclesiástica brasileira* 231 (September 1998): 618–33.

Tavares, Célia Cristina da Silva. "A cristanidade insular: Jesuitas e inquisidores em Goa, 1540–1682." Ph.D. dissertation, Universidade Federal Fluminense, 2002.

Tavora, Franklin. "Os patriotas de 1817." In *A república em Pernambuco*, ed. Leonardo Dantas Silva, 1–28. Recife: FUNDAJ, Editora Massangana, 1990.

Thurston, Herbert, and Donal Attwater, eds. *Butler's Lives of the Saints: Complete Edition*. 4 vols. New York: Kenedy and Sons, 1956.

Twinam, Ann. "Honor, Sexuality, and Illegitimacy in Colonial Spanish America." In *Sexuality and Marriage in Colonial Latin America*, ed. Asunción Lavrin, 118–55. Lincoln: University of Nebraska Press, 1989.

Vainfas, Ronaldo, ed. *Dicionário do Brasil colonial (1500–1808)*. Rio de Janeiro: Editora Objectiva, 2000.

———. *A Heresia dos índios: Catolicismo e rebeldia no Brasil colonial*. São Paulo: Companhia das Letras, 1995.

———. *Trópico dos pecados: Moral, sexualidade e Inquisição no Brasil*. Rio de Janeiro: Campus, 1989.

Veiga Torres, José. "Da repressão religiosa para a promoção social: A Inquisição como instância legitimadora da promoção social da burguesia mercantil." *Revista Crítica de Ciências Sociais* 4 (October 1994): 109–35.

———. "Uma longa guerra social: Novas perspectivas para o estudo da Inquisição portuguesa a Inquisição de Coimbra." *Revista de história das ideias* 8 (1986): 59–74.

---. "Uma longa guerra social: Os rítmos da repressão inquisitorial em Portugal." *Revista de História Econômica e Social* 1 (January–June 1978): 55–68.

Venâncio, Renato Pinto. "Nos limites da sagrada família: Ilegitimidade e casamento no Brasil colonial." In *História e sexualidade no Brasil*, ed. Ronaldo Vainfas, 107–24. Rio de Janeiro: Editores de Livros, 1986.

Venâncio, Renato Pinto, and Júnia Ferreira Furtado. "Comerciantes, tratantes e mascates." In *Revisão do Paraíso: Os brasileiros e o estado em 500 anos de história*, ed. Mary del Priore, 95–113. Rio de Janeiro: Editora Campus, 2000.

Viana, Isolina Bresolin. "Antonio José da Silva, 'o judeu', e as *Obras do Diabinho da Mão Furada*." In *Inquisição: Ensaios sobre mentalidade, heresias e arte*, ed. Anita Novinsky and M. Luiza Tucci Carneiro, 621–37. Rio de Janeiro: Expressão e Cultura, 1992.

Villalta, Luiz Carlos. "As licenças para posse e leitura de livros proibidos." In *De Cabral a Pedro I: Aspectos da colonização portuguesa no Brasil*, ed. Maria Beatriz Nizza da Silva, 235–45. Porto: Humbertipo, 2001.

Voltaire, François Marie Arouet de. *Candide and Related Texts/Voltaire*. Translated by David Wooton. Indianapolis: Hackett, 2000.

Wadsworth, James E. "Celebrating St. Peter Martyr: The Inquisitional Brotherhood in Colonial Brazil." *Colonial Latin American Historical Review* 12, no. 2 (Spring 2003): 173–227.

---. "Children of the Inquisition: Minors as Familiares of the Inquisition in Pernambuco, Brazil, 1613–1821." *Luso-Brazilian Review* 42, no. 1 (2005): 21–43.

---. "In the Name of the Inquisition: The Portuguese Inquisition and Delegated Authority in Colonial Pernambuco, Brazil." *Americas* 61, no. 1 (July 2004): 19–54.

---. "Joaquim Marques de Araújo: O poder da Inquisição em Pernambuco no fim do período colonial." In *De Cabral a Pedro I: Aspectos da colonização portuguesa no Brasil*, ed. Maria Beatriz Nizza da Silva, 309–20. Porto: Humbertipo, 2001.

---. "Os familiares do número e o problema dos privilégios." In *A Inquisição em Xeque: temas, controvérsias, estudos de caso*, ed. R. Vainfas, L. Lage, and B. Feitler, 97–112. Rio de Janeiro: Editora Universidade do Estado do Rio de Janeiro, 2006.

Walker, Timothy D. *Doctors, Folk Medicine, and the Inquisition: The Repression of Magical Healing in Portugal during the Enlightenment*. Leiden, Netherlands: Brill Academic, 2005.

Weber, Max. "Class, Status, and Party." In *Class, Status, and Power: Social Stratification in Comparative Perspective*, ed. Reinhard Bendix and Seymour Martin Lipset, 21–28. New York: Free Press, 1966.

Weber, Max. *Economy and Society: An Outline of Interpretive Sociology*. Edited by Guenther Roth and Claus Wittich. 2 vols. New York: Bedminster, 1968.

Wehling, Arno, and Maria José Wehling. "O funcionário colonial foi parte significativa da burocracia absolutista." In *Revisão do Paraíso: Os brasileiros e o estado em 500 anos de história*, ed. Mary del Priore, 141–59. Rio de Janeiro: Editora Campus, 2000.

Westphalen, Cecília Maria. "A milícia da comarca de Paranaguá e Curitiba." In *De Cabral a Pedro I: Aspectos da colonização portuguesa no Brasil*, ed. Maria Beatriz Nizza da Silva, 329–36. Porto: Humbertipo, 2001.

Whitaker, Arthur P. *Latin America and the Enlightenment*. 2nd ed. Ithaca: Cornell University Press, 1961.
Willems, Emilio. "Social Differentiation in Colonial Brazil." *Comparative Studies in Society and History* 12, no. 1 (January 1970): 31–49.
Wirth, John D. *Minas Gerais in the Brazilian Federation, 1889–1937*. Stanford: Stanford University Press, 1977.
Woodyard, George W. "A Metaphor for Repression: Two Portuguese Inquisition Plays." *Luso-Brazilian Review* 10, no. 1 (June 1973): 68–75.
Xavier, Ângela Barreto, and António Manuel Hespanha. "As redes clientelares." In *História de Portugal. O Antigo Regime*, ed. António Manuel Hespanha, 381–93. Vol. 4. Lisbon: Editora Estampa, 1993.

Index

Note: Page references in *italics* indicate a figure or photograph.

abandonment, applicants with background of, 109–12, 116n58, 117n63, 117n66
Abranches, Giraldo de, 22
accusations: impact on honor, 77–85; inquiries into, 58, 59–60
Adrian VI, 102
Africa, 19, 43, 50n11, 146, 200
Agreste: denunciations and punishments in, 48; region of, 6, 7,
Aguiar, João de, 195
Aires, José, 32
Alagoas: captaincy of, 5, 6, 7, 8, 9; denunciations and punishments in, 48; distribution of inquisitional officials in, *123*, *124*
Albuquerque, Britis de, 98, 99, 102
Albuquerque, Jerônimo de, 91n12, 98, 99, 102
Albuquerque, José de Sá de, 101
Albuquerque, Ventura de, 28
Albuquerque e Melo, Pedro de, 29
alferes, 178
Almeida, Antônio de, 101

Almeida, Bernardo Germano de, 152
Almeida, Gregório Xavier de, 84–85
Almeida Costa, Dionísio de, 193
alqueires, 66, 74n45
alvará, 74, 88
Alvares, Fernando Henrique, 104
Amaral, Manuel Garcia Velho do, 32, 33, 111
Amorim, Cipriano José de, 214
Amorim de Lima, Antônio de, 197
amulets, 195
Andrade, Antônio da Costa de, 154, 177
Andrade e Sousa, José de, 83
Angola, 43, 50n11, 146, 200
Antunes Correia, Roque, 176
Antunes Pereira, Domingos, 152
Anunciação, Gabriel da, 197
aposentadoria, 145
aposentador-mor, 146
applications: clergy excluded from, 82–83, 92n30; fees/costs associated with, 53, 62, 63, 68, 69n29, 70nn31–32, 70nn34–35, 79–90, 233;

256 ~ Index

qualifying for office, 53–68, 109–12; by women, 58–59, 69n18
appointments: accessibility to, 65–68; cheapening of, 95, 112, 113; costs/fees associated with, 62–64, 64, 65–68, 233; letters of, 60
Aranha, Francisco Xavier, 198, 199, 206n19
Arantes, Francisco José de, 79
Araújo, Antônio de, 193
Araújo, Correia da, 131
Araújo, Joaquim Marques de, inquisitional activities of, 58, 83, 111, 155, 169, 191, 200–204, 206n29, 207n38, 216, 217, 218, 219–20, 221, 223, 235
Araújo, Marianne de, 131
Araújo, Rosa Maria, 193
Araújo, Sebastião de Bras, 173
Araújo Barbosa, Antônio de, 131, 235
Araújo e Souza, João Silvestre de, 151
Araújo Lima, Domingos de, 83
Araújo Lopes, Antônio, 85–86
Arquivo Histórico Ultramarino (AHU), 5
Arquivo Militar, 5
Arquivo Nacional/Torre do Tombo (ANTT), 5
Arquivo Público Estadual de Pernambuco (APEJE), 5
autos-da-fé, 22, 46, 47, 108, 164, 179, 187
Ávila, Manuel de Rose de, 79
Azeredo Coutinho, José Joaquim da Cunha de, 201
Azevedo, Antônio Pereira de, 109
Azevedo, Belquior Mendes de, 187, 192–93
Azevedo, Leandro Ferreira de, 220
Azores, inquisitional offices in, 1

Bahia: bishopric and archbishopric of, 9, 21, 24; brotherhood activities in, 163, 182n22; captaincy of, 20; distribution of inquisitional officials in, 37, 38, *123*, *124*, 137n19, 152–53; *familiares* permitted in, 149, 152–53; influences of Enlightenment in, 212; militia companies in, 173, 175, 176–77, 184n57; New Christian populations in, 46
Bandeira, José Ferreira, 176
banishment, 46, 51n25, 189
baptisms: of Jewish children, 74; records of, 59, 65, 220
Barreto Velho, João Pais, 98, 99, 113n10
Barros, José Alves de, 222
Bastos, José Timóteo Pereira de, 87
Benedictine order, 21
benefice, 83, 144
Biblioteca da Ajuda, 5
Biblioteca Nacional (BNL), 5
bigamy, 28, 43, 46, 47
biography, collective, 4
blood, purity of. *See* purity of blood
Bluteau, Raphael, 120–21, 127
Board of Conscience and Orders, 20, 68, 81, 87, 99, 203
Boiça, Manuel Gaspar da, 221
Borborema plateau, 6, 7
Bragança, Duke of, 171
Bras de Araújo, Sebastião de, 173
Brazil: arrival of Inquisition in, 19–34; brotherhood activities in, 161–65, *165*, *166*, *166*, *167*, *167*, 168–71, 182n13, 233; captaincies and subordinate captaincies of, xvi, 6, 7, 8, 20; Church of, 21; colonial populations in, 2, 3, 19–34, 76–77, 230–32; disease and epidemics in, 146, 219; distribution of inquisitional officials in, 37–49, 119, 122–30, 138n21; Dutch settlements in, 7–8, 229–30; ecclesiastical jurisdiction over, 20–21; *familiares do*

número permitted in, 146, 147, 149, 150, 232; family models in, 131–36, 140n37; genealogies of colonial populations in, 96–112, 231; immigrants as inquisitional officials in, 119, 122, 129–30, 131, 137n16, 139n34, 139n35, 140n41, 231; Indian populations in, 7–8, 20, 29, 87–89, 93n57, 94n59, 95, 193; influences of Enlightenment in, 211–13; inquisitional authority delegated to, 45–46, 47, 49, 51n29, 229–35; legalized discrimination in, 73–77, 91n2; militia companies in, 172–73, *174*, 175–80; New Christian populations in, 23, 47, 49, 75–76, 85, 97–105, 113n6, 113n8, 127, 128; prisoners of Inquisition in, 32–33; slave populations in, 8, 65–66, 87–88; social hierarchies in, 3, 109–12, 116n58, 117n63, 117n66; sugar plantations in, 1, 6, 8, 23, 46, 98, 121, 122, 127; tribunal established in, 24
brazilwood, 20
breve da marea, 195
Brito, João Pereira de, 111
brotherhoods: entrance fees of, 163, 164, 169, 181n10; festivals celebrated by, 164–65, *165*, 166, 168–69, 170, 182n22; insignias of, 166–67, *167*, 168, 182n26; niche in inquisitional organization, 155, 164, 165, *165*, 166, *166*, 167, *167*, 168–71, 179–80, 182n23, 233; on purity of abandoned or illegitimate children, 110; of St. Peter Martyr, 63, 126, 150, 162–71, 218, 233; sermons by, 166, 168–69, 182n30; status and honor associated with, 161, 162–71, 233; symbolism and iconography of, 166–67, *167*, 168; trades or saints associated with, 162

cabelo torcido, 87
caboclo, 88
cabra, 89
caixeiros, 176
Calheiros, João Pacheco, 78
Calmon, João, 148
Calvinism, 43
câmara, 9
Campelo, Nuno, 102, 103
capitanias donatárias, 20
capitão agregado, 178
capitão-mor, 177
Carmelite order, 21, 25, 35, 80, 81–82, 83, 84, 111, 126, 170
Carmo, Order of, 86
Carneiro, Antônio Gonçalves, 1–2, 3, 67, 235
Carneiro, Joaquim Manuel, 89–90
Carneiro da Cunha, Ana Francisca, 111
Carneiro da Cunha, João, 104
Carneiro da Cunha, João Manuel, 111
Carneiro da Cunha, Manuel de, 103–4, 105
carta de familiar, 60, *61*, 65–66, 222–23
Cartagena, tribunal in, 24
Carvalho, José Antônio, 155
Carvalho, Paulo de, 114n37
Carvalho, Sebastião de, 103, 104
Carvalho e Gama, Lourenço Pereira de, 214
Carvalho e Melo, Sebastião José de, 88, 106
Carvalho e Mendonça, Paulo de, 106
Casio, Isidro de, 197–98
casta de negro, 87
Castilo, Pedro de, 163
Castro, Agostinho Fernandes de, 127
Castro, Antônio Alves, 110
Castro, Francisco de, 106, 163
Castro e Caldas, Sebastião, 97
Catarina, 172
Catholic Church, 10, 19, 43, 210
Cavalcante, Cosme Bezerra, 114n27

258 ~ Index

Ceará: captaincy of, 4, 7, 7, 8, 9, 15n15; denunciations and punishments in, 48; distribution of inquisitional officials in, *123*, *124*
censorship, 212, 225n7
Chagas, Antônio das, 84, 170
Chamba, Francisco, 193
Chaves, João Rodrigues, 23
Church of Brazil, 21
Clement IV, 162
clergy: excluded from appointments, 82–83, 92n30; inquisitional opportunities for, 79–80; privileges as *familiares*, 154–55; qualifications of, 79–80
Clerics of Saint Peter, 126
clothing, as qualifying issue, 78–79, 139n33
Coelho, Baltasar, 193
Coelho, Duarte, 20, 91n12, 98, 103
Coelho, Felipe, 26, 198
Coimbra: brotherhood activities in, 163, 181n9; tribunal in, xvi, 45, 55
collective biography, 4
comissários: appointments of, xv, 23, 41, 44; compensation and payment of, 63–64, 70n35; responsibilities of, 5, 43–45, 56, 57, 58
comissários delegados, 26, 81
Companhia dos Familiares: niche in the Inquisition, 171, 173, 174, 175, 176, 177, 183n45, 184n56, 184n59, 184n78, 218; privileges associated with, 171–72; uniforms of, 173, *174*, *175*
Conceição, Antônio Dias da, 80
confrarias, 74
congruas, 83, 93n36
Constitution of the Bahian Archbishopric of 1707, 27
Cordeiro, Antônio Raposo, 191–92
Correia, Roque Antunes, 176
Correia Góes, Antônio Dantas, 133

Correia Góes, Antônio Dantas (son), 133–34
Correia Paz, Antônio Raposo, 191–92
cor tostada, 87
Costa, Inácio Joaquim da, 132
Costa Andrade, Antônio, 154
Costa Bandeira, Francisco da, 84
Costa Braga, Domingos da, 177
Costa Cunha Souto Maior, Pascoal Martins da, 213
Costa de Andrade, Antônio da, 154, 177
Costa de Sá, Manuel da, 87
Costa Moura, Manuel da, 86
Costa Ribeiro, Manuel dae, 169
Council of Trent, 19
Coutinho, Azeredo, 205, 207n41, 212, 216, 219, 222, 224, 226n26
crusader crosses, 167
crypto-Jews, 42, 46, 97
cum ad nil magus, 19
Cunha, Francisco Inácio da, 190
Cunha, João Carneiro do, 80
Cunha, Paulo Carvalho da, 86
Cunha Souto, Antônio Martins da, 65

Dantas, Júlio, 10, 235
denunciations: mechanism of, 42, 43, 45–47, 48, 49; records of, 54
depositario dos bens do fisco, 158n21
deputies, xv
desembargador, 153
destituido de toda pureza, 178
Dias, Branca, 102, 103–4, 114n27
Dias, Felipe, 102, 103
Dias, Henrique, 173
diligências, 5, 55, 58, 63, 111, 201, 202, 203
Dinis, Jerônimo, 133
Dominic, Saint, 164, 166, 167, 168
Dominican order, 3, 13n1, 162, 166, 167, 168, 195
Duarte, Teodoro de Lemos, 31

Dutch wars, 13, 23
dyewood, poaching of, 20

ecclesiastical offices, inquisitional personnel in, 25–29, 126–27
Edicts of Faith (*éditos-da-fé*), 26, 42
endogamy, 132
engenho, 1, 103, 127
Enlightenment, 209, 210–16, 224n2
Episcopal Church: authority delegated to, 28; clergy working in Inquisition, 25
Espírito Santo, Felipe Neri do, 109–10
estado do meio, 120, 129
estilo, 54
estrangeirados, 211
Évora: brotherhood activities in, 163; prison in, 190; tribunal in, 45, 55
extrajudicial, as informal inquiry, 55–56
extranumerarios, 150, 159n30

fama pública, 59
familiares: applicants for positions of, 23, 39–45, 65, 130–31; appointed in Brazil, xv, 22–23, 37–49, 146, 147, 149, 150, 232; compensation and payment of, 63–64, 70n35; costs/fees associated with position of, 62–67, 69n29, 233; marriage and family strategies of, 130–34, *134*, 135, *135*, 136, 231; medallions worn by, 60, 69n21, 193; multigenerational, 133–34, *134*, 135, *135*, 136; privileges associated with appointment of, 146, 232–33; responsibilities of, 43–44, 45, 56; social and economic competition by, 127–29, *128*, 139n30; standards of modesty and decency for, 60–62; as witnesses, 57–58
familiares do número: in Companhia dos Familiares, 172; privileges of, 143–57, 157n1, 158n16, 176, 232–33
familiares do vinte, 150
family trees, 55, *55*, 56. *See also* genealogies
Farjado, Manuel Pereira Azevedo de, 63
Farjado, Pereira Azevedo de, 67
feitorias, 20
Fernandes, Diogo, 103
Fernandes Souza, Francisco, 79, 101, 199
Ferreira, Francisco, 195
Ferreira, José Rimígio, 67
Ferreira Bandeira, José, 176
Ferreira Frazão, João Ferreira, 79
Ferreira Peixoto, Vicente, 79
Ferreira Portugal, Bernardo Luís, 190–91, 200–204, 206nn27–28, 206n31, 207n36, 216, 219–20
Ferreira Souto, Miguel, 86
fidalgos, 99, 101, 112, 120, 128, 139n32, 231
finta, 86, 93n44
fire, as purifying, 49
fleur-de-lis, 166, 167, *167*, 168
Fonseca, Antônio José Victoriano Borges da, 30–31, 69n5, 101, 102, 103
Fonseca, Francisco da, 197
Fonseca Galvão, Cipriano Lopes da, 104–5
foro, 145, 218
foro militar, 172
foundlings, qualifying for appointments, 110–11
France: dyewood trade by, 20; invasion of Portugal by, 204, 213, 226n18
Franciscan order, 21, 74, 82
freemasonry, 43, 47
Freire, Henrique Louis Pereira, 176
Freitas Sacoto, José de, 133
Funchal: archbishopric of, 21; brotherhood activities in, 163

Gaio, Henrique Martins, 44, 58, 84–85, 171, 190–91, 200, 202, 219
Gaioso, Rodrigo, 58
genealogies: of abandoned or illegitimate children, 109–12, 116n58, 117n63, 117n66; of applicants, 55, 55, 56, 231; fraud and manipulation of, 95–113
General Council: colonial jurisdiction of, xvi, 1, 2, 21, 23, 28, 45; on composition of militia companies, 176; on delegated authority, 28, 29; expenses associated with processos in, 65–68; inquiries reviewed by, 59, 60; licenses issued by, 60–61; on local tribunals in Brazil, 23–24; on privileged *familiares*, 146, 148, 150, 151, 153, 154, 158n13; on purpose/activities of brotherhoods, 163
Goa, India: brotherhood activities in, 163, 181n6; edict for, 40n11, 43; tribunal in, 45, 108, 210
Góes, Inês de, 98, 101
Góes, Joanna de, 103, 104
Góes, José Dantas Correia, 133
Goiana, *comissários* in, 84
Gomes, Miguel Correia, 99
Gomes Pires, Antônio, 152
Gonçalves Bastos, Lourenço, 87
Gonçalves Carneiro, Antônio, 1–2, 3, 67, 235
Gonçalves Lima, Antônio, 220
Gonçalves Reis, Antônio, 67
Gorjão, Antônio Alves, 235
Gorjão, Vicente, Jr., 133
Gorjão, Vicente, Sr., 133
Grão Pará, captaincy of, 151
Gregory IX, 162
Gregory XIV, 110
Guardes, Inês, 98
Guerra, Antônio Alves, 28, 170, 220
Guerra dos Mascates, 9, 97, 113n4

Guimarães, Domingos Lopes, 65
Guimarães, José Lopes, 65

habilitações, 5, 6, 79, 84, 109, 221
Henrique, Infante D., 27
hereditárias, 20
heresy, 27, 28, 47, 52n35
Holanda, Arnão de, 102, 103
Holanda, Maria de, 98
Holanda Barreto, Arnão de, 98, 101
Holy Office of the Inquisition, xvi
homens de letras, 80
homens de negócio, 127
honor: as defense of social status, 77–85; investigation/qualification of, 53–68, 231; lost and regained, 77; qualifying for office and, 73–90, 231; role of public opinion in, 76, 91n16
honra, 76

Iberian Inquisition, 11
Iguareta, José, 194
Ilha Terceira, 1
illegitimacy, applicants with background of, 109–12, 116n58, 117n63, 117n66
incest, moral crime of, 28, 42
Inconfidência Mineira, 212
indulgences, 43, 169
Innocent IV, 162
inquiry: extrajudicial, 55–56; impact of delays on, 73; judicial, 56–57; in qualification process, 56, 69nn8–9
Inquisition: abolition of, 19, 64, 223; abuses of authority in, 145, 187, 189–92, 204–5, 233–34; application and qualification process in, 1, 2, 5, 23, 37, 49n2, 53, 54–68, 69n29, 70nn31–32, 70nn34–35, 231; arrival in Brazil, 19–34; as avenue to privilege, 41, 143–57, 232–33; corporate institutions within, 144,

155, 161–80; crimes under jurisdiction of, 27, 28–29, 30, 42, 43; decay and decline of, 155, 159n46, 209–23; delegated authority in Brazil, 23, 26–34; duration of, 4, 5; enforcement by, 42–45; evidence used by, 59–60; exclusionary procedures/criteria of, 53–68; executions associated with, 12, 22, 45–46; genealogical battles in, 97–113, 231; as Holy Office of the Inquisition, xvi; honor and prestige associated with, 53–68, 73–90, 231; impact of Enlightenment, 209, 210–16, 224n2; institution of, xvi, 2, 3, 37, 143; investigations of applicants by, 1, 2, 5, 25–26, 59–60, 100; literacy/education requirements of, 129; multigenerational service to, 133–34, *134*, 135, *135*, 136; myth of, 9–13; network of officials in, 21–29, 33; papal suspension of, 105–6; patron saint of, 162; primary purpose of, 42; prisoners of, 28, 29, 30, 32–33; property confiscated during, 3, 31, 32, 106; punishment determined by, 38, 45–47, 49, 51n29; records of activities by, 27, 54; reforms in, 95, 105–13, 114n34, 114n36, 155, 201, 209, 211, 233–34; repressive effects of, 1, 12–13, 235; secular and ecclesiastical personnel in, 25–29; standards of modesty and decency, 61–62; status and social promotion associated with, 3–4, 53–68, 77–85, 119, 122–30, 187–205, 230; studies of, 9–13
inquisitional, xvi
inquisitor generals, xv, 21
inquisitorial, xvi
Instituto Arqueológico Histórico e Geográfico Pernambuco (IAHGPE), xvii, 5–6

investigations: of applicants, 1, 2, 5, 25–26; non-inquisitional, 59–60; of purity of blood, 59, 100
Islam, discriminatory laws against, 43, 74, 75, 91n3
Itamaracá, captaincy of, 4, 8, 9

Jesuits: colleges in Brazil, 21, 32, 149, 196, 211; expulsion of, 198; inquisitional authority of, 26, 27, 29, 61, 126
Jesus, José Maria de, 190
Jesus, Teresa Maria de, 111
Jesus Gorjão, Maria José de, 133
Jesus Maria Souza, José de, 220, 221
Jewish populations: in Brazil, 73, 74, 75, 91n3; discriminatory laws against, 73, 74, 75, 91n7; inquisitional searches for, 23, 27, 30, 42, 43, 46, 47, 49, 98, 101; in Portugal, 111–12; in Spain, 19–20; stereotypes of, 97; taxes (*finta*) paid by, 86, 93n44. *See also* crypto-Jews
João, Prince Regent, 89, 215, 216
João II, 6, 20
João III, 74
João IV, 106, 171, 172
João V, 30, 96
João VI, 215, 216
Joaquina, Maria, 111, 132
José I, 88, 106
Judaism, practice as a crime, 23, 27, 30, 42, 43, 46, 47, 49, 98, 101
juiz comissário, 26
juiz conservador dos familiares, 148
juiz de fora, 30, 31
juiz do fisco, 45, 155
Junta de Comércio, 122

Koster, Henry, 217

lacaio, 79
Lacerda, João Ribeiro Pessoa, 103

uma lei para a inglês ver, 215
Lemos Duarte, Teodoro de, 31
Lemos Ribeiro, Manuel de, 86–87
libertinagem, 218
libertino, 218
Lima, Antônio de Amorim de, 197
Lima, Antônio Gonçalves, 220
Lima, tribunal in, 24
limpeza de sangue: of applicants, 85–90; requirement of, 75. *See also* purity of blood
Lisbon: brotherhood activities in, 163; militia companies in, 171, 172, 183n44, 183n47; receiving prisoners from Brazil, 28, 29; tribunal authority delegated by, xvi, 25, 26–27, 38, 39, 43, 45
Lopes, Antônio Araújo, 85–86
Lopes, Tomás, 187–88
Lutheranism, 43

Machado, Félix José, 97
Maciel, Anna Ferreira, 201
Maciel, Antônio da, 32–33
Maciel, Brás Ferreira de, 131
Maciel Monteiro, Manuel Francisco, 178
Madeira: archbishopric of, 21; brotherhood activities in, 163, 170
Madre de Deus, Felipe da, 86
Madre de Deus Convent, 89
Magalhães, José Valeiro de, 193
Magellan, Ferdinand, 19
Maio, Antônio Ribeiro, 29–30, 80
Maio, Inácio Ribeiro, 198–99
Maior, Antônio Martins da Cunha Souto, 65
mango negro, 87
manioc flour, 66, 74n46
Manuel, 74, 91n3
Maranhão: *familiares* in, 151–52; influences of Enlightenment in, 212
Margiocchi, Francisco Simões, 222

marriages: inquiries related to, 58–59; inquisitional involvement in, 130–34, 134, 135, 231; records of, 58, 59, 65, 220, 231; strategies of nobility with, 130–33, 135, 140n40, 231
massapé, 6
Mato Grosso, distribution of inquisitional officials in, 151
Matos, Antônio de, 26
mecânico, 77
medallions, 60, 69n21, 193
Melo, Ana Maria José de, 101
Melo, Angela Teresa de, 89
Melo, Antônio Vieira de, 89
Melo, João Gomes de, 102
Melo, José Gomes de, 102
Melo, Tomás José de, 200
Melo Bezerra, Manuel de, 89
Melo e Albuquerque, Josefa Francisca de, 101
Melo e Albuquerque, Pedro de, 100
Mendes, Beatriz, 98, 101–2, 103
Mendes, Henrique, 187
Mendonça, Heitor Furtado de, 22, 98, 103, 187
Mendonça, Manuel de, 220
merchants: as *homens de negócio*, 127; as inquisitional officials, 121–22, 127, 128, 131, 132, 232; as nobility, 122; settlements in Recife, 96, 97, 99, 102, 112, 132, 230
Mesa da Consciência e Ordens, 20, 68, 81, 87, 99, 203
mestre, 80
Mexico: brotherhoods in, 164, 182n18; tribunal in, 24
Milanese Inquisition, 162
milícia, 173
military service: privileges associated with, 144; social position with, 121, 127–28
militia companies: composition of troops in, 172–73, 184n53; in

Lisbon, 171, 172, 183n44, 183n47; niche in inquisitional organization, 155, 171–73, *174*, 175–79, 180; privileges associated with, 144, 172, 183n51, 234; on purity of abandoned or illegitimate children, 110; status and honor associated with, 161, 171–80, 234; uniforms of, 173, *174*, 175. *See also* Companhia dos Familiares

Minas Gerais: brotherhood activities in, 163; colonial populations in, 7, 8, 149, 150; influences of Enlightenment in, 212; inquisitional officials in, 149, 150

Miranda Montenegro, Caetano Pinto de, 203–4

misconduct, accusations of, 58, 59–60

moedeiros, 173

Monteiro, Manuel Alves, 132

Monteiro, Manuel Francisco Maciel, 178

Morais, Luís Inácio de, 29

Morais e Silva, Antônio de, 127, 219

Morim, Luís de, 149

Motta, Antônio Teixeira da, 30

Napoleonic wars, 214–15, 218

Nascimento, Caetana de, 132

Nascimento, Luísa da Paz do, 87

Nazi Germany, 11, 12

negociante, 127

Neves, Manuel Francisco da, 84

New Christians: impurity of blood associated with, 78, 85, 88, 95, 97, 98, 105, 177; investigations of, 23, 30, 31, 46, 47, 49, 61, 68, 69n9, 74, 78, 95, 187; as merchants, 127, 128; offices held by, 75; vs. Old Christians, 47, 49, 74, 96, 107, 108, 115n48; populations in colonial Brazil, 23, 75–76, 85–90, 96, 97–105, 113n6, 113n8; taxes (*finta*) paid by, 98, 99, 100, 107–8, 115n47

nobility: hereditary vs. civil/political, 120; new nobility in, 121, 137n9; privileges associated with, 144; professions as ennobling, 121, 137n9, 231; respectability and purity of blood associated with, 119–36

nobreza da terra, 122, 232

notários: compensation and payment of, 63–64, 70n35; qualifications of, xv, 23, 79–80; responsibilities of, 5, 44, 45, 55, 56, 69n7

Nova Colônia do Sacramento, settlement of, 194

Nova Vila de Soure, 198, 199, 206n19

Nunes, Guiomar, 104–5

obre serafico, 168, 182n31

Old Christians: vs. New Christians, 47, 49, 74, 96, 107, 108, 115n48; populations in colonial Brazil, 47, 49, 76; as witnesses, 57, 69n9

Olinda: brotherhood activities in, 163; captaincy of, 9, 43; distribution of inquisitional officials in, *123*, *124*, *125*, *126*, 149, 154; nobility in, 122; planter populations in, 96–97, 98, 99, 102, 112, 230; prisons/prisoners in, 30, 32, 199

Oliveira, Marcos Soares de, 58, 68, 104

Oliveira Gouvim, João de, 131

Oliveira Ribeiro, Zacarias de, 58

Oliveira Rosa, Domingos, 147–48

Oporto, brotherhood activities in, 163

oral testimony, in extrajudicial and judicial hearings, 59–68

ordenanças, 173, 176

Order of Carmo, 86

Order of Christ, 20, 74, 99, 100, 103, 112, 128, 176, 177

ouvidor geral, 31, 44

Pacheco Calheiros, João, 78

Pacheco Ferrás, Lourenço Gines, 60

padroado real, 20
Paes, Fernando Dias, 193
Pais Barreto, Antônio, 100–101, 114n9
Pais Barreto, Estêvão José, 101
Pais Barreto, Felipe, 1, 98, 99, 100, 101, 112, 235
Pais Barreto, João, 100
Pais Sarmento, Nicolau, 28, 30
Paiva, Britis de, 102
Paraíba: captaincy of, 4, 6, 7, 7, 8, 9, 15n15; distribution of inquisitional officials in, *123*, *124*; inquisitional activities in, 29, 46–47, 48, 51n25; New Christian populations in, 30–31
parda, 98
Parnaíba River, 6
pau-brasil, 20
Paul V, 162
Paz, Severino de, 131
Paz Barreira, Manuel de, 58
Paz do Nascimento, Luísa da, 87
Peddlers War, 97, 113n4
Pedro II, 96, 146–47
Peixoto, Vicente Ferreira, 79
Pereira Freire, Henrique Louis, 176
Pernambuco: abuses of inquisitional authority in, 187–88, 233; applications from, *64*, *65*; arrival of Inquisition in, 21–29; bishopric of, 9, 21; captaincy of, 2, 4–5, 6, 8, 230; colonial genealogies in, 96, 112, 113n2, 231; decline of Inquisition in, 216–17; distribution of inquisitional officials in, 37–49, 50n4, 123, *123*, 124, *124*, 125, 126, 135, 136, 149, 230, 233; influences of Enlightenment in, 212–13; militia company in, 173, 175, 176; New Christian populations in, 46, 85; nobility in, 120–22, 231, 232; prisoners in, 28–29, 32–33; slave populations in, 8; Suassunas conspiracy in, 213

Pessoa, Inês de, 102
Pessoa, José Campelo, 103
Pessoa, Maria, 102
Peter of Verona, martyrdom of, 162
Philip I, 74
Philip II, 74
philosophical heresies, 47
Pilar, Bartolomeu de, 78, 191
plantations, sugar, 1, 6, 8, 23, 46, 98, 121, 122, 127
planters: as aristocracy, 121, 122, 127, 137n14, 139n27; as inquisitional officials, 127, 128, 132, 232
Pombal, Marquis of, inquisitional reforms by, 88, 95, 106–7, 108, 109, 110, 111–12, 114n37, 115nn40–41, 115n43, 155, 201, 211, 222, 233–34
porteiro, 63
Portela, Antônio Rodrigues, 29
Portugal: arrival of Inquisition in, 20, 21, 22–23, 74; brotherhoods in, 179–80; discriminatory laws and practices in, 73–77, 91n7; explorations and trade by, 19; *familiares do números* permitted in, 145, 146, 147, 158n9; French invasion of, 204, 213, 226n18; influences of Enlightenment in, 211–13; Jewish populations in, 73–74, 91n7; as kingdom under Spanish crown, 24, 45, 75; military strength of, 171, 173; Moorish populations in, 74, 75, 91n7; split with Rome, 106, 114n34, 114n36, 115n38; treaties with foreign powers, 214
Portuguese Inquisition, xvi, 22–23
Prazeres, Margarida Maria dos, 79
pregadores, 80
"Presbyters of the Habit of Saint Peter," 126
processos, 5, 66
promotor, 63

promotor e defensor dos matrimônios, 201
prosopography, methodology of, 4, 15n9
Protestant Reformation, 19
provisão, 60
Purificação Jácome da, 81
De Puritate Sanguinis, 74
purity of blood: of applicants, 59, 85–90; certificates of, 41, 77; as formal requirement/enforcement of, 54, 55–56, 75–90, 222, 230; identifying African ancestry in, 87–88; ideology of, 41–42, 47; nobility based on, 119–36; proof of, 77, 78, 92n20; revocation of requirements of, 108, 109, 217

qualificadores, responsibilities of, 5, 44, 56
qualification: of applicants and honor, 53–68, 231; costs associated with, 53, 68, 69n29, 70nn31–32, 70nn34–35, 233; procedures and criteria of, 53–68, 69nn8–9

ranches/ranchers, in Brazil, 129
Raposo Cordeiro, Antônio, 191–92
real, xvi
Real Mesa Censória, 107, 115n44
Recife: brotherhood activities in, 163, 165, *165*, 166, *166*, 168, 169, 170, 171; Corpo Santo in, 165, *165*, *166*, 220; distribution of inquisitional officials in, *123*, *124*, 125, 126, 149; merchant populations in, 96, 97, 99, 102, 112, 213, 230; port city of, 9; prisons/prisoners in, 30
regimento dos nobres, 173
regimento dos privilegiados, 173
regimento dos úteis, 173
regimentos: discriminatory attitudes in, 75; on educational requirements of officials, 80; on inquisitional procedures/investigations, 22–23, 28, 53–54, 57, 63, 70n35; on New vs.

Old Christians, 108, 115n48; on oaths of office, 60; on requirements for appointments, 83; standards on modesty and decency, 61–62
Rego Barros, Francisco de, 98
Rego Barros, Francisco do, 101
Rego Barros, João do, 101
Rego Barros, Luís do, 98, 101
Reis, Antônio dos, 29
Reis, Antônio Gonçalves, 67
Reis, Isabel Maria dos, 200
Reis, José Pedro dos, 87
"Revolt of the Tailors," 212
Riba, Simão Ribeiro, 147
Ribeiro Maio, Antônio, 80
Rimígio Ferreira, José, 67
Rio de Janeiro: brotherhood activities in, 170; *familiares do número* in, 149, 150, 154; influences of Enlightenment in, 212; militia companies in, 172, 175, 176; New Christian populations in, 46; Portuguese royal court in, 213
Rio Grande do Norte: captaincy of, 4, 6, 7, *7*, 8, 29; distribution of inquisitional officials in, *123*, *124*; inquisitional activities in, 48
Rodrigues, Antônio, 195–96
Rodrigues Pais, Garcia, 193
Rodrigues Teixeira, João, 68
Rose de Ávila, Manuel de, 79
Rousseau, Jean-Jacques, 200

Sá, Duarte de, 98, 99, 100, 101
Sá, Luís Barradas de, 191
Sá, Manuel da Costa de, 87
Sá de Albuquerque, José de, 101
Saint George, cult of, 162
Saint Peter Martyr: brotherhood of, 63, 126, 150, 162–65, *165*, 166, *166*, 167, *167*, 168–71, 218, 233; celebrations/festivals of, 164–66; as servants of the Inquisition, 163

Salazar, Dr., 11
Sales Gorjão, Francisco de, 190
Salvador: *familiares do número* in, 149, 154; militia company in, 177
Sá Matias, Antônio de, 98, 99, 100
Sampaio, Gabriel José Pereira de, 213
sanbenito, 47
Santa Ana de Souza Barroso, João de, 214
Santa Cruz, José de, 82–83
Santa Inquisição (Dantas), 10
Santa Maria Jaboatão, Antônio de, 168–69, 182n31
Santareno, Bernardo, 16n22
Santa Teresa, Luís de, 206n19
Santos, Custodio Moreira, 122
São Felipe Neri, Congregation of, 89–90
São Francisco River, 6, 9
São João Baptista, convent of, 193
São José, Gonçalo de, 80
São José, Rodrigo Gaioso de, 81, 107
São Lourenço da Mata, 1, 29
São Pedro, Januário de, 193–94
São Tomás, Francisco de, 154, 155
São Vicente, captaincy of, 20
Sá Peixoto, Francisco de, 89
Sarafana, Francisco Lopes, 190
Sarmento, Manuel, 153
Sebastião, 144, 145
Sedrim, Antonio José, 220–21
Sedrim, José Duarte, 63
See of Olinda, 203
senhores e engenho, 127
Sertão: distribution of inquisitional officials in, 123, 124, 125; region of, 6, 7, 7, 43
Silva, Antônio da, 197
Silva, Francisco Pedro Cardoso da, 176
Silva, João Munis, 89
Silva, Manuel Ferreira da, 192
Silva Coutinho, Antônio da, 151
Silva e Azevedo, Joaquim Gomes da, 178
Silva Maciel, Antônio da, 32–33
Silva Sampaio, José da, 133
Silva Teles, Nunes da, 102
Silveira, Arcângela da, 98–99, 101
Simões Margiocchi, Francisco, 222
Siqueira, Manuel de, 26
slaves/slavery: cost of, 65–66, 127; populations in Brazil, 8, 65–66, 87–88
smallpox, 146
sodomy, crime of, 43, 47
Sousa, Martin Afonso de, 20
Sousa, Tomé de, 20
Souto, Miguel Ferreira, 86
Souza, Francisco Fernandes de, 58, 79, 87, 100, 101, 199
Souza Barroso, Antônio de, 66, 214
Souza Barroso, João de Santa Ana de, 214
Souza Barroso, José de, 214
Souza Barroso, Manuel Pereira de, 214
Souza Pereira, João de, 195
Spain: discriminatory laws/practices in, 74; Moorish kingdom of, 19; Portugal as kingdom under crown of, 24, 45, 75
Suassunas conspiracy, 213
sugar: cultivation and production of, 1, 6, 8, 23, 46, 98, 121, 122, 127, 137n14, 139n27; wealth and nobility associated with, 121, 127, 137n14, 139n27
supranumerarios, 150, 159n30

"Tailors Conspiracy," 212
Teixeira, Antônio Alves, 25
Teixeira, João Rodrigues, 68
Teixeira, Marcos, 22, 24
terços, 173
Third Orders, 170

Tordesillas, 20
Torres, José Veiga, 37
Treaty of Alliance and Friendship, 214–15
Treaty of Madrid, 88
tribunal(s): authority delegated by, xvi, 21, 25, 26–27, 38, 39, 43, 45; in Brazil, xvi, 23, 24, 45, 55; in Cartagena, 24; in Goa, 45, 108, 210; in Lima, 24; of Lisbon, 21, 25, 26–27, 34n3, 38, 39, 43, 45; in Mexico, 24
tropas da linha, 173

United States, McCarthy era in, 11

Vale, José de, 190
Valente, Manuel Bernardo, 80
Velho Barreto, Pedro, 101
Viana, José Lopes, 178
Viana, Manuel José, 200
Vieira, Francisco, 23
visitas, 22, 126

Vocabulario Portuguez e Latino, 120–21
Voltaire, 11, 212

witchcraft, 28, 43, 47, 193
witnesses, role in inquiries/investigations, 56–57, 68, 100
women: as applicants, 58–59, 69n18; marriage strategies and, 130–36, 231; qualification of, 55; as witnesses, 57

Xavier, Francisco, 110
Xavier da Cunha, Elias Francisco, 201, 202

yellow fever, 146

Zona da Mata: colonial populations in, 6, 7, *7*, 8; denunciations and punishments in, 47, 48, 49; distribution of inquisitional officials in, *123*, *124*, 125, 136, 233

About the Author

James E. Wadsworth is assistant professor of history at Stonehill College where he teaches Latin American history and world history. He received his Ph.D. in Latin American history and world history from the University of Arizona in May 2002. He publishes in scholarly journals including *History of Religion*, *Colonial Latin American Historical Review*, *Luso-Brazilian Review*, and *The Americas*. His research seeks to view the Inquisition from unique perspectives that deepen our understanding of this important institution and the societies that supported it.

www.ingramcontent.com/pod-product-compliance
Lightning Source LLC
Chambersburg PA
CBHW021847300426
44115CB00005B/48